GLOBOCNIK'S MEN

IN ITALY, 1943–45

Abteilung R and the SS-Wachmannschaften of the Operationszone Adriatisches Küstenland

Stefano Di Giusto
& Tommaso Chiussi

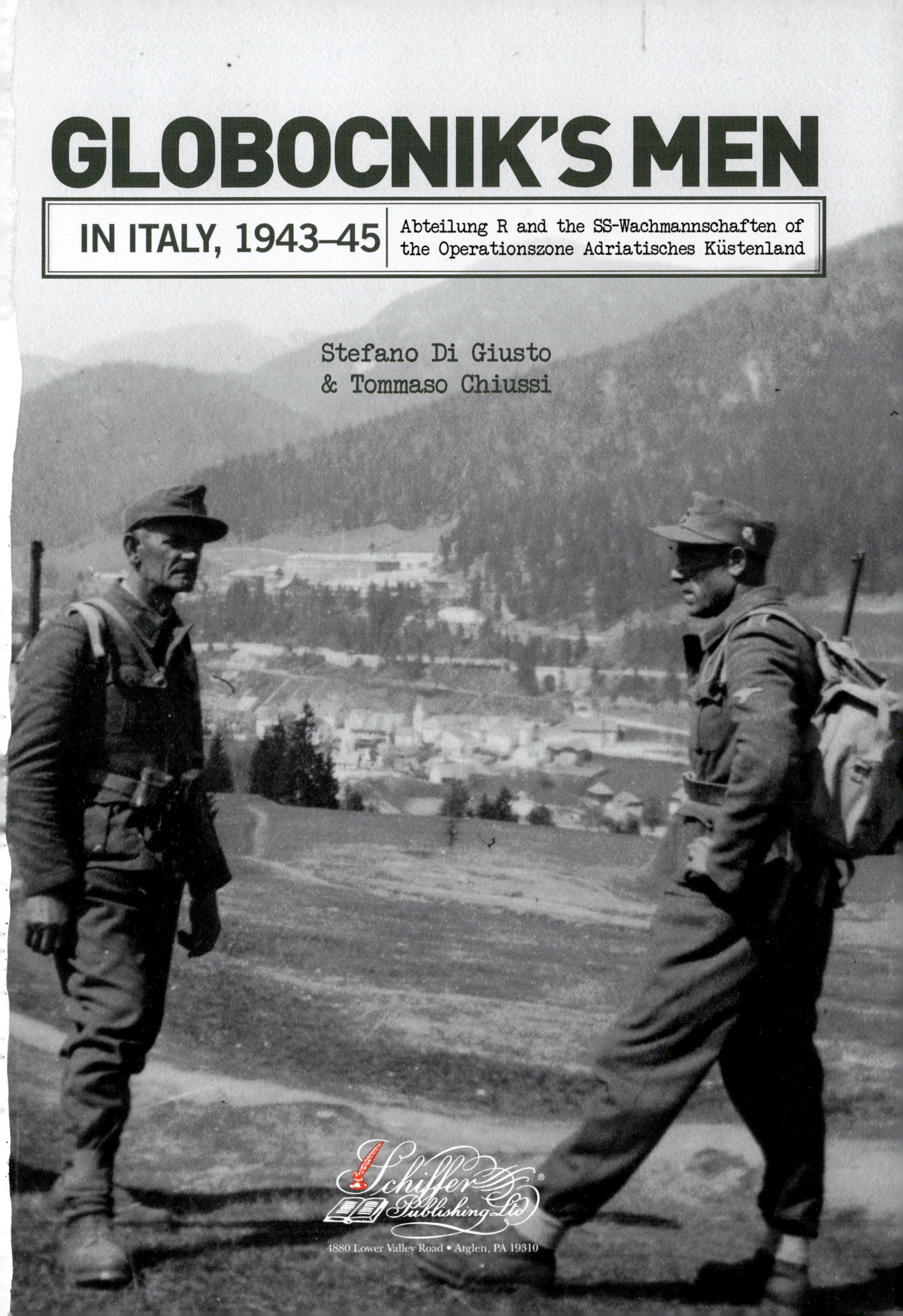

Schiffer Publishing Ltd
4880 Lower Valley Road • Atglen, PA 19310

Other Schiffer Books on Related Subjects:
Operation Drvar by Branislav Radovic (978-0-7643-3060-5)
Ukrainians in the Waffen-SS by Rolf Michaelis (978-0-7643-3349-1)
Himmler's Bosnian Division by George Lepre (978-0-7643-0134-6)

Library of Congress Control Number: 2016953716

Cover design by John Cheek
Type set in DIN Black/Times New Roman

ISBN: 978-0-7643-5254-6
Printed in China

Published by Schiffer Publishing, Ltd.
4880 Lower Valley Road
Atglen, PA 19310
Phone: (610) 593-1777; Fax: (610) 593-2002
E-mail: Info@schifferbooks.com

CONTENTS

INTRODUCTION

In recent years the extermination of the Jews perpetrated in Poland during 1942–43 in the framework of *Aktion Reinhard*, in the Belzec, Sobibor and Treblinka camps by a group of men who had previously taken part in *Aktion T4*, the killing of the mentally ill and disabled in Germany during 1940–41, has received a lot of attention in historical research circles.

The enormous scale of the crimes committed during *Aktion Reinhard* has relegated to the background the activities carried out by the same group of men after the extermination in the three Polish camps was stopped and the camps dismantled. Generally, in the books on *Aktion Reinhard,* and in the biographies of the men who took part in it, it is only mentioned that they were further active in Italy during 1943–45, but details are generally few or absent.

In autumn 1943, following Odilo Globocnik, who had been SS and police commander in Lublin and as such the person mainly responsible for the conduct of *Aktion Reinhard*, the men that had carried it out were transferred to occupied northeastern Italy. The region, whose main city was the port of Trieste, was called by the Germans *Operationszone Adriatisches Küstenland* (Operational Zone Adriatic Littoral, OZAK) and included also parts of the present-day Slovenia and Croatia (the Slovenian littoral, the Istria peninsula, the area of Fiume, now Rijeka). Here the group took up the name of *Abteilung R* and in the intentions of its commander, Christian Wirth (previously overseeing the three extermination camps in Poland), it was to have accomplished the task of making the region "*Judenfrei*" (free from Jews). And indeed in Italy *Abteilung R* devoted itself for the entire further duration of the war to tracking down and arresting the Jews, and even more to seizing their properties, which were confiscated by the German administration or sometimes just appropriated by the unit members to unlawfully enrich themselves. However, the fact that the number of Jews in the region was relatively limited, as well as the raging of the partisan war in the area and the unfavorable war development for Germany, all meant that the unit was used partly for other tasks: providing security to communication lines, fighting the partisans, setting up, training and leading locally recruited military units, and constructing defensive positions. All these activities though came in addition to the original one, never abandoned, of persecuting the Jews.

The reconstruction of these activities, on which so far little has been published, is the subject of this book. Its completion has been made difficult by the scarcity of available original documents: in practice the vast majority of documents produced by the SS and police headquarters and units in the OZAK is missing, probably lost or intentionally destroyed at the end of the war. The few exceptions (limited organic collection of documents or single papers) are of limited use to reconstruct the history of the SS and police and their activities in the region. The main source regarding the activities of *Abteilung R* is therefore the trial depositions, with the obvious significant limitations that are typical for such materials. Several trials for the crimes committed during *Aktion Reinhard* took place in Germany, while a trial regarding the Risiera di San Sabba, the detention and transit camp run by *Abteilung R* in Trieste (where many Jews and members of the resistance movement were detained to be later deported to Germany, but sometimes killed and incinerated in the prison crematorium), was celebrated in that city in 1976.

In the German trials, apart from a few exceptions, the Italian phase is generally dealt with only superficially, since the investigators concentrated their interest and their questions on the Polish extermination camps. During the Trieste trial only one former member of *Abteilung R* (Geng) was interrogated in court, while a few others were interrogated by German investigators on behalf of their Italian colleagues. In general it can be said that for obvious reasons the depositions are often reticent if not mendacious, imprecise, and generic, probably in the intention not to provide elements that may have been useful to incriminate anyone, sometimes perhaps also due to the long time passed since the events. The information provided in the depositions must therefore be carefully analyzed and when possible cross-checked. In any case they undoubtedly represent interesting and relevant material, which has been very useful during the research which led to this book.

Taking into account the limitations just described regarding the sources, we believe we have been able to provide a sufficiently complete picture of the activities of *Abteilung R*. From this research it appears clearly that the unit was employed for various tasks, which evolved according to wartime requirements. Among them it seems that the fight against the partisans and more generally the repression of the resistance movement were a significant component of the unit's activities, probably more than so far known, although only a part of the members of *Abteilung R* took part in it. To the fight against the partisans belonged also the reprisal actions carried out by *Abteilung R* against the civilian population, from which suffered especially the villages along the Trieste–Fiume road, an area of intense partisan activity. In this regard it has been ascertained that *Abteilung R* was almost certainly responsible for the massacre of Lipa (a village in Croatia, north of Fiume), on April 30, 1944; with almost 300 civilian dead it was the worst atrocity committed in the OZAK. The possibility is also analyzed here that the unit was involved as well in the massacre that took place in the village of Avasinis (north of Udine), where fifty-one civilians were killed on May 2, 1945.

In addition to *Abteilung R* it has been deemed interesting to also deal here with the *SS-Wachmannschaften* (SS guards units) of the OZAK, military units that were formed locally and had links with *Abteilung R*, since elements of the latter were seconded to the *SS-Wachmannschaften*. It is a topic which has so far almost been completely unknown. Also in this case the research has been particularly difficult due to the extreme lack of sources.

Since this book devotes considerable space to the anti-partisan activities of *Abteilung R*, as well as to other more "technical" subjects such as uniformology, it features a large number of photographs. In addition to images of *Abteilung R* and the *SS-Wachmannschaften* (and other units linked to them, such as the *Landschutz*, or territorial defense), a number of photographs taken during the anti-partisan operation *Unternehmen Braunschweig* (conducted in Istria and in the Fiume area in late April – early May 1944), in which also elements of *Abteilung R* participated, have been included. The analysis of the photographs has made in several cases a useful contribution to the research work, and considerable efforts have been put into finding out places and dates when they were taken; when possible present-day comparative photos have been included, in a "then and now" style. It is thought that the photographs, in addition to their historical interest, and despite the fact that they were often taken for propagandistic purposes, can illustrate the bleak reality, in particular for the civilian population, of the anti-partisan war conducted by German and collaborationist units.

The large space given in this book to the "military" activities of *Abteilung R* in the OZAK is not meant in any way to downplay the fact this unit remained also in Italy a central element of the implementation of the "final solution," and more generally of the repression of any political and military opposition to Nazi Germany, together with the other SS and police structures in the region. The Risiera di San Sabba still remains the symbol of the violence and brutality of that regime.

• • •

We would like to thank the following who have contributed to the research: Darko Cafuta, Stefano Commentucci, Mike Constandy, Hinrich-Boy Christiansen†, Rodolfo Decleva, Bojan Dimitrijevic, Giuliano Giorcelli, Marin Iljadica, French L. MacLean, Ivo Mileusnic, and Vinko Surina.

A particular thank you goes to Luca Cossa who has contributed substantially to writing the uniform appendixes and to researching where period photographs were taken.

Many thanks also to Ralph Riccio who proofread the English text and provided linguistic advice.

The source of photographs is credited at the end of each caption; where no credit is specified, the photo belongs to the authors' collection.

Note to the reader: Throughout the text, towns and villages which were inside the Italian borders at the time of the events and are now in Slovenia or Croatia, are called with their Italian names as used in the original documents and maps. In appendix 7, a table provides the corresponding present Slovenian or Croatian name.

CHAPTER 1

Aktion T4 and Aktion Reinhard

The personnel that belonged to *Abteilung R* in the *Operationszone Adriatisches Küstenland* (Operational Zone Adriatic Littoral, OZAK) had participated in one or (in most cases) both of two criminal operations planned and carried out by the Nazi regime in the previous years: *Aktion T4*, or "Euthanasia" program, the killing of the mentally ill and disabled, and *Aktion Reinhard*, the extermination of the Jews in occupied Poland, or *Generalgouvernement*.

Aktion T4 put into practice the Nazi eugenics and "racial hygiene" theories: based on them, from early 1940 to August 1941, around 70,000 mentally ill and disabled, rated as incurable, as well as Jewish patients, were killed with lethal gas in six establishments in Germany and Austria, and their bodies incinerated. The operation was led by the *Kanzlei der Führers* (Hitler's Chancellery), under the responsibility of Philipp Bouhler, head of the Chancellery, and Karl Brandt, Hitler's personal doctor; its implementation was entrusted to Viktor Brack, a high-rank official of the Chancellery. The offices of *Aktion T4*, from where the entire operation was coordinated, were based at the Tiergartenstraße 4 address in Berlin, hence the T4 abbreviation (the name *Aktion T4* was not used at that time, but was introduced after the war), and were directed by Gerhard Bohne, later by Dietrich Allers. In total around 500 men and women participated in the operation; in addition to the doctors there were also other personnel, both civilians (for instance nurses, drivers, technicians, etc.) as well as seconded from the police and the SS. The administrative personnel responsible for the management of the six establishments where the patients were killed generally belonged to the police. Although the operation was supposed to be secret, rumors about it started to spread and there were some protests, in particular from the church, so in August 1941 the operation was officially suspended (although the killing of disabled patients continued in the following years and the T4 establishments continued to be used for the suppression of concentration camp inmates who had become unable to work). After a few months of uncertainty on their further use, from early 1942 (a few, like Christian Wirth, even from late 1941) some of the men who had participated in *Aktion T4* were sent to the Generalgouvernement (occupied Poland) to be employed in the genocide of the Jews. The offices of the Tiergartenstraße continued their work under Allers' command (and of his superior in the Chancellery, Werner Blankenburg, who from summer 1942 replaced Brack), to further manage the former *Aktion T4* personnel.

Aktion Reinhard (or *Reinhardt*, as sometimes written also in original documents), that is the Jewish genocide in the Generalgouvernement, was carried out in the extermination camps of Belzec, Sobibor, and Treblinka from spring 1942 to autumn 1943, under the leadership of Odilo Globocnik, then SS and police commander in Lublin (*SS- und Polizei-Führer Lublin*). It seems certain that the name of the operation was a reference to Reinhard Heydrich, the head of the *Reichssicherheitshauptamt* (central office for the Reich's security, or RSHA), who was killed by Czechoslovak partisans in June 1942.

The extermination camps were active during different periods: the first to start the killing process was Belzec in March 1942, Sobibor followed in May 1942, Treblinka in July.[1] The killing was

A map dating from the 1930s showing the Italian regions at the northeastern border. From autumn 1943 to the end of the war, these regions, plus southern Slovenia, under German rule formed the Operational Zone Adriatic Littoral (*Operationszone Adriatisches Küstenland, OZAK*). Among the main cities, Fiume is now Rijeka, Pola is now Pula (both in Croatia).

stopped in Belzec in December 1942; summer 1943 the camp had been dismantled, the bodies had been exhumed from the mass graves and cremated, and the site had been turned into a fake farm in the attempt to remove all traces. Treblinka and Sobibor remained in activity until October 1943. In both camps there were prisoners' riots—on August 2, 1943, in Treblinka, on October 14, 1943, in Sobibor—during which hundreds of inmates escaped (in Sobibor some German guards from *Aktion Reinhard* were also killed); these episodes, with the ghetto uprising in Warsaw (April–May 1943) and Bialystok (August 1943) led to the decision to stop the operations, also because in the meantime the center of the killing activity had become Auschwitz-Birkenau. By the end of November 1943, Treblinka and Sobibor were also closed and dismantled, and like in Belzec, an attempt was made to conceal all traces of the extermination activity that had taken place there.

In the three camps the victims were mainly killed in gas chambers, with the exhaust fumes produced by engines. Altogether 1.5 million people, the majority Jews but also Sinti and Roma, were killed in the camps; 1.7 million were killed in total during the entire *Aktion Reinhard*, or around a quarter of the victims of the Holocaust. The Jews were mostly Polish, coming from the ghettos set up after the German occupation, but they also came from Germany and from other countries (in particular the Netherlands, France, Czechoslovakia, and Greece).

If Globocnik had the overall responsibility for the operation, the one who directed it was *SS-Hauptsturmführer* (later *SS-Sturmbannführer*) Hermann Höfle, an officer in charge of "Jewish affairs" at the SSPF headquarters, who coordinated the transports of the deported. A very prominent role in the implementation of *Aktion Reinhard* was also played by Christian Wirth, who directed the building of the Belzec camp and was its first commander. In spring 1942 he became formally the *Inspekteur der SS-Sonderkommandos beim SSPF Einsatz Reinhard(t)* (inspector of the SS special detachments of the SSPF operation Reinhard) with the task of coordinating the activities of the three camps. Wirth came from the criminal police (*Kriminalpolizei*), from which he had been seconded to *Aktion T4*; feared and loathed by his men, whom he treated very harshly (he was nicknamed by them *der wilde Christian*, or the wild Christian), in Poland he carried out the task of organizing the Jewish extermination with extreme fanaticism, determination, and brutality.

Aktion Reinhard personnel came almost entirely from *Aktion T4* and consisted of around 100 people, a surprisingly low number. To the around 100 Germans one must, however, add a considerable number of collaborationist auxiliaries, the so-called *Trawniki*, who not only had guard tasks inside and outside the camps (100–120 men per camp), but sometimes participated directly in the killings of the victims in the gas chambers (more on the *Trawniki* later). Additionally, in each camp there was a group of Jews who carried out the hardest work, such as removing the bodies and sorting the victims' belongings. In addition to the extermination camps, *Aktion Reinhard* also included some work camps that employed Jewish workers, who were mostly killed during operation *Erntefest* in early November 1943.

The conclusion of *Aktion Reinhard* can be set at October 1943, when the last extermination camp was closed. At that time Globocnik had already been transferred to the OZAK region with part of the men of his headquarters; among them was also a small group of men from *Aktion Reinhard*, including Wirth. Most of the personnel of *Aktion Reinhard* initially remained in Poland to complete the dismantling of Sobibor and Treblinka, and moved to Italy later.

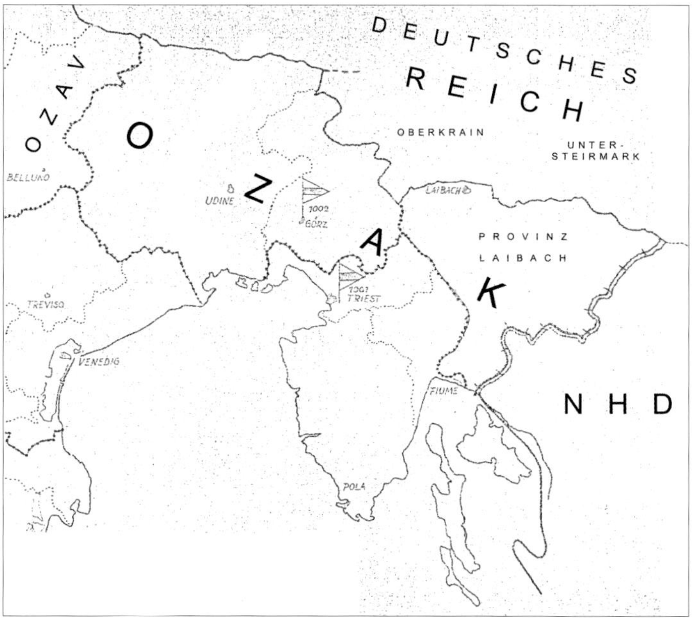

German wartime map of the OZAK area; region and state names have been added (NDH = Croatia). The tactical symbols and the numbers 1001 and 1002 indicate the *Militärkommandanturen* (territorial headquarters) in Trieste and Gorizia (respectively Triest and Görz, in German).

CHAPTER 2

Operationszone Adriatisches Küstenland (OZAK)

Following the armistice signed by Italy with the Allies and made known on the evening of September 8, 1943, German troops occupied northern and central Italy and all other areas previously controlled by the Italian army. On September 10, an ordinance by Hitler stipulated the formation in northern Italy of two *operationszone* (operational zone): *Alpenvorland* (Prealps Region, OZAV, with the provinces of Trento, Bolzano and Belluno) and *Adriatisches Küstenland* (Adriatic Littoral, OZAK). These regions were governed directly by the Germans, each through an *Oberster Kommissar* (Highest Commissar), and were de facto excluded from the sovereignty of the new Mussolini puppet state, the *Repubblica Sociale Italiana* (RSI). At that time the creation of the two *operationszone* was explained in terms of military necessity (protecting the communication lines from Italy and the Balkans to the *Reich*) but very likely it was just a way to prepare the annexation of the regions to the *Reich* as soon as politically feasible (an immediate annexation was not advisable because it would have damaged the relations with the RSI).

The OZAK was a fairly large area that included the regions at the then northeastern Italian border, including parts of present Slovenia and Croatia.[1] It included the following provinces: Trieste, Gorizia, Pola (now Pula, in Croatia; also called Istria province), Fiume (now Rijeka, in Croatia; also called Quarnero, or Carnaro, province), Udine (or Friuli province, with today's Udine and Pordenone provinces) and Ljubljana (the latter included the territories of southern Slovenia, annexed to Italy in 1941; it was called by the Germans Provinz Laibach, the German name for Ljubljana). The border with Croatia set in 1941 after the dissolution of Yugoslavia remained unchanged, save for a few minor alterations concerning some islands in the Quarnero gulf.

Oberster Kommissar in the region was nominated the *Gauleiter* (civilian governor) of the Austrian region of *Kärnten* (Carinthia), Friedrich Rainer. *SS-Gruppenführer und Generalleutnant der Polizei* Odilo Globocnik was nominated by Himmler to the post of *Höherer SS- und Polizei-Führer in der Operationszone Adriatisches Küstenland* (HSSPF OZAK), or higher SS and police commander in the OZAK (excluding the Provinz Laibach, which was under the authority of *HSSPF Alpenland*, Erwin Rösener). His nomination, dated September 13, 1943, took effect from September 17; Globocnik arrived in Trieste a few days later, where he established his office. The HSSPF had the tasks of combating political dissent, arresting and deporting the Jews and seizing their properties, guaranteeing public order and security, protecting communication lines and infrastructure, fighting the partisan movement. Subordinated to Globocnik in his area were headquarters, structures and units belonging to the two components of the German police forces:

- *Sicherheitspolizei und Sicherheitsdienst* (Sipo/SD, security police and SS security service),[2] whose tasks included fighting the opposition to Nazism, in particular the political organizations, as well as persecuting Jews.
- *Ordnungspolizei* (*Orpo*, order police),[3] had the task of maintaining public order and security, and whose units were largely employed in fighting against the partisans.

Subordinated to the SS/*Polizei* headquarters were also all RSI units based in the region and employed for public order tasks (police forces, militia units, and even some units of the RSI army), collaborationist units formed by the Germans in the OZAK with locally recruited elements as well as units formed with foreign volunteers.

Immediately after the Italian armistice, the partisan armed resistance (Italian, Slovenian, and Croatian) erupted in the region, and continued uninterrupted until the end of the war despite the efforts made by the Germans to eradicate it. Consequently, already on November 8, 1943, following Himmler's order the OZAK was declared *Bandenkampfgebiet*, or "area of combat against the bandits." The practical consequence of this order was the creation, in January 1944, of the *Bandenbekämpfungsstab Triest* (headquarters for fighting the "bandits" of Trieste), more commonly called *Führungsstab für Bandenbekämpfung* (FSBB, operational headquarters for fighting the "bandits"). Formally placed under the orders of Globocnik, the OZAK FSBB had the task of planning and conducting anti-partisan operations in the region. It was based in Trieste until the end of August 1944, when it was transferred to Gradisca d'Isonzo, near Gorizia.

As far as the *Wehrmacht* was concerned, the highest military rank in the OZAK was the *Befehlshaber in der Operationszone Adriatisches Küstenland* (Commander in the Operational Zone Adriatic Littoral). In September 1943, Hitler nominated *Befehlshaber* in the OZAK *General der Gebirgstruppen* (general of alpine troops) Ludwig Kübler, who took up this position in early December and remained in it until the end of the war. His primary mission (carried out through his *Stab*, in practice a corps' headquarters, called *General-Kommando Kübler*) was the protection and fortification of the coastline, its defense in case of an Allied landing, the protection of the communication lines, and (in cooperation with the SS/*Polizei*) guaranteeing security and fighting the partisans. All *Wehrmacht* units stationed in the region were subordinated to the *Befehlshaber*.

Due to the partial duplication of tasks between Globocnik and Kübler with reference to securing the territory, and the insufficient SS/*Polizei* forces, anti-partisan operations were often conducted in cooperation between these and *Wehrmacht* units.

A series of photos taken during the military parade in Trieste, on the quay, to celebrate Hitler's birthday on April 20, 1944. *General der Gebirgstruppe* Ludwig Kübler, military commander in the OZAK, talks to a *Kriegsmarine* officer. Behind him, partially visible on the right, is *SA-Oberführer* Werner Blankenburg, one of the main perpetrators responsible for the Euthanasia program (*Aktion T4*), and later for *Aktion Reinhard*, the extermination of the Jews in Poland. *MNZS, 7175_07*

Political and military authorities of the OZAK waiting for the military units to march past. Visible are Blankenburg, in the first row with spectacles, and behind him, Allers. Both wear *Sturmabteilung* uniforms. *MNZS, 7175_13*

The *Oberster Kommissar* in the OZAK, Friedrich Rainer, speaking with an NSDAP official (*Hauptbereichsleiter*). To the right of the latter is again Kübler, and in the background, between the two, *SA-Sturmbannführer* Dietrich Allers, director of the *Aktion T4* offices and, from June 1944, commander of *Abteilung R. MNZS, 7175_08*

On the platform, from the left, the *Höherer SS- und Polizei-Führer* (SS/*Polizei* commander) in the OZAK Odilo Globocnik, Rainer and Kübler watching the parade. Behind Kübler, on the right, the officer with the *Ritterkreuz* is *SS-Sturmbannführer* Walter Bestmann, commander of *SS-Junkerschule* Klagenfurt. Next to the platform, on the right, with helmet and *Ritterkreuz*, is *Generalleutnant* Harry Hoppe, commander of *278. Infanterie-Division*, at the time based in the region. *MNZS, 7175_14*

A unit of the *SS-Wachmannschaften* raised in the OZAK region, led by an SS officer, marching during the parade. Note the use by some soldiers of the newly introduced piped rhomboidal collar tabs, and SS-style arm eagle. *Biblioteca Nazionale Slovena di Trieste, Fondo Bubnic*

A Sd.Kfz. 253 armored half-track with registration number SS-642228, modified with a Fiat 35 machine gun mounted behind a rotating armored shield, used by an unidentified unit (possibly *Abteilung R*, which also took part in the parade; see appendix 4 for information on vehicles). *Courtesy Sergio Corbatti*

Troops lined up in front of the Palazzo di Giustizia (court house) in Trieste on April 20, 1944.

Globocnik reviewing soldiers from the *SS-Junkerschule* Klagenfurt, lined up in front of the Palazzo di Giustizia. In the background, on the right, in front of the grate, are Allers and Blankenburg.

Globocnik delivering his speech. It is interesting that he wears a *Reichsführung-SS* cuff band. On the right of the photo, looking down, is Blankenburg, on his right, Allers. *MNZS, 6832_3*

Globocnik before the Palazzo di Giustizia. On his left, wearing a helmet, *SS-Standartenführer und Oberst d.SchP.* Hermann Kintrupp, commander of the *Ordnungspolizei* in the OZAK. *MNZS, 7803/a*

Panoramic view of the troops lined up in front of the Palazzo di Giustizia (court house) in Trieste on April 20, 1944. The vehicle column parked in the foreground includes: an armored half-track, probably the Sd.Kfz. 253 with registration number SS-642228 also shown on page 12, and perhaps belonging to *Abteilung R*; the armored truck number 3 of *Abteilung R* (it seems to have a machine gun shield mounted above the driver's cabin), apparently towing a 2 cm *Flak* gun; a Fiat 626 truck armed with a machine gun mounted on the flatbed, and towing a 20 mm Breda 20/65 gun, most probably belonging to *Abteilung R*. On the other side of the square, on the left edge of the photograph, the armored truck number 1 of *Abteilung R* is visible. *Courtesy Kleine Berlin Archive–Trieste*

CHAPTER 3

Abteilung R in the OZAK

3.1: Arrival in Trieste

Nominated by Himmler to the position of HSSPF OZAK, on September 20, Globocnik set off from Lublin with a motorized column and arrived in Trieste a few days later (on September 23 it seems). In addition to some men from his staff,[1] he brought along the officer mainly responsible for the implementation of *Aktion Reinhard*, *SS-Hauptsturmführer* Christian Wirth,[2] and some of his men, in total only six people: Josef Oberhauser (who was the closest of Wirth's collaborators, as his assistant and escort),[3] Franz Stangl, Otto Stadie, Konrad Geng and Rudolf Baer.[4] Upon arrival in Trieste, Wirth and his men were billeted in the Hotel de la Ville (or Grande Albergo della Città), on the quay. All other men of *Aktion Reinhard* remained initially in Poland, where they worked to dismantle the Sobibor and Treblinka extermination camps. According to a trial deposition by Oberhauser, initially the men of *Aktion Reinhard* who had moved to Trieste did not have any defined tasks.[5] After a while, Wirth, Oberhauser, and some other people were sent to Pola to carry out criminal police tasks until a *Sipo*/SD commander in the city was nominated; at that moment, after spending three–four weeks in Pola, they went back to Trieste and were billeted in a villa, most probably Villa Segre on Via Murat. Also after going back to Trieste, their role still remained undefined. Oberhauser said that he was therefore employed as courier, using also seaplanes to travel to Pola and Fiume. Later he was employed as company commander and probably also as trainer for the recruits of the *SS-Wachmannschafts-Btl.* (*SS-WMS-Btl.*), the SS guard battalion which was being formed in Trieste under the respon-

Christian Wirth, inspector and main director, responsible for the implementation of *Aktion Reinhard* in Poland, and later commander of *Abteilung R* in the OZAK. This photo of him, wearing an *SS-Sturmbannführer* uniform, was taken in Marcossina (now Markovščina, Slovenia) on the Trieste–Fiume road (or Karststrasse), outside the Gostilna "Baša" ("Baša" restaurant) in early May 1944, during the anti-partisan *Unternehmen Braunschweig*. *LA NRW, Münster*

Gottlieb Hering, commander of section R I of *Abteilung R* in Trieste, as well as commander of the Risiera di San Sabba camp until July 1944, seen in the *Sipo*/SD uniform also used by the members of the *Kriminalpolizei*, to whom Hering belonged. In Poland, he was commandant of the Belzec extermination camp.

sibility of *SS-Untersturmführer* Johann Schwarzenbacher.[6] Also according to a trial deposition by Stadie, after arriving in Trieste the group had practically no tasks for around six weeks (perhaps Stadie did not go to Pola), then they set up a recruitment office for local volunteers (for the *Wehrmacht* as stated in the deposition, but more probably it was for the *SS-WMS-Btl.*); Stadie said he was then also employed as trainer for three or four months.[7] After some weeks, perhaps in late November or early December, Oberhauser took up again his position of Wirth's assistant (it is not known what Wirth's activities had been in the meantime, but it seems that he travelled often to Berlin and in early November he was back in Lublin to participate in operation *Erntefest*, the mass shooting of the remaining Jews in the area), since in the meantime the reconstitution of the entire *Aktion Reinhard* structure in the OZAK was looming.

A few weeks after taking up the HSSPF position in Trieste on October 27, 1943, Globocnik wrote to Berlin to complain about the lack of personnel and to ask for more people to be sent from Poland.[8] In the letter he also mentioned that in Lublin he had had at his disposal ninety-two people seconded from Hitler's Chancellery for *Aktion Reinhard*, of whom he had only taken six with him to Trieste (see above). In the course of the following weeks, thanks to Blankenburg's support, the personnel of *Aktion Reinhard*—then lacking specific employment, after dismantling the Treblinka and Sobibor camps and concealing the traces of the massacres, which was concluded by the end of November 1943—was therefore sent to Trieste.

The men's transfer from Poland to Italy happened at different times and in different ways, as the camp personnel was gradually reduced as the dismantling proceeded: sometimes they travelled in groups, some other times individually; sometimes they arrived directly from Poland, sometimes from Germany after a leave period. In addition to the personnel coming from Poland, also some elements from Germany previously active in *Aktion T4* (Euthanasia program) who had not been employed in the Polish extermination camps arrived in Italy. Information is rather confused but it seems that a first group arrived in Trieste around mid-November, others followed in early December; the most numerous group, apparently around 40–50 men, arrived at the end of December, and more in early 1944. By January 1944, most of the around 100 men who formed *Abteilung R* had arrived in the OZAK. Only a few unit members arrived in Trieste during 1944.[9] Also some female personnel, used for secretarial work, arrived in Trieste.

In Italy, Wirth's unit took the name of *SonderAbteilung R* (special unit R) or more commonly and simply *Abteilung R* (unit R).[10] Its men were subordinated to Globocnik for operational and disciplinary issues, but as far as administrative and financial matters were concerned they were subordinated as before to Hitler's Chancellery via the T4. Also during its stay in Italy *Abteilung R* maintained strong links with the Berlin T4 base, which evidently also had the task of keeping under strict control a group of men who knew

Josef Oberhauser, Wirth's assistant and later commander of section R I and the Risiera di San Sabba camp, as well as company commander in the *SS-Wachmannschafts-Btl.*, in two photographs taken in the late 1930s. He wears the uniform of the *2. SS-Totenkopf-Standarte "Brandenburg." StA München*

important state secrets. In this regard it is known that some leading T4 men, in particular Blankenburg (and for some unknown reason also his predecessor Brack) and Allers, came to the OZAK several times on visit. Both Blankenburg and Allers were photographed in Trieste at the military parade held for Hitler's birthday on April 20, 1944, and participated in Wirth's funeral in Opicina, near Trieste, at the end of May.

Direct subordination to Globocnik and at the same time the strong link to Berlin meant that *Abteilung R* could enjoy a high degree of operational autonomy in the OZAK. As already in Poland, Wirth was the commander of *Abteilung R*, officially again with the title of *Inspekteur*. The unit headquarters were based in the same Villa Segre on Via Murat where Wirth lived; here were billeted a few unit members, among whom some *Trawniki* men.[11]

Many of the men of *Aktion Reinhard* transferred in the OZAK were formally civilians, who (some, if not all) arrived in the OZAK wearing civilian clothes. At the arrival in Trieste they received *Ordnungspolizei* ranks and uniforms, which was probably meant to militarise them, due to their employment in a war zone. In practice it seems that the civilians were integrated in the *Ordnungspolizei* as reservists.[12] The rank attributed to them was probably the *Ordnungspolizei* equivalent of the SS rank they had in Poland. On the other hand, those men who belonged to the police (*Kripo* or *Orpo*) or to the *Waffen-SS*, and were already wearing the specific uniform (*Orpo*, *Sipo*/SD, SS/*Waffen-SS*), generally kept on using it in Italy and maintained the ranks they already had.[13]

Together with the German members of *Abteilung R* also a certain number of foreign collaborators, generally indicated as Ukrainians although some also belonged to other nationalities, moved to the OZAK. They were the so-called *Trawniki*, from the name of the *Ausbildungslager* (training camp) based in the locality by the same name, near Lublin, where their units—named *Wachmannschaften*, literally "guard units"—had been formed and trained by the SS.[14] The *Trawniki* were mainly former prisoners-of-war, in the majority Ukrainians but also from other nationalities of the Soviet Union, recruited by the Germans in the prisoners' camps where conditions were very harsh and the possibilities to survive very limited, at least during 1941–42. Some had also been recruited (sometimes voluntarily, other times following coercion) among the Polish or Ukrainian civilians. The *Wachmannschaften* units were created from late summer 1941 on Globocnik's initiative and trained for auxiliary police tasks. In practice, they were used for all tasks linked to the Jewish deportation and extermination in Poland: guarding labor and extermination camps, killing operations in the extermination camps, evacuating the ghettos, and mass executions. They were also used generally for security purposes (fighting the partisans, guard services, escorts, suppressing riots, etc.) in the

Franz Stangl, commander of section R III, based in Udine, later of R II in Fiume, and finally of R IV in the Veneto region. In Poland, he was commandant of Sobibor, and later Treblinka.

Arthur Walther, *Leutnant der Schutzpolizei*. For a short time he led section R III before being transferred to the outpost of Castelnuovo d'Istria (now Podgrad, Slovenia), on the Karststrasse.

Helmut Fischer, *SS-Untersturmführer*. He was a member of section R II, then from summer 1944 led section R III in Udine.

Gerhard Börner, commander of section R II in Fiume after Stangl.

Paul Rost, *Leutnant der Schutzpolizei* and *SS-Untersturmführer*, member of section R I.

Dietrich Allers in civilian clothes. From June 1944, he was Wirth's successor as commander of *Abteilung R* in the OZAK.

Generalgouvernement and later also outside it. The *Wachmannschaften* were organized in companies, where the company and platoon commanders were German officers or NCOs, while cadres and enlisted personnel were *Trawniki*; among the cadres, the highest ranks assigned to the *Trawniki* (NCO ranks) were generally held by *Volksdeutsche* (i.e., men of German origin not living in the Reich, such as those belonging to the German ethnic minorities of the Soviet Union), who were often squad leaders. In the specific case of the *Trawniki* who arrived in Trieste with the members of *Aktion Reinhard*, they were most probably men who had directly participated in the killing in the extermination camps in Poland, and it can be assumed that they were practically considered as belonging to the unit for all practical purposes (if not officially).[15] Around twenty names of *Trawniki* attached to *Abteilung R* in Italy are known, of whom probably at least one-third were *Volksdeutsche* (a list is provided in appendix 5; however, it is surely not complete and probably not completely correct). Some of them deserted, some died during employment in the OZAK. Also some Ukrainian women moved to Italy, where they worked as kitchen personnel.

A photo inside Globocnik's office in the Palazzo di Giustizia in Trieste on April 19, 1944, when awards were presented, mainly to members of *Abteilung R*. From the left: Hering, unknown (though not a member of *Abteilung R*), Stangl, Oberhauser, Schwarz, and Hackenholt.

Globocnik awards the Iron Cross Second Class to Lorenz Hackenholt. In the middle background is Schwarz, and partially visible at right is probably Schneider. It is not known what decorations were handed out to the other people, but they were probably less important since it was this photo that was chosen to be published in the Trieste German-language newspaper *Adria Zeitung* on April 20, 1944.

Members of *Abteilung R* congratulate Hackenholt for the award of the Iron Cross Second Class. From the left: Lambert, Löffler, Schiffner, Plikat, Girtzig, Hackenholt, Dubois, Bredow, and Schneider. The image was taken in the courtyard of the Locanda "Venezia Giulia" bar, which was (and is) in front of the Risiera di San Sabba in Trieste, probably the same day as the awards ceremony depicted previously. *StA München*

On the same occasion as the previous photo: from the left, Löffler, Schneider, and Jührs, photographed before the bar entrance. Löffler would be killed, and Schneider wounded shortly afterwards, on April 30, 1944, probably during the partisan attack at the Rupa junction. *StA München*

3.2: Sections R I, R II, and R III

Shortly after the arrival of the first groups of men of *Aktion Reinhard* from Poland, *Abteilung R* was divided in three sections (in addition to the headquarters), indicated as R I, R II, and R III. The most numerous section (R I) was based in Trieste, the other two were based in Fiume and Udine (R II and III respectively). The command of each section was entrusted to one of the former commanders of the Polish exterminations camps: initially section R I was led by Gottlieb Hering (commander in Belzec), R II by Franz Reichleitner (commander in Sobibor) and R III by Franz Stangl (commander in Sobibor and later in Treblinka). No original lists of personnel serving in the various sections have been found, additionally their composition varied over time with several transfers from one section to the other; the main source of information on the personnel allocation is therefore the trial depositions.

Apparently, each section was divided in sub-sections, with a specific activity field; it is documented for instance that a sub-section called *Abteilung Finanzen* existed, evidently in charge of economic affairs, primarily the seizing of Jewish properties. The name and tasks of other sub-sections are not known; it is however likely that at least from early 1944 an operational unit with military tasks existed in each section, used to escort convoys on the Trieste–Fiume road, to provide security on the same road and to conduct anti-partisan operations.

The funeral of Franz Reichleitner, first commander of section R II, in the German military cemetery of Opicina (near Trieste) in January 1944. Wirth, wearing spectacles, is seen in the middle. In Poland, Reichleitner was commandant of the Sobibor extermination camp. *LA NRW, Münster*

Section R I in Trieste was the most numerous: around fifty men probably served in it (there are around sixty names of men who were at some point in Trieste, but this includes also the personnel belonging to the *Abteilung R*'s headquarters). Its barracks and operational basis was the Risiera complex, in the Trieste neighborhood of San Sabba.[16] The Risiera di San Sabba was a former rice mill, with a number of large buildings and warehouses, which became a prison for Jews, political opponents, partisans and civilians captured or arrested during sweep operations, who were later deported to Germany or killed and cremated in the Risiera. In addition to being the barracks for R I and a prison, the complex was also the *Abteilung*'s *Hauptstützpunkt* (literally main support base), that is the operational center for the anti-partisan actions and sweep operations carried out by the unit in the region. Here the external sections of *Abteilung R*—R II in Fiume and R III in Udine—collected food, equipment, and fuel as well as received their operational orders in case of anti-partisan actions, and handed over any prisoners to be interrogated by Wirth and later by Allers (Wirth's successor in June 1944). It seems that for the management of the Risiera (guarding the prisoners and the complex, administration), a rather limited number of Germans from section R I was used, around 20–30 men, together with around 12–15 *Trawniki* men.

Hering commanded both section R I and the Risiera, where he lived. He was dismissed by Allers for reasons that are not completely clear in July 1944. According to Oberhauser, the reason for Hering's removal was that Globocnik had harshly reproached Wirth, Hering, and the *Gestapo* commander in the OZAK, August Schiffer, for the arbitrary executions of Jews, reminding them that Trieste was not Eastern Europe and such actions were not allowed. However, this explanation—referring to a conversation that

A photo probably taken in spring 1944 in the first courtyard of the Risiera di San Sabba. Wirth is in the middle, with Hering on his left, and other members of *Abteilung R. LA NRW, Münster*

Erwin Lambert, on the left, and Karl Pötzinger, with his back to the camera and carrying a Suomi KP/-31 sub-machine gun, probably at the Risiera. *LA NRW, Münster*

must have taken place at least two months before Hering's removal, being Wirth still alive—does not seem truthful and could have had the objective of blaming mainly Wirth and Hering for the Jewish persecution in the OZAK and downplaying the role of others in it. According to Gley, the reason for Hering's removal was different: it was caused by personal conflicts between he and Allers, but was officially motivated by Hering being blamed for being unable to keep discipline among his men. The pretext was a fight between Gley and Hackenholt on one side, Plikat and Häusler on the other side, following which Hering was dismissed and sent to Udine in July or early August 1944 (Gley, who as *spieß*, or senior NCO, was in practice Hering's second-in-command at the Risiera, was sent back to Germany). However, Hering remained only a short time in Udine where apparently he took up no command role; on Allers' orders he also went back to Germany in late August or early September.

After Hering the command of section R I and the Risiera was taken over by Oberhauser, who also went to live in the Risiera (moving from the city, where he previously lived, in an unknown place after the destruction of Villa Segre). At the same time Oberhauser was also company commander of *6. Kp./SS-WMS-Btl.* (later renumbered *1. Kp.*); this unit—formed in May 1944 with Italians formerly belonging to *Battaglione Patrioti Davide*—was billeted at the Risiera and was tasked with guarding the entrance to the complex, the first courtyard, and the external perimeter (on Oberhauser's company see the chapter on the *SS-Wachmannschaften*; more on *Battaglione Davide* later).

In addition to the commanders (Hering and later Oberhauser) the following men were in Trieste (the names with an asterix also served in other sections): Baer (later seconded to the *SS-WMS-Btl.*), Barbl, Bauer,* Bolender* (later seconded to the *SS-WMS-Btl.*), Bredow, Dachsel,* Dietze, Dubois, Eisold, Fettke, Forker, Franz (seconded to the *SS-WMS-Btl.* in Gorizia), Geis, Geng, Girtzig (later seconded to the *SS-WMS-Btl.*), Gley, Gringers, Grossmann, Hackenholt, Häusler, Hengst,* Horn, Jührs, Klier, Köhler, Koschewski, Lambert,* Löffler, Mätzig,* Matthes, Miete,* Nowak, Plikat, Post,* Rehwald, Riedel, Rose, Rost, Rum, Schiffner, Schluch, Schmidt, Schneider, Schulz, Schulze, Schwarz (seconded to the *SS-WMS-Btl.*), Seidel, Seifert, Siebert, Sporleder (later seconded to the *SS-WMS-Btl.*), Stadie,* Steubl,* Suchomel,* Tauscher, Unverhau, Vey (or Fey), Wendlandt,* Wolf,* Zänker; plus perhaps Arndt and Orlyewski.[17]

In addition to Hering and Oberhauser, Franz, Häusler, Rost, Schwarz, and Tauscher had officer rank. As far as it is known, the tasks carried out by these officers were: Franz and Schwarz, as mentioned, were seconded to the *SS-WMS-Btl.* where they were involved in propaganda activities for recruiting local elements, training of recruits, territorial security, and fighting the partisans. Häusler was *Rechnungsführer* (chief accountant), and was in charge of wages, supplies, leaves; from Trieste he was moved to Turin and Milan to seize Jewish properties for four to five months and in March 1945, he went back to Germany. According to his own deposition, Rost served in the *Wirtschaftspolizei* (economic police) while in Italy, and also in a deposition by another unit member he was reported as working at the customs; however, according to another deposition he was leading the seizure of Jewish properties in Trieste. Tauscher, according to his own deposition, was employed in fighting the black market and later (probably after *Abteilung R* got involved in the activities of the *Sonderauftrag Pöll*) in acquiring materials (fuel, tires, trucks); however, a photo taken near the Rupa junction shows him wearing a camouflage outfit, apparently confirming that he also participated in anti-partisan actions in spring 1944.

Regarding section R II, generally its seat is indicated as Fiume, but sometimes also as Sušak (the part of the city east of the Recina (Rječina) River, which before the outbreak of World War

Otto Stadie, wearing an *Ordnungspolizei* uniform, posing with a Suomi KP/-31 in the Risiera. *LA NRW, Münster*

Erich Bauer in Italy, in *Ordnungspolizei* uniform but wearing an SS belt. *LA NRW, Münster*

Karl Ludwig in Italy, wearing an *Ordnungspolizei* tunic with elongated collar and Italian-style cuffs; apparently produced specifically for *Abteilung R*. *LA NRW, Münster*

II was on Yugoslav territory; today both parts belong to Rijeka).[18] Its first commander, Reichleitner, was killed by partisans on January 3, 1944. His successor was Stangl (transferred from Udine), who during summer 1944, was moved to the Veneto region, where the new section R IV was set up. Stangl was replaced as R II commander by Gerhard Börner, who was already in Fiume. Section R II counted around 25-30 men, of whom – in addition to the commanders – only the following are identified (the names with an asterix also served in other sections): Bauer,* Bolender,* Dachsel,* Fischer,* Frenzel, Gomerski,* Hiller, Hödl,* Kamm, Ludwig, Richter, Stadie,* Steubl, Wagner,* Wendlandt,* Wolf,* Zierke; plus perhaps Lambert.[19]

Except the commanders (Reichleitner, Stangl, Börner), the only officer was Helmut Fischer (apparently promoted to officer rank—*SS-Ustuf.*—in late June 1944).

Section R III in Udine was initially based on Via San Martino, in the city quarter south of the train station, in a house requisitioned from the Jewish family of Roberto Gentilli. When the house was damaged by an air raid (probably on June 10, 1944), the R III moved to the *Sipo*/SD offices on Via Cairoli, in the city center. The section was initially commanded by Stangl, until his transfer to Fiume in January 1944. His temporary successor was Fritz Küttner (formerly responsible for the "unteres Lager" of Treblinka, or Treblinka 1, the camp "administrative" section) until the arrival of Arthur Walther (who had been temporary commander of Sobibor in 1942) from Germany in March/April 1944. After two or three weeks, during April 1944, Walther was transferred with most of the R III men to Castelnuovo d'Istria, to help provide security on the Trieste–Fiume road. It is not clear who replaced him in Udine, possibly again Küttner; later, perhaps in August or September, the command was taken up by Fischer, transferred from section R II. Section R III counted around 10–20 men, among whom—in addition to the commanders—the following are identified (the names with an asterix also served in other sections): Beelitz, Bollert, Fels, Gentz, Hengst,* Kielminsky, Lambert,* Mätzig,* Mentz, Miete,* Münzberger, Pötzinger, Suchomel*; plus perhaps Hirtreiter.[20]

This photo probably shows a member of *Abteilung R* (possibly Karl Ludwig) in *Ordnungspolizei* uniform, armed with a Suomi KP/-31.

Only the commanders (Stangl, Walther, Fischer) had officer rank. After most men were transferred to Castelnuovo with Walther, only a few people remained in Udine (under Fischer's command there were apparently only Beelitz, Miete, and Suchomel).[21]

During summer 1944, a new section R IV was additionally created with bases in Treviso, Mestre, and Venice, in the Veneto region, that is outside the OZAK territory, commanded by Stangl; apparently its members were at least Wagner, Hödl, Gomerski, Post, and surely Suchomel (who later went back to Udine in early 1945).[22] Its creation probably originated from the expansion of Rainer's and Globocnik's authority to the Veneto region as responsible for the construction of

Ernst Zierke in *Ordnungspolizei* uniform, probably in Trieste. *LA NRW, Münster*

defensive lines and the start of Sonderauftrag Pöll, in which also *Abteilung R* was involved (see section 3.4.5).

For some men it is not known which section they belonged to: Bischkopf, Möller, Müller, Schrottmayer, Seidler, Sporleder, Sydow, Thiel and Witt. Furthermore, the presence in Italy of two more people—Becher and Godenschweig—is possible but not confirmed.[23]

3.3: Personnel Evolution

After the arrival in Trieste of around 100 men of *Abteilung R* between late 1943 and early 1944, the personnel had limited variations during the stay in Italy due to transfers, deaths, and new arrivals. Information is surely incomplete but the following is ascertained.

At least fourteen or fifteen men left Italy before the German retreat at the end of the war, for reasons which are not always known: Siebert in early 1944 (within a couple of months after arriving in Trieste); Unverhau in March 1944 (he went to the Wehrmacht on own request); Gley in July or early August 1944 (for disciplinary reasons; he became instructor in the *Waffen-SS* in Prague); Hering in late August or early September (due to contrasts with Allers); Plikat in summer–autumn 1944 (for disciplinary reasons; he was transferred to the *Ordnungspolizei* and later to the *Wehrmacht*, was said to have died in the last days of the war in Berlin); Eishold and Horn in autumn 1944 (for disciplinary reasons, it seems); Rum in February 1945 (he went to hospital after a motorbike accident); Häusler, Küttner, Stangl, Wagner, and perhaps Post in March 1945 (for disciplinary reasons, it seems); Beelitz and Seidler at an unknown date.[24]

At least ten men died in Italy. Of these, seven were killed in ambushes or in a fight with the partisans: Reichleitner (1/3/1944), Gringers and Löffler (4/30/1944), Wirth (5/26/1944), Schwarz (6/19/1944), Richter (8/13/1944), Thiel (missing in action in March 1945, apparently captured by the partisans and probably killed). Pötzinger died after being wounded by a strafing airplane (he died at the Udine hospital on 12/22/1944 after being wounded in San Vito al Tagliamento; on the same day, probably on the same occasion, also Mentz was wounded). Wendlandt died on 12/28/1944 in Pordenone, probably during an air raid that hit the city on that day. Vey (Fey) died in unknown circumstances during the final retreat (it seems on 4/25/1945).[25] Also Börner is reported as missing or perhaps killed in Italy in the final phase of the war, but confirmation is missing.

Wirth was killed on May 26, 1944, in an ambush by Slovenian partisans belonging to the first battalion of the Istrski Odred (Istria detachment) near the village of Erpelle, on the Trieste–Fiume road; the exact place is indicated as near the village of Nazire di San Dorligo della Valle (according to a Carabinieri report) or near the so-called Vetta di Erpelle (Kozinski vrh) hill, aound one kilometer northwest of the twin villages of Cosina–Erpelle (according to a Yugoslav reconstruction).[26] Wirth, who a few weeks earlier had been nominated *Sicherungskommandant der Karststrasse* (security commander for the

This series of photos was taken at Wirth's funeral, held at the German military cemetery of Opicina a few days after his death on May 26, 1944. Military and civilian authorities walk towards the cemetery, among them are Blankenburg and Allers (indicated by crosses, respectively on the right and on the left of the first photo). Both wear *Sturmabteilung* uniforms. In front of Blankenburg, in the first photo, is Globocnik. *HHStA, Wiesbaden*

Military and civilian authorities during the ceremony. In the middle of the first photo Blankenburg and Globocnik can be recognized, with Allers at left. In the background on the right, wearing helmets, are members of *Abteilung R* in *Ordnungspolizei* uniforms and *Trawniki*. With their back to the camera, in the first row with the *edelweiss* on the tunic sleeve, are two SS soldiers (probably members of the *SS-Karstwehr-Btl.*). Behind them, with black berets, are soldiers of an unidentified Italian unit (possibly GNR officer cadets). *HHStA, Wiesbaden*

Trieste–Fiume road, called Karststrasse, or Karst road, by the Germans) was going to Fiume to discuss an anti-partisan operation and was travelling with his driver, Geng, who was lightly wounded; they did not have an escort. Wirth's body was transported to the Risiera, where a mortuary was set up. A few days later he was buried at the German military cemetery of Opicina with military honors and in the presence of Globocnik and other OZAK dignitaries, as well as of—as mentioned—Blankenburg and Allers, who came from Berlin. Immediately, rumors started to circulate that Wirth had been killed by his men, who feared and hated him; however, no concrete element to support this hypothesis has ever been presented, while Yugoslav sources confirm that he surely died in a partisan ambush.

Wirth's successor was *Oberregierungsrat der Verwaltungspolizei* (high-rank official of the administrative police, corresponding to the rank of *Oberstleutnant der Polizei*) and *SA-Sturmbannführer* Dietrich Allers, who at that time was director of *Aktion T4*. Allers arrived in Trieste in early June and took up all tasks previously carried out by Wirth, becoming Inspekteur of *Abteilung R* and *Sicherungskommandant der Karststrasse*. A few days after his arrival, on June 10, 1944, Villa Segre was destroyed in an air raid and the headquarters of *Abteilung R* moved to an apartment on the third floor of a building on Via Giustinelli 1, where a Jewish family used to live. Here lived Allers, and with him Häusler, Rum (Allers' orderly and guard), Geng (initially Allers' driver), three female clerks, a cook, and a cleaner.

In addition to Allers, some other men already active in *Aktion T4* arrived in the OZAK from Germany during 1944 to be integrated in *Abteilung R*; among the known names are Fischer (arrival date unclear),[27] Walther (arrived in March/April 1944), Köhler (in September 1944), and Geis (during autumn 1944). Also, this further arrival of personnel from *Aktion T4*, although very

Blankenburg giving the last salute to Wirth. Around the coffin is an honor guard made up of *Abteilung R* men wearing *Ordnungspolizei* and *Waffen-SS* uniforms. *HHStA, Wiesbaden*

Another photo taken at Wirth's funeral: the honorific salvos are fired. With their backs to the camera are members of *Abteilung R* and *Trawniki*.

modest, confirms the enduring links between this organization and *Abteilung R* in Italy.

As mentioned, in total around a hundred men serving in the OZAK with *Abteilung R* are identified; the list is in appendix 5. It is to be noted, however, that the list is probably not complete and not completely correct, and in some cases only surnames are known.

3.4: Tasks of *Abteilung R*

Abteilung R carried out various tasks in the OZAK, which evidently evolved over time in particular because of the evolution of the general war situation. The following activities have been identified:

- Tracking down and arresting Jews, identification and seizure of their properties (from autumn 1943)
- Management of the Risiera di San Sabba prison complex (*Polizeihaftlager* San Sabba; probably from the end of 1943 – early 1944)
- Contribution to the setting-up, training, and leading of locally formed military units (*landeseigene Verbände*; from autumn 1943)
- Providing security on the Trieste–Fiume road (Karststrasse), including setting up outposts on this communication line (from early 1944)
- Participation in sweep operations and anti-partisan actions (apparently from early 1944)
- Contribution to the construction of the defensive lines built in the region (under the responsibility of the Sonderauftrag Pöll; from summer 1944)

Although the management of the Risiera only fell upon section R I, all three sections R I, II, and III took part in the other tasks (section R IV only in the first and the last). Apparently, each section was divided in sub-sections, to which different activity fields were assigned. Although it is difficult to be certain due to the fragmentary information, it seems that some unit members were employed only or almost exclusively for one of the listed activities, while others changed roles several times.

The following sections deal with the various aspects of the *Abteilung R* activities in the OZAK.

3.4.1: Tracking and Arrest of the Jews, Identification and Seizure of Property

Probably right after the arrival in the OZAK of the first group of *Abteilung R* men in November 1943, the primary tasks assigned to them were tracking down and arresting the Jews, and the identification, cataloguing and seizure of their properties.[28]

Tracking down and arresting the Jews were carried out in parallel also by the *Sipo*/SD. Only a (non quantifiable) part of the arrests made in the region was therefore effectuated by *Abteilung R*. The first preserved detention form (*Haftschein*) concerning three arrested Jews issued by the unit (in particular by section R I, signed by Rost) is dated December 30, 1943.

There are very few specific details regarding operations conducted by the unit for arresting Jews. Some trial depositions by former members of *Abteilung R* mention an important round-up of Jews carried out in Abbazia at an undefined date during 1944.[29] This is perhaps the same episode described in his memoirs by an Italian soldier of the *SS-Wachmannschaften*, based at the Risiera, who took part in it with around fifty of his Italian comrades: on June 6–7, 1944, they escorted German personnel during a series of searches in some villas in the seaside resorts of Abbazia and Laurana, which probably preceded the actual round-ups. The same Italian soldier also recalls in his memories the participation of a group of Italian soldiers—again as escort—to a night round-up action in the Trieste ghetto, probably in June 1944, possibly also together with some members of *Abteilung R*, during which several people were arrested.[30] *Abteilung R* most probably carried out other similar operations, in Trieste and in other areas, on which, however, specific information is missing. Other arrests were for sure also made during targeted searches in the houses of Jewish families. The Jews arrested by *Abteilung R* were detained in the Risiera awaiting deportation (on the Risiera see the next section). Apparently, the transports of Jews to the concentration, extermination and labor camps were exclusively organized by the Sipo/SD, and *Abteilung R* was not involved.

According to several depositions or accounts by former *Abteilung R* elements, the persecution of the Jews was stopped or strongly reduced in the OZAK due to the initiative of Globocnik as well as Allers. According to Oberhauser, Globocnik harshly reproached Wirth, Hering, and the *Gestapo* commander Schiffer for the arbitrary killing of Jews, stating that the OZAK was not Eastern Europe and the same methods used in the latter were not allowed to be applied in the former.[31] According to Suchomel, Allers told him that he would not let any Jews be deported to Germany, rather he would have them work on site; in Allers' intentions, *Abteilung R* should not waste energy in chasing the Jews, but concentrate itself on more urgent tasks (fighting the partisans, securing the Trieste–Fiume road).[32] Although it is possible that Globocnik wanted to avoid arbitrary executions (but is seems very unlikely that he was opposed to arrests and deportations), these reconstructions could have been agreed among former unit members to mitigate their own responsibilities, blaming mainly the deceased Wirth for the persecution of the Jews. It is in any case possible that, after the first months of German occupation, the number of Jews in the OZAK provinces, already not high, had been extremely reduced by arrests and flights, limiting therefore further actions of *Abteilung R* in this area. After the creation of section R IV, during summer–autumn 1944 Jews were also arrested outside the OZAK, in particular in the Veneto region; they were detained in the Risiera before being deported to Germany.

The seizure of properties carried out by *Abteilung R* consisted both in the clearing of Jewish houses, apartments, and shops (an inventory was made of their content, which was then stored in the storehouses in the Risiera complex),[33] as well as the seizure of bank deposits and safes. Generally, teams of two men of *Abteilung R* visited the houses and apartments reported to belong to Jewish families; if someone was found there they were arrested, but in the great majority of cases the inhabitants had fled or had already been arrested. On Wirth's orders the components of the teams rotated regularly, and each house or apartment was visited by two teams at different times, so that one team verified the work of another. Like for the arrests, the confiscation of Jewish property by *Abteilung R* also took place sometimes outside the OZAK, probably after the creation of section R IV: some trial depositions mention such activity in particular in Milan and Turin, where for instance shops and commercial activities owned by Jews were searched.[34] The seizure of Jewish properties continued certainly until the last phases

Two *Haftschein* (detention forms) produced by *Abteilung R* and dated January 20, 1944, respectively signed by Hering and Oberhauser. One concerns a Jew, Dr. Carlo Morpurgo from Trieste, deported to Auschwitz where he died. Note that the forms bear the heading "*Der Befehlshaber der Sipo und des SD in der OZAK*," crossed out by hand and replaced by "R 1."

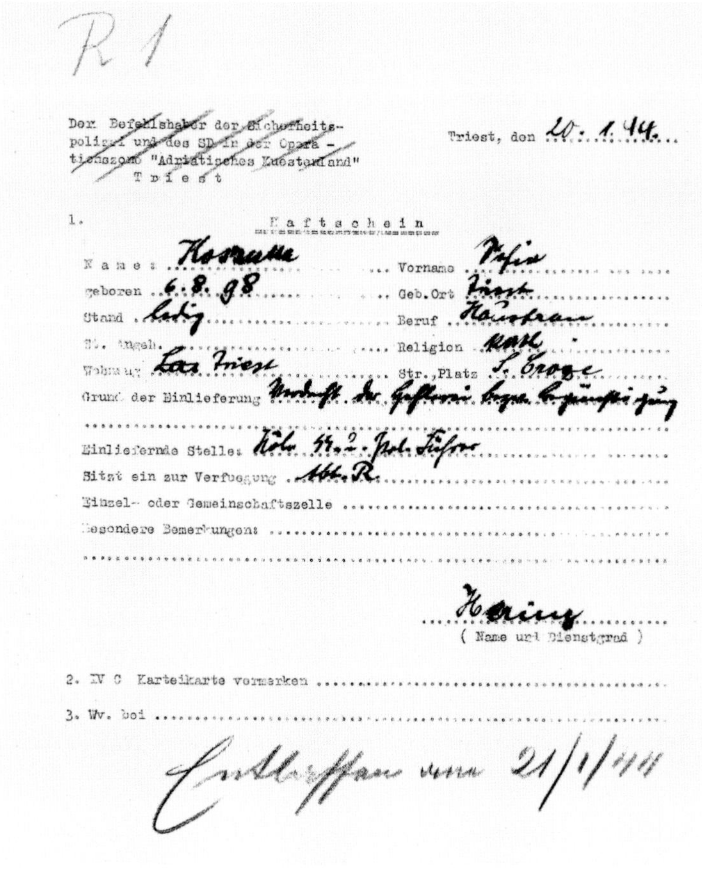

R 1

Der Befehlshaber der Sicherheitspolizei und des SD in der Operationszone "Adriatisches Kuestenland" Triest — Triest, den 20. 1. 44.

1. Haftschein

Name: ... Vorname ...
geboren 6.8.98 ... Geb.Ort Triest
Stand ledig ... Beruf Hausfrau
St. Angeh. ... Religion kath.
Wohnung ... Triest ... Str., Platz S. Croce
Grund der Einlieferung ...
Einliefernde Stelle: ...
Sitzt ein zur Verfügung Abt. R.
Einzel- oder Gemeinschaftszelle ...
Besondere Bemerkungen: ...

Hering
(Name und Dienstgrad)

2. IV C Karteikarte vormerken ...
3. Wv. bei ...

Entlassen am 21/1/44

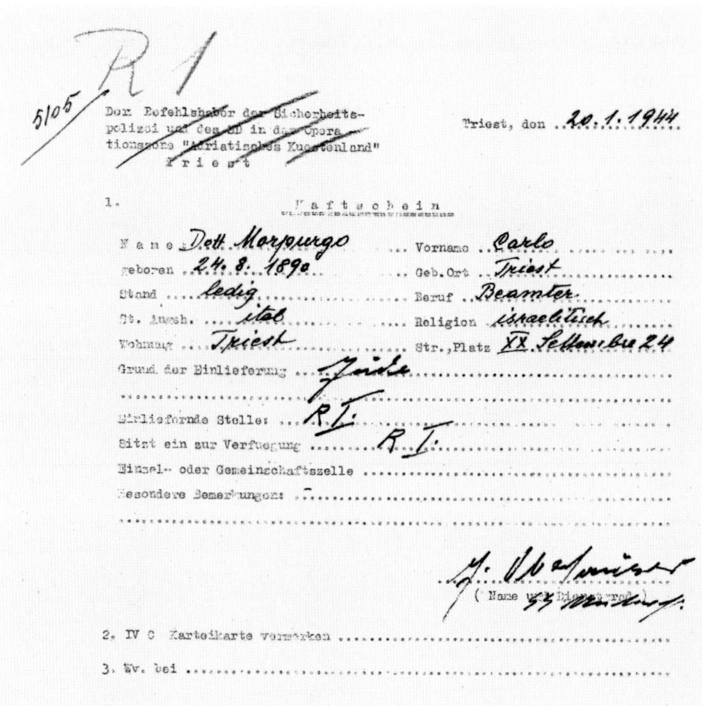

5105 R 1

Der Befehlshaber der Sicherheitspolizei und des SD in der Operationszone "Adriatisches Kuestenland" Triest — Triest, den 20.1.1944

1. Haftschein

Name: Dott. Morpurgo ... Vorname Carlo
geboren 24.8.1890 ... Geb.Ort Triest
Stand ledig ... Beruf Beamter
St. Angeh. ital ... Religion israelitisch
Wohnung Triest ... Str., Platz XX Settembre 24
Grund der Einlieferung Jude
Einliefernde Stelle: R.I.
Sitzt ein zur Verfügung R.I.
Einzel- oder Gemeinschaftszelle ...
Besondere Bemerkungen: –

(Name und Dienstgrad)

2. IV C Karteikarte vormerken ...
3. Wv. bei ...

of the war. These activities very probably offered several members of the unit the opportunity to take possession of abandoned goods and unlawfully enrich themselves.

3.4.2: The *Polizeihaftlager* in the Risiera di San Sabba

The Risiera di San Sabba, often still wrongly defined as an extermination camp, was actually a *Polizeihaftlager*, that is a police prison from where people were sent to concentration, extermination, and work camps in Germany. However, many prisoners were killed in the complex, and their bodies incinerated in a crematory to eliminate any traces.

Originally a rice mill, the Risiera had been turned into a warehouse and later barracks for the Italian army. It was a large complex, divided into two separate parts, made up of buildings gathered around two adjacent courtyards, linked by a covered passageway. During the German occupation and the use of the site by *Abteilung R*, the area of the first courtyard was mainly used as barracks, while the area of the second courtyard was where the prisoners were detained and sometimes killed. The first courtyard included the main entrance, with the building for the guards on the left; this building also hosted the apartment of the camp commander, initially Hering and later Oberhauser. On the right of the entrance was a large three-floor building, used as billets for the German and *Trawniki* personnel, offices, kitchen and canteen. Also on the right of the first courtyard was a garage. Directly in front of the camp entrance was a large six-floor building, initially used as a warehouse and from May 1944 as billets for the *SS-Wachmannschaften* unit formed by Italians based at the Risiera (*6. Kp./SS-WMS-Btl.*, formerly *Battaglione Davide*); the ground floor hosted a canteen. Adjacent to this building on the left there was a smaller one, used also as a storeroom for seized goods; through it went a passageway that led to the second courtyard. The passageway was closed by a gate that was constantly guarded and only those who were authorized to access the second courtyard could pass; access, as well as any contact with the prisoners, was strictly forbidden to the Italian soldiers of *6. Kp./SS-WMS-Btl.*

The second courtyard was much larger and included several buildings, most of them used as warehouses, including for Jews' properties. The second building on the left after the passageway was the main prison: it included two large rooms (on the second and third floor) where the prisoners were detained in groups; on the first floor another large room hosted a tailor's and a shoemaker's workshop where groups of prisoners were employed as forced labor. On the ground floor there were seventeen small cells. In front of this building

The Risiera di San Sabba in an image dating from the 1950s. *IRSML-FVG*

was the former kiln, with chimney, which was adapted as a crematory. The presence of this crematory represents the Risiera's peculiarity compared to all Nazi prisons in Western Europe. It was built by Lambert presumably in early 1944, and was used to burn the bodies of people killed in the Risiera or elsewhere. Various depositions mention that on one occasion several dozen bodies were transported from Opicina to the Risiera, where they were incinerated; these were probably the bodies of the seventy-one hostages shot at the Opicina shooting range on April 3, 1944, as a reprisal for a bombing attack perpetrated against a cinema in the town, where seven German soldiers were killed. The ashes resulting from the burning were dispersed in the sea facing Trieste.

For the Jews the Risiera was a place of incarceration and transit, with a few exceptions they were not killed there. According to the most recent estimates, around 1,450 Jews (originating from the OZAK region, from Veneto and from Croatia) passed through the Risiera on their way to the extermination camps, mainly Auschwitz and Ravensbrück; at least twenty-eight of them are confirmed killed in San Sabba. For the political prisoners (who included members of the resistance movements, partisans, civilians accused or suspected of supporting the partisan movement, hostages, etc.) the Risiera was a prison (where they were questioned, sometimes tortured), a transit camp, and often a killing camp. Several thousand people—there are only estimates—passed through the Risiera on their way to the extermination, detention, or labor camps in Germany; a considerable number of people—estimated between 2,000 and 5,000—were killed in the San Sabba complex.

The prisoners remained in San Sabba generally for short periods, after a few days or weeks they were deported or killed. The only exception was around thirty Jewish prisoners, who occupied the first floor of the detention building on the second courtyard, and remained in the camp until its demise as workers (tailors, shoemakers, cleaners, in the warehouses, etc.). The tailor's workshop, active from June 1944 to the end of the war, not only produced uniforms for the officers on order and made repairs on of clothing items, but probably also produced in (small) series some uniform items used by *Abteilung R* (see appendix 1).

The prisoners had sometimes been arrested by *Abteilung R*, sometimes they were transferred to the Risiera from other prisons in the region; in general it is not possible to ascertain the reasons for which a prisoner was moved to the Risiera. During their stay they were subject to constant terror and anguish because of the ever-present physical and psychological ill-treatment. What

The entrance to the Risiera site. *IRSML-FVG*

The first courtyard, with the covered passageway (during the war closed by a gate) leading to the second courtyard, where the prisoners were detained. The large building in the middle was used for storage as well as to billet the Italian *SS-Wachmannschaften*. *IRSML-FVG*

In the first courtyard, view to the right: in the middle the garage, on the right the building that hosted the billets for the Germans and the *Trawniki*, the offices, the canteen, and the kitchen. *IRSML-FVG*

In the first courtyard, view to the left: on the right the covered passageway leading to the second courtyard, in the middle a small building where Wirth's body was placed immediately following his death. *IRSML-FVG*

The Risiera entrance, seen from the first courtyard: the house on the right hosted the entrance guards and the lodging of the camp commander, Hering, and later Oberhauser. *IRSML-FVG*

The second courtyard, with the debris caused by the explosions that destroyed the crematorium.
IRSML-FVG

criteria caused a prisoner to be killed at the Risiera or deported there is no sufficient information; it seems likely that in most cases the killings were arbitrary, without any court decision. The killings were carried out in different ways: according to accounts by former prisoners, it seems that blows delivered with a bludgeon, hanging, or perhaps sometimes firearms were used. Oberhauser stated in a deposition that prisoners were also executed by means of suffocation via exhaust fumes.[35] During the killings, which generally took place at night, shouts or sounds were covered by artificially produced noises, such as running engines or music played at high volume by loudspeakers. According to a deposition, the peak of the executions was between August and November 1944, but they continued frequently until February–March 1945. Apparently, the executioners were generally (but not exclusively) *Trawniki* men (indicated as "Ukrainians" in the depositions), who also burned the bodies. In addition to being warders and executioners, the *Trawniki*—there were apparently 12–15 of them—were employed at the Risiera to guard the complex.

It seems that the German personnel active in the management of the prison complex (watching over the prisoners, guarding, administration) numbered around 20–30 people. After the camp

German military vehicles parked in the second courtyard garage, crushed by the explosion.
IRSML-FVG

An external view of the complex, probably in the 1960s. *IRSML-FVG*

commander, the highest position was that of the *Spieß* (senior NCO); it was initially covered by Gley, who was removed by Allers together with Hering. He was replaced as *Spieß* by Stadie (apparently after a short transition period covered by Dubois). Regarding the warders, only some are known by name thanks to the depositions of former prisoners: they are Stadie, Koschewski, Dachsel, Geis, Horn, Schneider, Schulz;[36] there was also a particularly cruel warder who was missing a forearm, but he is not identified (perhaps Orlyewski). Active at the Risiera, although not as warders but rather in offices, in the management of the warehouses or in other occupations, were at least Barbl, Bauer, Dubois, Girtzig, Hackenholt, Köhler, Plikat, Riedel, Schiffner, Schneider, another Schulz, and Seidel.

The Risiera was not only a prison, a transit, killing and forced labor camp, and a warehouse of seized goods. It was also the base of section R I and the barracks of its operational unit active against the partisans and for guaranteeing security on the Karststrasse (and additionally, from May 1944, the barracks of the Italian soldiers of the former *Battaglione Davide* who formed *6. Kp./SS-WMS-Btl.*). It was also the *Hauptstützpunkt* for the entire *Abteilung R*, i.e., the main support base for section R II and R III, from which the anti-partisan actions and the sweep operations set off. In addition to the above mentioned men employed for managing the camp, all other components of section R I were billeted at the

The entrance to the Risiera today; the complex has been heavily modified and transformed into a museum.

The second courtyard of the Risiera today. On the right are the buildings where the prisoners were detained; in the middle are the traces left by the building that held the crematorium.

Risiera but in general did not occupy themselves with the prisoners. This explains why former inmates knew for instance the names of Hackenholt and Bolender, who were based at the Risiera but had apparently no responsibility as far as the prisoners were concerned.[37]

The Risiera continued its activity in practice almost until the last day of the German presence in Trieste.[38] The camp was closed on April 29, 1945. On the evening of that day the last Jewish prisoners still in the camp (around thirty, those who worked at the tailor's and shoemaker's shops, etc.) were freed; Oberhauser even shook their hands. After their release most of the camp personnel left the Risiera heading for the city center, while groups of partisans were already in the area. A little later, during the night, the crematorium and the chimney exploded (apparently with a time charge), in an attempt to hide what had happened there.[39]

3.4.3: Contribution to the Setting-Up, Training, and Leading of Locally Formed Military Units (*landeseigene Verbände*)

Around the end of 1943, the setting-up of local auxiliary units, the so-called *landeseigene Selbstschutzverbände* (literally self-defense local units, or *organizzazioni per la difesa territoriale*—territorial defense organizations—in the official Italian translation; for brevity they were also called *landeseigene Verbände*, or local units) was started in the OZAK. They were military units formed by locally recruited elements indicated by the Germans with the term *landeseigene Kräfte* (literally local forces, but it was officially translated into Italian as *forze territoriali*, or territorial forces). Components of the *landeseigene Verbände* were the *SS-Wachmannschaften of the OZAK* (consisting in practice of the *SS-Wachmannschafts-Bataillon*), the *Landschutz* (territorial defense) units and other units.

Elements of *Abteilung R* were used for recruiting and training of the *landeseigene Kräfte*, and as cadres in the *SS-WMS-Btl.* In autumn 1943, at least Franz, Schwarz, and probably Oberhauser were employed as trainers for the recruits of the *SS-WMS-Btl.* in the Via Combi barracks in Trieste. Later, Franz led the *Landschutzschule* (school for *Landschutz* troops) in Gorizia, where he was transferred in early 1944 as commander of a detachment of the *SS-WMS-Btl.* (called *Kommando G.*). Franz also took part in propaganda and (voluntary or forced) recruiting actions for local units in the Gorizia province together with *Sonderkommando "Adria"* of the *SS-Standarte "Kurt Eggers,"* a *Waffen-SS* propaganda unit.[40] Also, Stangl in his trial depositions declared that he was tasked with setting up *Landschutz* units formed by local elements in Udine and later in Fiume, in cooperation with an SS propaganda unit (evidently the mentioned *Sonderkommando "Adria"*).[41]

The *SS-WMS-Btl.* (in particular one of its parts, the *Wachmannschaft II*) was mainly formed by locally recruited personnel, but its cadres consisted of elements (Germans and *Trawniki*) coming from a company of *Wachmannschaften* that had arrived in Trieste from Lublin, as well as elements of *Abteilung R* (Germans and *Trawniki*

Kurt Franz, member of *Abteilung R* but seconded to the *SS-Wachmannschaften* of the OZAK, in the uniform of an SS-*Untersturmführer*. In Poland, he had been deputy commandant and, in the last phase, commandant of the Treblinka extermination camp.

Two photos of Gottfried Schwarz, in the uniform of an *SS-Oberscharführer* probably in the early 1940s. Note the right collar tab with the *Totenkopf.* In Italy, with the rank of *SS-Untersturmführer*, Schwarz was a member of *Abteilung R* but was seconded to the *SS-Wachmannschaften*.

attached to *Abteilung R*). The members of *Abteilung R* that—in unknown number—were permanently inserted in the *SS-WMS-Btl.* were apparently seconded to the battalion but remained full members of *Abteilung R*. Only very few names are known: among them three officers (*SS-Ustuf.* Franz, Oberhauser, and Schwarz) and four NCOs (*SS-Uscha.* Baer, Bolender, Girtzig, and Sporleder). For sure in the case of the three officers and of the first three NCOs, they were *Waffen-SS* members and as such they had undergone at least some degree of military training; this was evidently the reason they were chosen to be seconded to the *SS-WMS-Btl.*, a unit with military tasks. For the *Trawniki* attached to *Abteilung R*, five men seconded to the *SS-WMS-Btl.* are known (Schmidt, E. Kostenko, A. Rosenke, Dahlke, and Siewert).

Oberhauser was company commander and probably trainer in the *SS-WMS-Btl.* for a short time during autumn 1943, then he was assigned to other duties in *Abteilung R*; in May 1944, he was again seconded to the battalion as commander of the newly formed *6. Kompanie*, based at the Risiera. To this company belonged also the four NCOs. Schwarz was commander of *2. Kompanie* of the *SS-WMS-Btl.*, probably from autumn 1943, and as such (as well as probably *Sicherungskommandant* in the Gemona area, in the Udine province) he was killed by partisans on June 19, 1944. Franz, as mentioned, was commander of a detachment of the *SS-WMS-Btl.* (called *Kommando G.*) sent to Gorizia in early 1944, and later apparently expanded to a company (additionally from June 1944 he was also *Sicherungskommandant* for the San Daniele del Carso sector).

On the *SS-WMS-Btl.*—which in summer 1944 numbered up to six companies in the *Wachmannschaft II*—only little information is available. Apart from the secondment of some personnel, it seems that it did not have operational links with *Abteilung R*, except for the mentioned *6. Kompanie*, which was involved in the activities of *Abteilung R* in several ways:

- It performed guard duties at the Risiera;
- In some occasion its elements participated as escort in search and round-up operations carried out against the Jews (see the episodes in Abbazia and Laurana and in the Trieste ghetto);
- From May 1944 some elements of the company were moved to the *Stützpunkt* (outpost) Castelnuovo d'Istria, and later (apparently from July) also to the *Stützpunkt* Mattuglie, both on the Trieste–Fiume road, side by side with *Abteilung R* men, and together with them they also took part in anti-partisan operations (see next section).

More information on the *SS-Wachmannschaften* of the OZAK and on the other *landeseigene Verbände* is provided in chapter 4.

Two views of the village of Castelnuovo d'Istria (now Podgrad, Slovenia) on the Karststrasse at around midway between Trieste and Fiume, in the 1930s. An outpost of *Abteilung R* was based there at least from April 1944 to early 1945, under Walther's command. From mid-May 1944, a detachment of Italians from *6. Kp./ SS-Wachmannschafts-Btl.* (former *Battaglione Davide*) was also based there. It was also the headquarters of a company of Italian *Guardia di Finanza* (Finance Guard) employed for security purposes and fighting the partisans.

Partial view of Mattuglie (now Matulji, Croatia), near Fiume, in a photo from the 1930s (view to the west). On the left is the town hall, on the top right the train station.

The town center and main road of Mattuglie, in a photo from the 1930s (view to the east). On the top left of the picture are several buildings belonging to the train station (among them, one which is visible on a photo showing men of *Abteilung R*, reproduced in the section on the *Braunschweig* operation, page 54).

Pre-World War II image of the ONMI hospital in Mattuglie. The building (still standing) was on the main road, at the town's western entrance. Probably in 1944–45, it hosted an outpost created by section R II of *Abteilung R* from Fiume, which was active on the Karststrasse. From July 1944, a detachment of Italians from *6. Kp./SS-Wachmannschafts-Btl.* (former *Battaglione Davide*) was also based in this building, and at least from October 1944 it hosted the headquarters of the *2. Compagnia of 3. Rgt. MDT. Photo G. Petricich via www.croinfo.net*

3.4.4: Providing Security on the Karststrasse, Participating in Sweep Operations, and Anti-partisan Actions

The Trieste–Fiume road, called Karststrasse (Karst road) by the Germans,[42] was one of the main communication lines in the region and had therefore great importance. At the same time, practically for its entire length it drove through areas of strong partisan activity, and ambushes against German vehicles were a daily occurrence since the start of the German occupation, so that it became necessary to drive on it in convoy, preferably with the escort of armored cars or armored vehicles. Reichleitner, the commander of section R II based in Fiume, was killed on January 3, 1944, while driving by car on this road towards Trieste, in a Partisan ambush 3.5 kilometers northwest of Castelnuovo d'Istria.[43]

Providing security on the Karststrasse and contrasting the partisan activity in areas along the road were among the main tasks of *Abteilung R* during its stay in the OZAK. The reason why this task was assigned to the unit, although few of its men had received proper military training, is not known. Among the reasons one could put forward the following:

- The scarcity of German security forces, which made it necessary to use all available men;
- The impossibility of employing all 100 men of *Abteilung R* for tracking down the Jews and seizing their properties, given the

This photo taken in Càrie (now Harije, Slovenia), a few kilometers northeast of Castelnuovo d'Istria, in spring 1944, perhaps during *Unternehmen Braunschweig*, shows Globocnik near an armored car, an Italian-produced AB 41, belonging to *I. Btl./SS-Pol.Rgt. "Bozen." MNZS, 2378_10*

Karl Ludwig (left) and Philip Post (right), both armed with Suomi KP/-31s, at the permanent check point at the Rupa junction, towards the end of winter 1944 (probably in the second half of March). Behind them are some Italian soldiers, including some *Carabinieri*, probably belonging to the MDT detachment manning the outpost. *LA NRW, Münster*

relatively limited number of Jews still in the region;

- The necessity for the unit to protect its own transports between Trieste and Fiume.

The starting date for the involvement of *Abteilung R* in the security of the Trieste–Fiume road and in anti-partisan activities is not precisely known. According to a trial deposition,[44] the anti-partisan employment started immediately after the death of Reichleitner, but other confirmations in this regard are missing. Schneider said that already by the end of April 1944 (when he was wounded) he had taken part in several anti-partisan operations, during which his unit searched villages and arrested suspects, who were taken to the Risiera.[45]

Apparently during the first quarter of 1944, the unit set up at least one outpost on the Karststrasse, in the village of Sappiane, which existed at least from the end of March: at least this can be inferred by the fact that in that period commander of the outpost was a certain Fischer, who can possibly be identified with Helmut Fischer of *Abteilung R*.[46] It is also known that probably in the first months of 1944 the unit acquired some (three or perhaps four) jury-rigged armored trucks, built using armored plates from various sources (see appendix 4). These vehicles were used to escort convoys travelling on the Trieste–Fiume road and to patrol the road. Some photos showing two of these trucks in action at the end of April 1944, represent the first evidence of the engagement of *Abteilung R* in patrolling the Karststrasse (see below).

In order to help secure the road, later the unit built some other outposts on the Trieste–Fiume road, the main ones being Castelnuovo and Mattuglie; it seems that there were also smaller outposts in other localities, but none are identified

Men of *Abteilung R* wearing the characteristic camouflage outfits used by the unit, produced in Italian mod. 29 camo fabric. *LA NRW, Münster*

Men of *Abteilung R* slaughtering a calf, somewhere in Istria. *LA NRW, Münster*

Willi Wendlandt during an action in Italy. *LA NRW, Münster*

with the probable exception of Starada, likely a sub-post of Castelnuovo, some three kilometers southeast of this village.[47] There is no certain information on the dates when these outposts were set up, but their creation was probably linked to the nomination of Wirth to the position of *Sicherungskommandant der Karststrasse*, made by Globocnik evidently with the objective of improving the security on this important communication line.[48] Not even the exact date of Globocnik's order nominating Wirth *Sicherungskommandant* is known, but it probably dated to the second half of April 1944 or to early May. It was probably the first security commander nominated in the OZAK,[49] to whom many more followed (see the specific section). Globocnik's order is transcribed in the following:

> In accordance with my order 15/44, I nominate *SS-Stubaf.* Christian Wirth security commander for the Trieste–Fiume road (*Sicherheitskommandant für die Strasse Triest–Fiume*). To it belong also the areas left and right of the road itself. He will himself suggest the borders [of his responsibility area] after identifying the area from which the enemy intervenes on the road. A plan on this regard is to be submitted to me by May 14. [Wirth] must agree his actions with the provincial *SS-u.Polizei-Kommandeur* [of Trieste, Fiume and Istria]. In particular I underline the necessity of collaborating with the *Wehrmacht* and the *Deutscher Berater* [head of civilian administration] of the provinces of Trieste, Fiume and Istria.

This nomination represented probably the acknowledgment of the already ongoing engagement of *Abteilung R* in providing security on the

Three photos taken during an operation probably on the Carso plateau east of Trieste during spring 1944. The *SS-Sturmbannführer* in the middle is Ernst Lerch, carrying a Suomi KP/-31 sub-machine gun on his shoulder, seen together with other SS and *Polizei* officers.

Karststrasse, but also a leap forward because of the attribution to Wirth and his unit of extensive military functions, involving the use of fixed outposts; these were added to the other tasks—never abandoned but carried out in parallel—of chasing the Jews and seizing their properties, as well as further tasks that were assigned to the unit later.

In his new function Wirth had to coordinate himself with the *SS-u.Pol.Kommandeur* of the provinces crossed by the road or near it (Trieste, Fiume, and Pola), to whom he was subordinated; additionally he had to cooperate with the *Wehrmacht* and the civilian authorities. In practice at operational level he got his instructions from the *Einsatzkommandeur der Ordnungspolizei* (*Orpo* operational commander) of the provinces, who in their turn were subordinated to the respective provincial *SS-u.Pol.Kommandeur*. Operational orders also came from the *Führungsstab für Bandenbekämpfung* of the OZAK.[50]

Following the issue of this order, then, it is likely that *Abteilung R* set up the outposts on the Trieste–Fiume road. The date of their creation could fall during the days of the *Unternehmen Braunschweig* anti-partisan operation, which started in the last week of April, or during the days immediately following its conclusion, in early May.

The Castelnuovo outpost of *Abteilung R* was set up by moving most of the men belonging to section R III from Udine, led by *Leutnant d.SchP.* Arthur Walther. According to Walther,[51] during the month of April he was sent out from Udine with his men to participate in an anti-partisan operation organised by the *Wehrmacht*, in which section R III members had to carry out security tasks on the Trieste–Fiume road. The operation was in all probability the mentioned *Unternehmen Braunschweig*. The presence of *Abteilung R* elements on the Karststrasse in the days of

Soldiers resting near a house: standing on the left is again Lerch, while the third man from the right, wearing a *Waffen-SS* uniform and the rank of an *SS-Hauptscharführer* (and also carrying a Suomi KP/-31), is most probably Hackenholt from *Abteilung R*. The other men wear *Ordnungspolizei* uniforms except the one near Lerch who is a *Waffen-SS Gebirgsjäger*, probably a *Karstjäger*, who wears a camouflage smock and an *edelweiss* on the side of his cap.

Another scene taken on the same occasion: a group of men belonging to the SS and *Polizei* prepare for action.

Karl Frenzel, wearing a camouflage tunic, and Erich Bauer, in *Ordnungspolizei* uniform, in Italy. *LA NRW, Münster*

Two men of *Abteilung R*, identified as Ernst Zierke (right), and Rudi Kamm, wearing a camouflage tunic and hat. *LA NRW, Münster*

Unternehmen Braunschweig, as well as the participation of the unit and its commander Wirth in the operation, are photographically documented. Photos taken in those days show two armored trucks belonging to *Abteilung R* driving on the road, and men of the unit in a nearby village, Bergut Grande; also, some photos show Wirth and Oberhauser in the village of Marcossina together with the commander of *I. Btl./SS-Pol. Rgt. "Bozen," Major d.SchP.* Oskar Kretschmer, probably in early May.

On April 30, hence during the *Unternehmen Braunschweig*, the deaths of two members of *Abteilung R*, Max Gringers and Alfred Löffler, are registered, as well as the wounding of another unit member, Gerhard Schneider. On the same day German units, together with Italian troops, destroyed the village of Lipa, southeast of Rupa, near the Karststrasse, and massacred its population. With at least 280 dead (of whom seventy-two were children), but perhaps up to 300 if the number of those officially still missing is added, it is the worst massacre carried out in the OZAK during the war. It seems certain that the perpetrators of the tragic episode included elements of *Abteilung R*, and it is likely that the massacre was linked to the deaths. The Lipa massacre is dealt with in a separate section.

Still according to Walther, after the conclusion of the anti-partisan operation to which his unit had been called in to participate, he and his men remained there setting up a series of small outposts along the Karststrasse, the main one being in Castelnuovo, where also Walther himself was based.[52] The Mattuglie outpost may have been created in the same period (but it is not excluded that it existed even earlier) by seconding there men from section R II in Fiume, perhaps under the command of Stangl; this group was probably billeted at the ONMI obstetrical hospital, where later also soldiers of the *SS-Wachmannschafts-Btl.* and the headquarters of *2. Compagnia* of *3. Rgt. Milizia Difesa Territoriale* (MDT; more on this company later) were billeted.[53] None of the other smaller outposts set up by *Abteilung R* on the Karststrasse are identified (except probably Starada).

The main tasks assigned to the newly set-up outposts of *Abteilung R* were to escort convoys that travelled between Trieste and Fiume, patrol and secure the road, intervene to help vehicles or outposts attacked by partisans, and fight the partisan movement by participating in combat actions and sweep operations in nearby areas in cooperation with other units, together with detachments of section R I and R II that intervened from the Risiera or from Fiume. Later the outpost garrisons were also used for the surveillance and protection of the building sites of the defensive positions being built along the Karststellung line, which ran through the region known as Ciceria (Ćićarija), in northeastern Istria (see section 3.4.5). For escort and transport services, the Castelnuovo outpost had at its disposal one of the armored trucks of *Abteilung R*. Also R II in Fiume had an armored truck available, used for the connections to Trieste, while another armored truck, or perhaps two, were probably based at the Risiera and used by section R I.

In addition to the *Abteilung R* detachments, the *Sicherungskommandant der Karststrasse* had at his disposal also a company of the *SS-Wachmannschafts-Btl.* (its *6. Kompanie*) and two Italian units: a company of the *Guardia di Finanza* (Finance Guard) and *2. Compagnia* of *3. Rgt. MDT*.[54]

The *6. Kompanie/SS-Wachmannschafts-Btl.* had been formed in mid-May 1944, at the Risiera from elements of the former *Battaglione Patrioti Davide* (on the company see the chapter on the *SS-Wachmannschaften*; on *Battaglione Davide* see the specific section in that chapter). It remained based at the Risiera until the end of the war, but company troops were sent in turns to at least two main outposts, Castelnuovo (with elements apparently also in Starada, a village nearby) and

This and the following twelve photographs were taken by a member of *Abteilung R*; they probably all date from late April or early May 1944, during the anti-partisan operation *Unternehmen Braunschweig*. This photo shows a commanders' meeting in an unidentified village, probably on the Karststrasse (perhaps Rupa). Recognizable are Globocnik, Wirth and Oberhauser, respectively the second, third, and fourth from the left (the fifth man is indicated as Hering in the original photo caption but the identification does not seem correct; the first on the left is identified as Michalsen, but the photo is not sufficiently clear to be sure). *StA München*

Another unidentified officer joins the group. *StA München*

Men of *Abteilung R* in the village of Sappiane (now Šapjane, Croatia), on the Trieste–Fiume road, just west of the Rupa junction (see Lipa map, Then and Now point "E"). The first on the left is Hering, while according to the original photo caption the other men are Ukrainians (i.e., *Trawniki* attached to *Abteilung R*), among whom the first two on the right were present in Belzec (the second from the right is possibly Rosenholz). The photo was taken from the balcony of a house on the opposite side of the road. *StA München*

Mattuglie; it is not known if elements were also sent to other outposts. The first company detachment was transferred to the *Stützpunkt* Castelnuovo already on May 18, joining the elements of *Abteilung R* who were already there. It seems that company men were sent for the first time to Mattuglie, where there was also an outpost of *Abteilung R*, only on July 16.[55]

On the *Guardia di Finanza* company the available information is scarce and confused. According to one source, an independent company which was based in Trieste was sent on the Karststrasse in early June 1944, led by a *tenente* (probably Francesco Rolleri); apparently only around fifty men reached Castelnuovo and were distributed also in the outposts of Matteria, Gradischie and Obrovo, while thirty-eight refused to move out and were therefore arrested and deported by the Germans.[56] From other information it seems, however, certain that a company of the *Guardia di Finanza*, indicated as *Compagnia Autonoma di Sicurezza* (independent security company), had manned some outposts on the Trieste–Fiume road (perhaps only on the stretch between Trieste and Sappiane; one outpost was surely in Matteria) at least since December 1943; it had its headquarters in Castelnuovo and apparently it was initially led by *Capitano* Antonio Rosito, later by *Capitano* Carabelli (until late June 1944).[57] The men sent to the Karststrasse in early June were perhaps only reinforcements for the company already deployed along the road. The *Guardia di Finanza* company was later led by *Tenente* Rolleri and it also participated in sweep operations together with German units.[58]

The *2. Compagnia "Arditi" of 3. Rgt. MDT* (the regiment headquarters was based in Fiume) was already deployed on a stretch of the Trieste–Fiume road (probably between Mattuglie and the Rupa junction) before being subordinated to the *Sicherungskommandant der Karststrasse*; in April 1944, it was led by *Tenente* Oscar Battestin, who was based in Giordani–Mucici. Already at the beginning of April, its men were manning the outpost at the Rupa junction (just south of the village of the same name), where the roads coming from Postumia–Ljubljana and from Clana met the Karststrasse, under the command of *Sottotenente* Aurelio Piesz. A preserved order of the day from *3. Rgt. MDT*, dated August 1, 1944, reports the text of a letter by Allers to the regiment commander, *Colonnello* Porcu, where Allers praised the elements of the unit employed "for road security" tasks on the Karststrasse, and in particular *Sottotenente* Piesz.[59] Promoted to *tenente*, Piesz took up command of *2. Compagnia* already before October 1944. From the end of 1944 to the end of April 1945, among the localities of the Karststrasse manned by elements of his company were at least Mattuglie (where the company headquarters was), Giordani–Mucici, the *Casa cantoniera* of Vele Lasi (road inspector's house, near the train station of Bergut) and the Rupa junction.[60]

On the same spot in Sappiane: on the right is Hering, on the left a *Heer Gebirgsjäger*, perhaps belonging to *2. Kompanie/ Reserve-Gebirgs-Jäger-Regiment 138* which in that period was based in the village. *StA München*

Men of *Abteilung R* cleaning their weapons on the balcony from where the first photo with Hering was taken. Second from the right is Heinrich Gley; according to the original photo caption the other men were Ukrainians (i.e., *Trawniki*). The first man on the left, not identified, with his trousers tucked inside the boots, is probably present on a photo taken in Lipa during the massacre (see page 83). *StA München*

After the creation of the *Abteilung R* outposts along the Trieste–Fiume road in the context of the responsibilities attributed to the *Sicherungskommandant der Karststrasse*, some men of *Abteilung R* were primarily employed for security and repression tasks in this area, including participating in anti-partisan and sweep operations. For larger operations the unit received operational orders from the *Führungsstab für Bandenbekämpfung* of the OZAK, while local level actions were probably conducted independently or in cooperation with other units (*Wehrmacht* or SS/*Polizei*) based in the same area.[61] There is very little information on this employment, which must have been relatively intense. As an example, the proposal for awarding Walther with the *Eisernes Kreuz II. Klasse* (Iron Cross Second Class) drafted at the end of 1944 mentioned that Walther was in "*Bandeneinsatz*" (in action against the partisans) since April 1944 as commander of an outpost and of an operational platoon (*Stützpunktkommandant und Führer eines Einsatzzuges*) and had participated in more than twenty operations against the partisans.[62]

In the following, the available information is provided on anti-partisan operations in which the participation of *Abteilung R* is documented or probable.

Just after mid-May, the Germans conducted an anti-partisan operation in the Brkini area, immediately north of Castelnuovo. Few details are available but it is known that on May 16, *III. Btl./SS-Pol.Rgt. 15* attacked partisan positions in Pregara (the village had been fortified with road cuts and bunkers).[63] On the next day, a four vehicle column on which travelled the *Befehlshaber der Sipo*/SD in Italien (commander of *Sipo*/SD in Italy), *SS-Brigadeführer und Generalmajor der Polizei* Wilhelm Harster (based in Verona), and the *Befehlshaber der Sipo*/SD in the OZAK, *SS-Obersturmbannführer* Ernst Weimann, was ambushed by partisans on the Karststrasse near Starada; the Germans—twenty-five men in total, one of whom was killed, three wounded and five missing in action during the firefight—were forced to abandon the road and take shelter among the rocks, and only with difficulty managed to break through the encirclement and reach Castelnuovo. Men of the *Sipo*/SD who accompanied Harster and Weimann were in action in the area of Castelnuovo also on May 18, perhaps during retaliation for the attack on the convoy.[64] In the days between May 18–21, six villages of the Brkini area were burned: Pregara, Cuie, Gabrega, Zaielse, Pobese and Tomigna, and around seventy civilians were killed (among which thirty-three in Tomigna, most of them gathered in three houses which were then set on fire, similarly to what happened in Lipa). Although not proven, it seems likely that elements of *Abteilung R* participated in these actions in the Brkini area. It should also be recalled that on May 18, the first elements of *6. Kp./SS-WMS-Btl.* were transferred to the *Stützpunkt* Castelnuovo, probably in connection with the operations in the Brkini area or with the attack to the convoy near Starada.

Men of *Abteilung R* resting near the Rupa junction, on the stretch of the road leading north from the junction towards the village of Rupa and Villa del Nevoso (see Lipa map, Then and Now point "D"). They all wear the characteristic camouflage outfits used by the unit, produced in Italian mod. 29 camouflage fabric. The only one identified on the basis of the original photo caption is Tauscher, first on the right; the collar tab with the rank of *SS-Untersturmführer* is just visible inside his camouflage tunic. The man in the foreground with his back to the camera, with trousers tucked inside his boots, armed with a Suomi KP/-31 sub-machine gun, is also present in a photo taken in Lipa during the reprisal, as well as probably in the photo with the men cleaning their weapons taken in Sappiane. *StA München*

Judging by these actions carried out in the weeks after *Braunschweig*, it appears that the Germans had the intention to make scorched earth of some areas along the Karststrasse, at least those with very high presence of partisan units, in order to deprive these of the possibility to attack the road. Although there is no specific information, it is possible that the tactics applied in the area were proposed and applied by Wirth, whose brutality was underlined by many former members of *Abteilung R*. He had in any case not too much time to devote himself to the new task of *Sicherungskommandant*, because he was killed on May 26, 1944. Probably in order to try and capture the perpetrators and punish the population, considered supportive of the partisans, on the same May 26, an action was organised by the HSSPF OZAK and carried out by forces of the *Befehlshaber der Sipo/* SD in the OZAK (probably with elements of *Abteilung R* also) in the area of Basovizza–Cosina–San Pietro di Madrasso–Occisla–Becca, near the place where Wirth died; in reprisal the village of Becca and part of Occisla were set on fire and destroyed. During the night between May 27–28, and the day of May 28, under the leadership of Weimann, the nearby villages of San Dorligo, Gabrovizza (which was also set on fire) and Villa Decani were searched; in this action, in addition to German forces, elements of the Italian police (*Ispettorato Speciale di Pubblica Sicurezza*, a special unit active against the political opposition) and of the *Milizia Confinaria* also participated. As said, the tasks of the *Sicherungskommandant* were taken over, probably from early June, by Wirth's successor, Allers.

Going back to the anti-partisan operations on June 19, men of *Abteilung R* from the Castelnuovo outpost went into action in the area of Tatre–Slivia–Calcizza (north of the Castelnuovo–Matteria stretch of the Karststrasse) together with *2. Kompanie/3. Rgt. Brandenburg*; the action started in the night between June 18–19, and ended in the morning of June 19.[65]

Around August 7–10, a sweep operation took place in the Ciceria region, with the participation of parts of *III. Btl./SS-Pol.Rgt. 15*, Italian units (a platoon from the *Milizia Confinaria* based in Pisino—belonging to *2. Compagnia of I. Battaglione Milizia Confinaria DT*—and elements of *3. Rgt. MDT*) and probably elements of *Abteilung R*. Having noticed that partisans had found hospitality in some of the villages, the civilian populations of Vodizze di Castelnuovo, Danne, Trestenico di Raspo, Clenosciacco, Raspo, and Racia were evacuated (they were transported to Trieste) and the villages were set on fire. According to accounts by some civilians arrested and transported to the Risiera, the action was led by Allers.[66] A few days later, on August 13, Richter fell in Starada (on the Karststrasse, southeast of Castelnuovo); the circumstances are not known but he probably died in a partisan ambush on a truck, mentioned by an MDT report. On August 19, Bolender and his men participated in an action on Mount Lisina (in the Ciceria, northwest of Mattuglie); although the action was probably conducted by elements of *6. Kp./SS-WMS-Btl.*, it is possible—but not certain—that elements of *Abteilung R* not seconded to the *SS-WMS-Btl.* may have participated too (see also the chapter on the *SS-Wachmannschaften*).

On September 2, elements of *Abteilung R* coming from Trieste and from the Castelnuovo outpost (as well as elements of *6. Kp./SS-WMS-Btl.*) took part in an action to relieve the *Wehrmacht* outpost of Elsane, attacked by partisans. These forces were led by an unidentified *Oberstleutnant*, probably Allers himself; after fierce fighting by the end of the day they managed to repel the partisan attack (for more details on this episode see the chapter on the *SS-Wachmannschaften*).

On September 14, near Tatre (northwest of Castelnuovo) an action took place with the participation of Walther and his men, who repelled a partisan attack against the village (which had probably been temporarily occupied by the Germans).

The memoirs of an officer from *2. Compagnia of 3. Rgt. MDT*, based in Mattuglie, later (from late January 1945) in Giordani and finally (from the second half of March) at the Rupa junction, mention numerous anti-partisan actions carried out by the company between October 1944 and March 1945, sometimes together with SS troops from Castelnuovo or

Oberhauser (on the right, in standard *SS-Untersturmführer* uniform) and Gley sitting on the same wall as seen in the previous photo. It is possible, although not proven, that this photo and the previous one were taken on the day of the Lipa massacre. In addition to fitting the place and time, a hint is the fact that some men are dressed in exactly the same way as seen in the photos taken in Lipa during the reprisal. *StA München*

This and the two following photos, perhaps taken during the same action as the previous two, show the unit during a transfer; also here the men wear the camouflage outfits made in Italian mod. 29 camouflage fabric. On this first photo, the third man from the left is Gley. The vehicle is a Spa CL 39 light truck; note the cartoon-style drawing painted on its front. *StA München*

Trieste and elements of the *Guardia di Finanza*, mentioning in particular the presence of Walther. The places where these actions were conducted are not always specified in the memoirs, but among those mentioned are Tatre, Tomigna, and the triangle Gabrega–Succorie–Prelose (all villages north of Castelnuovo) and upper Istria (i.e., probably the Ciceria south of Castelnuovo).[67]

Some changes to this setup were made in late 1944 or early 1945. Allers said in some depositions that from this period he was additionally put in charge of the security for the Trieste–San Pietro del Carso–Fiume railway line, but also that he was replaced as *Sicherungskommandant der Karststrasse* and took command of the *Sicherungsbereich* (security sector) of Duttogliano, a village north of Trieste, on the railway line to Gorizia.[68] This seems in accordance with the fact that in early 1945 Walther and his men abandoned Castelnuovo and moved to the area of Sesana, with the task of protecting the Trieste–San Pietro del Carso railway;[69] they remained in this sector until the general retreat of the end of April 1945, but no information on their activities is available.

Another Spa CL 39 light truck being recovered. In the middle, bent down and wearing binoculars, is again Gley. The two soldiers in the foreground, their backs to the camera and wearing helmets, are Italians, perhaps Blackshirts from *3. Rgt. MDT*. *StA München*

The same vehicle as the previous photo. According to the original photo caption, the man on the vehicle is Hackenholt, but the image is not sufficiently clear to be sure. *StA München*

Men of *Abteilung R* in an unidentified location. From the right are Seidel (wearing the camouflage outfit, helmet with cover and motorcycle goggles), Oberhauser (in standard *SS-Untersturmführer* uniform), Pötzinger (in camouflage outfit), Bredow (in camouflage trousers and *Ordnungspolizei* tunic), and Gomerski (with motorcycle overcoat). *StA München*

It seems that Allers maintained some responsibility as regards the security of the Karststrasse (or of the building sites of the Karststellung line; see section 3.4.5); the memoirs of the MDT officer recall a meeting with Allers which took place in Rupa on April 17, to discuss the security of the road. Additionally, one source also mentions that in the last days of April 1945, when the Yugoslav troops were approaching Trieste, Allers ordered the *Guardia di Finanza* company based in Castelnuovo to set up a defense outpost in Marcossina; the Italian unit commander, however, disregarded this order and retreated to Trieste.[70] It is possible (but not confirmed) that, despite the transfer of Walther and his men, parts of *Abteilung R* remained in action along the Karststrasse also during the first months of 1945.

Kurt Seidel (on the right in camo outfit), who was evidently a motorcycle courier, with an unidentified *Wehrmacht* officer. The Benelli motorcycle carries the registration number SS-965075. *StA München*

In the last weeks of the war, elements of *Abteilung R* were apparently employed in anti-partisan operations in other areas. In March–April 1945, the Germans organized the largest anti-partisan operations carried out in the OZAK during their occupation. The progressive advance of the southeastern front made it necessary to try and eliminate the threat that the partisans represented in the immediate front rear areas, using all available means. To this aim two parallel operations were conducted, the *Unternehmen Winterende* (winter end) and *Frühlingsanfang* (spring start): *Winterende* was carried out on the mountain area of the Bainsizza (Banjšice) plateau, the Chiapovano valley (Čepovanski dol) and the Tarnova plateau (Trnovski gozd), north and east of Gorizia, under the command of the FSBB OZAK; *Frühlingsanfang* was led by the *HSSPF Alpenland* and was carried out in the area around Circhina (northeast of Gorizia), including large mountain areas across the border between Italy (OZAK region) and the German Reich (Oberkrain region, i.e., part of the annexed northern Slovenia). Since areas belonging to the OZAK, the Provinz Laibach and the Reich were involved, the operations were conducted in cooperation between the two FSBB of Globocnik and Rösener, and with the participation of units subordinated to both headquarters; they started on March 19 and ended around April 5, 1945.

Seidel, Bredow, and Gomerski (from the left) photographed in Mattuglie. The photo was taken on the present Ulica Viktora cara Emina street, on the corner with Kastavska cesta (see Braunschweig map, Then and Now point "B"). The building in the background was part of the train station. According to the original caption, the photo was taken around May 1, 1944, and the men in the background belonged to the *Wehrmacht*. (StA München)

Among the units employed in *Unternehmen Winterende* there was a *Kampfgruppe Lerch* (led by *SS-Sturmbannführer* Ernst Lerch, close collaborator of Globocnik)[71] which was made up by elements of the HSSPF headquarters (*Stabseinheit des HSSPF*) and parts of the Cetnik–Dinara Division.[72] It is confirmed that around March 27, when it was in action in the area of Monte Signi (Sinji vrh), just north of Aidussina, *Kampfgruppe Lerch* included a *Kompanie Allers*;[73] this name most probably indicated parts of *Abteilung R* and / or elements of the *SS-Wachmannschaften*. A soldier (Italian) from *1. Kp./SS-Wachmannschaften* is reported as fallen northwest of Monte Signi on March 27; again on Monte Signi is reported as missing, probably during the same action, a member of *Abteilung R*, Thiel. In the further phases of the operation, *Kompanie Allers* was subordinated to the HSSPF Alpenland until April 3 (when it went back to HSSPF OZAK), but no specific information is available on its employment. In the fight around Easter 1945 (April 1) were wounded also Bolender (apparently on March 31; he was initially transported to the Ljubljana hospital) and Oberhauser (probably lightly). Additionally, in March 1945, probably during these operations, a *Trawniki* attached to *Abteilung R*, Arnold Rosenke, was reported as missing in action. The result of the *Winterende* and *Frühlingsanfang* operations was to temporarily weaken and disorganize the units of the partisan *IX. Korpus* operating in the area, but overall they ended in failure: the partisan units were not destroyed and in a relatively short time they managed to acquire again their operative capacity, so that they were able to take the initiative in the closing phase of the war, at the end of April and early May 1945.

Showing the intense anti-partisan employment, some members of *Abteilung R* were awarded the *Bandenkampfabzeichen* (anti-partisan guerrilla warfare badge) and participated in courses on fighting against the partisans.[74] In addition to the killed and wounded already mentioned, several men of *Abteilung R* were wounded in unspecified combat actions, among them at least Franz and Frenzel (the latter was wounded by a mortar splinter).

3.4.4.1: Operation *Unternehmen Braunschweig* (Late April - Early May 1944)[75]

The Progression of the Operation

The anti-partisan operation *Unternehmen Braunschweig* took place in the last week of April and the first week of May 1944 (several original documents variably date its start on April 24, 25, or 26, its conclusion on May 5, 6, or 7), and was subdivided in three phases: *Braunschweig* I, II, and III.[76] Its objective was to eliminate the partisan presence from the area of the Monte Maggiore (Učka) massif (defined as "the bandits' sacred mountain" in a German document) and to destroy the so-called "bandits' supply base" in the area of Mune–Lanischie–Monte Alpe Grande (Planick)–Mattuglie, in the eastern Ciceria region. Additionally, in early May some units mopped-up a large area of central Istria, advancing to the west from the area of Chersano towards Pisino–Antignana and farther towards Rovigno. It seems that in early May operations also took place in the area of Clana and in the areas along the Trieste–Fiume road, or Karststrasse.

The operation was organized by the *Führungsstab für Bandenbekämpfung* in the OZAK and directed by Globocnik. The following units participated in *Braunschweig*:

Wehrmacht units:[77]

- Elements of *278. Infanterie-Division* (two reinforced companies and the *Pionier-Zug of II. Btl./Grenadier-Rgt. 992*; two reinforced companies of *Grenadier-Rgt. 993*; 4. and *7. Batterie/Artillerie-Rgt. 278; 3. Kp./Pionier-Btl. 278*),
- Elements of *188. Reserve-Gebirgs-Division* (*I. Btl./Reserve-Gebirgs-Jäger-Rgt. 138* and probably other smaller units)

Waffen-SS and SS/*Polizei* units:

- *SS-Karstwehr-Btl.*
- *III. Btl./SS-Polizei-Rgt. 15*
- *I. Btl./SS-Polizei-Rgt. "Bozen"*
- *Polizei-Kompanie z.b.V. "Alpenland"* (based in Pisino)

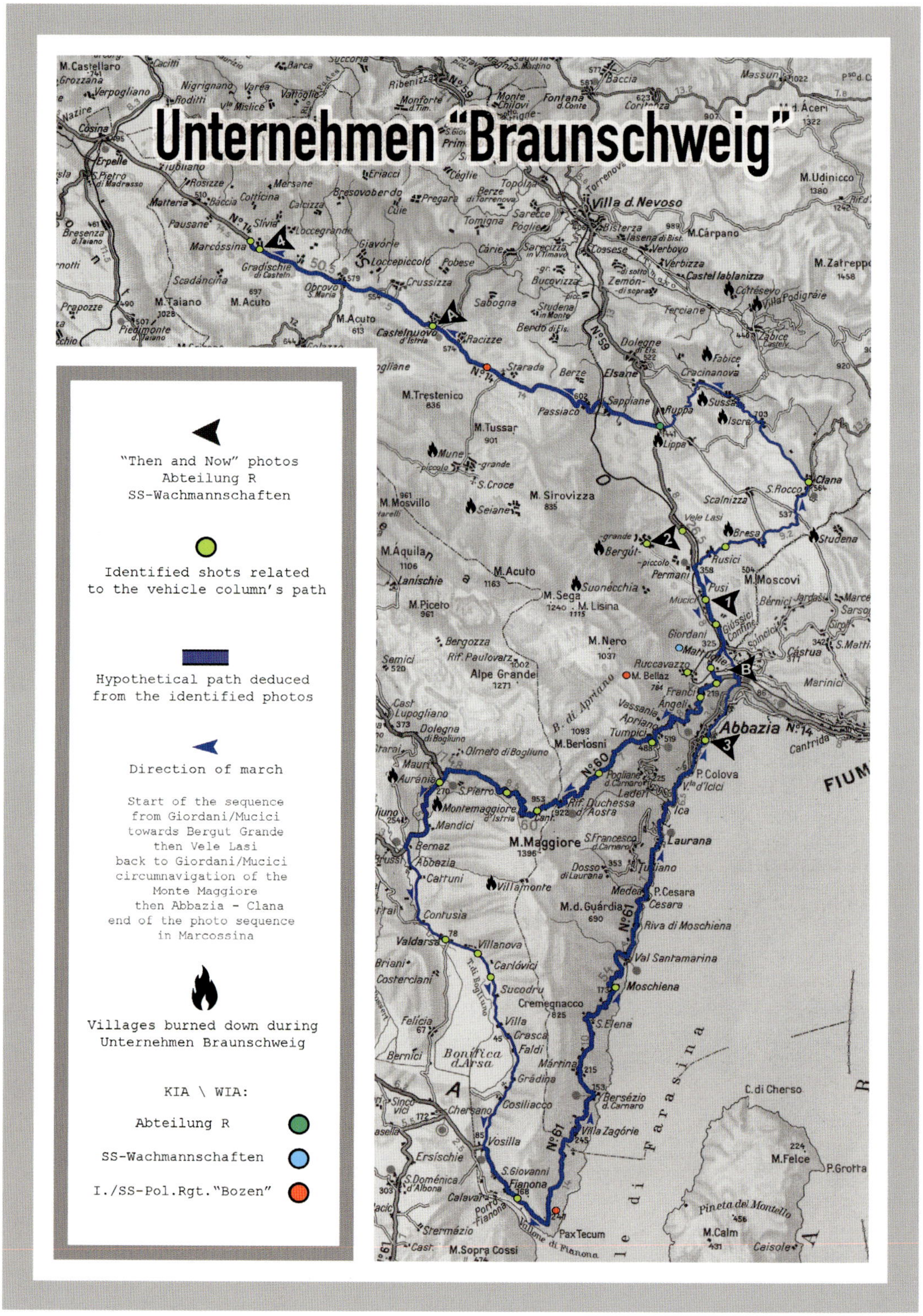
Unternehmen "Braunschweig"
"Then and Now" photos
Abteilung R
SS-Wachmannschaften
Identified shots related
to the vehicle column's path
Hypothetical path deduced
from the identified photos
Direction of march
Start of the sequence
from Giordani/Mucici
towards Bergut Grande
then Vele Lasi
back to Giordani/Mucici
circumnavigation of the
Monte Maggiore
then Abbazia - Clana
end of the photo sequence
in Marcossina
Villages burned down during
Unternehmen Braunschweig
KIA \ WIA:
Abteilung R
SS-Wachmannschaften
I./SS-Pol.Rgt."Bozen"

- An *Einsatzgruppe* (task force) of the *Sipo*/SD (led by *SS-Obersturmbannführer* Weimann and made up also by elements of the *Ski-Kommando* and the *Bandenjagdkommando* of the *Befehlshaber der Sipo*/SD in Italien)
- A detachment from the *Befehlshaber der Sipo*/SD – *Aussenkommando Pola* (led by *SS-Obersturmführer* Helmut Prasch, whose report on the operation is reproduced below)
- Elements of *Abteilung R* and of the *SS-Wachmannschafts-Btl.*, identified on the basis of photographic material

Also included were some Italian troops consisting of around 150 men of the *Milizia Difesa Territoriale* (among which—in various phases—elements of *2. Rgt. MDT* from Pola, of *3. Rgt. MDT* from Fiume, and of the *Milizia Confinaria*).

The few preserved original documents do not allow us to follow in detail the development of the operation.[78] From the Prasch report (see later) it is known that the detachment of the *BdS – Aussenkommando Pola*, after leaving the city on April 26 at dawn, via Arsia–Albona–Chersano–Valdarsa (where it sustained a firefight with the partisans) reached the western slopes of Monte Maggiore, where it searched the villages of Brdo, Cattuni, Abbazia and Bogliuno; it then proceeded to Aurania, where probably in the night between April 28–29, it made contact with another motorized column coming from the direction of Mattuglie.

As far as this second column is concerned, no documents have been found that provide information on its actions; however, the itinerary it followed during the last days of April could be precisely reconstructed on the basis of a large number of photographs produced by a *Kriegsberichter* (war correspondent) attached to *I. Btl./SS-Pol. Rgt. "Bozen."* The photo sequence develops throughout these locations, identified thanks to the images: Giordani–Mucici,[79] deviation to Bergut Grande, return to Giordani–Mucici (presumably on April 27); Mattuglie, Ruccavazzo (presumably on April 28); circular path around the Monte Maggiore through Apriano, Učka Pass, Aurania, Valdarsa, Villanova, Fianona Valley, Moschiena (presumably on April 28–30); Abbazia.[80]

In practice this motorized column drove around Monte Maggiore, setting fire to several villages (see later), while detachments on foot marched to the top of the mountain trying to engage partisan units. According to the photographs, this motorized column consisted with certainty at least of considerable forces from *I. Btl./SS-Pol.Rgt. "Bozen"* (among which surely its *3.* and *4. Kp.*),[81] parts of the *SS-Karstwehr-Btl.* (among which at least parts of its *1., 2.* and *4. Kp.*)[82] and *Wehrmacht Gebirgsjäger* units.

The photographs show also that from Abbazia, probably in the first days of May, a motorized column of *I. Btl./SS-Pol.Rgt. "Bozen"* drove though Mattuglie, Giordani–Mucici, Clana (leaving therefore temporarily the Karststrasse to head eastwards, making a detour to reach then again the Karststrasse, probably at the Rupa junction), Castelnuovo and Marcossina, where the photo sequence ends.

The photo sequence shows elements of *Abteilung R* and the *SS-Wachmannschafts-Btl.* In particular, Wirth and Oberhauser appear in some images taken in Marcossina probably in early May. Other photos show two armored trucks from *Abteilung R*, probably patrolling the Karststrasse and escorting vehicle columns: one was photographed in Giordani–Mucici at the beginning of the photo sequence, the other one in Marcossina at the end of the sequence. Other elements of *Abteilung R* appear in photos taken in Bergut Grande, probably on 27 April. Finally, images taken in Abbazia probably in early May (possibly on May 2) show a column of vehicles carrying troops belonging to the *SS-Wachmannschafts-Btl.*[83]

After making contact with the column of *I. Btl./SS-Pol.Rgt. "Bozen"* in Aurania during the night between April 28–29, the detachment of the *BdS – Aussenkommando Pola* was employed farther south, in the area of Sumbresi–Veliacchi (west of Chersano) and in the area of Fianona, on April 30. Thereafter, for three days in early May, together with *III. Btl./SS-Pol.Rgt. 15,* it mopped-up the area from Vosilla–Felicia near Chersano towards the west to Pisino–Antignana. At the end of this phase, the *BdS – Aussenkommando Pola* went back to Pola on May 5. But evidently German activities on the Istria peninsula proceeded farther to the west, since on May 6, elements of *III. Btl./SS-Pol.Rgt. 15* assaulted and took point 198, a hill six kilometers north of Villa di Rovigno

Giordani–Mucici (now Jurdani–Mučići, Croatia), view towards the northwest (see the *Unternehmen Braunschweig* map, Then and Now point "1"); probably early on April 27, 1944. The armored truck of *Abteilung R* with registration number SS-965034 stopped next to the Lancia 1ZM armored car of *I. Btl./SS-Pol.Rgt. "Bozen,"* parked near the Milizia Difesa Territoriale (MDT) fortified outpost, which was located between the villages of Giordani and Mucici, just north of the Giordani train station (in the following it is indicated as outpost of Giordani–Mucici). The building was directly on the Karststrasse, the road running from Trieste to Fiume. It probably hosted the headquarters of *2. Compagnia* of *3. Rgt. MDT*. The two vehicles are heading in the direction of Fiume.

(two kilometers south of Braicovici); in this fight 15–20 partisans were killed.[84]

According to photographic documentation, units from *I. Btl./SS-Pol.Rgt. "Bozen"* (at least the same units that in the last days of April had participated in the operations around Monte Maggiore) were subsequently in action in the area of Clana and along the Karststrasse, probably in the first days of May. As shown by the photos, it seems that these forces were mainly used to escort away civilians that had been forcibly evacuated from nearby villages, which in some cases were set on fire (see below), in cooperation with elements of *Abteilung R* led by Wirth himself.[85] Since no documents on this last phase of the operation have been found, no precise data is available, with the exception that on May 3, *Kp./SS-Pol.Rgt. "Bozen"* had a firefight with partisans in Cacitti (north of Cosina–Erpelle). Also in the first days of May, several villages in the area east of Rupa were set on fire after the civilians were evacuated.

The final outcome of the operation according to *Wehrmacht* sources was 250 enemy dead and 770 arrested (draft dodgers and people suspected of supporting the partisans), while the Germans had eleven dead and twenty-four wounded. According to SS/Polizei sources, there were 392 enemy dead and 1,865 arrested.

The Village Burnings

During the *Unternehmen Braunschweig*, in order to contribute to the objective of making it impossible for the partisans to get supplies from the villages, or as a measure of collective punishment of the population when proof was found that the partisans had been in the village, several villages were set on fire and partially or completely destroyed. Their population was hauled away, partially arrested and deported, partially moved to other areas.[86] The following villages were affected (the list is probably not exhaustive):

- Bergut Piccolo and Bergut Grande, and partially Suonecchia, in the eastern Ciceria region, emptied of their population and burned on April 27.
- Seiane, Mune Piccolo and Mune Grande, in the eastern Ciceria region, emptied of their population on April 27 and later burned on May 5.[87]
- Montemaggiore d'Istria piccolo (also known as Villamonte) and Montemaggiore d'Istria

A few moments later, *Major d. SchP.* Oskar Kretschmer, in the middle, commander of *I. Btl./SS-Pol.Rgt. "Bozen,"* talks to the crew of the Lancia 1ZM. The officer behind Kretschmer, looking at the damage caused by bullets on the armored car's painting, is probably *Leutnant d.SchP.* Krauss (later *Oberleutnant*), commander of *3. Kp./SS-Pol.Rgt. "Bozen."*

Giordani–Mucici, view towards the southwest; probably early on April 27, 1944 (as also the next four photos). Elements of the motorized column of *I. Btl./SS-Pol.Rgt. "Bozen,"* stopped in front of the Giordani–Mucici outpost, wait to move towards Monte Maggiore (Učka). The Lancia 1ZM is followed by a truck with registration number Pol-39724, the Volkswagen *Kübelwagen* Pol-113302 (probably the personal vehicle of *Maj.* Kretschmer), and finally truck Pol-76129, transporting an Italian 47/32 mod. 35 anti-tank gun on the flatbed, and towing another.

grande (area of Monte Maggiore), burned on April 30.
• Lipa and Iscra (east of Rupa), burned respectively on April 30 and May 1.
• Aurania (area of Monte Maggiore), burned on May 1.
• Sussa and Fabice (east of Rupa) and Studena (south of Clana), burned on May 4.
• Cottesevo and Villa Podigraie (northeast of Rupa), burned on May 6.

Note how the sequence of village evacuations and sometimes burnings (in particular Bergut Piccolo and Bergut Grande, Suonecchia, Montemaggiore d'Istria piccolo and grande, Aurania) corresponds with the path followed by the motorized column around Monte Maggiore, as reconstructed on the basis of the photo sequence. On the other hand, the village fires of early May involved the eastern Ciceria region (Seiane, Mune Piccolo and Mune Grande) and the areas south of Clana and east of Rupa.

In the list are also included for completeness the fire of Lipa, whose population was massacred, and the one of Iscra, although the destruction of these two villages was apparently not directly part of the Braunschweig operation. The Lipa massacre is dealt with in a separate section.

Report on Unternehmen Braunschweig *of the* Sipo/SD Aussenkommando *Pola*

On the activity of the detachment from the *Befehlshaber der Sipo/SD (BdS) – Aussenkommando Pola* during the *Unternehmen Braunschweig* the following report has survived. It was written by its commander, *SS-Obersturmführer* Prasch, and was dated May 9, 1944:[88]

Giordani–Mucici, view towards the south. Italian *Milizia* soldiers belonging to the Giordani–Mucici outpost, members of *I. Btl./SS-Pol.Rgt. "Bozen"* (among whom Maj. Kretschmer, are first on the right, standing in the middle of the road), and *Gebirgsjäger* from a unit of *188. Reserve-Gebirgs-Division* (with mules) in front of the MDT outpost.

Giordani–Mucici, view towards the northwest. In the foreground, wearing boots, is a *Milizia tenente* who seems to have been the outpost commander. He could be *Tenente* Oscar Battestin, at this time commander of the *2. Compagnia* of *3. Rgt. MDT*. Working in the background are some *Carabinieri* (recognizable from the white collar tabs), attached to the MDT detachment manning the outpost.

To the *Befehlshaber der Sipo u.d. SD* in der OZAK, Trieste
Subject: Activity report on the *Unternehmen Braunschweig* 1, 2, 3

(...) The *BdS – Aussenkommando Pola* has taken part to the *Unternehmen Braunschweig* with one officer and 18 men, two *Pz.-LKW mit 2 cm Kanone* [armored trucks armed with a 20 mm gun], six light machine guns, two heavy machine guns and two light mortars.

I. phase [of the *Unternehmen Braunschweig*, in the area south and west of Monte Maggiore]:

The *BdS – Aussenkommando Pola* [detachment] is assigned to *Sicherungsgruppe Lins* [perhaps *2. Kp./SS-Pol.Rgt. Bozen*, apparently commanded by *Hptm*. Erwin Lins] and leaves Pola on 26 April 1944 at 5.00 o'clock. From 8.00 o'clock march from Arsia to Chersano, via Albona–S. Domenica. The *BdS – Aussenkommando Pola* becomes an

Giordani–Mucici, view towards the northeast. Men of *I. Btl./SS-Pol.Rgt. "Bozen"* and *188. Reserve-Gebirgs-Division* marching towards Monte Maggiore. In the background is the MDT fortified outpost of Giordani–Mucici.

Giordani–Mucici, view towards the east. Men of *I. Btl./SS-Pol.Rgt. "Bozen"* repair telephone lines in front of the outpost. Note the makeshift loopholes on the balconies and windows, the Italian flag and the propaganda writings, some made with a stencil.

One of the slogans, reading "*Con la Germania per la pace!*" ("With Germany for peace"), was also written in the Croatian language ("*Sa Njemàćkom k miru!*") on a wall not visible on this image.

independent group under the command of *SS-Ostuf.* Prasch. In Chersano two persons are killed while trying to escape. On one of them communist propaganda leaflets are found. Six prisoners are taken. After Chersano three bridges and 36 road cuts are provisionally repaired. While approaching the village of Valdarsa our group receives fire from the terrain before the village. With guns, heavy machine guns and mortars the resistance is broken, a bandit is killed and four are taken prisoner. Taking advantage of the fight *SS-Schütze* Udo from the *Hitlerjugend* division, on leave from Paris, who had been taken prisoner by the bandits, frees himself. He joins the group as a soldier. The bandits' group, numbering around 50 men, withdraws across the river and 4 km north of Valdarsa they fire on the road with three machine guns. The enemy positions cannot be spotted. Our column remains under fire for four hours. Seven men from the *Milizia* are wounded. They are evacuated, as well as [the wounded from] the *Polizei*, using tanks. By methodically covering the terrain with explosive grenades, mortar rounds and machine gun fire seven bandits are killed. The nearby villages of Brdo, Cattuni, Abbazia and Bogliuno are searched, two fleeing men are killed, 16 are taken prisoners. The march continues up to the destroyed and impassable bridge of Aurania, the road is checked by patrols. Five prisoners, working to remove obstacles, are killed by the bandit's fire. The *Einsatzkommando* (task force) is relieved in the night on 29 April 1944.

The 8 ton. *Pz.-LKW* falls down a ravine near Felicia. The place of the accident is visited by the *Gruppenführer* [Globocnik] on 29 April.

On 30 April the *BdS – Einsatzkommando Pola* sends a scouting group towards Sumbresi; in the woods near Veliacchi eight bandits are taken by surprise. One manages to flee, seven are killed. Some materiel is captured. Among the killed is the *Ceta*

Bergut Grande (now Veli Brgud, Croatia), view towards the northwest (see the *Unternehmen Braunschweig* map, Then and Now point "2"); probably the late morning of April 27, 1944. Men of *Abteilung R* (probably belonging to the crew of the armored truck SS-965034), *I. Btl./SS-Pol.Rgt. "Bozen"* and probably *Pol.Kp. z.b.V. "Alpenland"* on the central square in the village, which was set afire on April 27, 1944. The policeman on the far left wears on his forearm the "*Kreuz des Südens*" shield, an award honoring the *Polizeitruppe Deutsch-Ostafrika* (colonial police of German East Africa), distributed to members of the *Kolonialpolizeischule* Oranienburg (school for colonial police). Apparently, some of the members of *Pol.Kp. z.b.V. "Alpenland"* came from one of the training courses held at this school. On this policeman's left are: a member of *Abteilung R* (perhaps Jührs; probably he was on the armored truck SS-965034 when photographed in Giordani–Mucici, note the light-colored shirt, and the characteristic camouflage tunic); an unidentified soldier; probably another member of *Abteilung R*, wearing boots (possibly Girtzig); a member of *I. Btl./SS-Pol.Rgt. "Bozen"*; *Hauptmann d.SchP.* Grünewald (commander of *4. Kp./SS-Pol.Rgt. "Bozen,"* with the camouflage helmet cover); three unidentified soldiers; *Oblt.* Krauss (wearing the *Ordnungspolizei* eagle on his sleeve); *Maj.* Kretschmer (with pipe) and his adjutant (or driver).

Bergut Grande, view towards the southwest. In this photo taken on the same occasion are visible from the left: a member of *I. Btl./SS-Pol.Rgt. "Bozen"*; seen from the side, carrying a MAB mod. 38 sub-machine gun, the member of *Abteilung R* already visible of the previous photo (possibly Girtzig); *Hptm*. Grünewald; *Maj*. Kretschmer (with his back to the camera) talking to a man who might be *SS-Ustuf*. Schwarz of *Abteilung R/SS-Wachmannschafts-Btl.*; an unidentified officer of *I. Btl./SS-Pol.Rgt. "Bozen"*; an unidentified *Heer* officer (half-hidden); *Oblt*. Krauss; the *Milizia tenente* already seen in Giordani–Mucici (with the *Alpini*-like hat); Kretschmer's adjutant (or driver); a Milizia NCO also from the Giordani–Mucici outpost (with his back to the camera, wearing an Italian mod. 33 helmet) and another man of *I. Btl./SS-Pol. Rgt. "Bozen."*

Bergut Grande, view towards the south. From the left: an unidentified officer of *I. Btl./SS-Pol.Rgt. "Bozen"*; *Maj*. Kretschmer; possibly *SS-Ustuf*. Schwarz; the already seen *Heer* officer; a member of *I. Btl./SS-Pol.Rgt. "Bozen"*; Kretschmer's adjutant (or driver); another man of *I. Btl./SS-Pol.Rgt. "Bozen"* (half-hidden); the *Milizia tenente* and NCO. In the background, on the right, *Hptm*. Grünewald talks to two of his men.

[company] commander. Departure at 3.00 o'clock, return at 8.00 o'clock. Removal of a road block made of tree trunks near Fianona and climb [to the area above the Laesme] around 11.00 o'clock with three companies of *III./Pol. 15* [= *III. Btl./SS-Pol.Rgt. 15*].

In the II. phase of *Braunschweig* the mopping-up of the mountain terrain above the Laesme [river?], carried out autonomously [by the *BdS – Aussenkommando Pola*], results in three dead and eight prisoners, one of which is a deserter. Various material, one light machine gun and a rifle are captured. Eleven huts, [on] "Point 7," are burned, several caverns are set on fire. In the operation *Braunschweig* phases I. and II. the *BdS – Aussenkommando Pola* scores 25 enemy killed and 34 prisoners.

In the III. phase of *Braunschweig* the groups of SS men [of *BdS – Aussenkommando Pola*] are again divided among the companies of *III./Pol. 15*. Mopping-up actions take place from Vosilla and Felicia to the west. After three days Pisino–Antignana

Bergut Grande, view towards the southwest. Again on the same square, from the left: the *Milizia tenente* and NCO; *Hptm*. Grünewald; *Maj*. Kretschmer; *Oblt*. Krauss; the *Heer* officer and two men of *I. Btl./SS-Pol.Rgt. "Bozen."*

The *Milizia tenente* and the *Heer* officer leave the village on a motorbike, possibly heading to Vele Lasi, where other photographs show the arrival of the civilian population forcibly evacuated from the Ciceria (Ćićarija) region. On their right are *Oblt*. Krauss and the *Milizia* NCO, and two men of *I. Btl./ SS-Pol.Rgt. "Bozen."*

Unidentified place, probably on April 27,1944. Visible in this photo is the man seen on previous images and dubiously identified as Girtzig (first on the left), together with at least another member of *Abteilung R* (fifth from the left, wearing the characteristic camouflage outfit used by the unit, produced with Italian mod. 29 fabric). The others are mostly members of an unidentified *Ordnungspolizei* unit, probably *I. Btl./SS-Pol.Rgt. "Bozen,"* but there is also a *Waffen-SS Gebirgsjäger* armed with a MAB sub-machine gun (second from the left). The location is not identified, but it is possible that the photo was taken near Bergut Grande on the same day as the previous images.

are reached. In this phase 12 prisoners receive the "special treatment" [= execution], four bandits are killed in action. Return to Pola on 5 May without any friendly losses.

Total results: 41 enemy killed, 34 prisoners, arms, ammunitions and propaganda material [captured]. These figures have not been reported by *Pol. 15*.

Lessons learned

Our units do not engage in any scouting or short-range reconnaissance. For this reason the bandits, who are always watchful, manage to retreat on time when they hear the noise of troops approaching. Colored signal flares are used in an excessively wasteful manner. On every hill, in every valley, even when there is visual contact, white signal flares are fired. The enemy is then exactly informed kilometers away the movements of our units. Any quick pursuit of the retreating enemy is also forsaken. Troops go mainly into the houses (beer!) while the terrain around the villages remains untouched. The bandits know well that the houses are searched, so they avoid them. The heavy *Pz.-LKW* have proven themselves only partially, because of the many road cuts. The soldiers' shoes are inadequate. At the end of the operations some shoes were no longer fit to wear.

"Casa Cantoniera" (road inspector's house) of Vele Lasi, view towards the north; probably April 27, 1944. Civilians evacuated from a Ciceria village, perhaps Bergut, arriving at the "Casa Cantoniera," which was then a *Milizia Confinaria* outpost. Nearby was the Bergut train station, from where the civilians were probably transported away. On the left of the image is the *Heer* officer already seen in Bergut. *Milizia* soldiers are visible both in the foreground (among whom a *brigadiere*, probably belonging to the *Milizia Confinaria*, judging from the *Alpini*-like hat), as well as in the background, escorting the civilians.

Pol-76129

Pol-39725

This page and opposite: Mattuglie (now Matulji, Croatia), probably in the last days of April 1944. Vehicles of *I. Btl./SS-Pol.Rgt. "Bozen"* leaving Mattuglie in the direction of Monte Maggiore. Presently, this road is called Ulica 43. Istarske divizije.

Photos taken during the itinerary around Monte Maggiore, probably still during the last days of April 1944. The first image shows vehicles of I. Btl./SS-Pol. Rgt. "Bozen" in Ruccavazzo (now Rukavac); the armored truck visible in the background, coming in the opposite direction, probably belonged to the Italian unit 14. Battaglione Costiero da Fortezza (coast fortress battalion) (see also page 89).

The second image, taken just after Montemaggiore d'Istria Grande (now Vela Učka), shows soldiers of *I. Btl./SS-Pol.Rgt. "Bozen"* marching in the direction of Aurania (now Vranja), escorted by the Lancia 1ZM, together with some elements of the *SS-Karstwehr-Btl*. The massif of Monte Maggiore is in the background.

In the third image the column is seen in Valdarsa (now Šušnjevica). On the right, looking at the photographer, is *Hptm.* Grünewald.

The last two photographs taken during the itinerary around Monte Maggiore show vehicles of *I. Btl./ SS-Pol.Rgt. "Bozen"* at a road cut on the Villanova–Sucodru (now Nova Vas–Jasenovik) road.

Moschiena (now Mošćenice, Croatia), probably in the last days of April 1944. *Maj*. Kretschmer (with binoculars) and other soldiers in the village square; the man in the middle of the photo, with his hands behind his back, resembles the *Befehlshaber der Sipo*/SD in the OZAK, *SS-Ostuf.* Weimann. Behind the group is a car with registration number SS-950087. It is documented that on April 29, 1944, Globocnik was in Felicia (now Zatka Čepić), not far from Moschiena, where he visited the place where an armored truck belonging to the *SD-Aussenkommando Pola* had fallen down a ravine.

Still in Moschiena, Kretschmer and the SS officer from the previous photo (probably Weimann) talk to some young *Gebirgsjäger*, perhaps belonging to *I. Btl./Res.Geb.Jg.Rgt.138*.

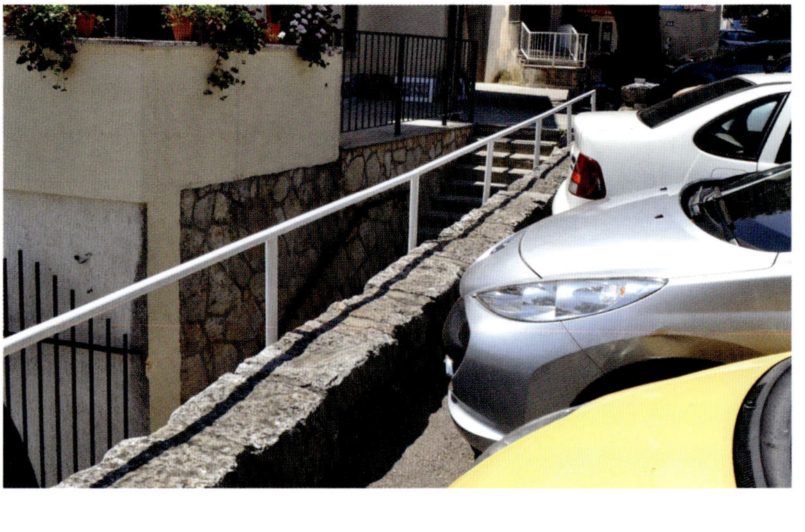

Abbazia (now Opatjia, Croatia); view towards the north (see the *Unternehmen Braunschweig* map, point Then and Now "3"); probably early May 1944, late morning. An Alfa Romeo 350 truck with registration number SS-963035 used by the *SS-Wachmannschaften* drives south passing by the then Hotel Regina Elena (presently Hotel Imperial), which at that time seems to have hosted the headquarters of *I. Btl./SS-Pol.Rgt. "Bozen."* On the cabin roof is a Breda mod. 37 machine gun. The second man sitting on the flatbed side seems to be wearing a three-color shield on his sleeve. Presently, this street is called Ulica Maršala Tita.

A few dozen meters to the south of the previous photo, a column of vehicles has stopped on the right side of the open space in front of the Hotel Principe (presently Hotel Millennium), heading north. In the foreground, is a Fiat 621P truck with registration number SS-965047 transporting men belonging to the *SS-Wachmannschaften*. In front of it is a car with no registration plate but carrying an insignia, barely visible on the right fender, probably the "Globus" used by the *SS-Wachmannschaften* and by *Abteilung R*; it is towed by an Alfa Romeo 350 truck with registration number SS-965035. On the left of the photo vehicles from *I. Btl./SS-Pol.Rgt. "Bozen"* are parked in front of the Hotel Regina Elena.

Around a hundred meters farther south, the Fiat 621P truck with registration plate SS-965047, visible also in the previous and next photo, is seen on the left. The column parked on the right, heading north, is probably made up of vehicles of the *SS-Wachmannschaften*, although some have *Polizei* registration plates. Judging from the uniforms, the soldiers are in fact mostly from the *SS-Wachmannschaften*, but some are probably members of *Abteilung R*. One can see an armored truck with registration number Pol-4711 (a Fiat 626 with jury-rigged armor, missing on the driver's cabin sides), a car with *Polizei* registration plate and another truck with SS registration plate towing a 20 mm Breda 20/65 gun.

The photographer has gone back to find again the Fiat 621P truck with registration number SS-965047, now in front of the Hotel Regina Elena, heading north. Note on the back of the truck the "Globus," the insignia used by the *SS-Wachmannschaften* and by *Abteilung R*. The *SS-Wachmannschaften* on board seem to be all wearing red collar tabs with white piping and sidecaps with *Totenkopf* and SS eagle sewn onto the front. The truck on the right has a *Polizei* registration plate with an illegible number.

Marcossina (now Markovščina, Slovenia), on the Trieste–Fiume road (now Road E61), km. 181, view towards the east (see the *Unternehmen Braunschweig* map, Then and Now point "4"); probably early May 1944. The photographer has left Abbazia with the column from *I. Btl./SS-Pol.Rgt. "Bozen."* After passing through Giordani–Mucici, Bresa, Clana, and Castelnuovo d'Istria (itinerary documented on the basis of the photographic sequence), the vehicles are seen here stopped on the Karststrasse at the exit of Marcossina in the direction of Trieste. In both photos, battalion commander *Maj.* Kretschmer is recognizable in the middle.

Marcossina, on the Road E61, km. 181.5; probably early May 1944. This photo, taken outside the present Gostilna "Baša" ("Baša" restaurant) in Marcossina, directly on the Trieste–Fiume road, shows Wirth (in the middle) talking to Kretschmer (on the right) in the presence of Oberhauser (on the left). *MNZS, 2482/5*

On the same occasion, outside the present Gostilna "Baša," Kretschmer (looking at the photographer) is seen together with his adjutant while discussing the operations. *BA, 101 I-005-0008-27*

Two images of the Gostilna "Baša" of Markovščina, as it appeared in the 1960s. Today, the building has been completely renovated and is unrecognizable. *Courtesy Gostilna "Baša"*

Marcossina, view towards the west; probably early May 1944. A motorized column of *I. Btl./SS-Pol. Rgt. "Bozen"* stopped on the Karststrasse, direction Fiume, a few meters from the Gostilna "Baša." The trucks are loaded with civilians, probably deported from the Ciceria villages in order to stop them helping the partisans. On the right, one can just make out the Lancia 1ZM of *I. Btl./SS-Pol.Rgt. "Bozen,"* parked just off the road. *BA, 101 I-005-0008-34 and 36*

Marcossina, view towards the east. The Lancia 1ZM parked off the Karststrasse, near the Gostilna "Baša" and the road junction to Loce Grande (now Velike Loče; the dirt track to this village is visible left of the armored car). The crucifix on the side of the road, although moved and modified, is still there today.

Marcossina, view towards the southeast. An armored truck belonging to *Abteilung R* photographed in front of the Gostilna "Baša" while it drives on the Karststrasse in the direction of Trieste. The vehicle carries an SS registration plate with an illegible number. On the other side of the road are vehicles from *I. Btl./SS-Pol.Rgt. "Bozen"* loaded with soldiers, heading towards Fiume.

More vehicles belonging to *I. Btl./SS-Pol.Rgt. "Bozen,"* among which the Lancia 1ZM, again in front of the Gostilna "Baša" while they set off towards Fiume. Judging from the camouflage outfit produced with Italian mod. 29 fabric, the man walking on the left of the photograph was probably a member of *Abteilung R*.

Marcossina, view towards the west. The armored truck of *Abteilung R* has made a u-turn and is now parked before the Gostilna "Baša" in the direction of Fiume. Several members of the unit are recognizable: on the truck, from the left is Hackenholt (or perhaps Hirtreiter, the two resembled one another), possibly Bredow, then Münzberger and Frenzel; on the ground, second from the left with the sidecap is perhaps Dubois, behind him possibly Kamm. The men on the left and on the right are from *I. Btl./SS-Pol.Rgt. "Bozen."*

Detail view of the armament of the armored truck (an 8 mm Saint Etienne mod. 07T16 French machine gun from World War I) and of two crewmembers, Hackenholt (or perhaps Hirtreiter), and behind him Münzberger.

A comparison of the man on the truck with Hackenholt (right) and Hirtreiter (left).

On and near a civilian bus parked in front of the Gostilna "Baša" are three policemen from *I. Btl./SS-Pol.Rgt. "Bozen,"* the civilian driver (with the dark uniform) and the same man seen before in front of the armored truck, tentatively identified as Dubois (with the sidecap). The bus, probably belonging to the Fiume public transport service (it had registration number FM-1342), had been used to transport men of *I. Btl./SS-Pol.Rgt. "Bozen"* from Giordani–Mucici.

Taken on the same occasion, still in front of the Gostilna "Baša," this photo shows Wirth (on the right) again talking to Kretschmer (on the left) in the presence of Oberhauser (in the middle). Behind them is the civilian bus of the previous photo, and on the right a camouflaged Fiat 1500A car. *BA, 101 I-005-0008-39*

Achievements

The enemy's offensive plans have been frustrated. The enemy has been dispersed and eliminated, we have demonstrated endurance, dynamism and strength. The nimbus of Monte Maggiore has disappeared. Rumours about an enemy landing, strikes and sabotage for 1 May have not come true. Fear and respect for the German troops are now widespread.

The operation has been tactically very well planned. The enemy was unable to guess our intentions. Many have abandoned the bandits and presented themselves to the German units. Further propaganda initiatives to present the success [of the operation] and the treatment of those who have abandoned the bandits are necessary.

The forced transfer of recruits to Croatia is not carried out. The recruits are sent back home.

More harassment missions in Istria promise to bring success.

The commander of the action
SS-Obersturmführer [Prasch]

SS-Obersturmführer Helmut Prasch wearing the *Bandenkampfabzeichen* in Gold, which he was awarded in February 1945.

3.4.4.2: The Lipa Massacre (April 30, 1944)

The Massacre

The village of Lipa (or Lippa, as it was also called in the period where it was on Italian territory, between the two world wars) is not far from the main road that from Fiume runs to Trieste and Postumia/ Ljubljana, a couple of kilometers southeast of the village of Rupa (or Ruppa), on a secondary road leading in the direction of Clana and farther towards Fiume. At the end of the 1930s its population was around 500 people, most of them ethnic Croats; many worked in agriculture, other in various economic activities in Fiume, which could be reached by public transport. In 1944, only women, children, and elderly people remained in the village, probably little more than 300 people; men who were able to carry arms were fighting with the partisans (the great majority) or with the Italians or the Germans.

In the afternoon of April 30, 1944, in a reprisal action the village was set on fire and destroyed, and its inhabitants killed for the most part. Only uncertain information is available on how the massacre was conducted, since only very few survived among those that were in the village when the soldiers arrived.[89] Apparently, the soldiers surrounded the village, fired at it with machine guns and mortars and around 1600, entered it, starting to brutally kill civilians on the streets and in their homes, looting houses and stables and then setting them on fire. The surviving civilians were ordered to take a few necessary items and set out towards Rupa; however, they were all locked up in the last house at the northwestern exit of the village where they were then slaughtered with firearms and hand grenades. The house was then burned and it seems also blown up to try and cancel the traces of the massacre. According to some sources, German soldiers came back to the village a couple of days after the event, and burned and blew up the houses that were still standing, perhaps in order to eliminate any traces or to complete the destruction. The entire village with eighty-seven houses, and eighty-five other buildings was destroyed.

An Italian officer from *3. Reggimento MDT*, *Tenente* Torquato Dalcich from Fiume, commander of the outpost at the Rupa junction from the second half of March 1945, visited the remains of the village on 29 March 1945. In his memoirs he described it:

> With my colleague Pizzarotti, deputy commander of the Vele Mune [= Mune Grande] outpost, I went to see, for the first time, Lipa and its ruins. The scene was beyond description. In the middle of the ruins of the houses appeared human bones, burned clothes, pottery, even orthopaedic appliances. The entire village, although it is on the road to Clana, is off limits for everybody, since that terrible April.[90]

The number of the victims is not precisely known, but according to the most recent research at least 280 dead (among them seventy-two children) have been identified; considering the number of those that are still officially missing, the real number could go up to 300.[91] In numerical terms it is the largest massacre of civilians that took place in the OZAK region during the war. Despite this it has received little attention both in Italy and in Yugoslavia, as well as later in Croatia, and there has never been a serious attempt to identify the perpetrators.[92]

No known original document of German origin mentions the episode. However, some photos exist that were taken during the massacre; it seems that a photographer in Villa del Nevoso, who was asked to develop and print them, kept some copies, which can be found today in various Slovenian and Croatian archives and in the small Lipa memorial. Since one soldier visible on one of these photos wears an *edelweiss* insignia (used by the *Gebirgstruppe*, or mountain troops) on his cap, the responsibility for the massacre was attributed at some point to the *Waffen-SS* of the *SS-Karstwehr-Btl.*, who wore this insignia and were in the general area at that time as the unit was participating in the anti-partisan operation *Unternehmen Braunschweig*.[93] However, the man wearing the *edelweiss* in the photo belongs clearly to the *Heer* (German army), not to the *Waffen-SS*. Also, no evidence proves that during *Braunschweig* the *SS-Karstwehr-Btl.* was in action in the Lipa area (it is known that it was employed in the

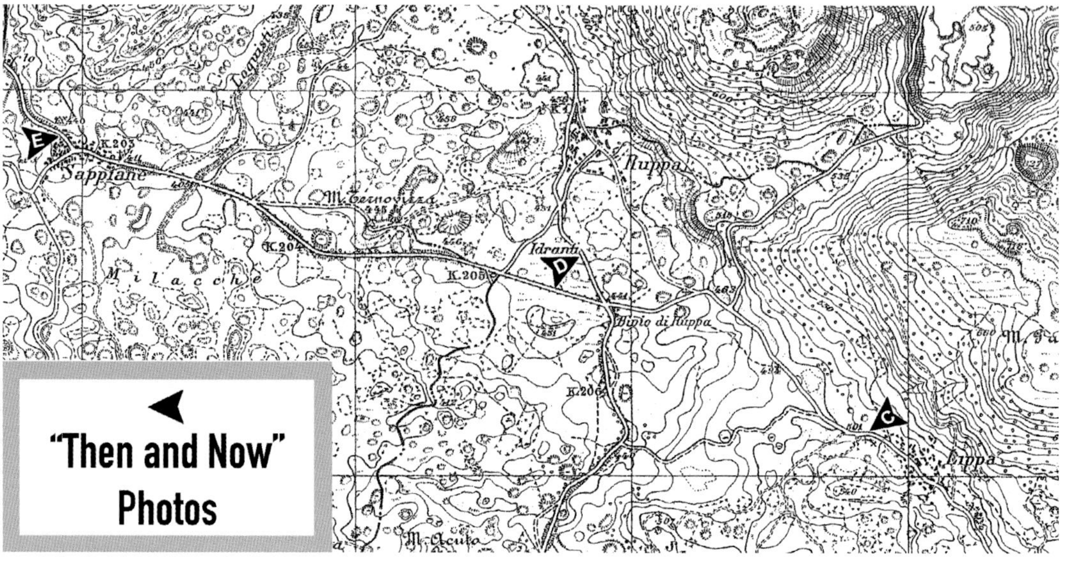

Map from the 1930s showing the area of Lipa (indicated as Lippa, as it was then also called, see point "C") and the location of some "Then and now" photos.

Monte Maggiore area). On the other hand, other soldiers visible in at least two other photos wear the characteristic camouflage outfits used by the members of *Abteilung R*; also, it is practically certain that the SS officer well visible in the photo with the *Gebirgsjäger* is *SS-Ustuf.* Josef Oberhauser. *Abteilung R*, together with elements of other German, Italian, and apparently also Chetnik units, is in fact almost certainly responsible for the massacre.[94]

The Context

In order to understand causes and responsibilities of the Lipa massacre it is necessary to describe the situation in the area and the events of that day, April 30, 1944.

The presence and activity of the partisans in the area between Trieste and Fiume was very strong; they controlled the territory outside the towns and villages where the Germans and their allies had outposts. In addition to trying to cut the railway line, the partisans regularly ambushed vehicles driving in particular on the Trieste–Fiume road (Karststrasse) and attacked the outposts. These were concentrated along the main roads and the railway lines, and their main task was to ensure the protection of the communication lines. The main German outposts in the area in April 1944, for what is known, were in Villa del Nevoso (where the *I. Btl./Res.Geb.Jg.Rgt. 138* was based), Sappiane (where a *Gebirgsjäger* company, probably *2. Kp./Res.Geb.Jg.Rgt. 138* led by *Hptm.* Koser, and apparently also elements of *Abteilung R* were based), Castelnuovo (here also probably with elements of *Abteilung R* a.o.),[95] Mattuglie, Clana (outpost of *I. Btl./SS-Pol. Rgt. "Bozen"*), Castua (probably also an outpost of *I. Btl./SS-Pol.Rgt. "Bozen"*).

The Italian forces in the area are not known in detail, but there were at least the following units:

- *2. Compagnia of 3. Rgt. MDT di Fiume*, commanded in April 1944 by *Tenente* Oscar Battestin, which was based in Giordani–Mucici and probably manned a series of outposts between Mattuglie and the Rupa junction.[96]
- Elements of *14. Battaglione Costiero da Fortezza* (coast fortress battalion; previously known as Battaglione Castelli, it was formed

Rupa junction, view towards the north. These three photos, probably taken in February or early March 1944, show two *Pz.Kpfw. III Ausf.* Ns of *3. Panzer-Sicherungs-Kompanie* posted there with their crews (recognizable from their black uniform). In addition to the tankers, also visible are some policemen from *I. Btl./SS-Pol.Rgt. "Bozen,"* and some Italian MDT and army soldiers (with white collar tabs, in the third photo; probably *Carabinieri* or *Granatieri* from the *Battaglione Volontari di Sardegna*, a unit which had recently been disbanded). The MDT officer in the middle of the first photo wears the red "M" collar tabs of the *Milizia* elite battalions, and may have belonged to *14. Battaglione Costiero da Fortezza* (coast fortress battalion), which was formed around elements of the *Milizia Confinaria* and included members of the former *Battaglione Volontari di Sardegna*. The house on the right is the restaurant from where Vinko Surina saw the bombardment on the junction on April 30, 1944. Behind the house the road coming from Lipa arrived at the junction. The Fiat 665 NM armored truck belonged to a *Wehrmacht* unit, the other truck probably to the "*Bozen*."

by soldiers coming partly from the *Milizia Confinaria* and partly from the RSI army), which protected the railway line between Mattuglie and Sappiane (at least until early May, when it was moved to Gorizia); its commander was *Maggiore* Oscar Soravito.
• A company of the *Guardia di Finanza* (Finance Guard), with outposts along the Trieste–Fiume road (perhaps only in the stretch between Trieste and Sappiane) and headquarters in Castelnuovo.
• Elements of an unidentified battalion of the *Milizia Confinaria*, probably based in Fiume.
• Elements of the *Carabinieri* (military police), probably small groups assigned to various outposts of other units.

Additionally, a Croatian Chetnik unit was also present in the area, billeted in Giordani and Mattuglie.[97]

Just south of the village of Rupa, which laid on the Fiume–Postumia road only a couple of kilometers away from Lipa, there was a junction where the roads coming from Trieste, Fiume, Postumia/Ljubljana and from the direction of Clana (the latter passing through Lipa) met. Given its strategic location, at the Rupa junction (where there were a few houses, including a restaurant) there was a constantly manned check point. Since December 1943, it had been manned by German tank soldiers, when they left in mid-March 1944, the task was taken over by soldiers from the *2. Compagnia of 3. Rgt. MDT*. It was a platoon with around thirty men, among whom a few *carabinieri* (less than ten, attached to the MDT unit), led by *Lieutenant* Aurelio Piesz, from Fiume. The junction was frequently attacked by the partisans with mortar fire, often coming from the direction of Lipa or Novocracina (the latter village was a couple of kilometers northeast of Rupa).

Causes of the Massacre and Its Perpetrators

In the last week of April, the Germans began the anti-partisan operation *Unternehmen Braunschweig* in the Ciceria region and in the area of the Monte Maggiore massif (see above). Initially the military operations did not involve the area of Lipa, however, partisans in the area showed themselves active, perhaps to try to hamper German operations taking place farther south. In an ambush, they destroyed a German motorized column around two kilometers from Vele Lasi–Casa Cantoniera (on the Trieste–Fiume road, between Sappiane and Mucici) on April 25; at the same time they also attacked the *Milizia Confinaria* outpost of the Casa Cantoniera (near the Bergut train station).

Furthermore, in the morning of April 30, a partisan unit belonging to the *"Ivan Gortan" Brigade* carried out an action against the Rupa junction, described in the brigade history:

> 04/30/1944: early in the morning a small detachment of 2nd battalion attacked Rupa [actually the junction], while the rest of the battalion deployed in an ambush position on the road from Fiume and the 1st battalion on the road from Ilirska Bistrica [Villa del Nevoso]. Enemy reinforcement arrived from the direction of Fiume but the waiting unit did not manage to intercept them and they arrived in Rupa [junction], where they were bombarded by mortars. Enemy losses are not known. The enemy did not intervene from the direction of Ilirska Bistrica, so the 1st battalion was not employed. On the same day the enemy entered Lipa and killed all inhabitants.[98]

This reconstruction is probably reliable but incomplete. Integrating the report is the account by the former officer of *3. Rgt. MDT*, Dalcich. Based on what he was told by Piesz himself in March 1945, Dalcich described after the war the events preceding the massacre:

> No Italian soldier participated in the German raid [on Lipa]. (...) According to what Relly (Piesz) told me in March 1945, the outpost he led [at the Rupa junction] was the object of continuous provocations [by the partisans], in particular bombardments with 81 mm mortar rounds. Nobody ever knew if the mortar was placed in Lipa, Graccina Nova [= Novocracina] or in a depression nearby but it is a fact that despite the hail of mortar shells, some of which did not explode, the men of *3. [Rgt.] MDT* never reacted. (...) But we, meaning the outpost soldiers, had

> not considered the Nazis, the SS based in Castelnuovo. In the morning of 30 April an armored car stopped at the junction to fill its radiator up with water. There were three crew members. At that moment a mortar round arrived and exploded a few steps away from the vehicle. Two Germans die, the third one runs to Castelnuovo. In the afternoon an SS column arrives in Rupa. It is led by First Lieutenant Arthur Walter [sic]. Piesz and his men are asked to remain in the outpost. We were not aware of what would happen. And the massacre took place. (...) It was carried out by the SS only.[99]

Very interesting in this writing is the information that on the morning of April 30, a mortar round fired by the partisans killed two Germans belonging to the crew of an armored car stopped at the Rupa junction. The death of two soldiers and the wounding of a few more by a mortar round that fell on the junction is confirmed by a firsthand witness, Vinko Surina, at that time a teenager. He then lived at the restaurant on the junction, and had hidden in the cellar with his family during the bombardment. According to Surina, the Italian soldiers of the outpost, worried that an infantry assault would follow the bombardment, halted the passing German column to ask for help. Through a small window at street level, Surina saw some trucks stopped at the junction and a shell exploding on the wall of a house in front of the restaurant (this house, now gone, was on the opposite side of the junction, where today there is a petrol station). Some soldiers who had dismounted from the vehicles were struck by the splinters, causing two dead and some wounded.[100]

This photo was taken at the western entrance of Lipa during the massacre of April 30, 1944 (see Lipa map, Then and Now point "C"). A *Heer Gebirgsjäger* is looking inside the last village house where part of the population has been locked up; they would be killed shortly afterwards. On the ground outside the house is the baggage that the civilians, thinking they were leaving the village, had taken with them. The other men in the photo are members of *Abteilung R*, wearing the characteristic camouflage outfit used by the unit; the man in the foreground with his back to the camera, armed with a Suomi KP/-31 sub-machine gun, is also visible in a photo showing personnel of *Abteilung R* near the Rupa junction and probably in a photo taken in Sappiane (see pages 49–50). The house was partially destroyed after the massacre but a section of the external walls has been preserved; inside the remains of the building is a memorial. *MNZS, 2366/6*

Another photo taken in the same place as the previous one, but looking towards the village (in south-east direction). In the foreground on the left is *SS-Ustuf.* Oberhauser, armed with a MAB mod. 38 sub-machine gun, looking at the house filled up with the civilians. Also visible is another member of *Abteilung R* (second from the right, with the characteristic camo outfit), a *Heer Gebirgsjäger* (in the foreground in the middle, with the *edelweiss* insignia on his cap), and an Italian (with his back to the camera, in the middle between Oberhauser and the *Gebirgsjäger*; from his uniform he probably belonged to the MDT). Also in this photo the abandoned civilians' baggage is visible. *MNZS, 2366/7*

A *Heer Gebirgsjäger* (probably the same as on the previous photo) setting fire to a house.

Lipa victims of the reprisal.

Lipa houses on fire.

On April 30, 1944, the death of two members of *Abteilung R*, Max Gringers and Alfred Löffler was registered, while another unit member, Gerhard Schneider, was wounded.[101] Although the place of death of Gringers and Löffler is officially given as Opicina, Cosina or generally as the Trieste area, it is indeed possible that the two men were killed at the Rupa junction.[102] This is also consistent with the fact that for both of them the cause of death is indicated as "*Granatsplitter*" (grenade splinters). The armored car near which the mortar round fell could have been one of the armored trucks used by *Abteilung R* to patrol the Trieste–Fiume road. Apart from the coincidence of the date and cause of death and wounding of Gringers, Löffler and Schneider, another element that supports this hypothesis is that fact that, according to Surina, the soldiers who came into his house to dress their wounds and wash themselves right after the shell exploded spoke Russian; they may have been *Trawniki* attached to *Abteilung R*.

Photographs taken in Lipa during the massacre show that personnel of this unit surely took part in it, among them was Oberhauser. *Abteilung R* may therefore be at the origin of the massacre, as well as its main perpetrator. It is plausible that the action was carried out in retaliation for the partisans' attacks on the outposts and the convoys on the Trieste–Fiume road in the area, and that the immediate pretext was the death of Gringers and Löffler. Lipa was probably singled out since it was in the general direction of the incoming mortar rounds and because its inhabitants were accused of supporting the partisans.[103] More generally, the objective was clearly to terrorize the population of the region and setting its mind against the partisans.

Other elements that point towards *Abteilung R* are to be found in the investigations carried out by the Yugoslav authorities, which mention the participation in the Lipa massacre of German troops based in Sappiane. As commanders of this outpost (as well as of the one of Castelnuovo) they cite "Captain Fischer" and "Lieutenant Walter" (sic). Although the Yugoslav prosecution files do not mention their first names or their units, it seems very likely that for the latter they refer to *Leutnant d.SchP.* Arthur Walther, and for the former possibly (despite the rank difference) to *Polizeimeister* (later *SS-Ustuf.*) Helmut Fischer, both from *Abteilung R.*[104] Also the memoirs by the former officer of *3. Rgt. MDT*, Dalcich, links directly *Abteilung R* to the massacre, mentioning the participation of Walther and the "SS based in Castelnuovo."

To the reprisal participated probably elements of the group led by Walther (members of section R III from Udine, recently transferred in the area to take part in anti-partisan operations) and possibly also of section R II from Sappiane or Fiume.[105] Since Oberhauser was present in Lipa, probably also Wirth was there or in the vicinity; it seems likely that Wirth gave the reprisal order, perhaps after consultation with Globocnik. The personal participation of Walther or Fischer in the massacre is, however, not proven.

In addition to *Abteilung R* some German army *Gebirgsjäger*, Italian soldiers and apparently also some Chetniks participated in the reprisal action.[106] The active participation of *Gebirgsjäger* elements results from the photos taken in Lipa; they probably belonged to the company based in Sappiane (probably *2. Kp./Res.Geb.Jg.Rgt. 138*) and perhaps also to other units of *I. Btl./Res.Geb. Jg.Rgt. 138* from Villa del Nevoso.[107]

The Lipa massacre memorial.

A Chetnik unit, probably Croatian Chetniks from the Lika region, photographed in the area of Clana (north of Fiume) during spring–summer 1944. Note in the background the AB41 armored car from *I. Btl./SS-Pol.Rgt. "Bozen." BA, 101 I-005-0018-07*

As far as the Italians are concerned, although the writing by Dalcich states the opposite, their presence during the massacre is also proven, both through accounts[108] as well as on the basis of the photo with Oberhauser taken during the action.[109] The investigations of the Yugoslav authorities accuse Piesz and his men from the Rupa junction outpost to have participated in the massacre, underlining in particular the leading role that the officer allegedly had in it; they also mention the presence of soldiers from the Giordani outpost, among them the commander of *2. Compagnia*, Battestin.[110] Regarding the Chetniks, they may have been Croatian Chetniks based in Giordani–Mattuglie, but this is probably impossible to verify.

Apparently, according to a declaration made to the Yugoslavs by an Italian soldier that had belonged to the Rupa junction outpost, around 150 men participated in the reprisal, of whom around eighty were Germans, forty Italians and thirty Chetniks.[111]

Although the massacre took place in the days of the *Unternehmen Braunschweig*, it does not seem that it was planned as part of this operation. On the contrary, on the basis of the description of the events presented, it seems that it can be concluded that there was no direct link between *Braunschweig* and the reprisal, which was rather caused by a single episode, the death of two men of *Abteilung R*.

Search for the Perpetrators

The partisans and the Yugoslav authorities collected affidavits concerning the massacre and its perpetrators with a view to identifying and punishing the culprits. Immediately after the end of the war the Croatian and Istria commissions for war crime investigations put together prosecution files on Piesz, accused of having participated in the reprisal.[112] The Yugoslavs gathered also the names of many Italian soldiers belonging to the Rupa junction and Giordani outposts, who at least in part participated in the action in Lipa or were suspected of having taken part in it.[113] The accusations were based on testimonies from civilians from the area as well as on statements by at least two former soldiers from the Rupa junction outpost, arrested and detained in Yugoslavia. It seems that none of the accused was ever formally put on trial, excepting perhaps some soldiers taken prisoner by the Yugoslavs at the end of the war (but at least the two detained soldiers who made statements on the episode were acquitted of having participated in the reprisal and set free).

Several sources state that Piesz was arrested by the Yugoslavs in Trieste (where he retreated with his unit in late April 1945) in May 1945, and executed for having participated in the Lipa massacre; according to some sources he was hanged at the Rupa junction, but this is denied by Surina. However, the files from the Croatian and Istria commissions for war crime investigations on Piesz indicate that he had fled to Italy (in the Gorizia province), and nothing is mentioned about his execution. Also Battestin is reported by Italian sources as captured by the Yugoslavs in Fiume at the end of the war, transferred to Castua and then disappeared.

Neither of the two German commanders indicated by the Yugoslavs as active in the Sappiane and Castelnuovo area (Walter/Walther and Fischer) was identified, nor had *Abteilung R* been so far associated with the Lipa massacre.

Members of *Polizei-Kompanie z.b.V. "Alpenland"* and of the *Milizia Confinaria* seen before the main gate of the Pisino (now Pazin, Croatia) castle in spring–summer 1944. The Italians probably belonged to *2. Compagnia* of *I. Battaglione Milizia Confinaria DT* and operated together with the German company, to which they were perhaps attached. Note the *Orpo* eagle worn on the chest by a Blackshirt (the first one sitting on the left).

Two more photos of members of *Pol.Kp. z.b.V. "Alpenland"* in Istria, together with Italian *Milizia Confinaria* soldiers. The church in one of the images is Sv. Matej in the village of Cere, on the road Barbana–Gimino (now Barban and Žminj, Croatia).

Elements of *Pol.Kp. z.b.V. "Alpenland"* near the Pisino boarding school (now Pazinski Kolegij), perhaps the company billets.

This photo taken in Matteria (Materija, Slovenia) on August 10, 1944, shows men and a radio vehicle of *Polizei-Nachrichten-Kp. 21* (police signals company) with members of the Italian *Guardia di Finanza* (Finance Guard). It is possible that they were participating in operations that were being conducted under Allers' command in the nearby Ciceria region that day.

Armored truck used by *14. Battaglione Costiero da Fortezza* (coast fortress battalion), an Italian unit formed in Fiume right after the Italian armistice with elements of the *Milizia Confinaria*, later supplemented by soldiers from the RSI army. Second from the left, with the black shirt and *Alpini*-like hat, is the unit commander, *Maggiore* Oscar Soravito. The photo probably dates from spring–summer 1944. The truck is a jury-rigged realization based on a Fiat 626 chassis; very unusual is the presence of a shield or a turret for using a machine gun, mounted behind the driving cab and covered by a camouflage cloth. This is probably the same vehicle visible in the distance in a photo taken in Ruccavazzo during *Unternehmen Braunschweig* (see page 68).

3.4.4.3: Structure of the *Sicherungskommandant* in the OZAK

The *Sicherungskommandant* (security commanders)[114] were officers responsible for maintaining security and protecting communication lines and potential objectives of sabotage actions in specific and particularly threatened areas, which were called *Sicherungsabschnitt* or *Sicherungsbereich* (security sector or area). When the areas were particularly large they were divided into a number of sub-sectors, led by officers called *Sicherungsführer*.

The network of the *Sicherungskommandant* in the OZAK was created by the HSSPF and all *Sicherungskommandant* were subordinated to the *SS- und Polizeikommandeur* of the respective province. The *Sicherungskommandant* were experienced officers belonging mostly to the SS/*Polizei*, in some cases also to the *Wehrmacht*. The forces at their disposal were generally static units, based in outposts; they were mainly SS/*Polizei* forces or collaborationist units, rarely also Wehrmacht units.[115] These forces were complemented when needed by *Jagdkommando* (partisan-hunting squad; these were mobile and well-armed strike forces formed with personnel from units based in the area) and *Alarm–Einheit* (alarm unit; these were emergency units that intervened in case of surprise enemy attacks, formed with all available forces, including support units), also including *Wehrmacht* forces.

The first *Sicherungskommandant* in the OZAK was nominated by Globocnik for maintaining security along the Trieste–Fiume road, the Karststrasse, in the person of Wirth.[116] The precise date of this nomination is not known but probably dates to the second half of April or perhaps in early May 1944. After his death, which occurred only a few weeks later, Wirth was replaced by Allers.[117]

Later many other *Sicherungskommandant* were progressively nominated in the OZAK. Information on this regard is very scarce and surely incomplete, but those identified are:

In the Udine (or Friuli) Province:
Sich.Kdt. Udine; *Sich.Kdt. Pordenone*, to whom were subordinated (at least in December 1944) the *Sicherungsführer Sacile*, *Aviano*, *Pordenone* and *Spilimbergo*; *Sich.Kdt. Palmanova*; *Sich.Kdt. San Giorgio di Nogaro*; *Sich.Kdt. Gemona*;[118] *Sich.Kdt. Tolmezzo*; *Sich.Kdt. Villa Santina*; *Sich.Kdt. Paularo*; *Sich.Kdt. Paluzza*.

In the Gorizia Province:
Sich.Kdt. Tolmino–S. Lucia (responsible for a stretch in the middle part of the Isonzo (Soča) River valley and for the Baccia (Bača) River valley); *Sich.Kdt. Plezzo–Caporetto* (responsible for the upper Isonzo River valley and for the Natisone River valley); *Sich.Kdt. Aidussina*; *Sich.Kdt. San Daniele del Carso* (responsible for the road and the railway Gorizia–Montespino–Rifembergo–San Daniele del Carso–Duttogliano–Opicina).[119]

In the Trieste Province:
Sich.Kdt. Trieste; *Sich.Kdt. Castelnuovo d'Istria*; *Sich.Kdt. Monfalcone* (responsible for the road and the railway Gorizia–Monfalcone–Aurisina–Barcola); *Sich.Kdt. Postumia* (responsible for the road Opicina–Postumia–Planina and the railway Opicina–Postumia–San Pietro del Carso–Rakek; apparently it was later divided in four parts, each with a *Sich.Kdt.*: Sesana, Senosecchia, Postumia and San Pietro del Carso).[120]

In the Fiume (or Quarnero) Province:
Sich.Kdt. Villa del Nevoso.

In the Pola (or Istria) Province:
Sich.Kdt. Pola; *Sich.Kdt. für das Kohlegebiet Arsia* (*Sich.Kdt.* for the coal mining area of Arsia); *Sich.Kdt. für das Bauxitgebiet in Istrien* (*Sich.Kdt.* for the bauxite mining area in Istria).

Additionally, across the provinces of Udine and Gorizia there was a *Sicherungskommandant* responsible for the Udine–Gorizia road.

There were undoubtedly more security sectors which are not identified. On the basis of the number of copies of documents sent by the SS/*Polizei* headquarters in the OZAK to the *Sicherungskommandant*, it seems that there were fifteen on August 30, 1944, augmented to thirty-seven (probably including the subordinated *Sicherungsführer*) in February 1945.[121]

To the sectors listed, one should add from mid-1944 the security sectors created for the protection of the building sites for the defensive lines built under Rainer's responsibility; these sectors were subordinated to the *Höherer Sicherungsstab*, the headquarters specifically created for this task (see the specific section).

This series of photos, although not directly linked to *Abteilung R* or the *SS-Wachmannschaften*, has been included because it shows—in addition to *Wehrmacht* and *Ordnungspolizei* troops—men probably belonging to the *SS-und Polizei-Kommandeur Istrien* based in Pola, to which reference is made in the text. All photos (except one) were taken between August 5–9, 1944, near the village of Prodol, on the D66 road running from Pola to Abbazia. On August 5, near Magnadorsi (now Manjadvorci, Croatia), a village a few hundred meters from the place where these photos were made, a sweep operation was carried out by the *SS-u.Pol.Kdr. Istrien*, with the participation of elements of *Polizei-Freiwilligen-Btl. "Pola."*

A jury-rigged armored truck with SS runes painted on the left fender, probably belonging to *SS-u.Pol. Kdr. Istrien*; note the writing painted on the cab, apparently containing the date "24-7-44." On the right, is the only AB 41 armored car used by *I. Btl./ SS-Pol.Rgt. "Bozen."*

A group of SS/*Polizei* men, likely from *SS-u.Pol.Kdr. Istrien*, follow the armored truck. The car in the background carries the insignia of *188. Reserve-Gebirgs-Division*, the *Steinbock*, painted on its right fender.

Immediately afterward, on the same road stretch, another jury-rigged armored truck, based on a Fiat-SPA 38R chassis, makes a detour to bypass a road cut. Note the lightning "M" insignia used by the *Guardia Nazionale Repubblicana* (called MDT in the OZAK) painted on the cab. The vehicle belonged perhaps to the motorized company "Mazza di Ferro" of *2. Rgt. MDT*, based in Pola.

On the same road near Prodol, what remains of an armored truck from *2. Rgt. MDT* is overtaken by a column from *I. Btl./SS-Pol.Rgt. "Bozen."* This photo was probably taken in late June–July 1944. The destroyed vehicle hit a mine on June 15, 1944, causing nine dead among the crew; it had been sent to recover the bodies of MDT soldiers killed on June 13, during the partisan attack against the MDT outpost of Santa Domenica di Albona (now Nedešćina, Croatia).

Again on the same road between August 5–9, 1944: the side armor of the truck destroyed on June 15, is used as a platform to overcome a road cut. The Prodol area was probably ideal for partisan ambushes: in the same area an armored vehicle used by the *SD-Aussenkommando Pola* hit a mine on October 30, 1944, among the dead were two Byelorussian *SS-Schutzmänner* (probably belonging to *3. Kp./ Schutzmannschafts-Btl. 13*), a German *SS-Oberscharführer* and an Italian *SS-HiWi* (volunteer) from Istria (the latter two belonging to *SD-Aussenkommando Pola*).

The column from *I. Btl./SS-Pol.Rgt. "Bozen"* photographed near Prodol in early August 1944, drove farther to northeastern Istria, where between August 7–10, units of *188. Reserve-Gebirgs-Division*, *Luftwaffe* ground units, and Italian MDT units carried out the anti-partisan operation *Unternehmen Prien*. This sweep operation took place from the area of Erpelle (now Hrpelje, Slovenia) towards Grisignana–Buie (now Grožnjan and Buje, Croatia), through the Risano (Rižana) and Dragogna (Dragonja) River valleys. These photos, also taken between August 5–9, show soldiers and civilians working to make passable the bridge on the Dragogna River near Sicciole (now Sečovlje, today the border crossing between Slovenia and Croatia) destroyed by the partisans, and vehicles belonging to *I. Btl./SS-Pol.Rgt. "Bozen"* (AB 41, Lancia 1ZM, various trucks) and to the SS (the car being pushed has registration number SS-965092) overcoming the road cut.

The southern approaches to the road cut are guarded by soldiers with a very rare anti-aircraft gun model; a 2 cm *Gebirgsflak* 38. Near the weapon are an Italian officer (probably from the MDT) and a German soldier. Repair work to the bridge is going on in the background, at the end of the road.

3.4.5: Contribution to the Construction of Defensive Lines (*Sonderauftrag Pöll*)

Istria was always considered by the Germans as a possible Allied landing zone, since landing there would have allowed bypassing the Italian front and conducting an attack towards the Ljubljana plain and the Reich, or towards Zagreb. Immediately after the occupation of the region, one of the main tasks of the German forces was coastal security and defense, including building fortifications: these were to concentrate on the ports of Trieste, Pola, and Fiume and on a defensive line along the "neck" of Istria, approximately between Trieste and Abbazia.

The reconnaissance of possible defensive positions in Istria was made during winter 1943–44. The path of the defensive line, known as *Karststellung* (Karst defensive line), was initially set out as follows: Risano (Rižana) River valley (between Muggia and Capodistria)–Villa Decani–Pinguente–Castel Lupogliano–Valdarsa–Adriatic coast near Moschiena, west of the massif of the Monte Maggiore, the highest Istria mountain and one of the main partisan areas. Although precise information is missing, it seems evident that the path was subsequently changed in its southeastern part, which was moved farther east, on the mountains of the Ciceria region; probably this new line was indicated as *Tschitschenbodenstellung* (Ciceria defensive line), although it seems that also for this adjusted line the name of *Karststellung* continued to be used. Construction was started in the first half of 1944, but advanced slowly. By the beginning of June 1944, the course had been explored along its entire length, but fortification work had not been started yet.

The pulling back of the Italian front during spring–summer 1944 forced the Germans to start building defensive lines north of the Grün–Linie on the Appennini mountain range (the so-called Gothic Line). On July 27, with the *Führerweisung 60* (*Führer*'s directive No. 60, completed in the following days by directives Nos. 60a and 60b), Hitler ordered the construction of a rear defensive system in northern Italy, which included the following defensive lines:

1. The *Voralpenstellung* (Prealps defensive line, also known as Blaue Linie or Blau–Linie,

Blue Line): it ran from the Italian border with Switzerland to the Adriatic Sea; it started at the Stelvio Pass, touched the northern tip of Lake Garda, passed through the Alps north of Belluno (Longarone), the Carnia Prealps (in the OZAK region, approximately following the line Cimolais–Claut–Tramonti–Gemona), the line Gemona–Caporetto, the eastern shore of the Isonzo River via Tolmino down to Gorizia, and from here south to the Adriatic coast between Monfalcone and Duino, following for long stretches the front of World War I;

2. The *Karststellung* (Carso defensive line): it ran from Trieste to Fiume (or more precisely from the area south of Trieste to the area of Volosca, just north of Abbazia), through the Ciceria region, and should have stopped the enemy in case of a landing in Istria, avoiding the *Voralpenstellung* being bypassed from the east;

3. Two intermediary containment lines (*Riegelstellung*), respectively from Ala and Belluno to the Gulf of Venice, and the highest possible lines of additional intermediary lines, in particular along the rivers, aiming at keeping the enemy far away from the Udine area, protecting the air bases there and gaining time to complete the main defensive positions.

The responsibility for the construction of the defensive line was given to the two highest commissars of the OZAK and OZAV, Rainer and Hofer, also outside the two *Operationszone*, on the territory of the RSI. They were given "free hand" as far as the employment of men and material was concerned. The specialists, qualified workers, and equipment would come from the Organisation Todt, but simple workforce had to be found through a popular mobilization led by the political authorities, who in this case had to prove to be able to "improvise." The highest commissars were given permisson to find workers with the help of the army, by means of sweep operations, also carried out outside the *Operationszone*.[122] The protection of the building sites was also a task assigned to the highest commissars with the forces at their disposal (SS/*Polizei*, including collalborationist units), to which they were allowed to add up to 40% of the personnel of all *Wehrmacht* headquarters and offices which had no tactical function. Fighting against the partisans remained the task of the *HstSSPF Italien* (Karl Wolff), through the SS/*Polizei* commanders in the respective areas. As far as the military aspects of the construction works were concerned (definition of the operative and tactical course, decision on the priority sequence for executing the work and on the type of fortifications to build, etc.) the *Oberbefehlshaber*

The commander of the Italian front (*Oberbefehlshaber Südwest*) *Generalfeldmarschall* Kesselring, the *Oberster Kommissar* for the OZAK region Rainer and the region military commander (*Befehlshaber in der* OZAK) *General der Gebirgstruppe* Kübler during an inspection to the building sites for the defensive lines built in the region.

Südwest/Heeresgruppe C (i.e., *Generalfeldmarschall* Albert Kesselring, commander of the Italian front) was responsible. The *Oberbefehlshaber Südwest/ Heeresgruppe C* (not the Highest Commissars) maintained responsibility for the construction of the coastal defenses.[123]

On September 4, the *Oberbefehlshaber Südwest/Heeresgruppe C* communicated to the *Oberkommando der Wehrmacht* the priority sequence it had decided for the defensive lines listed in the *Führerweisung 60*, which was set as follows:

1. *Blaue Linie* (from the Swiss border to the area north of Verona), *blaue Vorfeldlinie I* (first advanced line of the Blue Line, from Lake Garda to the Adriatic Coast), *Karststellung* and area of Fiume.[124]
2. In-depth defense of the Adriatic coast (second and third coast lines, for the defense in case of landing).
3. Containment line along the Piave River (Piave–Riegel) [from Belluno to the Adriatic Sea].
4. Containment line along the Isonzo River (Isonzo–Riegel);
5. Containment line along the Tagliamento River (Tagliamento–Riegel).
6. Containment line along the Brenta River (Brenta–Riegel).[125]

Many of the defensive lines which the Germans planned to man to slow down the Allied advance in Italy were, at least partially, in the OZAK. The priority attributed to the *Karststellung* and to the Fiume area was probably a consequence of the worries about a possible Allied landing in Istria, caused by intelligence reports received by the *Oberkommando der Wehrmacht* in late August.[126]

The *Führerweisung 60* left to the two highest commissars to define the border between the respective competence areas on RSI territory. It is not known where this border was set, but it seems certain that Rainer's area extended to the entire Veneto region (excluding the Belluno province, which was part of the OZAK) until the *blaue Vorfeldlinie I*.

Additionally, to the tasks related to the defensive lines listed in the *Führerweisung 60*, with the *Führerweisung 60a* Rainer was also given responsibility for building the in-depth coastal defensive lines, in cooperation with the military headquarters.

In the following weeks, the Soviet advance in the Balkans forced the Germans to plan the defense of the *Reich*'s southeastern borders. On September 12, Hitler issued the *Führerweisung 65*, which ordered to start building a *Grenzstellung* (border defensive line, also called *Grenzstellung Südost*, or *Südost–Linie*) in the *Reich* southeastern regions. This line was meant to protect the border of the Austrian regions of Carinthia and Styria;

Another photo taken on the same occasion, in which Globocnik is also visible.

A civilian car used by the *Sonderauftrag Pöll*. Note the registration plate starting with the organization name.

Elements from the *Technische Nothilfe* (police technical assistance) working in the building sites for the defensive lines in Jamiano, near Monfalcone, in early 1945.

it was to start in the OZAK and follow the following path: north of Gorizia [probably at the entrance of the Isonzo River valley, where it probably met the Blaue Linie]–Vipacco (Vipava) River sector–Postumia–Višnja Gora–*Reich*'s border south of Litija. Also in this case the responsibility for the construction of this line was given to the regional governors, Rainer and Uiberreither (the latter was *Gauleiter* of Styria), and the workforce was to be recruited among the civilian population.

Additionally, on December 4, the *Oberbefehlshaber Südwest/Heeresgruppe C* ordered the extension of the Südost-Linie by creating the so-called *Linie B* (also known as *B-Stellung*, *Ingrid–Linie* or *Ingrid–Stellung*), which was to run from Fiume to Postumia/Cerknica, using as much as possible the old Italian border fortifications.

During the month of August, Rainer created a special centralized structure, directly subordinated to him, tasked with building the defensive lines, called *Sonderauftrag Pöll* (special task Pöll, also indicated as *Unternehmen Pöll*, operation Pöll).[127] Directing the *Sonderauftrag* was a *Planungsstab Stellungsbau* (headquarters for planning the construction of the defensive lines), at whose head Rainer nominated Globocnik; he became hence the *Gauleiter*'s representative for

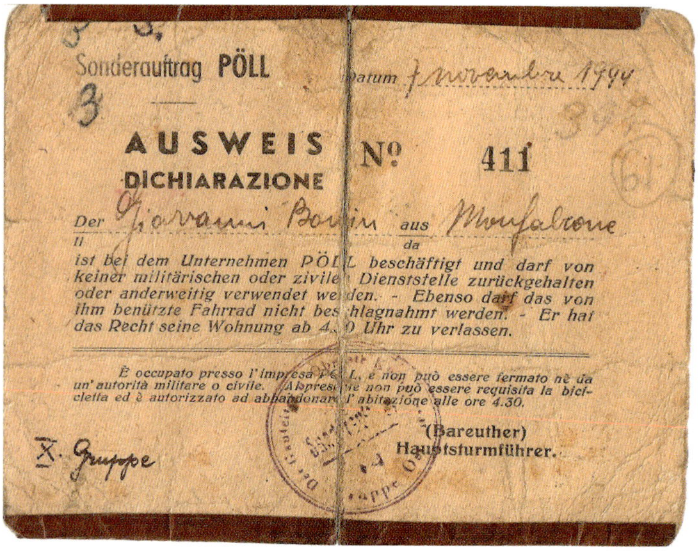

Sonderauftrag PÖLL

Datum 7 novembre 1944

AUSWEIS No. 411

DICHIARAZIONE

Der / Il Giovanni Bonin aus / da Monfalcone

ist bei dem Unternehmen PÖLL beschäftigt und darf von keiner militärischen oder zivilen Dienststelle zurückgehalten oder anderweitig verwendet werden. - Ebenso darf das von ihm benützte Fahrrad nicht beschlagnahmt werden. - Er hat das Recht seine Wohnung ab 4.30 Uhr zu verlassen.

È occupato presso l'impresa PÖLL, e non può essere fermato nè da un'autorità militare o civile. All'presente non può essere requisita la bicicletta ed è autorizzato ad abbandonare l'abitazione alle ore 4.30.

X. Gruppe

(Bareuther)
Hauptsturmführer.

An *ausweis* (identity card) issued by the *Sonderauftrag Pöll* to a worker in November 1944. Note the stamped signature of *SS-Hstuf.* Bareuther, belonging to Globocnik's staff already in Lublin and later in Trieste.

the realization of the defensive lines. The *Sonderauftrag*, in cooperation with the civilian offices of the *Oberster Kommissar*, the HSSPF, the *Wehrmacht* and the Organization Todt, had to deal with all aspects of the operation, from planning and executing the works, to providing materials and workforce, to watch over the workers, to protect the building sites from possible attacks by the partisans, etc. It was composed of four sections, called *Gruppe* or *Gruppenstab* (group or group headquarters), each responsible for a different area, of which three are identified: the *Gruppe West*, probably responsible for the works in the Veneto and Friuli regions; the *Gruppe Ost*, probably responsible for the Provinz Laibach; and the *Gruppe Nord*, based in Klagenfurt, responsible for the fortifications along the Austrian border. The *Gruppe Süd* was perhaps responsible for the building sites in Istria. Each *Gruppe* was divided in a number of *Oberabschnitt* (main sector), in their turn made up of *Abschnitt* (sector) where the building sites were located.

The sector corresponding to the *Karststellung* was divided into two *Oberabschnitt*, named *Wirth-West* and *Wirth-Ost* (west and east), evidently in honor of the *Abteilung R*'s commander killed in that area. The *Oberabschnitt Wirth-West* was responsible for the northwestern stretch of *Karststellung*, from the Muggia peninsula to the village of Mune Grande (with the building sites of Villa Decani, Antignana, San Sergio, Prapozze, Sasseto, Piedimonte del Taiano, Gelovizza, Vodizze, Mune Grande and Mune Piccolo). The *Oberabschnitt Wirth-Ost*, in its turn sub-divided in sector A and B, was responsible for the southeastern stretch of the defensive line (the building sites of Seiane, Suonecchia, Mattuglie, Ruccavazzo, and Volosca are known).

The surveillance and protection of the building sites was assigned to a *Höherer Sicherungsstab* (higher security headquarters), subordinated to the *Sonderauftrag* (see the specific section).

Also *Abteilung R* was called upon to contribute in several ways to the efforts of *Sonderauftrag Pöll*. It seems that the men involved in this operation (probably only a part of *Abteilung R*) took the name—it is not known if officially or not—of *"Einsatzstab beim Gruppenstab Pöll"* (operational headquarters by the group headquarters

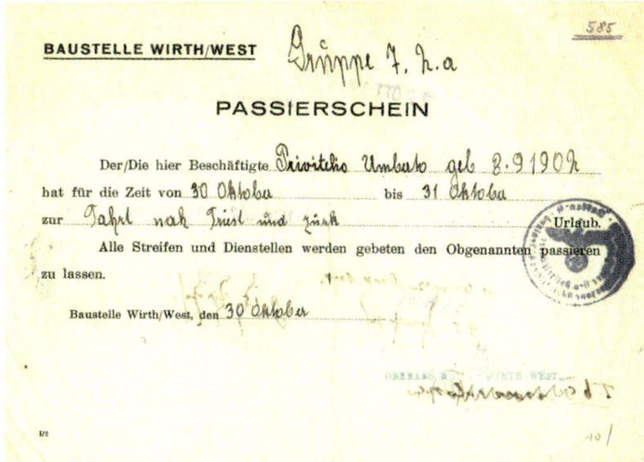

BAUSTELLE WIRTH/WEST

PASSIERSCHEIN

Der/Die hier Beschäftigte ...
hat für die Zeit von 30 Oktober bis 31 Oktober
zur ...
Alle Streifen und Dienststellen werden gebeten den Obgenannten passieren zu lassen.
Baustelle Wirth/West, den 30 Oktober

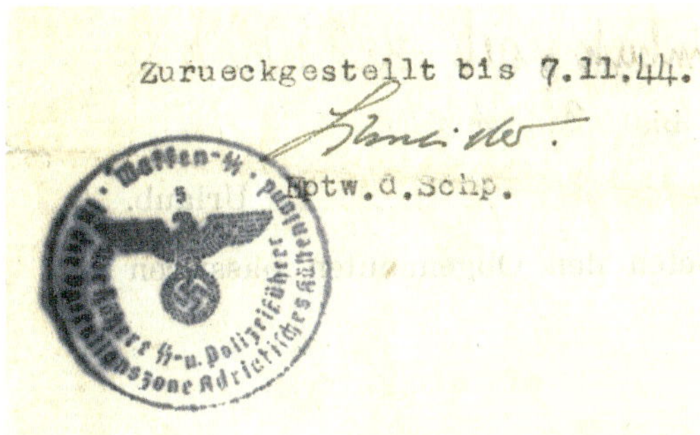

Zurueckgestellt bis 7.11.44.

...tw.d.Schp.

Passierschein (pass) for going to Trieste and back issued in October 1944, to a worker of the *Baustelle* (building site) Wirth-West. On the reverse side there is a note signed by Schneider from *Abteilung R* and the round stamp HSSPF OZAK number 5 used by *Abteilung R*.

Pöll).[128] An important set of tasks for the unit derived from the nomination of Allers as head of the *Oberabschnitt Wirth-West*;[129] as a consequence, he became responsible for the construction of the defensive positions in the building sites in this main sector. To this aim Allers and *Abteilung R* had to manage the civilian workers forcibly recruited to work on the building sites of *Oberabschnitt Wirth-West*. According to Allers he had around 5,000 workers at his disposal.[130] In several accounts it is mentioned that the workers' personal documents were confiscated and kept in the offices of *Abteilung R* on Via Giustinelli in Trieste, to limit the risk of fleeing. In exchange for their personal documents they received an identification card (*Ausweis*) issued by *Abteilung R*; a certificate (*Bescheinung*) was issued to the workers who for various reasons were exempted from work.[131]

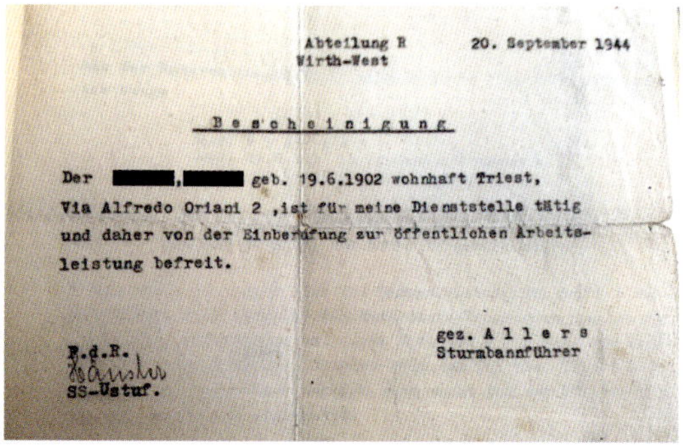

Abteilung R 20. September 1944
Wirth-West

Bescheinigung

Der ■■■, ■■■ geb. 19.6.1902 wohnhaft Triest, Via Alfredo Oriani 2, ist für meine Dienststelle tätig und daher von der Einberufung zur öffentlichen Arbeitsleistung befreit.

F.d.R. Häusler SS-Ustuf.

gez. Allers Sturmbannführer

A document with heading *Abteilung R* – Wirth-West issued to a man working for this entity in September 1944, signed by Allers and countersigned by Häusler.

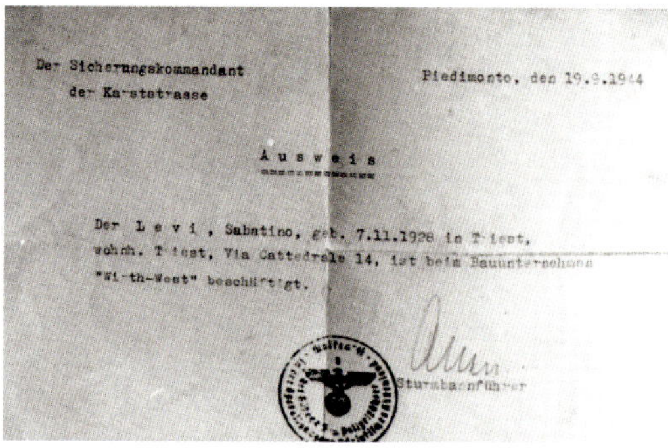

Der Sicherungskommandant der Karststrasse

Piedimonte, den 19.9.1944

Ausweis

Der Levi, Sabatino, geb. 7.11.1928 in Triest, wohnh. Triest, Via Cattedrale 14, ist beim Bauunternehmen "Wirth-West" beschäftigt.

Sturmbannführer

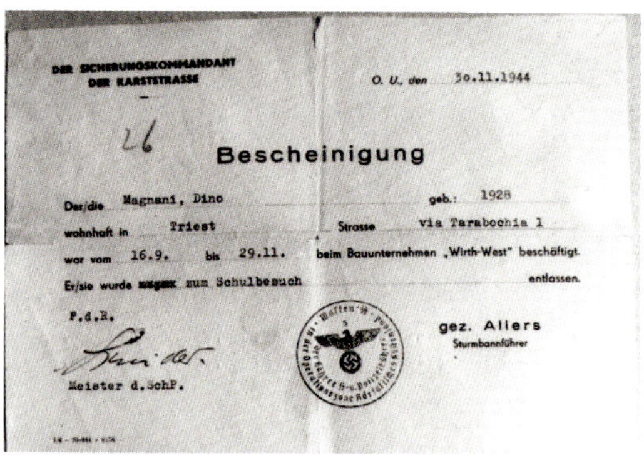

DER SICHERUNGSKOMMANDANT DER KARSTSTRASSE

O. U., den 30.11.1944

Bescheinigung

Der/die Magnani, Dino geb.: 1928
wohnhaft in Triest Strasse via Tarabochia 1
war vom 16.9. bis 29.11. beim Bauunternehmen „Wirth-West" beschäftigt.
Er/sie wurde zum Schulbesuch entlassen.

F.d.R. Meister d.SchP.

gez. Allers Sturmbannführer

Two documents from September and November 1944, issued to workers of the *Bauunternehmen* (building company) Wirth-West on headed paper of the *Sicherungskommandant der Karststrasse*, signed by Allers. One of the two documents is countersigned by Schneider from *Abteilung R*. *Courtesy Roberto Spazzali*

Despite all efforts, work on the *Karststellung* did not respect the planned schedule and by the end of the year the results were largely behind expectations, primarily because of the insufficient number of workers. In a report dated December 26, 1944, Kesselring informed the *Oberkommando der Wehrmacht* that the *Karststellung* was not yet ready. But actually work advanced slowly on all planned defensive lines in northeastern Italy and Slovenia, which remained largely incomplete and did not represent a significant obstacle to the advance of the Allied forces in the last weeks of the war.

In addition to his task of guaranteeing security on the Trieste–Fiume road as *Sicherungskommandant der Karststrasse*, Allers was also responsible for providing surveillance and protection of the building sites, apparently not only on the *Oberabschnitt Wirth-West*, but along the entire *Karststellung*, that is also on *Oberabschnitt Wirth-Ost*. For this, elements of *Abteilung R* were employed (Walther confirmed in a deposition that the Castelnuovo outpost was employed for this), but it is likely that primarily concerned were SS/*Polizei* (including collaborationist) units, put at Allers' disposal for this task. It is for instance known that for guarding the building sites of *Oberabschnitt Wirth*, elements of *41. Brigata Nera "Tullio Cividino"* from Trieste were used; from October to end of December 1944, they were present at building sites in the area from Trieste to Fiume (detachments of the *Brigata Nera* are identified in Criva–Ruccavazzo, Volosca, Castua, Piedimonte and Mune).[132] In December, the *Brigata Nera* was reorganized and its three companies were put at the disposal of the *Sicherungskommandant der Karststrasse* (who also had to provide for their training), and probably again used to protect the building sites.[133]

Abteilung R was also involved in obtaining and transporting all types of materials for the building sites, not only for the *Oberabschnitt Wirth-West* but probably of the level of the entire *Sonderauftrag*. Several member of *Abteilung R* (among them Tauscher and Stangl) were active in tracking down and purchasing, also on the black market, building materials, fuel, vehicles, tires, food, uniforms, shoes, etc.[134] Others mentioned in their trial depositions to have been employed as

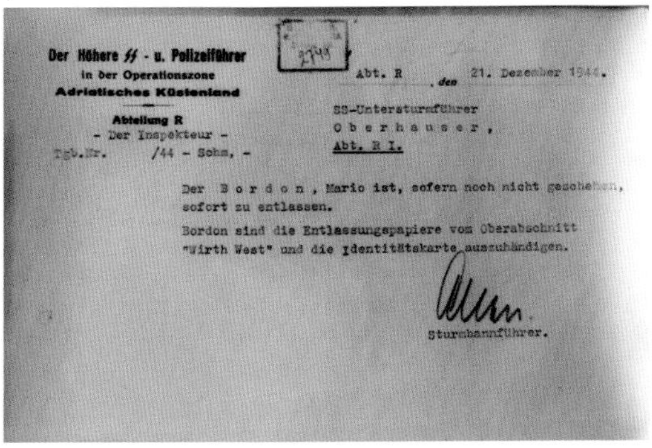

Der Höhere SS - u. Polizeiführer
in der Operationszone
Adriatisches Küstenland

Abteilung R
- Der Inspekteur -
Tgb.Nr. /44 - Schm, -

Abt. R , den 21. Dezember 1944.

SS-Untersturmführer
O b e r h a u s e r ,
Abt. R I.

Der B o r d o n , Mario ist, sofern noch nicht geschehen, sofort zu entlassen.
Bordon sind die Entlassungspapiere vom Oberabschnitt "Wirth West" und die Identitätskarte auszuhändigen.

Sturmbannführer.

A document drafted on *Abteilung R* headed paper, signed by Allers and sent to section R I, to the attention of Oberhauser, in December 1944. It concerns the release of a man working on the building sites of the *Sonderauftrag Pöll*, in the sector *Oberabschnitt* Wirth-West; this sector was under Allers' responsibility.

drivers to transport materials to the building sites of the *Sonderauftrag*, including in the Veneto region.[135] Also the large warehouses of the Risiera were used to stock construction materials.

It is likely that the setting up of the section R IV, led by Stangl, was a consequence of the extension of Rainer's influence area to the Veneto region in the framework of the *Sonderauftrag Pöll*. The section was active both in the arrest of Jews and seizure of their properties, as well as in finding and acquiring materials for the *Sonderauftrag*.

Still in relation with the defensive works in the OZAK, it seems that elements of *Abteilung R* were employed to work on defensive positions and prepare some sites of military interest for destruction. Indicatively from October 1944, some men of the unit worked to prepare the explosion of rock overhang in the Fella River valley, between Resiutta and Chiusaforte, north of Udine on the road to Austria, probably meant to block the valley at the arrival of the Allies. It seems that they were mainly men belonging to section R III from Udine, led by Fischer, who had served in an SS engineer unit (with him were Bollert, Fels, Geis, Lambert, Miete, Münzberger and around sixty Italians). These works, often interrupted by aircraft attacks, continued until the end of the war, but the explosion never did happen.

In an order issued by the HSSPF OZAK – *Operationsstab* (= FSBB) on March 11, 1945, signed by Globocnik and regarding the cooperation between the Wehrmacht and the SS/Polizei, one can read: "The *Sonderkommando 'Allers'* prepares for destruction the objects entrusted to it. Their destruction can only be carried out following my orders."[136] There is no information on what specific tasks this *Sonderkommando Allers* had, or on which were the objects entrusted to it.

Although not related to defensive positions but generally to the war effort, it should also be mentioned that at some point Allers was put in charge of a workshop in Tolmezzo (north of Udine) that recalibrated Italian rifles to German ammunition; probably in connection with this task, men from *Abteilung R* manned a *Stützpunkt* in Tolmezzo, at least in March 1945 (when Hackenholt was present; Grossmann and Lambert also served there).

3.4.5.1: The *Höherer Sicherungsstab*

The surveillance and protection of the building sites of the defensive lines built under the responsibility of the *Sonderauftrag Pöll* was assigned to a *Höherer Sicherungsstab* (higher security headquarters). Its setting up and command was entrusted to *SS-Brigadeführer und Generalmajor der Polizei* Karl Herrmann, who was sent to the HSSPF OZAK especially for this task in mid-August 1944. The *Höherer Sicherungsstab* was subordinated to the *Sonderauftrag Pöll* (in particular to its *Abteilung VI – Sicherungskräfte*, section VI – security forces) and it was initially based in Galzignano (near Padova), then in Ponte di Piave (at least between November 1944 and January 1945) and later in Trieste (at least in March 1945).

Of all the areas where defensive lines were built under the responsibility of the OZAK *Oberster Kommissar*, it seems that the *Höherer Sicherungsstab* was responsible only for the Veneto region (and only later also for the province of Udine, or the Friuli region, bordering Veneto on the east); at least initially it did not operate in the OZAK, where the building sites' protection was possibly assured directly by the security forces of the HSSPF OZAK.

Every *Oberabschnitt* and *Abschnitt* of the *Sonderauftrag* had a *Sicherheitsführer* (security commander, sometimes also indicated with the equivalent term of *Sicherungsführer*), generally respectively a battalion and company commander.

From mid-August 1944, the following *Ordnungspolizei* units were subordinated to Herrmann, all operating in Veneto: *III. Btl./SS-Pol. Rgt. 12, I. Pol.Freiw.Btl. "Italien," III. Pol.Freiw. Btl. "Italien"* and *IV. Pol.Freiw.Btl. "Italien."*[137]

After the four existing *Pol.Freiw.Btl. "Italien"* were consolidated in two battalions only (*I.* and *II. Pol.Freiw.Btl. "Italien"*) during September 1944 and following the assignment of other units, on October 8, the following units were subordinated to the *Höherer Sicherungsstab*: *III. Btl./SS-Pol. Rgt. 12* [in the area of Este–Monselice–Albettone–Lonigo], *I. Pol.Freiw.Btl. "Italien," II. Pol.Freiw. Btl. "Italien"* [only two companies, *2.* and *3. Kp.*],[138] *Gendarmerie-Kp. "Umbrien," Gendarmerie-Kp. "Toscana"* [in the area of Mira], *II. Brigata Nera* (mobile) [based in Padova], *Wasserschutzpolizei-Kommando "West-Adria"* [naval police unit *"West Adriatic See,"* based in Venezia], *4. Batterie/leichte Flak-Abt. 843 (v)* [in San Donà di Piave], *Flak – I. Pol.Freiw.Btl. "Italien"* [the battalion's anti-aircraft battery] and *[12.] Pol.Freiw.Kp.* of *III. Btl./SS-Pol.Rgt. 12*.

On the same date, the *Höherer Sicherungsstab* controlled three main security sectors: *Oberabschnitt "Erika"* (based in Este, probably responsible to protect the building sites on the blaue Vorfeldlinie I), *"Friedl"* (area of San Donà di Piave, probably responsible to protect the building sites on the Piave River and on part of the *Seestern I* line) and the *Oberabschnitt "Seestern I"* (based in Mira, probably responsible to protect the building sites on the *Seestern I* line and on the Brenta River). *Sicherheitsführer* for the *Oberabschnitt "Erika"* was the commander of *III. Btl./SS-Pol.Rgt. 12*, *Major d.SchP.* Karl Ludwig Bölsche.[139]

Additionally, in mid-September 1944, the *leichter Flakzug* and a *Vierling* quadruple anti-aircraft gun of the *SS-WMS-Btl.* were also under the *Höherer Sicherungsstab*.[140]

Apparently at the end of October, Herrmann's area of responsibility was extended to the Udine province (or Friuli region, in the OZAK), where *III. Btl./SS-Pol.Rgt. 12* was transferred; the unit was assigned to the *Oberabschnitt "Heidelore"* (perhaps already existing), presumably with the task of protecting the building sites on the defensive line by the same name on the Tagliamento River, in addition to the normal police tasks of controlling the territory and fighting the partisans. The battalion's headquarters were based in San Giorgio della Richinvelda, and *Major* Bölsche was designated as *Sicherheitsführer im Oberabschnitt* "Heidelore"; the battalion's sub-units were based in various towns and villages along the Tagliamento, from Venzone down to Codroipo. At the end of November it was followed by another unit, *I. Pol. Freiw.Btl. "Italien,"* which deployed in a not precisely known area across Veneto and Friuli, with headquarters in Pravisdomini.

In the second half of December, Bölsche was also designated as *Sicherheitsführer im Oberabschnitt "Feuerstein."* This was probably a newly created larger security sector, whose extension is, however, not precisely known (the "Heidelore" sector was inserted into it, as from that month it was simply indicated as *Abschnitt*, not as *Oberabschnitt* anymore). It seems that in addition to the area along the Tagliamento River, Bölsche was also responsible for the security in the area where the *Seestern I* and *II* lines met in Varmo, and beyond along these two defensive lines.[141]

On January 19, 1945, four *Oberabschnitte* (perhaps *Erika*, *Friedl*, *Seestern I*, and *Feuerstein*) were subordinated to the *Höherer Sicherungsstab*, whose *Sicherheitsführer* had the following units at their disposal: *III. Btl./SS-Pol.Rgt. 12, I. Pol. Freiw.Btl. "Italien," II. Pol.Freiw.Btl. "Italien"* [only two companies], *Gendarmerie-Hauptmannschaft "Umbrien"* and *Gendarmerie-Hauptmannschaft "Toscana."*[142]

On March 18, 1945, only two *Sicherheitsführer*, *Major* Bölsche (for *Oberabschnitt "Feuerstein"*) and *Hptm.* Keller (no further information known) were subordinated to the *Höherer Sicherungsstab* with the same units already present on January 19.[143] It is not clear if the decrease in the number of the sectors meant that the area of responsibility of the *Höherer Sicherungsstab* was also reduced; if so, it is possible that it abandoned part of the Veneto region and transferred some of its operations to the southeastern area of the OZAK (Provinz

Laibach, Fiume sector), where the building activity continued at full speed since by this time the threat from the Balkan front was approaching.

3.5: Retreat to Austria, and the Breakup of *Abteilung R*

Around mid-March 1945, the awaited Yugoslav offensive along the Dalmatian coast, conducted by the Yugoslav Liberation Army, had started from the region of Knin–Gračac. The weak German forces in Dalmatia could not offer any effective resistance and fell back progressively northwards along the coast, reaching the area of Fiume/Sušak just after mid-April. Due to the constant Yugoslav pressure, by April 20, the German units had to abandon Sušak and retreat behind the Recina River, taking up positions on the fortified defensive belt around Fiume. North of the city the front line continued to Monte Trestenico (Trstenik) following the partially fortified defensive positions of the Ingrid Line, where the German defense resisted relatively well until the end of April. Decisive developments took place during the last days of the month: Yugoslav units managed to pierce the German lines both north of the Fiume sector (in the area of Monte Nevoso (Snežnik), where there were only weak German forces) as well as southwest of it (landing on the Istria peninsula), and started to approach Trieste, their final and main objective. Starting from April 28–29, fighting between Yugoslav and German troops took place in several areas of the Trieste external defense belt, and by April 30, the city was surrounded.[144]

Regarding the activities of *Abteilung R* in this phase there is no information, but it is likely that when the Yugoslav army approached Fiume, any elements of section R II still in the city retreated to Trieste. As far as the men of the outposts on the Carso plateau east of Trieste or those possibly still in action on the Karststrasse are concerned, it can be supposed that they were also pulled back to Trieste. There are in any case no accounts of any clashes between elements of *Abteilung R* and Yugoslav forces east of Trieste.

At the same time as the Yugoslav forces entered the OZAK region from the southeast, from the west arrived British and New Zealand units advancing from the Italian front after breaking through the Gothic Line and crossing the Po River. On April 30, elements of the British 6th Armoured Division entered Pordenone, and crossed the Tagliamento River the following day; in the afternoon of May 1, Udine was reached. Also, the 2nd New Zealand Division, which was advancing farther south, crossed the Tagliamento River on May 1, advancing on Trieste, where the division entered the following day.

Globocnik abandoned Trieste at the last moment. Just a few hours before the city was cut off, in the night between April 28–29, the HSSPF left the city with the SS/*Polizei* headquarters and units and the civilian personnel still present, heading north in a motorized column, towards Austria. With Globocnik's vehicle column abandoned the city, and also the remaining men of *Abteilung R*. Geng, who was in it, mentioned the presence of Allers and Oberhauser. The latter set free the last Risiera inmates on the evening of April 29; shortly afterwards the complex was abandoned by the last elements of *Abteilung R* and later the crematorium was blown up.[145]

Probably driving around Udine, where an insurrection was brewing and the risk of partisan attacks was high, Globocnik's motorized column drove towards the entrance to the Tagliamento River valley, but near Tarcento, by the light of the day (April 30), it was attacked by Allied aircraft and temporarily scattered.[146] In the following hours the column reached the Carnia region (northwestern part of the Udine province, on the border with Austria): the HSSPF set up his command post in the village of Arta, a few kilometers from the Monte Croce Carnico Pass (Plöckenpass, on the Austrian border). It seems that also *Abteilung R* took up base in the same village.

Abteilung R had sustained some losses during the retreat: Fey/Vey died, Hödl was heavily wounded; for both the circumstances are not known, possibly during an aircraft attack or a firefight with the partisans, who sometimes attacked the retreating German columns.[147]

At least from May 1, the German forces in the Friuli region had passed under the subordination of the *Oberbefehlshaber Südost* (responsible for the Balkans sector) and did not consider themselves bound by the surrender signed with the Allied by the *Oberbefehlshaber Südwest* on April 29, which came into force in the Italian war theatre from the afternoon of May 2. The surrender negotiations that the British started in this sector with the Germans were therefore not successful. The *Oberbefehlshaber Südost*, who aimed at protecting its right flank, had nominally assigned command of this sector to Globocnik, who left the conduct of combat operations to the military (among whom *SS-Brigadeführer* Heinz Harmel) and after a few days (it seems in the night between May 3–4) he moved to Austria.

Three photos taken on the same occasion, one of which was used as cover for the weekly magazine *Adria Illustrierte*, published by the Germans in Trieste, on the issue dated April 7, 1945. They show *SS-Sturmbannführer* Ernst Lerch, another unidentified German officer (an *SS-Hauptsturmführer*), and a Serbian Chetnik commander before the cloister of Santa Croce di Aidussina (now Vipavski Križ), in the Vipacco (Vipava) River valley, east of Gorizia, during the anti-partisan operation *Unternehmen Winterende*, carried out in the last days of March and the first days of April 1945. In this operation, Lerch led a *Kampfgruppe* which included a *Kompanie Allers*, the latter made up by elements of *Abteilung R* and/or the *SS-Wachmannschaften*; he probably set up his command post in the village, from where one had a good view of the valley and the southern slopes of the Tarnova plateau, where the partisans had their basis. *MNZS, 3404_1 and NI11_491*

A photo taken in the last days of March 1945 during the *Unternehmen Winterende*. This mixed SS/*Polizei* unit belonged to *Kampfgruppe Hellinger* (*Zug Oblt.d.SchP.d.Res*. Brenner), formed by elements from the OZAK SS/*Polizei* headquarters. According to the photo's original caption, the *Kampfgruppe* was in action in the area of Podicrai–Zolla–"Monte Spizza" (probably Monte Spicco, now Špiček, just north of Zolla), between March 19–30, 1945, probably as part of the *Kampfgruppe Lerch*. *Hauptmann d.SchP*. Hellinger was *Luftschutz-Offizier* (officer responsible for protection against air raids) in the headquarters of the *Befehlshaber der Ordnungspolizei* in the OZAK.

On May 2, British forces advanced northwards from the area between Codroipo and Udine, heading to the entrance to the Tagliamento River valley, which leads towards Austria. The British advance was momentarily halted just after Gemona: at the entrance to the valley the Germans had set up an improvised resistance line, manned by some *Karstjäger* Division units (around 200–300 men, according to British sources), supported by some tanks and artillery, dug in at the north entrance of the village of Ospedaletto. Other, more numerous units were concentrated in Venzone, a few kilometers north, where the main defense line ran.

On the same day, May 2, a massacre took place in Avasinis, a village in a small valley parallel to the Tagliamento River, west of Gemona. During the massacre, fifty-one inhabitants, in the great majority women, elderly, and children, were killed by soldiers in German uniforms, and others were wounded. Despite the investigations made and the various hypotheses proposed during many years since the events, the perpetrators of the massacre have never been identified with certainty. On the basis of the information available on *Abteilung R*, the possibility that its men carried out the massacre cannot be discarded. The episode is dealt with more in detail in a later section.

The front line remained static between Gemona and Venzone from May 2–6; the British waited for the Germans to surrender or to be granted free passage to Austria, while the Germans aimed at gaining time to organize the resistance on a defensive line farther to the rear.

This photo was taken in a studio in Tricesimo, north of Udine, probably towards the end of 1944. It shows two men in German police uniform, one of whom wears a Lithuanian national arm shield. He was probably a former member of the Lithuanian *Schutzmannschaft* units, at the time of the photo perhaps belonging to *SS-Polizei-Regiment 10*, a unit which surely counted some Lithuanians in its ranks (together with several other nationalities: documented are Hungarians, Ukrainians, Russians, Poles, Alsatians, Croats, and Serbs). The photo shows the presence of men of different nationalities in the German units operating on the OZAK. *Courtesy Diego Franzolini, "Kazacja Zemlja," Aviani Editore*

The Germans abandoned Venzone and started to retreat towards Austria only in the early afternoon of May 6, probably with the intention of setting up a new defensive line on the border. The retreating German forces were followed with difficulty by the British advance elements, because of the numerous road cuts made by the Germans. In the meantime, however, in the night between May 6–7, the German capitulation had been signed in Reims: the cease fire was scheduled for midday of May 9. On May 7, the German headquarters on the southern front decided therefore to give unrestricted passage to the British to allow them to enter into Austria and advance eastwards as much as possible. Until that moment this measure had been delayed since it was feared that the presence of the British in Carinthia could be an obstacle to the retreat of *Heeresgruppe E* from Yugoslavia. When the general capitulation was signed it became clear that a part of *Heeresgruppe E* would not be able to reach Austria and would have to surrender to the Yugoslavs. At this point it was therefore decided to allow the British to advance freely, as their occupation was considered very much preferable than the dreaded arrival of the Soviets and Yugoslavs. In the afternoon of May 8, British advance elements reached Klagenfurt, where the German surrender in this sector was signed.

Globocnik went into hiding but a few weeks later he was tracked down by the British in an Alpine hut near the Weissensee Lake, where he was hiding with Rainer and a few close collaborators (Lerch, Michalsen, Höfle); when he was captured, on May 31, Globocnik committed suicide with poison.

In the first days of May, *Abteilung R* also passed the Monte Croce Carnico Pass and entered Austria (perhaps with Globocnik). Its last base was in Kirchbach, between Mauthen and Hermagor, where around May 7–8, it was officially disbanded by Allers. The men attempted to go back to their homes in small groups; some perhaps succeeded, but many were taken prisoner by the Allies. According to some depositions, some were captured by the British who let them go after disarming them, since they were wearing *Polizei* uniforms; when captured by the Americans, as a rule they were declared prisoners of war and put in camps.[148] After various detention periods the former members of *Abteilung R* were released and went back to civilian life. Fearing to be called to account for their actions in *Aktion T4* and in *Aktion Reinhard*, some took up false identities and disappeared (Hackenholt, Post) and some fled abroad (Stangl, Wagner).[149]

3.5.1: The Avasinis Massacre (May 2, 1945)

In the final days of the war, on May 2, 1945, a massacre took place in Avasinis, a village of the Valle del Lago valley, which runs parallel to the Tagliamento River Valley, a few kilometers west of Gemona, northwest of Udine. The perpetrators have never been identified, but on the basis of testimonies by the survivors it is known that they wore camouflage uniforms with mountain shoes, spoke German, Italian (also with an accent from Trieste and Istria) and Friulian (the language spoken in Friuli); one of them told the civilians that he was Croat, another one that he was Polish. Generally, in personal accounts from survivors and in reconstructions they are indicated as belonging to the SS. Admittedly, civilians could not necessarily tell an SS uniform, unless the collar tabs with the runes were clearly visible, which was not necessarily the case in particular if camouflage uniforms or smocks were worn. However, some accounts mention in a quite precise way the presence of SS collar tabs and caps with a skull insignia (as used by the SS), it seems therefore credible that at least some of the perpetrators belonged to the SS.

Also from contemporary accounts it is known that the German unit that perpetrated the massacre crossed the Tagliamento coming from the Gemona area on May 1, and took up position in Trasaghis and on the mountain behind the village (Montisel), as well as, it seems, on the Col del Sole hill, just south of Avasinis. Apparently, this unit numbered around 200–300 men. In the morning of the following day, the Germans attacked towards Avasinis, with the supporting fire of mortars placed on the Montisel; after dispersing the few and insufficiently armed partisans positioned near the new cemetery of Avasinis, they entered the village and carried out an indiscriminate reprisal, killing fifty-one persons and wounding several others, mostly women, children, and elderly. It seems that the slaughter was stopped when an officer arrived. The Germans remained in the village until the following morning (May 3), they

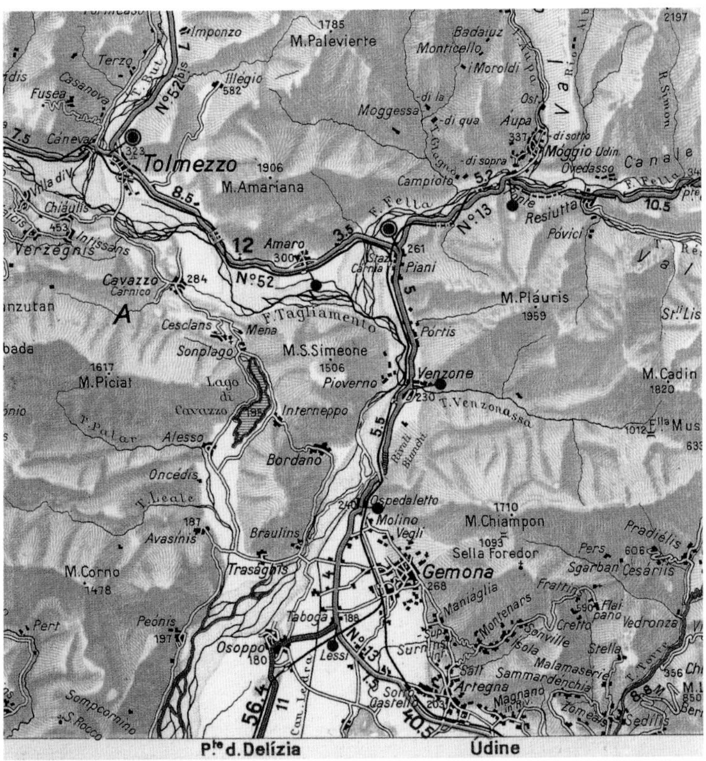

Map from the 1930s of the area of Gemona–Tolmezzo (north of Udine), with the Valle del Lago valley and the village of Avasinis, where the massacre of May 2, 1945, took place.

then retreated northwards along the Valle del Lago Valley.

The following are the two most significant accounts related to the phases that immediately preceded the attack on Avasinis:

> Memorial book of the Avasinis parish, drafted by the priest, Don Francesco Zossi:
>
> On May 1 in the morning, a long Cossack column advances on the road from Peonis. A partisan youngster from Oncedis and a man from here, Ridolfo Giacomo Ten, go to have a look but are captured by the Cossacks who bring the two with them to Tolmezzo; it is a miracle that they later come back home alive. There are many partisans, youngsters and men around. On the same morning around 200 German SS crossed the bridge on the Tagliamento and then blew it up behind them; they stopped in Trasaghis, climbing up on the Montisel. Already in the evening of the same day they try to approach Avasinis, but are slowed down by their own carefulness and by a long rain shower. In the morning of May 2, around 6.30 o'clock our partisans start to fire from the ridge above the cemetery towards Trasaghis. The German SS consisting of the military scum from every race and nation, even including some from Friuli, advance towards Avasinis![150]

Report by professor Mario Di Gianantonio, dated May 6, 1945:

> On May 1, some SS patrols were spotted on the hills around Trasaghis. A column came from Peonis [the Cossacks], but it was not molested. After the column had passed it was tried to disperse the SS troops who were still on the Trasaghis hills. These however asked for reinforcements and during the night they tried to encircle the partisans' positions. In the morning of May 2, some mortar rounds fired on Avasinis meant that the enemy had decided to break through at all costs. The partisans withdrew.[151]

Various hypotheses have been formulated as to the possible motivations for the massacre, among them the main ones are: a partisan attack to the German columns retreating on the State Road 13 "Pontebbana" (leading north from Udine, towards Austria) near Gemona; the kidnapping of German personnel that worked on the building sites of the Organisation Todt and *Unternehmen Pöll* in the area of Avasinis; the disarming and capturing of the Cossack detachments of Avasinis and Oncedis, carried out by the partisans on April 29, and the request to surrender made to other outposts in the Valle del Lago valley, which left in the direction of Tolmezzo on the next day.[152]

Among the various hypotheses the first one, that is a reprisal for a partisan attack on the Pontebbana road, is advocated in particular by Pier Arrigo Carnier.[153] He wrote—apparently on the basis of information obtained after the war by Erich Kühbandner, former officer of the *Karstjäger* Division—that the Germans saw the partisans who had attacked them retreat towards the area of Avasinis, and hence decided to carry out a reprisal there (the area was already known for the strong partisan presence). However, this reconstruction does not look very plausible, since Avasinis is not visible from the other side of the Tagliamento, and the partisans, once they had passed the bridge, could have reached several other villages. Therefore, the link between Avasinis and an attack on the Pontebbana does not necessarily seem very strong. Additionally, no clear confirmation of a partisan attack has been found in any accounts originating from the partisan side, although a hint about this is in the diary of the village priest, Don Zossi:

> The [Pontebbana] state road is an endless jam of fleeing Germans. Some partisans have the bad idea of carrying out a final action and go to harass their flight on the state road near the junction to the road leading to our village. They should have never done it. (...) They [the Germans] chase the partisans and follow them on the road, coming to this area; they understood that if they remained on the state road they would have been caught up with by the Allies who were arriving in Osoppo and Gemona. It is May 1, 1945.[154]

Another possible reconstruction is based on the hypothesis that the German unit which took up position in the area of Trasaghis on May 1, was not pursuing partisans that had attacked the Germans on the Pontebbana, but that it deployed there with the task of defending the access to the Valle del Lago Valley, which leads to Cavazzo and for the Allies was one of the possible access routes to the Carnia region, on the border with Austria. In December 1944, elements of the *Karstjäger* Division had carried out an exercise in this area, which consisted of defending the sectors of Venzone (on the Tagliamento Valley) and of Lake Cavazzo (in the Valle del Lago Valley) in case of an Allied attack coming from the Udine area.[155] Much as the German positions on Ospedaletto (just north of Gemona) in early May 1945, were a forward defense screen in front of the main resistance line which ran by Venzone, it is possible that similarly the area of Trasaghis–Col del Sole was planned as a forward defense line in front of the stronger positions around Lake Cavazzo. The German unit occupied the area of Trasaghis for less than two days, retreating towards Lake Cavazzo in the morning of May 3. Since in the meantime, on May 2 at dawn, its positions in Trasaghis had been fired at by partisans from the ridge near the Avasinis cemetery, it is possible that the Germans feared an ambush and decided to clean out the partisans to be able to retreat without interference. Following this logic the reprisal on Avasinis could have been the follow-on to the German attack on the partisans' positions near the village. Its impossible to ascertain whether the reprisals against the civilians was decided and planned in advance (perhaps even ordered by higher headquarters, as sometimes suggested) as a final act of revenge against the partisans and the population, or if the slaughter was an unplanned aftermath of the attack on the partisans. Beyond what the real cause of the reprisal may have been, it is evident that the widespread German loathing for the partisans, their feelings of vendetta and the frustration and rage for the defeat which all saw was near were unleashed on the innocent and unarmed civilians.

Suspicions about the responsibility for the massacre have been concentrated for a long time on units belonging to the *Karstjäger Division*.[156] It is known that in early May, parts of its *I. Btl.* were in the area of Lake Cavazzo, in the Valle del Lago Valley, where they occupied defensive positions around the lake at least until the early hours of May 6. The *Karstjäger* wore the typical *Waffen-SS* smock (*tarnjacke*) over the normal tunic, and mountain boots. The division had received a number of recruits from the OZAK (from Friuli, Gorizia, Istria, etc.), who at least in part had been inserted in some of the companies of the two *Gebirgsjäger* battalions which made up the division's nucleus. According to what is outlined above, it seems possible, although not certain, that the unit which attacked Avasinis may have been part of the *I. Btl. of the Karstjäger-Division*.[157]

However, it cannot be excluded that elements of *Abteilung R* and of the *SS-Wachmannschaften* may have participated in the massacre or may even have been its main perpetrators. The following facts may point towards them: they were in the area of Gemona on May 1–2; the members of *Abteilung R* wore camouflage outfits (tunics, trousers, helmet covers, fieldcaps) produced with the Italian mod. 29 cloth, and sometimes march or mountain boots;[158] in the *SS-Wachmannschaften* there were local personnel who spoke Italian, the dialects from Friuli, Trieste and Istria, as well as Croat, who at least partially followed *Abteilung R* during the retreat towards Austria. Additionally, there is the precedent of the Lipa massacre, carried out almost certainly by *Abteilung R*, which also has an element of similarity with Avasinis: in both cases the civilian population that had survived the slaughter was assembled in a few houses, but while in Lipa they were later all killed, in Avasinis they were finally spared.

It may be plausible that elements of *Abteilung R* and of the *SS-Wachmannschaften* were attached to units of the *Karstjäger* Division deployed in the area of Trasaghis to protect the access to the Valle del Lago Valley, or that they were sent in as reinforcement when the presence of partisans positioned near Avasinis was noted.[159] Once the partisans who had tried to stop the Germans before the village had been dispersed, *Abteilung R* and the *SS-Wachmannschaften* may have carried out the reprisal to "punish" the population for supporting the partisans.

It has to be finally underlined, however, that all hypotheses on which unit carried out the massacre are only based on circumstantial evidence; there is to date no concrete proof that identifies the perpetrators or their unit.

3.6: Epilogue

Beginning in 1949, the investigation started in Germany on the crimes committed in the framework of *Aktion Reinhard*.[160] By that date, of the more than 120 men identified as having taken part in the action in Poland, at least forty-six had died or were declared dead (among those that were in the OZAK, in addition to the dead already mentioned also Hering had died at the end of 1945). In the then German Federal Republic nine trials concerning *Aktion Reinhard* were held, during which forty-four people were investigated and interrogated. All the remaining people, although their names were known, could not be found. Of those investigated, twenty-seven were tried: nine of them were convicted to a life sentence; ten to light prison sentences; seven were acquitted; and one (Bolender) committed suicide during the trial.

The trials were the following: Landesgericht (state court, LG) Berlin, 1950 (for crimes committed in Sobibor; accused: Bauer); LG Frankfurt am Main, 1950 (for crimes committed in Sobibor; accused: Gomerski and Klier); LG Frankfurt am Main, 1951 (for crimes committed in Treblinka; accused: Hirtreiter); LG München I (for crimes committed in Belzec, 1965; accused: Oberhauser); LG Düsseldorf, 1965 (for crimes committed in Treblinka; accused: Franz, Matthes, Mentz, Miete, Münzberger, Stadie, Suchomel, Lambert, Rum, Horn); LG Hagen, 1966 (for crimes committed in Sobibor; accused: Frenzel, Bolender, Wolf, Fuchs, Ittner, Dubois, Lambert, Jührs, Lachmann, Schuett, Unverhau, Zierke); LG Düsseldorf, 1970 (for crimes committed in Sobibor and Treblinka; accused: Stangl), plus two retrials for Gomerski and Frenzel in the 1970s and 1980s.

Some of the participants to *Aktion Reinhard* were also involved—and sometimes convicted—during some of the numerous trials on the "Euthanasia" program held in East and West Germany and in Austria.

During the investigations for the trials, the activities of *Abteilung R* in the OZAK were often mentioned in the depositions of the accused and witnesses, but since they were not directly linked with the object of the investigation or trial the matter was not investigated further. In Germany no specific trial on the crimes committed in the Risiera di San Sabba has ever been held.

In Italy, the first investigations on the Risiera were started by the Italian police in 1945, but were not followed up by the authorities of the Allied Military Government (AMG) which until October 1954 ruled Trieste.[161] On the reason of the inactivity of the AMG various hypotheses have been made: on one extreme, the intention to block the investigations to avoid discussions on politically sensitive topics (like the collaboration with the German occupiers), which may have worsened the heavy local political tensions, all centered on the destiny of Trieste, claimed both by Italy and Yugoslavia; on the other extreme, a simple lack of attention by the AMG for the Risiera, given the other more pressing problems. But it has to be underlined that the local political forces also avoided for several years to discuss anything about the Risiera, whose memory remained confined to minorities (the survivors, their families, former partisans and members of the resistance movement, and the Jewish community). Only in the second half of the 1950s, and then in the 1960s, were the first personal accounts and historical studies on the Risiera published. In 1956 the complex (heavily modified with the demolition of some buildings and the construction of a large entry "corridor") was declared a "national monument."

Only in 1970, following the *Aktion Reinhard* trials held in Germany during which some information regarding the Risiera emerged, the Trieste tribunal opened an investigation on the crimes committed in San Sabba. After avoiding the transfer of the procedure to a military tribunal (which would have meant the immediate archiving of the procedure because war crimes had been granted an amnesty), the trial was held in Trieste in 1976. Some former members of *Abteilung R* were interrogated in Germany by German investigators on behalf of their Italian colleagues; during the investigation phase and at the trial many former prisoners and deportees also came to give their depositions.[162] The only accused in the trial was Oberhauser; the other people identified in the indictment were either already dead (Wirth, Hering, Stangl) or died before the start of the trial (Allers, in 1975). The charges had been limited to the killing of people that "for certain had not participated to activities contrary to the military interests of the occupying military authority" (i.e., the Germans). This meant that the charges did not include the killing of those who had participated in political or military activities which were punishable according to war law (a statute of limitation applied to these killings). The result was to create a distinction between victims whose killings was considered legitimate according to war law, and "innocent" victims, which was often criticized, at that time and later. Also, during the trial any discussion on the collaborationism with the Germans was carefully avoided, so that on the basis of a decision by the court no member of the Italian *SS-Wachmann-schaften* based in San Sabba was interrogated (only a former member of *Battaglione Davide*, deported to Germany after a short imprisonment in the Risiera in May 1944, was heard as witness). Oberhauser, who did not present himself in court, was convicted to a life sentence (confirmed on appeal), but did not go to prison because on the basis of the international agreements between Italy and Germany he could not be extradited.

In order to remedy the insufficiencies of the trial, a second investigation was started already in 1976 (those investigated were Lerch, Weimann, Michalsen, Franz, Schiffer, Stadie; to them was later also added Ivan Demjanjuk, a Ukrainian suspected of being "Ivan the Terrible" in the Treblinka extermination camp, on the basis of—most probably incorrect—rumors which said that he had been in Trieste during the war). Suspended and later restarted at a slow pace, this second investigation was archived in 1992 without a second trial being held.

The result of the Trieste trial for the crimes committed in San Sabba was disappointing for those that awaited justice for the Risiera victims. It had, however, at least the merit of gathering a large number of accounts and a body of knowledge useful for historical research.

Photos taken in Montespino (now Dornberk, Slovenia), in the Vipacco (Vipava) River valley, east of Gorizia, probably during the anti-partisan operation *Unternehmen Spitz* in late May 1944. Globocnik, in the middle, and Werner Mundhenke, on his right, talk to soldiers from the *SS-Karstwehr-Btl. Courtesy Sergio Corbatti*

On the same occasion, Globocnik speaking with *SS-Ustuf.* Erich Kühbandner from the *SS-Karstwehr-Btl.*, see from the side just left of Globocnik. *Courtesy Sergio Corbatti*

Globocnik, Mundhenke and an unidentified officer looking at the camera. The man with the black beret belonged to an unidentified Italian unit (possibly a GNR officer cadet). On the vehicle on the left are apparently two *SS-Wachmannschaften* soldiers wearing "simil-Sipo/SD" uniforms, perhaps *Trawniki* belonging to Globocnik's escort. *Courtesy Sergio Corbatti*

SS-Sturmbannführer und Major d. SchP. Werner Mundhenke. He was *Chef des Stabes* (Chief of Staff) of the commander of the *Orpo* in the OZAK (Kintrup) and of Globocnik's *Führungsstab für Bandenbekämpfung* (operational headquarters for fighting the "bandits").

CHAPTER 4

The *SS-Wachmannschaften* of the OZAK

The name *Wachmannschaften* (literally guard units)[1] was used by the Germans in Poland to indicate some auxiliary units created by the SS. Formed mainly by former Soviet prisoners-of-war, they were used to guard the extermination and labor camps and for a series of other actions related to the deportation and killing of the Jews. From the name of the place where the training camp for these units was based, their men were commonly indicated as *Trawniki*.[2]

Probably taking inspiration from the *Wachmannschaften* formed in Poland, the same name, but with the addition of the SS- suffix,[3] was used in the OZAK to indicate a number of units which will be dealt with here because they were more or less closely linked with *Abteilung R*. In this analysis, the name of *SS-Wachmannschaften of the OZAK* is meant to include:

- The company of *Wachmannschaften* that arrived in the OZAK from Poland under the command of Schwarzenbacher, formed in the majority by *Trawniki* and by some *Reichsdeutsche* (it will be indicated in the following as *Trawniki* company); at least initially it was integrated in the *SS-Wachmannschafts-Bataillon* (see next point) and indicated as *Wachmannschaft I* (*Ostvölker*),[4] later it was probably detached from the battalion and named *SS-Wachmannschafts-Kompanie*.
- The *SS-Wachmannschafts-Bataillon* (*SS-WMS-Btl.*, SS guard battalion), a battalion made up (at least initially) by two parts: the *Wachmannschaft I* (*Ostvölker*) and the *Wachmannschaft II* (*landeseigene Kräfte*). The latter consisted of several companies and was formed—in addition to some *Reichsdeutsche* and *Trawniki*—in the majority by locally recruited elements, called by the Germans *landeseigene Kräfte* (literally local forces, but the official translation in Italian was *forze territoriali*, or territorial forces). This term, which for clarity is also used in this analysis, included both soldiers recruited in the OZAK region and belonging to its various ethnic groups (Italians, Slovenes, Croats, as well as some *Volksdeutsche*, ethnic Germans living outside the Reich's borders), as well as Italians from other regions (like for instance the former members of *Battaglione Patrioti Davide*).

In practice the *SS-Wachmannschaften* of the OZAK were equivalent to the *SS-WMS-Btl.*, as long as this existed (as it will be seen later, in late 1944, the battalion was apparently disbanded as such, although some of its company continued to exist); later, they consisted of the remaining companies that had been part of the battalion.

The story of the *SS-Wachmannschaften* of the OZAK remains mostly obscure. Nearly all documents produced by the HSSPF OZAK have been lost, thus making it extremely difficult to reconstruct the history of the SS/*Polizei* structures and units in the region. For the entire years 1943–44 one single (rather sketchy) organization chart of the SS/*Polizei* forces operating in the OZAK has been found, dating from February 1944 and drafted by a *Wehrmacht* officer who was sent to the region on an official fact finding mission by the *Oberkommando des Heeres* (OKH, the Army Supreme Headquarters); additionally, some *Verteiler* (lists for the distribution of documents to the various headquarters and units subordinated to the HSSPF OZAK) have also survived.[5] For 1945, more information is available: from January to April 1945, several organization charts and *Verteiler* for the SS/*Polizei* units in the OZAK are available. However, the picture of the *SS-Wachmannschaften* of the OZAK becomes less clear after August 1944, since after this date no known document mentions the *SS-WMS-Btl.*[6] The absence of the *SS-WMS-Btl.* from all documents after August 1944 is not clear: it is possible that the battalion as such was disbanded, but it is certain that at least some of the companies that had been part of it continued to exist until the end of the war. The following sections provide the available information on the *SS-Wachmannschaften* of the OZAK, investigating their links with *Abteilung R.*

4.1: Formation and Development of the *SS-Wachmannschafts*-Btl. until Mid-1944

At the same time as Globocnik, his staff, and part of *Aktion Reinhard* personnel moved from Lublin to Trieste a few days after mid-September 1943, the same journey (but by train) was made by a company of *Wachmannschaften* (*Trawniki* company). In this unit the cadres were composed of Germans (Reichsdeutsche) belonging to the SS (probably a very limited number), while enlisted personnel and some NCOs were made up of *Trawniki*, mainly Ukrainians.[7] Immediately before leaving Lublin, Globocnik nominated commander of this company *SS-Untersturmführer* Johann Schwarzenbacher.[8] The company strength is not known with certainty: in a letter from October 1943, Globocnik wrote that he brought from the *Ausbildungslager Trawniki* to Trieste seventy men belonging to the *Wachmannschaften*; however, according to Oberhauser, who defined the unit as a "reinforced company," it counted about 200 men.[9] The unit strength is therefore not certain, but it seems probable that Globocnik (also considering his complaints about the scarcity of personnel available in Trieste compared to Lublin) may have tried to give lower figures than was the reality[10] and therefore the figure quoted by Oberhauser could be more plausible.[11] In Trieste the company was billeted in the "Dante Alighieri" schools on Via Giustiniano, opposite the Palazzo di Giustizia, or court house. Its specific tasks mainly included providing guards for the buildings where German headquarters or offices were based in the city of Trieste, as well as escorts during journeys in the operational areas.

In the weeks immediately following Globocnik taking up office in Trieste, on the HSSPF's initiative the setting up of a security battalion was initiated. The battalion was to be formed by locally recruited forces, indicated as *landeseigene Kräfte*, using as a basis the *Trawniki* company.[12] The unit was called *SS-Wachmannschafts-Bataillon*, but as mentioned the indication (*SS-*) *Wachmannschaften* (or *SS-Wachmannschaften Triest*) to indicate its constituent units or its men was also used.[13]

The task of forming and training the battalion was given to Schwarzenbacher, who became its temporary commander as *Btl.Führer*.[14] Despite the low rank (he was promoted *SS-Obersturmführer* (*Allgemeine-SS*) on January 30, 1944), Globocnik considered him particularly competent for this task, since already in Poland he had shown good skills at commanding units formed of foreign personnel. The setting up of the battalion took place in Trieste and had already started in October 1943.[15] The battalion headquarters and offices were based partly in the "De Amicis" schools on Via Combi 13, partly in the "Dante Alighieri" schools on Via Giustiniano and inside the Palazzo di Giustizia. The battalion recruits were also billeted in the "De Amicis" schools, where training took place. Later on the battalion also occupied buildings on Via Besenghi 16 (former *Carabinieri* barracks, also used by the Landschutz in early 1944) and on Via dell'Istria 58. When these barracks were hit by bombs during air raids (on an unknown date), the battalion was concentrated in the schools on Via Giustiniano.[16]

The battalion's companies were formed progressively between autumn 1943 and spring 1944. The cadre personnel for all these new companies were taken from the *Trawniki* company, transferring mainly German (Reichsdeutsche) personnel but also some *Trawniki*.[17] Such transfers were extremely limited in numbers, and probably

Himmler visiting *Trawniki* on July 19, 1942, reviews a *Wachmannschaften* unit. In the background, indicated with a cross is Johann Schwarzenbacher, with a circle Hermann Höfle.

Wirth (in the middle) together with Schwarzenbacher (on the left) and another officer, probably in Lublin during 1943. Schwarzenbacher was tasked with setting up the *SS-Wachmannschafts-Btl.* in the OZAK and was the first battalion commander. He was killed by partisans on June 2, 1944. *StA München*

for this reason *Abteilung R* was also called in to help (see later). Despite this the battalion formation was achieved in a way that Globocnik considered satisfactory[18] and actually by the end of February 1944 three companies had been formed (although it is not confirmed whether they were all operational). Additionally, the *Trawniki* company that arrived from Poland under Schwarzenbacher was also integrated in the battalion, although somehow as a unit on its own. In an organization chart dated February 22, 1944, the structure of the *SS-WMS-Btl.* was indicated as follows:

- *Wachmannschaft I (Ostvölker)*, with one company, in Trieste
- *Wachmannschaft II*, with three companies:
    1. *Kompanie* in Trieste and Gorizia
    2. *Kompanie* in Trieste
    3. *Kompanie* in Fiume and Pola[19]

As can be seen, the battalion was divided into two parts: the first one, indicated as *Wachmannschaft I (Ostvölker)*, was what was left of the *Trawniki* company, whose strength had been reduced to less than 100 men after the personnel transfer to the new companies of the *SS-WMS-Btl.*, as well as to another unit subordinated to the HSSPF and based in Pola.[20] In early 1944, the company is reported to have had around eighty-five men, most were *Trawniki* but there were also six Germans (including the commander) and a few locally recruited personnel sent as reinforcement.[21] Schwarzenbacher had handed over the command of the *Trawniki* company to a young officer, *Leutnant* (later *Oberleutnant*) *d.SchP.* Kurt Eibisch, a few weeks after arriving in Trieste, probably when the formation of the battalion started.

The other part of the battalion, the *Wachmannschaft II*, included the newly formed companies, made up mainly by locally recruited personnel. The chart seems to indicate that part of two companies had already been transferred to some of the main cities in the OZAK: Gorizia, Fiume and Pola. Sometime later—probably by the end of April 1944—a *4.* and *5. Kompanie* were formed, as well as a *Stabskompanie* and a *Kraftfahrstaffel* (transport section). A *6. Kompanie* was formed around mid-May 1944, at the Risiera di San Sabba in Trieste, using some of the soldiers belonging to an Italian

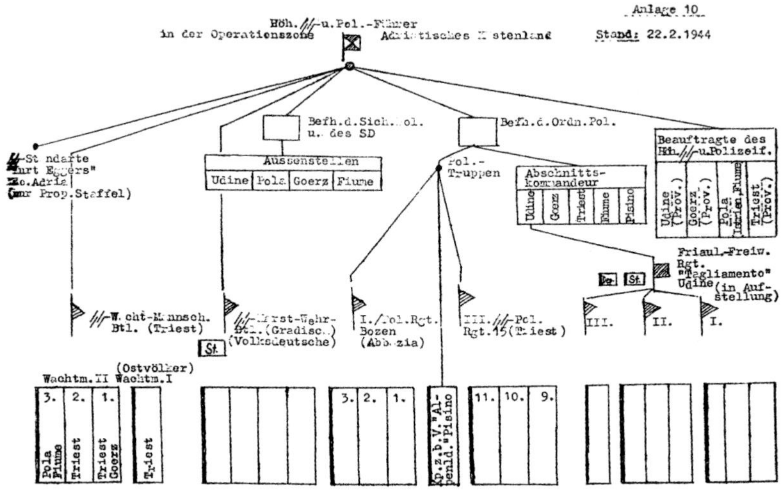

Organizational chart showing the headquarters and units placed under the HSSPF OZAK on February 22, 1944. The chart shows the *SS-Wachmanschafts-Btl.* as divided into two parts: *Wachmannschaft I (Ostvölker)*, with one company, and *Wachmannschaft II*, with three companies.

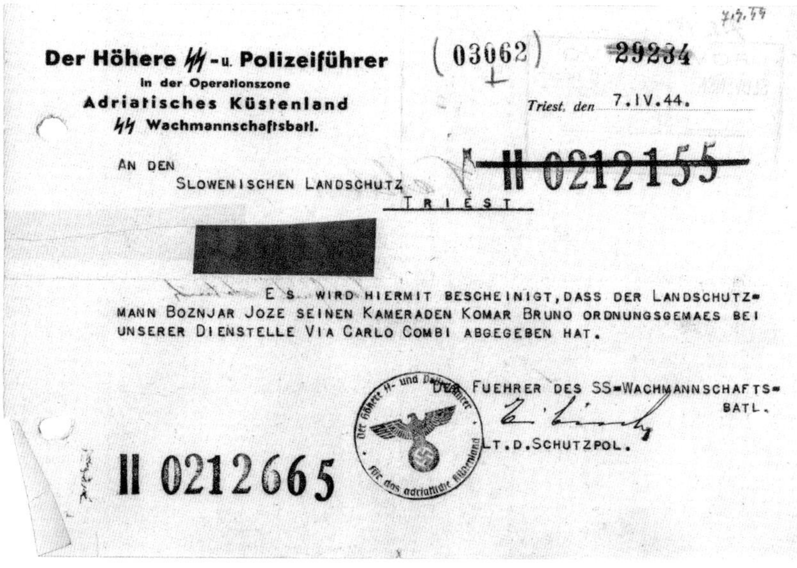

Der Höhere SS-u. Polizeiführer
in der Operationszone
Adriatisches Küstenland
SS Wachmannschaftsbatl.

(03062) 29234

Triest, den 7.IV.44.

AN DEN
SLOWENISCHEN LANDSCHUTZ
TRIEST

II 0212155

ES WIRD HIERMIT BESCHEINIGT, DASS DER LANDSCHUTZMANN BOZNJAR JOZE SEINEN KAMERADEN KOMAR BRUNO ORDNUNGSGEMAES BEI UNSERER DIENSTELLE VIA CARLO COMBI ABGEGEBEN HAT.

FUEHRER DES SS-WACHMANNSCHAFTS-BATL.
LT.D.SCHUTZPOL.

II 0212665

The only known document on headed paper of the *SS-Wachmannschafts-Btl.*, dated April 7, 1944, and signed by *Leutnant d. SchP*. Eibisch as "*Führer des SS-Wachmannschafts-Btl.*," i.e., acting battalion commander. The document mentions the battalion's base in Via Combi, Trieste.

unit, the *Battaglione Patrioti Davide*, which had been disarmed because the Germans suspected that it was about to switch sides to the partisans (on this unit see the specific section). Later on, probably during summer, at least one leichter *Flakzug* (light anti-aircraft platoon) was formed; it was probably armed with some 20 mm anti-aircraft guns.

In early 1944, a detachment from the *SS-WMS-Btl.*, called *Kommando G.*, was sent to Gorizia, probably with the main task to train *Landschutz* recruits. At the latest during the month of May, *2. Kompanie* was sent to the Udine province for operational employment, while *4. Kompanie* was transferred to outposts along the Trieste–Postumia road. For *1.*, *3.* and *5. Kompanie* information is missing to establish where they were based and operated. On the basis of the February 1944 chart and other data, it seems certain that at least parts of *1. Kompanie* were in Gorizia, while it is possible (but confirmation is missing)

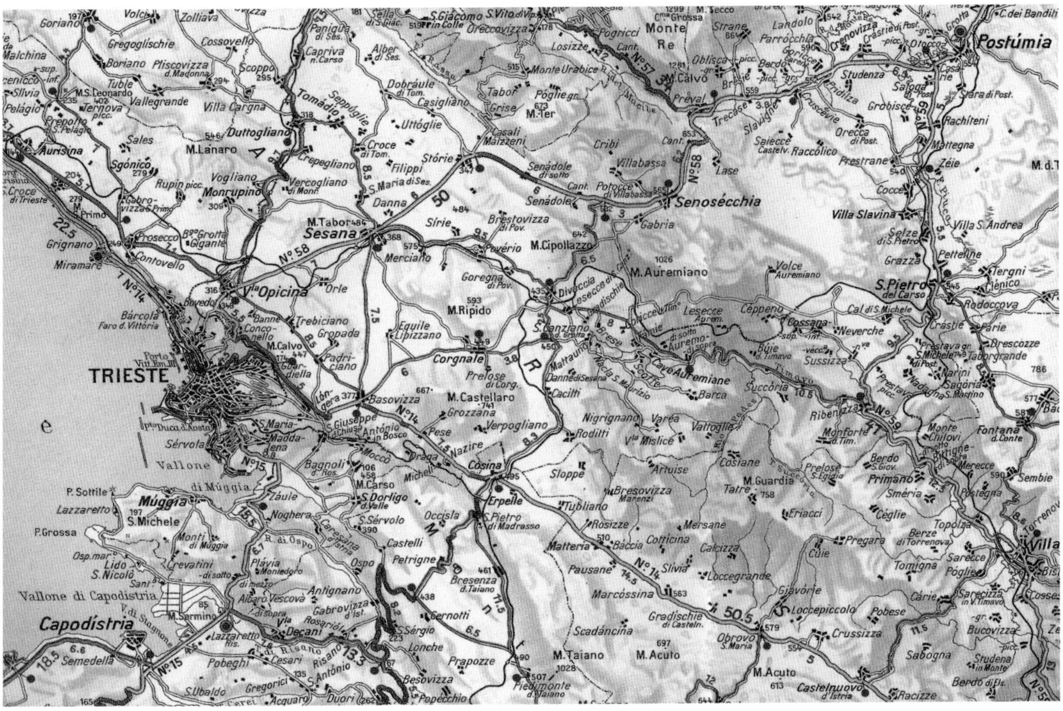

Map from the 1930s of the area east of Trieste, showing the road to Postumia and part of the Karststrasse (until Castelnuovo d'Istria).

that *3. Kompanie* was based partly in Pola and partly in Fiume. The *6. Kompanie* was based at the Risiera and was mainly used for guarding the prison/barracks complex, but it also provided personnel for outposts along the Trieste–Fiume road. For more details see the section on the battalion's operational employment.

At the beginning of June 1944, the numbers of the battalion's *erkennungmarke* (identity tags) had arrived at least to 544 (attributed to a soldier from *2. Kompanie* wounded on June 2); this figure included probably almost only the locally recruited personnel (and apparently part of the *Trawniki*) but excluded most Germans, who kept the *Erkennungsmarke* they already had (if any). The highest known number for a battalion's *Erkennungsmarke* is 1399, attributed to a soldier (Italian) who apparently joined the unit in late 1944 or early 1945. The battalion may have reached a maximum strength of not more than 1,000 men, but probably on average it numbered around 700–800 men. From very partial information it seems that it sustained considerable losses (for instance more than sixty dead, wounded and missing in action are counted only for the period from end of May to mid-July 1944). Information on desertions is extremely scarce. The *Trawniki* company is reported to have had four deserters (not counting the last days before the German retreat from Trieste, when several men left the unit and hid in the city). As far as the *Wachmannschaft II* is concerned, it is known that *6. Kompanie* was abandoned by at least forty-five men of the around eighty-five that initially belonged to it (but this is probably not representative for the entire battalion, this company being atypical as far as its origin is concerned). As far as the other companies are concerned, it is just known that four men from *2. Kompanie* deserted to the partisans in the area of Gemona in October 1944; in January 1945, one was killed and three captured by the Germans, the latter were later all executed in Trieste on April 28, 1945.[22]

Nikolaus Gorobej, a Russian in SS uniform who served in the headquarters of the HSSPF OZAK as attendant to *SS-Hstuf.* Blum, an officer in Abt. IVa (supplies). He also worked as shoemaker in the barracks at the "Dante Alighieri" schools near the Palazzo di Giustizia (court house), although it is not clear if he was integrated in the *Wachmannschaften I (Ostvölker)*, or *Trawniki* company (he was probably not a *Trawniki* himself). Evidently, he also participated in operations like that shown in this photo, taken in Istria during 1944. Here he is guarding a section of the Quieto River aqueduct, a few kilometers west of Pinguente. He seems to be wearing a standard *Waffen-SS* uniform. After the end of the war he lived in Trieste, where he died in 1980 as an Italian citizen.

In this photo taken on the same occasion, Gorobej is with a German *SS-Rottenführer* from the headquarters of the HSSPF OZAK.

For sure some personnel was transferred from the battalion to the *24. Waffen-Gebirgs (Karstjäger)-Division der SS* which was being formed (on the basis of the *SS-Karstwehr-Btl.* using local recruits from the OZAK) in the Udine province starting from July 1944, and was short of men; the number of transfers from the *SS-WMS-Btl.* to the *Karstjäger Division* is not known.

In addition to the organization chart from February 1944, no other document has been found that shows the structure of the battalion for any following period. At the moment of its maximum expansion, probably in summer 1944, it seems likely that the *SS-WMS-Btl.* had the following structure:

- *Wachmannschaft I (Ostvölker)*, with one company
- *Wachmannschaft II (landeseigene Kräfte)*, with,
  - *Stabskompanie*
  - *1., 2., 3., 4., 5.* and *6. Kompanie*
  - *Kraftfahrstaffel*
  - *leichter Flakzug*
  - *Kommando G.*

The data available on the evolution of the *SS-WMS-Btl.* after mid-1944 are analyzed in a later section.

4.2: Personnel

There is little information on the battalion's personnel. For the German personnel (*Reichsdeutsche*), including officers, only a few names are known; the same applies for the *Trawniki*. More information is available on the soldiers recruited in the OZAK (Italians, Slovenes, Croats and *Volksdeutsche*). The personnel of the *SS-WMS-Btl.* had at least the following origins:

1. *Reichsdeutsche* and *Trawniki* belonging to the company of *Wachmannschaften* (*Trawniki* company) arrived in Trieste from Poland; most of them remained in the same unit which was indicated as *Wachmannschaft I (Ostvölker)*, but some were transferred to the *Wachmannschaft II (landeseigene Kräfte)*.
2. *Reichsdeutsche* from *Abteilung R* as well as some *Trawniki* attached to *Abteilung R* (seconded to the *Wachmannschaft II*, but remaining full members of *Abteilung R*).
3. *Reichsdeutsche* coming from the *Schutzpolizei*.
4. Local personnel recruited in the OZAK, who made up part of the cadres and most of the enlisted personnel of the *Wachmannschaft II* (a few were also in the *Wachmannschaft I*).
5. Italian soldiers from other regions of Italy (also mainly in the *Wachmannschaft II*).
6. Perhaps more *Trawniki* arrived in the OZAK during 1944.

Of the first group, the only known names are those of the first battalion commander, Schwarzenbacher and some *Trawniki*. The second group included three officers—*SS-Ustuf.* Kurt Franz, Josef Oberhauser, and Gottfried Schwarz—and an unknown number of cadres and enlisted personnel. The third group was formed by a certain number, not precisely known, of additional German (*Reichsdeutsche*) officers and cadres sent to the battalion probably in order to increase the insufficient strength; known names are those of Eibisch and four NCOs, all belonging to the *Schutzpolizei*. As far as the fourth and fifth groups are concerned, they made up the so-called *landeseigene Kräfte*, that is local elements from the OZAK (Italians, Slovenes, Croats and *Volksdeutsche*) and Italian soldiers originating from other regions of Italy. The latter included—in addition to a certain number of single cases, probably soldiers who were in the area that would later become the OZAK at the time of the Italian armistice and then remained in the region—in particular the former members of *Battaglione Davide* (most originating from the Piedmont region) integrated in *6. Kompanie/ SS-WMS-Btl.*, but not only: one account mentioned that in July–August 1944, a group of around 100 young people, perhaps draft dodgers, many from the Emilia and Romagna regions (especially from the Cesena area), were prisoners in San Sabba and were then for the most part drafted in the SS.[23] The sixth group in the list is probable but not certain. It is known that on May 4, 1944, Himmler ordered that a further fifty *Trawniki* be sent to Trieste to be employed as "cadres for the creation of local units."[24] It is thus likely, although not confirmed, that more *Trawniki* arrived in the OZAK around mid-1944 and it is possible that at least part of them were inserted in the *SS-WMS-Btl.*

In the following more information is given on the battalion members, according to nationality and ethnic group.

The Germans (Reichsdeutsche)

There is only very little information about the battalion's German personnel, meaning the so-called *Reichsdeutsche*, or Germans from the *Reich* territories. The only known names in addition to those of the commander Schwarzenbacher and of his probable successor Allers, are Eibisch and three *SS-Untersturmführer* coming from *Abteilung R*: Franz, Oberhauser, and Schwarz.

Schwarzenbacher was killed by Slovenian partisans in an ambush on the evening of June 2, 1944, on the road between Senosecchia and Storie, east of Trieste. According to a partisan account, the ambush targeted a convoy formed by a truck, a car, and three motorcycles and took place near the village of Sinadole; the vehicles were returning to Trieste from Senosecchia, after a raid in the village of Villabassa, during which two partisans

Gottfried Schwarz, member of *Abteilung R* seconded to the *SS-Wachmannschafts-Btl.*, in which he was company commander, seen here still as an *SS-Hauptscharführer*, probably in early 1943. He was killed by partisans on June 19, 1944.

SS-Unterscharführer Kurt Bolender, member of *Abteilung R* seconded to the *SS-Wachmannschafts-Btl.* (in particular to its *6. Kompanie*, based in the Risiera).

The building hosting the *Landschutzschule* (school for *Landschutz* units) led in Gorizia by Kurt Franz, member of *Abteilung R*, detached to that city with the *Kommando G.* of the *SS-Wachmannschafts-Btl.* The school was in the then Opera Balilla (Fascist youth organization) building, which today—situated in Largo G. Culiat—still hosts a school. *MNZS, NI11_614, 618*

and four civilians had been killed.[25] In the report on Schwarzenbacher's death (*Verlustmeldung*), the cause of death was indicated as firearms wounds to the head and legs; it is additionally noted that his identity tag was taken by the partisans. According to German data, together with the officer ten soldiers from the battalion were killed, four were wounded (one of whom died shortly afterwards) and eleven were reported missing; curiously, the men belonged to the *Stabskompanie* and to all the first five companies of the *SS-WMS-Btl.*, with a prevalence from *2.* and *4. Kompanie*.[26] After the death of Schwarzenbacher, by order of Globocnik dated June 7, the battalion's command was temporarily assigned to *SS-Hauptsturmführer und Hauptmann d.SchP.* Guido Hornof, who at that time was the Ia (operations' officer) in the *Führungsstab für Bandenbekämpfung*.[27] Later, Hornof went back to his former position in the FSBB. Apparently, the command was then taken up by Allers, at least according to his own declaration.[28] According to another source, Schwarzenbacher's successor may have been Eibisch.[29] Despite the low rank (*Leutnant d.SchP.* at least until end of May 1944, later *Oberleutnant*) this officer had a relatively important role at least from early April 1944, when he signed documents as *Führer des SS-Wachmannschafts-Btl.*, that is acting battalion commander (probably in Schwarzenbacher's absence).[30] Perhaps the battalion's command was formally assigned to Allers, but the unit daily management was delegated to Eibisch.

The three officers seconded to the *SS-WMS-Btl.* from *Abteilung R*, all members of the *Waffen-SS* (and as such they had undergone at least some military training), were *SS-Ustuf.* Kurt Franz, Josef Oberhauser, and Gottfried Schwarz. All had been promoted to officer rank in recognition of their role in *Aktion Reinhard* after Himmler's visit to Lublin in February 1943, and all became company commanders in the *SS-WMS-Btl.*

Franz had been trainer and commander of the *Trawniki Wachmannschaften* in the Belzec camp; later he was first deputy commander in Treblinka and then, after Stangl's departure to Italy, camp commander. According to his declarations, Franz arrived in Trieste in late November – early December 1943; initially he remained confined in the "Grande Albergo della Città" hotel on Wirth's orders, who—still according to Franz—was reproaching him of being responsible for the escape of some Jewish prisoners during the Treblinka uprising on August 2, 1943. Probably in December he was then assigned to the school (on Via Combi) where the *SS-WMS-Btl.* was being set up and trained, as trainer and commander of a platoon of Italian recruits. In January 1944, with his platoon, already trained, he was transferred to Gorizia where the unit (later progressively expanded to the size of a company) took up the name of *Kommando G.* In Gorizia, Franz created and led a *Landschutzschule* (school for *Landschutz* troops) where Slovene recruits were trained; he also engaged in propaganda and recruitment activities. On March 17, 1944, he was awarded the *Eisernes Kreuz II. Klasse* (Iron Cross Second Class). In mid-1944, Franz was also *Sicherungskommandant* for the sector of San Daniele del Carso (see later). He was wounded in a fight against the partisans probably in October 1944, and sent to hospital. He came back to Italy after convalescence only in February 1945, being assigned again to Gorizia, where he was apparently used again as *Sicherungskommandant* and as trainer for a *Brigate Nere* (Republican Fascist party militia) unit.[31]

This page and next: Franz inspecting Slovenian recruits of the *landeseigene Selbstschutzverbände* (local units) in the *Landschutzschule* in Gorizia, probably in early 1944. Note that the sidecaps and "*Heer* M40/M41 style" tunics worn by the recruits do not display any insignia, except for the characteristic shoulder boards piped with white *Waffenfarbe*. It can be assumed that, until the draft of March 1944, all recruits of the *landeseigene Selbstschutzverbände*, including the *SS-Wachmannschaften* and the *Landschutz*, used this uniform pattern, with no distinctive insignia. *MNZS, NI11_616, 621*

Oberhauser, after having been commander of a platoon of *Trawniki* at the Belzec camp and in Lublin, became a close collaborator (as assistant and escort) of Wirth as they were still in Poland; he still had this position when they arrived in Italy. Like Franz, during the set up phase of the *SS-WMS-Btl.* he was seconded to the school where the battalion was billeted and employed as company commander and probably as trainer; after some time he was replaced by Schwarz in the *SS-WMS-Btl.* and went back to his functions as Wirth's right hand. Later on he was given command of *6. Kompanie* of the *SS-WMS-Btl.*, probably right after its formation in May 1944; he kept this function until the end of the war (by when the company had been renumbered *1. Kompanie*). The company was billeted at the Risiera di San Sabba but initially Oberhauser remained in his accommodation in the city center. After Allers' arrival and Hering's removal in July 1944, Oberhauser became commander of the Risiera and moved there, living in the apartment formerly occupied by Hering, in the building on the left of the entrance to the site. He was promoted to *SS-Obersturmführer* in January 1945, and remained at the Risiera until the Germans abandoned the city in the night between April 29–30, 1945, when the last prisoners were released and the complex was partially destroyed.

Schwarz had been deputy commander of the Belzec camp; after the camp closure in early 1943 he became responsible for the labor camp in Dorohucza. Transferred to Italy, he became commander of *2. Kompanie/SS-WMS-Btl.* probably in winter 1943–44. With this company he moved to the Udine province, and in mid-May 1944, he was based in Gemona, where he probably had the task of *Sicherungskommandant*. He was killed in a firefight with partisans on June 19, 1944, near San Pietro di Ragogna (northwest of Udine).[32]

Other Germans were seconded from *Abteilung R* to the *SS-WMS-Btl.* Only a few cases are known, all NCOs inserted in *6. Kompanie* (later *1. Kp.*):

Franz wearing the *SS-Untersturmführer* uniform in Gorizia, in spring or summer 1944.

A Slovenian soldier of the *landeseigene Selbstschutzverbände* probably during the first quarter of 1944. It is not clear if he belonged to the *SS-Wachmannschaften* or to the *Landschutz*, since there was apparently no difference initially between the uniforms of these two units. The tricolor Slovenian national arm shield, in this case unusually worn on the right sleeve, appears different from the outlined national arm shields specifically produced for the *SS-Wachmannschaften*. *MNZS, XII_31*

A truck from the *SS-Karstwehr-Bataillon* photographed in Sambasso (now Šempas, Slovenia) in late January 1944. The man on the road behind the vehicle is a member of the *SS-Wachmannschaften* or the *Landschutz*, as said it seems that in this timeframe the uniforms of these two units cannot be distinguished; he wears a gray-green greatcoat with black collar and cuffs. The soldiers on the left of the photo belong to the *Waffen-SS*, except for the first man from the right on the truck, who also seems to be a member of the *landeseigene Selbstschutzverbände*.

SS-Uscha. Baer, Bolender, Girtzig, and Sporleder. Also in this case, at least the first three had served in the *Waffen-SS*.

With reference to German NCOs serving in the *SS-WMS-Btl*. not coming from *Abteilung R*, four names are confirmed, all belonging to the *Schutzpolizei*. Worth noting is that two of them originally belonged to *Polizei-Begleit-Btl. Steiermark*, Himmler's escort battalion; one was seconded from the *Feldkommandostelle* (Field Command Staff) of the *Reichsführer-SS*.[33]

Trawniki

Trawniki made up the majority of the *Trawniki* company, or *Wachmannschaft I (Ostvölker)*. As some of them (including *Volksdeutsche*) were transferred from this unit to the *Wachmannschaft II*; their number is not known but seems to have been relatively limited. It is likely that NCOs were used as section leaders. The names of at least seven *Trawniki* that served in the *Wachmannschaft II* are confirmed.[34] Of these, at least five (Schmidt, E. Kostenko, A. Rosenke, Dahlke, Siewert) were attached to *Abteilung R* and were probably seconded to the *SS-WMS-Btl.* in the same way as the Germans belonging to *Abteilung R*; the other two came probably from the *Trawniki* company. In the list used to note down the pay (*Auszahlungsliste*) to the non-German soldiers belonging to the *Wachmannschaft II* (*Stabskompanie*, *2.*, *3.* and *4. Kompanie* and *Kraftfahrstaffel*), presumably referred to the month of April 1944 (see section 4.3), there are only two names identifiable as probable *Trawniki*, both in the *Stabskompanie*.[35]

Locally Recruited Soldiers (Italians, Slovenes, Croats, *Volksdeutsche*)

Apart from some possible cases of Germans and a certain number of *Trawniki*, the bulk of the enlisted personnel (and also some of the NCOs) in the *Wachmannschaft II* (*landeseigene Kräfte*) was made up of elements that were locally recruited in the OZAK: Italians, Slovenes, Croats, and some *Volksdeutsche*. A few were also present in the *Wachmannschaft I*. The soldiers of this category can be subdivided in three sub-categories:

- Italians, Slovenes, Croats, and *Volksdeutsche* recruits originating from the OZAK, who joined the *SS-Wachmannschaften* voluntarily or forcibly up to March 1944, and after that month on the basis of the obligatory draft introduced by the *Oberster Kommissar*.
- Italians originating from other regions, probably soldiers who were in the area that would later become the OZAK at the time of the Italian armistice, remained in the region after the German occupation, and later joined the *SS-Wachmannschaften*.
- Groups of soldiers or recruits transferred by the Germans from other regions of Italy to the OZAK and integrated in the *SS-Wachmannschaften* (*Battaglione Davide*, and the previously mentioned recruits from the Emilia and Romagna regions).

On November 29, 1943, an ordinance issued by Rainer introduced in the OZAK the "obligatory war service" (*Kriegsdienstpflicht*): on the basis of this ordinance all Italian citizens born in the years specified in the (Italian) law on civilian mobilisation of October 31, 1942, were declared "obligated to perform war service." Rainer's ordinance set out that the war service could be performed with or without weapons, in the following ways:

- In the landeseigene *Selbstschutzverbände* (literally local self-defense units; in the Italian translation of the ordinance, *organizzazioni per la difesa territoriale* or territorial defense organizations),
- In the *Aufbaudienst* (construction service),
- In the German armed forces: *Wehrmacht*, *Waffen-SS* or *Polizei*,
- In the Organisation Todt (OT, work service for the construction of military projects),
- In the units of the new Italian army (i.e., the RSI army).

Or it could be replaced by working in Germany.[36]

A few days later, on December 6, 1943, Rainer issued another ordinance (retroactively in force from October 1, 1943) on the creation of the *landeseigene Selbstschutzverbände*, according to which these units were to operate "in order to contribute to maintaining public order and security in the OZAK." The ordinance set out that these units were to be subordinated to the respective HSSPF (OZAK and *Alpenland*), who were to issue the necessary orders for their creation. It also indicated that serving in these units was on a voluntary basis and that this constituted war service according to the ordinance of November 29, 1943, on the obligatory war service.[37]

Inside the category of the landeseigene *Selbstschutzverbände* (also called, more simply, *landeseigene Verbände*, or local units) fell the *SS-Wachmannschaften* of the OZAK (the *SS-WMS-Btl.* was almost certainly the first unit of this type formed in the OZAK, even before Rainer's ordinances),[38] the *Landschutz* (territorial defense) units and other units.[39]

Three propaganda photos showing members of the *Landschutz* of the Udine province during training, probably near San Gottardo, at the edge of Udine in spring 1944. The tunics carry the provincial arm shield but not yet the red rhomboidal collar tabs; note the characteristic shoulder boards piped with white *Waffenfarbe* used by the majority of the *landeseigene Selbstschutzverbände* units. The sidecaps, probably produced in Grigioverde wool cloth imitating the cut of the *Feldmütze für SS* M34, do not carry any insignia. *MNZS, NI7_62, NI11_877, 903*

It is useful to provide in the following some information on the *Landschutz*, since it had links with the *SS-Wachmannschaften*: it was probably created already in December 1943, but its strength became significant only after the introduction of the conscription in the OZAK from March 1944, as described later.[40] It was divided into an *Aktiver Landschutz* (active territorial defense) and a *Reserve-Landschutz* (auxiliary territorial defense). The latter was a civic guard formed by all people of any age able to carry arms, who had to take part in guard and surveillance services in the town or village of their residence, mainly during the night; they generally wore civilian clothes and an armband with the inscription "*Difesa Territoriale – Landschutz*" (at least for the Italian-speaking units), had few weapons and practically no combat value. The *aktiver Landschutz* on the other hand had a formal military structure and was billeted in barracks. Limiting the analysis to the five provinces under Globocnik's authority,[41] it is evident that it was organized on ethnic basis. It included:

- The Italian units of the *Difesa Territoriale* (territorial defense)[42] created on provincial level at least in the provinces of Udine, Fiume and Pola (there is no confirmation that an Italian Difesa Territoriale existed in the province of Gorizia, while for Trieste it was probably replaced by the Guardia Civica di Trieste).
- The Slovenian units of the *Slovenski narodni varnostni zbor* (SNVZ, Slovenian National Security Corps, or *Slowenischer Landschutz* in German; it was also called *Primorsko Domobranstvo*, or National Guard of the Slovenian Littoral), formed from winter 1943–44; the SNVZ reached the maximum size of a regiment in summer-autumn 1944, and.
- One Croatian regiment (*Kroatisches Landschutz-Rgt.*) based in Sušak (the part of the city of Fiume east of the Recina River).

To oversee the local units a special inspectorate was created, later transformed into a *Leitstab für landeseigene Verbände* (command headquarters for territorial units, later renamed *Leitstab für landeseigene Kräfte*), under the command of *Oberleutnant* (later *Hauptmann*) *d.SchP.* Dr. Rossbacher, who was directly subordinated to Globocnik.[43] Subordinated to Rossbacher were the commanders of the territorial defense in the provinces (*Landschutzführer*), who on their turn controlled the area commanders (*Landschutzkre-*

Members of the *Landschutz* of the Udine province cleaning their weapons. The tunics carry the provincial arm shield and the red rhomboidal collar tabs. *MNZS, NI11_884*

Men of the *Landschutz* of the Udine province photographed in Udine in June 1944. They wear the Italian mod. 40 fatigue tunic and sidecaps bearing no insignia.

Two men belonging to the *Landschutz* of the Udine province in summer uniforms. Note the red collar tabs and the provincial arm shield carried on the shirt.

Members of the *Landschutz* of the Istria province photographed in late spring or summer 1944. The provincial arm shields depicting the Istrian goat are visible. The tunics have shoulder boards piped with white *Waffenfarbe* and red rhomboidal collar tabs. Curiously, the tunics of the two seated soldiers seem to be made with Tipo 343 cloth, a fabric used by the Italian Royal army from 1942. The sidecaps are probably produced in Grigioverde wool cloth imitating the cut of the *Feldmütze für SS* M34; they carry a simple silver button as cockade. *Courtesy Roberto Spazzali*

The only known photo so far showing a man of the *Landschutz* of the Fiume province, seen in October 1944 in Abbazia (now Opatija). He wears an Italian mod. 40 tunic with modified collar, red rhomboidal collar tabs and shoulder boards piped with white *Waffenfarbe*.

Men from the *Landschutz* of the Istria province, together with some *Waffen-SS* and *Ordnungspolizei* members, among whom apparently some *Kriegsberichter* (war correspondents), at the Duino castle.

Landschutz soldiers of the Istria province marching together with a medic belonging to the *SS-Wachmannschaften* (wearing a "transitional" tunic).

isführer); in all known cases they were German officers belonging to the *Gendarmerie*, the police for extra-urban areas. The responsibilities of the *Landschutzführer* were probably limited to creating, training and supervising the units, excluding their operational employment, which pertained to the provincial *SS- und Pol.Kommandeur*. Also subordinate to the Leitstab were the various schools for the territorial defense units (*Landschutzschule*) set up in various cities and towns in the OZAK; of these, two were *Landschutzführerschule*, which trained the officers and the NCOs, based at the Duino Castle (on the coast north of Trieste)[44] and in Cividale. These schools served probably not only the *Landschutz* but also the other units of the *landeseigene Selbstschutzverbände*, including the *SS-Wachmannschaften*. In Duino there was also a *Bandenkampfschule*, or school for fighting the "bandits," where anti-guerrilla tactics were taught; it was managed by the HSSPF OZAK and trained elements of all SS/*Polizei* units active in the region (as well as of *Abteilung R*).

Although Rainer's ordinance of November 29, 1943, established a general obligation, only the 1923–1924–1925 classes were actually drafted for military service, by ordinance of the *Oberster Kommissar* dated February 22, 1944 (in force from March 5).[45] Therefore, until March 1944, recruitments in the landeseigene *Selbstschutzverbände* units were only voluntary or took place following

Men from the *Landschutz* of the Istria province on a truck with registration number Pol-76129 from *I. Btl./SS-Pol.Rgt. "Bozen"* near Fianona (now Plomin, Croatia), in spring 1944.

The same truck transporting *Landschutz* soldiers; in the foreground is a *Sipo*/SD man (perhaps a trainer). *BA, 101I-005-0028-45*

A soldier of the Slovenian *Landschutz* (SNVZ) wearing a German-style tunic and an *Einheitsfeldmütze* M43 with German-style cockade. He carries the specific arm shield of the SNVZ, introduced at least from April 1944, depicting a red Illyrian ship on a white/blue background. *MNZS, PL_11490*

Soldiers of the Slovenian *Landschutz* (SNVZ) wearing different types of locally produced tunics made with Italian mod. 29 camouflage fabric and at least in one case the Slovenian national arm shield. Triangular or oval metal badges with the Slovenian flag colors are carried on the sidecaps. The photo was taken before the San Giusto castle in Trieste. *MNZS, XII_32*

Men of the Slovenian *Landschutz* (SNVZ), among whom an NCO, on an Italian-produced L3 tankette in Clana (now Klana, Croatia), north of Fiume, in front of the outpost manned by men from *I. Btl./SS-Pol.Rgt. "Bozen"* (*Case Incis*) probably in spring–summer 1944. The soldiers are not wearing national shields nor collar tabs.

An officer of the Slovenian *Landschutz* (SNVZ) wearing a locally produced tunic made with Italian mod. 29 camo fabric and the Slovenian national arm shield specifically produced for the Slovenian *SS-Wachmannschaften*, rarely worn by the SNVZ. On his sidecap he wears the oval metal badge with the Slovenian flag colors. The metallic triangular badge carried on his breast seems to be Royal Yugoslavian mountain troops' badge, depicting the Triglav three white mountain peaks. The picture was taken in the San Giovanni barracks in Trieste. *MNZS, XII_2_II*

These portraits of members of the Slovenian *Landschutz* (SNVZ) show the use of rhomboidal unpiped collar tabs made with a very light colored cloth, possibly white or yellow, carried on the collars of Italian mod. 40 fatigue tunics; at present the meaning of these insignia is not known.

some kind of pressure or coercion, but in any case they were not formally recruitments made on the basis of the obligatory conscription. In the case of the volunteers, they were probably both former soldiers of the Italian army as well as young men not previously drafted, hostile to the partisan movement and sometimes ideologically supportive of Nazi Germany. It is proven that in other cases (probably the great majority) forced recruitments took place.[46] The recruits that formed the first three companies of the *SS-WMS-Btl.* (*Wachmannschaft II*) fall in the categories of volunteers and forcibly recruited. After March 5, 1944, medical examinations started for the 1923–1924–1925 classes and slightly later the recruitments took place and the draftees were sent to the units. The draftees could opt for the *Wehrmacht*, the *Waffen-SS*, the *Milizia per la Difesa Territoriale (MDT)*, the RSI armed forces or the *Landschutz*, otherwise they were sent to the Organisation Todt. The volunteering for the RSI units (which in any case was an option only for the Italians) was discouraged in any possible way by the Germans. Many, especially among the Italians, ended up working for the Organisation Todt, by choice or following a decisions by the Germans, who needed workers and tended to trust the Italian in arms to a limited degree, unless they were volunteers.

Hauptmann d.SchP. Hans-Georg Bartholdi from *I. Btl./SS-Pol.Rgt. "Bozen"* together with a member of the Croatian *Landschutz* (wearing the gray uniform of the Hrvatsko Domobranstvo) seen in Istria during 1944.

An unknown but not negligible number of *Landschutz* soldiers were forcibly moved by the Germans to other SS, *Waffen-SS* or *Polizei* units: known are the case of soldiers transferred from the *Landschutz* to the *SS-Wachmannschaften*, the *Karstjäger Division* and the *Polizei-Freiwilligen-Btl. "Fiume."* On the personnel transfers to the *SS-WMS-Btl.* a specific account is available: forty-five young Italian draftees from the town of Pirano, in Istria, who chose to join the *Landschutz* at the end of March 1944, were trained for a month together with recruits from other villages in the "De Amicis" school on Via Combi in Trieste by *Gebirgsjäger* trainers. After the end of the training, probably in May they were all transferred to the *SS-WMS-Btl.* (and from this unit a part was further transferred immediately to the *Karstjäger* Division).[47]

In addition to the more or less voluntary recruitments and transfers from the *Landschutz* units, the personnel of the *SS-Wachmannschaften* was in part also formed by people who had been arrested because they had dodged the draft or work service or by people who had been forcibly taken from the building sites where they worked at the construction of defensive lines. These forced recruitments seem to have been relatively numerous

Soldiers belonging to the *Selbstschutz* of the Valcanale, probably during training, in the fields around Rutte Grande, near Tarvisio, visible in the background. Three army *Gebirgsjäger*, wearing awards, probably trainees, also appear in one photo.

in the last months of the war; there are two accounts of such episodes referring to the end of 1944 and April 1945.[48]

Among the *SS-Wachmannschaften* personnel recruited in the OZAK, the last of the three categories mentioned at the start of this section included soldiers transferred by the Germans from other Italian regions to the OZAK: it is referred here in particular, to *Battaglione Davide* and to the group of draftees, mainly from the Emilia and Romagna regions, kept prisoner in the Risiera in summer 1944 and then drafted in the SS. On the recruits from Emilia and Romagna no specific information is available. As far as *Battaglione Davide* is concerned, part of its soldiers, after several selections that took place during the first period in San Sabba in May 1944, formed *6. Kompanie/SS-WMS-Btl.* (see also the specific section on *Battaglione Davide).*

4.3: Ethnic Composition

A list used to note down the pay (*Auszahlungsliste*) of the non-German soldiers of the *Wachmannschaft II*, containing the names of the NCOs and enlisted personnel (*Unteroffizierie* and *Mannschaften*) belonging to the *Stabskompanie*, *2.*, *3.* and *4. Kompanie* and *Kraftfahrstaffel*, has been found.[49] The list is not dated but it is probably from April 1944 (before the formation of the *5.* and *6. Kompanie*), as confirmed by cross-verification with data on losses.

This list provides information on the strength and ethnic composition of the companies; as a rule only the surnames are indicated (the first names only in case there were several people with the same surname), so the ethnic origin is not always evident (in addition to the fact that sometimes people of Italian ethnicity had Slovenian or Croatian surnames, and the other way round), but indicative and plausible data can still be extrapolated. In addition to the personnel locally recruited in the OZAK the list contains a few names that are recognizable as Ukrainian (in the *Stabskompanie*), but apparently no Germans (*Reichsdeutsche*); it is not known if the reason for this was that there were no Germans in the companies (but this seems unlikely, especially for the *Unteroffizierie*) or if—more likely—there were separate lists for the pay of the German personnel (officers, NCOs and enlisted personnel), as it was also the case for the list of losses, which were reported separately for the Germans and for the battalion's *fremdvölkische Angehörige* (foreign members). The lack of data for *1. Kompanie* is not clear; it is possible that for this company—as in this period it was partly or fully in Gorizia—data were not available, or that it was administratively independent.

On the basis of the list, in the *Wachmannschaft II* NCOs and enlisted personnel (excluding the

Reichsdeutsche, as said) were present in the following strength and had the following ethnic origin in April 1944:

- *Stabskompanie*: 4 *Unteroffizier*, 33 *Mannschaften*; in the majority ethnic Italians, some Croats, at least three *Trawniki*
- (*1. Kompanie*: not listed in the document)
- *2. Kompanie*: 7 *Unteroffizier*, 98 *Mannschaften*; all seem to be ethnic Italians
- *3. Kompanie*: 1 *Unteroffizier*, 70 *Mannschaften*; the majority seem to be ethnic Italians
- *4. Kompanie*: no *Unteroffizier*, 109 *Mannschaften*; in the majority ethnic Croats, some Italians, some *Volksdeutsche* from the OZAK region
- *Kraftfahrstaffel*: 1 *Unteroffizier*, 15 *Mannschaften*; the majority seem to be ethnic Italians.

With reference to the two companies formed later, for *5. Kompanie* there is no information regarding its composition (with the exception of the names of two Ukrainian *Trawniki*). As mentioned, *6. Kompanie* was made up (in addition to its commander Oberhauser and a small number of German and *Trawniki* NCOs) only by soldiers formerly belonging to *Battaglione Davide*, at least initially.

It can be supposed that the ethnic composition of the various units of the *SS-WMS-Btl.* was—at least in the phase of its maximum expansion during summer 1944—the following:

Wachmannschaft I (Ostvölker):
- *Reichsdeutsche*, *Trawniki*, a few locally recruited personnel

Wachmannschaft II:
- *Stabskompanie*: *Reichsdeutsche*, *Trawniki*, for the enlisted personnel (and some NCOs) in the majority ethnic Italians and some Croats
- *1. Kompanie*: *Reichsdeutsche*, *Trawniki*, for the enlisted personnel (and some NCOs) probably in the majority ethnic Italians and Slovenes
- *2. Kompanie*: *Reichsdeutsche*, *Trawniki*, for the enlisted personnel (and some NCOs) in the majority ethnic Italians
- *3. Kompanie*: *Reichsdeutsche*, *Trawniki*, for the enlisted personnel (and some NCOs) in the majority ethnic Italians and some Croats
- *4. Kompanie*: *Reichsdeutsche*, *Trawniki*, for the enlisted personnel (and some NCOs) in the majority ethnic Croats and some Italians
- *5. Kompanie*: *Reichsdeutsche*, *Trawniki*, for the enlisted personnel no data available
- 6. *Kompanie*: *Reichsdeutsche*, *Trawniki*, for the enlisted personnel (and some NCOs) ethnic Italians, in the majority from the Piedmont region (former *Battaglione Davide*)
- *Kraftfahrstaffel*: *Reichsdeutsche*, *Trawniki*, for the enlisted personnel (and some NCOs) in the majority ethnic Italians and some Croats
- *Kommando G.*: *Reichsdeutsche*, Italians and Slovenes (?).

4.3.1: The *Battaglione Patrioti Davide*

The Davide unit in the Piedmont region

The *Battaglione Patrioti Davide* (Davide Patriots' Battalion, also simply called *Battaglione Davide*), was a very unique unit, which escapes simple categorizations.[50] It developed around the charismatic figure of Enrico Ferrero, aka "*Capitano Davide*" (the rank was self-attributed, so that later it became "*Colonnello Davide*")[51] who after the Italian armistice of September 8, 1943, managed to gather around himself a numerous group of former soldiers and RSI draft dodgers in the area around the village of Canelli (in the Asti Province, Piedmont region, in northwestern Italy).

The members defined themselves as "patriots," thus in principle adhering to the resistance movement against Fascism and the Nazi occupation. The hostility against Fascism of many of its men results clearly from their behavior on many occasions; several reports from RSI authorities mention attacks and provocative acts by members of the unit towards RSI soldiers and institutions. However, the "*Davide*" unit defined itself not only as anti-Fascist, but also as anti-English and anti-communist, and in early 1944, "Davide" put his unit at the Germans' service.

Although it cannot be known for certain, siding with the Germans may have been a tactical move: in fact "Davide" told his men often that they would sooner or later go back to the partisans' side. In any case, "Davide"'s ambiguous and opportunistic attitude makes it difficult to formulate a clear judgment of his unit, which seem to have rather belonged to a gray zone between collaboration with the Germans and resistance against them. In addition, beyond "Davide"'s manoeuvring, little is known about the motivations and orientations of his men beyond their hostility to Fascism; however, according to the few available personal accounts, in the majority they seem to have been hostile to the Germans as well.[52]

In the initial phases of the unit's existence, "Davide" struck an alliance with other partisan units of various ideological orientations, for instance a nationalist (*badogliano*) unit led by Pietro Balbo "Poli" and a social-communist unit led by Giovanni Rocca "Primo," as well as with other small groups of unknown political orientation, such as those led by Angelino Piras, Piero Audano, Ernesto Sarzano and a certain Ruggero (first name unknown), who all later became officers in Battaglione Davide (but not Balbo and Rocca). However, in January 1944, "Davide" tried to accredit himself with the RSI authorities, offering them the services of his unit. At the same time he also had contacts with the Germans, with whom he reached an agreement whereby the units of "Davide" and "Poli" would be allowed to recruit soldiers, taking them away from the RSI draft, in exchange for guaranteeing security in their operational area (Langhe del Belbo and Bormida). The units, which took up the name of "*Patrioti delle Langhe*" (Patriots of the Langhe Region), received from the Germans arms and uniforms. Responsible for liaising with the two groups was the SD office in Asti (*SD-Aussenstelle Asti, SS-Ustuf.* Otto Grieser).

According to some sources, following a German request, "Davide"'s unit swore allegiance to the RSI in Asti on February 21, but this can not be verified. Such an oath seems unlikely given the clear and fierce hostility to Fascism shown by the unit's men.

According to the agreement between "Davide" and the Germans in early March, his men and those of "Poli" were to have moved from Canelli to Pinerolo; it seems that the Germans had the intention of turning them into a regular unit, with formal military organization. However, during the night of March 1–2, the billets of the "Davide" group in Canelli and in other nearby villages were attacked by the men of "Poli," who did not accept the agreement with the Germans. "Davide"'s men were dispersed; some of them joined other partisan units, others—chased by the Germans who arrived the following morning—later came back to the unit. Although the Germans suspected that "Poli"'s attack may have been agreed upon with "Davide" to avoid the transfer, after some days the roughly 300 men left with "Davide" were moved to Venaria Reale, near Turin. Here the men of the unit were again participants in some instances of hostility against the local RSI Fascists.

Some sources report that on March 25, Battaglione Davide swore allegiance to Hitler, but the information is not verified. For propaganda purposes the Germans circulated among the population a leaflet which announced that, "the known partisan leader "Davide" has sided with the Germans with his entire unit on March 7, 1944." The leaflet included two photographs, one which showed "Davide" shaking hands with the *SS- und Polizei-Führer Oberitalien-West, SS-Brigadeführer und Generalmajor der Polizei* Willy Tensfeld.[53]

It seems that in this phase the battalion was considered by the Germans (probably with "Davide"'s agreement, but perhaps without the knowledge of many of his men) as a unit attached to the *Waffen-SS*. This can be in any case deduced by the stamps used by the unit in April 1944: a round stamp reading *"Battaglione Patrioti 'Davide' – Venaria – 1ª Brigata d'Assalto"* ("Davide Patriots' Battalion – Venaria – 1st Assault Brigade") and one linear stamp reading *"Legione Volontari Italiani – 1ª Brigata d'Assalto – Battaglione Patrioti 'Davide' – Comando"* ("Italian Volunteer Legion – 1st Assault Brigade – 'Davide' Patriots' Battalion – Headquarters"). The name *1ª Brigata d'Assalto della Legione Volontari Italiani* (1st Assault Brigade of the Italian Volunteer Legion) was the Italian translation of *1. Sturmbrigade der Italienischen Freiwilligen Legionen*, the name of a unit set up in early 1944, on the basis of the *Milizia Armata* battalions, which had been formed in late 1943 with Italian volunteers willing to fight on with the Germans; they were considered attached to, but not exactly belonging to the *Waffen-SS*.[54]

At the end of March, the Germans ordered the battalion to move to the Gorizia area, in northeastern Italy and in the OZAK region. The transfer was decided because of the complaints by the RSI authorities about the unit's behavior. Perhaps other considerations also played a role, such as the lower risk of desertion by the soldiers, who in the majority were from the Piedmont region (with some from the Lombardy and Emilia regions). In order to convince his men to accept the move, "Davide" told them he had the intention to go over to the Yugoslav partisans, and subsequently to reach liberated southern Italy; in view of his ambiguity, it is impossible to know if he spoke sincerely. It seems, however, that before the departure numerous soldiers abandoned the unit.

Regarding the officers in the battalion in this phase, the following thirteen names are known, in addition to the commander "Davide" (Enrico Ferrero):

- *Capitano*: Ruggero (first name unknown), Angelo Piano, Ernesto Sarzano, Franco Gonella, Angelino (?) Piras, Piero Audano (Sarzano was the adjutant of "Davide," Audano and Ruggero apparently commanded respectively 1. and 2. Company; all three had been officers in the *Regio Esercito*);
- *Tenente*: Mario Ferrero (brother of "Davide"), Gino Spaccaferro, Aldo Cerrato, Luigi Fulmine, Enrico Sgambati.
- *Sottotenente*: Gino Ranalli, Gabriele Sanfelice.

All followed the unit to the Gorizia area, with the only uncertainty concerning *Capitano* Piras and Audano.

Transfer to the OZAK and Disarmament

The *Battaglione Davide*, which apparently numbered around 200 men (of whom a dozen were officers), arrived in the town of Gradisca d'Isonzo, near Gorizia, on April 6.[55] After a few days in the town the unit was divided in two parts, billeted in school buildings in the nearby villages of Sagrado (where the commander "Davide" was based) and Fogliano (under the orders of the Adjutant, *Capitano* Sarzano).

Immediately, the unit drew attention to itself because of its confrontational attitude towards RSI units and authorities, leading to several incidents; its men were described as, "a bunch of braggarts and overbearing individuals motivated by anti-Fascist feelings" in the war diary of the RSI military command for the Gorizia province.[56] The behavior of the battalion's men also attracted the attention of the Germans. On April 19, the commander of *278. Infanterie Division* suggested to the *Befehlshaber* in der OZAK to disarm the unit, forbid leave, and keep its barracks under surveillance; also, put on trial the soldiers responsible for episodes which were not specified in the document (but were evidently considered serious by the Germans), and send all the rest to work in Germany. The response of the *Befehlshaber* dated April 23, stated that Kübler had asked Rainer and Globocnik to relocate the unit elsewhere, indirectly confirming that the unit was subordinated to the region SS/*Polizei* headquarters.[57]

It all came to a head at the beginning of May. On May 2, in Gradisca members of the battalion arrested *Colonnello* Urbano Rocco, commander of *4. Reggimento MDT*, and some other people (*Milizia* officers and a local member of the Fascist party). Officially, the arrest was motivated as a retaliation for the disarmament of a group of *Battaglione Davide* soldiers (led by *Capitano* Sarzano) who did not know the password at an MDT checkpoint in Savogna. However, according to rumors that immediately circulated, "Davide" had ordered the kidnapping of the group in order to hand them over to the partisans in exchange for some prisoners and a sum of money. According to some sources, the planned exchange was attempted but did not happen due to a mishap. The prisoners held by *Battaglione Davide* were released the next day following an energetic intervention by the Germans.[58]

It is not clear if the partisans' prisoners really existed or if "Davide" was only trying to accredit himself with the Yugoslav partisans, handing them some hostages, in preparation for the battalion joining the partisans. In any case it was probably this episode, and the suspicion (probably well-

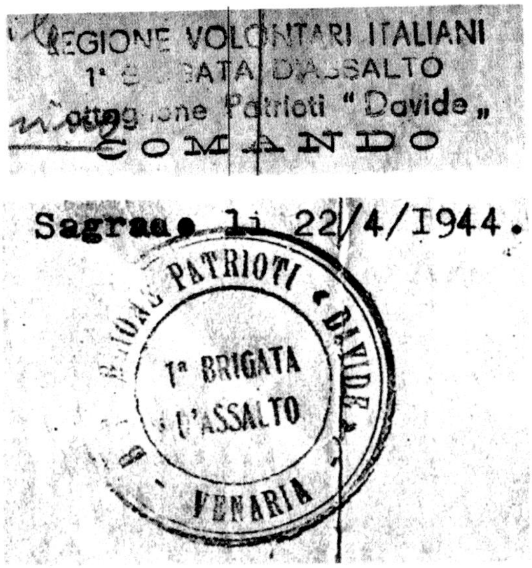

The round and linear stamps used by *Battaglione Davide*.

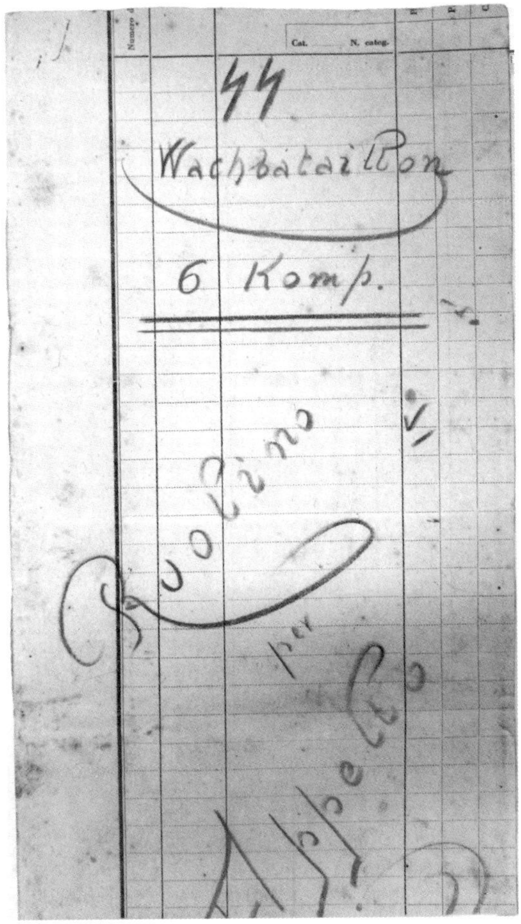

The cover page of the *Ruolino per appello* (roll call roster) of *6. Kp./SS-Wachmannschafts-Btl.* (formerly *Battaglione Davide*) dating from mid-May 1944.

founded) that "Davide" was in contact with the partisans, that convinced the Germans to act, especially so when they learned that on May 3–4 (the exact date is not certain) the battalion, having left only a few sentries to guard its barracks, went off for a training march on the Carso plateau. Evidently, the Germans feared that the battalion was going to defect to the partisans, and it is in fact possible that this was "Davide"'s intention (it seems the unit was accompanied by two women, who were partisan guides). Four trucks loaded with *Wehrmacht* soldiers (probably from *278. Infanterie Division*) were sent to disarm the battalion. They caught up with it in the area of Opacchiasella and monitored its movements from a distance; noticing that his unit was under observation, "Davide" decided to carry out a normal exercise and then march back to the barracks. However, on its way back, near the Redipuglia military sacrarium, the battalion was surrounded and—under the threat of German machine guns—forced to lay down its arms. Separated from their officers, the men were marched to their barracks in Sagrado, where they were kept under German surveillance.

San Sabba: Detention, Selection, and Integration in the *SS Wachmannschafts*-Btl.

On May 5, the soldiers—in total it seems 186,[59] excluding the officers (except *Sottotenente* Mario Ferrero and Cerrato, who for some reason remained in the group)—were brought by truck to the Risiera di San Sabba complex in Trieste. They were locked in a room on the second floor of the building used as a prison in the second courtyard.

On the floor below there were Jewish prisoners, with whom the soldiers managed to speak through some slits in the wooden floor.

The soldiers immediately found themselves in a condition of fear and intimidation. During the first days of detention some selections took place among the imprisoned soldiers; the first and most numerous was carried out randomly, then those who seemed to have manifested sympathy for the partisans were eliminated (for instance those that had pro-partisan writings on their caps); then another dozen men were eliminated after replying positively to Wirth's (false) offer to be transferred to another unit. In this way several dozen soldiers disappeared without a trace; it is likely that they were all sent to concentration camps in Germany.[60] The commander "Davide" was deported to Dachau; the same fate was probably met by some other officers, believed to be responsible for the unit's "betrayal" together with their commander.[61] Also the women who were with the unit when it was disarmed (it seems they were two partisan guides and "Davide"'s woman) apparently disappeared, probably killed or deported.

After a few days some officers, deemed trustworthy and not involved in the attempt to defect to the partisans, were united with the other ranks, but they were all still imprisoned.[62] After around a week of detention, that is around May 10, the soldiers were let out of prison and billeted in the central building on the first courtyard, which at that time was used for storage and the soldiers themselves had to clear. The Germans had evidently decided to use what was left of the unit, inserting the men in the *SS-Wachmannschaften*, as *6. Kompanie* of the *SS-WMS-Btl*. The company command was given to *SS-Ustuf.* Oberhauser from *Abteilung R*. The Italian officers were assigned German NCO ranks: *Capitano* Sarzano became *SS-Oberzugwachmann*, the *tenente* got the ranks of *SS-Zugwachmann*.

The soldiers soon had to experience Wirth's ferociousness and strictness. In his presence and probably on his orders, in the first days after the soldiers' liberation (it seems on May 13 or 14) two men, Antonio Pairolero and Achille Battistini, had to be executed by their own comrades, evidently to set an example: the reason for this punishment is not clear, according to one version it was because they had shown disrespect towards an Italian officer of their unit, according to other versions they had urged their fellow soldiers to rebel against the Germans or they had tried to desert.

From the period immediately after this execution is dated a list of Italian members of *6. Kp./SS-WMS-Btl.*, in which there are 122 names, of whom nine officers, twenty-one NCOs, and ninety-two enlisted personnel.[63] This list was compiled before the last of the selections carried out by the Germans: a medical examination conducted during May eliminated as not fit for service numerous men, who were probably sent to Germany to work. By the end of May, the company was therefore left with around eighty-five men, of whom five officers (*Capitano* Ernesto Sarzano, *Tenente* Mario Ferrero, Luigi Fulmine and Aldo Cerrato, *Sottotenente* Gino Ranalli).[64]

In the meantime on May 18, a first group of Italian soldiers—perhaps those considered more trustworthy—were sent to the outpost of Castelnuovo d'Istria, on the Trieste–Fiume road, where there was already an *Abteilung R* detachment, which was reinforced by the newcomers. More men belonging to the company were sent to Castelnuovo on May 28, among them Sarzano, who took up command of the company's group in the village. The transfer to Castelnuovo is documented on some of the forty-two personal registration cards belonging to Italian members of *6. Kompanie/SS-WMS-Btl.* that have been found. May 18 or 28 is indicated on the cards of these soldiers as the dates of enrollment in the SS. The soldiers who were not sent to Castelnuovo remained in San Sabba, where in the following weeks—without leaving the Risiera, except for some marches in the surrounding area—they were intensively trained, under the orders of Oberhauser and Bolender. Additionally, the unit started to guard the entrance to the Risiera complex, the first courtyard and the external perimeter (not the second courtyard, where the prisoners were kept and only authorized members of *Abteilung R* could enter).

Further information on the unit is given in the section relating to *6. Kompanie/SS-WMS-Btl.*

4.4: Operational Employment

It seems that the one company of the *Wachmannschaft I (Ostvölker)*, or *Trawniki* company, continued to be used mainly for guard and escort duties until the end of the war. On the other hand, after the training period almost all companies of the *SS-WMS-Btl.* formed by local elements (*Wachmannschaft II*) or at least part of them were moved out of Trieste for operational employment. Apparently, this consisted mainly in the manning of outposts (*Stützpunkt*) located in strategic locations along main communication lines or near important infrastructure, and their protection against sabotage and partisan attacks.[65]

The little available information shows that at least some of the companies were integrated in the *Sicherungskommandant* structure: this was the network of commanders responsible for the security of the communication lines and infrastructure, which was progressively created in the region starting from spring 1944 (see the specific section). As already mentioned, Wirth, and after him Allers, were nominated *Sicherungskommandant* for the Trieste–Fiume road (the Karststrasse), and had *6. Kp./SS-WMS-Btl.* under their command for this task. Employment under the orders of a Sicherungskommandant is also documented for the battalion's *4.* and probably *2. Kompanie*. Sometimes, as already mentioned, officers from the *SS-WMS-Btl.* (at least Franz and probably Schwarz) became *Sicherungskommandant* in the respective activity areas.

For almost all companies, the little information available on their employment comes mainly from the list of losses, which is largely incomplete: for the German personnel data have been found (although probably fragmentary) only for the period from late May to mid-June 1944, for the non-German personnel (indicated as "*fremdvölkische Angehörige*") there are data for the period from early May to mid-July.[66] An

Men of the *SS-Wachmannschaften*, probably Slovenian. Two types of tunics are worn, the Italian mod. 40 tunic produced for the Italian Royal army (rarely used by the members of this unit instead of the "*Heer* M40/M41 style" tunic) and the "transitional" tunic with the black collar. On this basis, the photo is likely to have been taken in January or February 1944. The man in the *Ordnungspolizei* uniform is probably a German trainer. *MNZS*

Trainers (wearing the "transitional" tunic with black collar) and recruits belonging to the *SS-Wachmannschaften* of the OZAK, seen probably before March 1944. On the right edge is partly visible a man from the *Ordnungspolizei*, perhaps the unit commander.

Two photos showing young Italian soldiers of the *SS-Wachmannschaften* training with a Brixia mod. 35 light mortar in March 1944. Note that the soldier holds the shell upside down, and that there is a security cap on the fuse; this shows clearly that these are propaganda pictures. *MNZS, NI5_628*

Soldiers of the *SS-Wachmannschaften* seen in a propaganda photo taken near the Duino castle, near Trieste, probably during the first quarter of 1944. They wear SS and *Ordnungspolizei* helmets. *MNZS, NI5_1292*

The uniform pattern visible on this and the above photo ("*Heer* M40/M41 style" tunics) was worn until around March 1944. Although it was apparently used with no distinctive features by the *SS-Wachmannschaften* as well as the *Landschutz*, the presence of a helmet with double SS decals seems to confirm that these soldiers belonged to the *SS-Wachmannschaften*. Visible are the outlined Italian national arm shield and the shoulder boards piped with white *Waffenfarbe*. *MNZS, Nemci30*

Four photos showing an anti-aircraft unit of the *SS-Wachmannschaften* (perhaps the *leichter Flakzug* of the *SS-Wachmannschafts-Btl.*) during an exercise at the Trieste port. They wear "transitional" tunics without collar tabs, it is therefore likely that the photos were taken between March and April 1944. Some soldiers wear tricolor Italian national arm shields. *MNZS, NI11_683, 684, 815, 816*

exception is *6. Kompanie*, on which there is information (although in any case very scarce and incomplete) from some personal accounts.

Information on employment for the various units is given in the following sections. Additionally, on the basis of photographic evidence it is known that unidentified elements of the *SS-WMS-Btl.* (among which, based on the list of losses, at least parts of *4. Kompanie*) participated between the end of April and early May 1944 to the *Unternehmen Braunschweig*, which is dealt with in a specific section.

Stabskompanie/SS-WMS-Btl.

There is no information on its employment, but it seems likely that it was based in Trieste, perhaps on Via Combi. The only known data is that a

Members of the *SS-Wachmanschaften*, at least partially Slovenian (according to the national arm shield worn by the first man on the right), probably photographed between March and April 1944. They all seem to be wearing "transitional" tunics, except maybe the second from left. One of them is a medic according to the specific arm band. *Courtesy Branko Čermelj*

This photo, probably taken in Trieste between March and April 1944, shows Globocnik (third from the right) during a ceremony together with SS and *Polizei* officers; the *SS-Ustuf.* in the middle might be Franz. The young soldiers in the room should be *landeseigene Kräfte* (local) recruits belonging to the *SS-Wachmannschaften*, perhaps still undergoing training; they wear "transitional" tunics, with black collar and piped shoulder boards, but without collar tabs. The waiter on the left wears a tricolor Italian national arm shield. *MNZS, NI11_843*

Another photo of Globocnik and an unidentified *SS-Ustuf.* taken on the same occasion.

soldier belonging to the company was killed and one was wounded during the ambush between Senosecchia and Storie where Schwarzenbacher was killed on June 2, 1944.

1. Kompanie/SS-WMS-Btl.

At the end of February 1944, it was apparently based partly in Trieste and partly in Gorizia.[67] Any precise information on the company is missing. It seems that still in late May 1944, it had elements in Gorizia, since on May 23, one of its members was reported as missing, after he had not come back from an anti-partisan action in the village of Vertoiba.[68] It is also known that some Slovenes belonging to the *SS-WMS-Btl.*, probably from this company (or perhaps from *Kommando G.* or the *Flakzug*) were used to man the *Flak* weapons at the Gorizia airport.

Two men from the company were captured by partisans during the ambush between

Senosecchia and Storie where Schwarzenbacher was killed on June 2, 1944.

Since after summer 1944, *6. Kp./SS-WMS-Btl.* was renumbered *1. Kompanie*, it can be deduced that the original *1. Kompanie* had been disbanded in the meantime.

2. Kompanie/SS-WMS-Btl.

The company or at least part of it was moved to the Udine province probably already in early March 1944, when partisan sources mention the arrival of German troops in the village of Pinzano (northwest of Udine), who protected the train station and part of the railway line Gemona–Sacile. These troops also manned the fortified outpost on the Colle Pion hill, just east of Pinzano, which dominated the road bridge over the Tagliamento River between Pinzano and Ragogna and the Pinzano–Gemona railway line. This fortified position had been created using the uncompleted construction of a mausoleum that was to have hosted the remains of German fallen from World War I. On the basis of the data on losses mentioned further down (although referred to a later period), it seems likely that these were elements of *2. Kp./SS-WMS-Btl.*

The presence of this company in the Udine province is certain at least since mid-May 1944, when it is confirmed that *SS-Ustuf.* Schwarz had its command post in Gemona del Friuli; as mentioned, the officer (who was killed in San Pietro di Ragogna on June 19) had probably the role of a *Sicherungskommandant*. In addition to *2. Kp./SS-WMS-Bt*l., Schwarz had at its disposal in Gemona also an Italian *Compagnia Autonoma di Sicurezza* (independent security company) belonging to the *Guardia di Finanza* (Finance Guard); it was subdivided in outposts from Reana del Rojale to Gemona, from Gemona to Sacile, and from Pinzano towards Casarsa, with road policing tasks.[69]

Three Italian soldiers from *2. Kp./SS-WMS-Btl.* were captured by the partisans and then killed near Gemona on May 30, while on the same day another Italian soldier from the company died in an accident on the road Cusano–Pordenone.

Elements of the company were probably still in Trieste in early June; the unit in fact suffered six dead, two wounded (one of whom died later), and three missing during the ambush between Senosecchia and Storie where Schwarzenbacher was killed on June 2, 1944.

Part of the company was in Udine in mid-June: three of its soldiers billeted in the city were killed, one was wounded, and one taken prisoner in a fight against the partisans near Ravosa, near

A photo published in the issue number 14 of the periodical *Adria Illustrierte* of April 24, 1944, showing, from the left, Rainer, Globocnik, and Schwarzenbacher while inspecting a unit of the *SS-Wachmannschaften* during training on the Carso plateau.

Rainer and Schwarzenbacher reviewing the soldiers, who are wearing "transitional" tunics.

SS-Wachmannschaften recruits, perhaps Slovenian, during training with an Italian 81 mm mod. 35 mortar on the Carso plateau. The trainee, wearing an *Ordnungspolizei* uniform, is probably a *Reichsdeutscher*. Since "simil-*Sipo*/SD" tunics are worn, the photo was probably taken after mid-April 1944; the rhomboidal piped collar tabs were probably red. The truck transporting the soldiers is a Büssing NAG with registration number Pol-11697. *MNZS, 2393_2, 2393_4, 2393_?, 2387_5*

Members of an *Ordnungspolizei* unit (on the left), likely from *I. Btl./SS-Pol.Rgt. "Bozen,"* with soldiers from the *SS-Wachmannschaften* (on the right, wearing "simil-*Sipo*/SD" tunics) photographed probably in Istria near a German truck which hit a mine. On the right, in the background, a soldier seems to be wearing a camo outfit in Italian mod. 29 fabric, perhaps he was a member of *Abteilung R*. Near the truck, bandaged, is possibly the driver, probably belonging to *I. Btl./SS-Pol.Rgt. "Bozen." MNZS, 5881_12, 13*

Savorgnano al Torre (north of Udine) on June 12, after they had looted a house looking for comestibles.

At least from mid-June the Germans created outposts also in Ragogna, San Pietro di Ragogna and one protecting the road bridge on the Tagliamento River between Pinzano and Ragogna, which were probably all manned by soldiers of *2. Kp./SS-WMS-Btl.*

Following a firefight, the Germans captured two partisans, who were detained in the house-turned-barracks where the troops of the *Stützpunkt Pinzano* were based, near the village train station. The house was attacked by the partisans in the afternoon of June 20, to free the captured partisans, since their execution had been announced for the same day. The attack was successful: after a heavy firefight the garrison was forced to temporarily abandon the house and the prisoners were freed;[70] a soldier from *2. Kp./SS-WMS-Btl.* was reported as missing after the fight. The following day, June 21, the Flagogna outpost was also attacked by a partisan unit and four Italians soldiers of the company were wounded. Elements of *2. Kp./SS-WMS-Btl.* probably protected also the "Cimano" railway bridge over the Tagliamento River, between Cornino and Majano: on June 8, one Italian soldier belonging to the company was wounded in Cornino, while on July 13, a soldier fell and four were wounded (all Italians) on the Cimano bridge during an air raid. This bridge was damaged beyond repair by Allied aircraft towards the end of the month and the outpost was probably withdrawn.

There is no more information on *2. Kp./SS-WMS-Btl.* after mid-July. The following two episodes of partisan attacks on Pinzano and Colle Pion in early September, may concern the company, but this is not certain. On September 2, 1944, the commander of the partisan *3. Osoppo Brigade* communicated to his divisional headquarters that seven "Russians" who had been part of the German outpost in Pinzano had deserted and gone over to the partisans; perhaps they were *Trawniki* of the *SS-WMS-Btl.*, or perhaps Cossacks.[71] In the evening of September 5, the German fortified positions of the Colle Pion mausoleum were attacked by two partisan detachments belonging to the "*Giustizia*" and "*Italia*" battalions from *3. Osoppo Brigade*; the partisans captured several light weapons among which some machine guns indicated as "Skoda," and the defenders had some (however not quantified) losses.[72]

At an unknown date, but perhaps at the end of August or during September, a Cossack squadron moved to Pinzano, probably replacing the elements of *2. Kp./SS-WMS-Btl.* that had been based there. At the end of October also *10. Kp./SS-Pol.Rgt. 12* arrived in the area: it took up its base in San Daniele del Friuli and had the tasks of protecting the bridge of Villuzza and patrolling in particular the roads around San Pietro di Ragogna, Pinzano, Valeriano, Lestans, and Sequals, in cooperation

These five photos show recruits of the *SS-Wachmannschaften* during training in spring or summer 1944. Visible are two German trainers, one of whom wears a cap with an *Ordnungspolizei* eagle, the other a cap with a *Totenkopf*. Also the recruit taking his food wears a tropical sidecap with an SS eagle and a *Totenkopf*. *MNZS, NI11_689, 691, 692, 694, 966*

with the Cossack squadron of Pinzano.[73] It seems likely that the Cossack squadron and the Schutzpolizei company had replaced *2. Kp./SS-WMS-Btl.* in the area of Ragogna–Pïnzano.

There is no information on the further employment of *2. Kp./SS-WMS-Btl.* after mid-July 1944, but it is likely that it remained at least for some time in the area of Gemona, since four of its men deserted to the partisans in that area in October 1944.

3. Kompanie/SS-WMS-Btl.

At the end of February 1944, it was apparently based partly in Pola and partly in Fiume.[74] For later periods no data are available on its dislocation and employment. The only information is that a soldier from the company (a *Reichdeutscher*) was wounded by partisans during the ambush between Senosecchia and Storie where Schwarzenbacher was killed on June 2, 1944.

In February 1945, among the units under the orders of the *Kampfkommandant Fiume* (*Oberst* Josef Brandl, commander of *Reserve-Gebirgs-Jäger-Rgt. 138*) there was an SS company from the *SS-u.Pol.Kommandeur* for the Quarnero Province (who was *SS-Obersturmbannführer* Wilhelm Traub),[75] which may have been a company of *SS-Wachmannschaften*, although this is not confirmed.

4. Kompanie/SS-WMS-Btl.

This company was probably formed by the end of April 1944. At least from the second half of May it was transferred to Senosecchia, on the Trieste–Postumia road; it was put at the disposal of the *Sicherungskommandant* in Adelsberg (the German name of Postumia), *Hptm.d.Gend.* Rieck, and tasked with manning some *Stützpunkt* on the Trieste–Postumia road together with other units. The *Sicherungskommandant* in Adelsberg—who despite its name had its seat in Senosecchia in this period, then in Storie (June – mid-July), then again in Senosecchia (from mid-July) and later in Postumia—had the responsibility of ensuring the protection of the Opicina (excluded)–Sesana–Storie–Senosecchia–Postumia–Planina road, and of the Opicina (excluded)–Sesana–Divaccia–San Pietro del Carso–Postumia–Rakek (excluded) railway line. He had at his disposal, in addition to *4. Kp./SS-WMS-Btl.*, some Slovenian companies belonging to the SNVZ, coordinated by the *Stab des slowenischen Landschutzes* based in Postumia: these were *4.*, *5.*, and *7. Kompanie*, respectively based (on June 1) in Postumia, Prevallo (or Preval), and San Pietro del Carso.[76] The forces of the SNVZ and *4. Kp./SS-WMS-Btl.* manned some outposts together: in late May, the SS company had a heavy weapons platoon (*schwerer Zug*) in Prevallo together with two platoons (three officers and eighty NCOs and enlisted personnel) of *5. Kp./SNVZ*, while a platoon of *5. Kp./SNVZ* was in Senosecchia with the rest of *4. Kp./SS-WMS-Btl.* Perhaps already in this period elements of *4. Kp./SS-WMS-Btl.* were also in the village of Storie.

Parts of the company probably took part in the *Unternehmen Braunschweig* between the end of April and early May; a Croatian soldier belonging to the unit was wounded on May 3 in Mattuglie.

The commander of the *SS-WMS-Btl.* Schwarzenbacher was killed during the ambush between Senosecchia and Storie on June 2, 1944, and *4. Kompanie* had two dead, one wounded, and five missing.

In the late evening of June 5, 1944, partisan units belonging to the Slovenian *XVII Brigade "Simon Gregorčič"* and the Italian Assault Brigade "Trieste" attacked the Prevallo outpost. According to a report by an SNVZ officer, the *Stützpunkt* consisted of eight defensive positions, each equipped with a heavy machine gun, which were occupied in turns by the Slovenes of the SNVZ and the Croats of *4. Kp./SS-WMS-Btl.*; the former were replaced by the latter every evening at 1800. The partisan attack was very violent and came from all sides; the defenders abandoned some positions and the partisans entered the village, but after a four-hour fight they were pushed back.[77] According to the war diary of the *"Trieste" Brigade* the defenders suffered five dead and eleven prisoners and the Partisans captured three Breda heavy machine guns, three 81 mm mortars with 400 shells, and twenty-five rifles with 3,000 rounds of ammunition. However, according to the list of losses of the *SS-WMS-Btl.*, the unit only had four wounded and six missing.[78]

After the battle, since the majority of the buildings in Prevallo were destroyed or damaged, the outpost was abandoned and *5. Kp./SNVZ* was moved to Storie. On June 20, the *Stützpunkt Storie* was manned by the following units under the command of *Hptm.d.Gend.* Lehnick (who held the position of *Sicherungskommandant* in Adelsberg and had his seat in Storie):

- *SS-Wachmannschaften* (evidently parts of *4. Kp./SS-WMS-Btl.*): one officer, one NCO, forty-seven enlisted personnel, armed with three Italian heavy machine guns, one Italian light machine gun, three Italian mortars, one Italian sub-machine gun, forty-four rifles, sixty-nine hand grenades.
- *5. slowenische Kompanie* (of the SNVZ; probably these were the two platoons formerly in Prevallo): one officer, seventy-six enlisted personnel, armed with four Italian light machine guns, one light Italian mortar, six Italian sub-machine guns, seventy-seven rifles, and 158 hand grenades.[79]

A little later *5. Kp./SNVZ* was replaced in Storie by *11. Kp./SNVZ* and apparently, for unknown reasons, *4. Kp./SS-WMS-Btl.* abandoned Senosecchia and was gathered in Storie. In fact on July 10, 1944, an order by the *SS-u.Pol. Kommandeur* for the Trieste province, *SS-Brigadeführer* von Malsen-Ponickau, set out that:

- *4. Kp./SS-WMS-Btl.* and *11. Kp./SNVZ*, based in Storie under the command of *Hptm.d.Gend.* Lehnick, were to be transferred under the command of *Rev. Ltn.d.SchP.* Mechold.
- On a date that would be further communicated by von Malsen, the *Stützpunkt Senosecchia* was to be occupied and *Ltn.* Mechold was to become its commander; after completing the organization of the *Stützpunkt Senosecchia*, Lehnick was to move to Postumia.

The *11. Kp./SNVZ* was transferred to Senosecchia on July 20, probably around the same date also *4. Kp./SS-WMS-Btl.* moved there. On August 4, von Malsen-Ponickau assigned the command of the *Stützpunkt Senosecchia* to Mechold and subordinated to him all forces in the town, that is the two companies and unspecified elements of *SS-Pol.Rgt. 10*.

After this date there is no more information available on the company, with the exception that it was included (with the name *4. SS-Wachmannschafts-Kompanie*) in a list of units subordinated to the *Befehlshaber der Orpo* in the OZAK on March 17, 1945, with the indication that it was still based in Senosecchia.[80]

5. Kompanie/SS-WMS-Btl.

It was probably formed by the end of April 1944. No information is available on its dislocation and employment. A Ukrainian *Trawniki* belonging to the company was reported missing in Starada near Castelnuovo on May 24, 1944. Additionally, another Ukrainian *Trawniki* from the company fell during the ambush between Senosecchia and Storie where Schwarzenbacher was killed on June 2, 1944.

6. Kompanie/SS-WMS-Btl.

It was formed around mid-May 1944 at the Risiera di San Sabba complex, using some of the Italian soldiers of the disbanded *Battaglione Davide*. The company numbered initially (June) around eighty-five men from *Battaglione Davide*, all Italians (among them five officers), as well as a limited number of Germans and *Trawniki* as cadres. Its commander was *SS-Ustuf.* Oberhauser; deputy commander was *SS-Uscha.* Bolender (at least in 1945, but probably already before).[81]

The company remained based at the Risiera until the end of the war. Its men were billeted in the building facing the entrance, on the right, on the first courtyard. The unit guarded the entrance to the complex, the first courtyard, and the Risiera external perimeter but not for the internal section around the second courtyard, which was separated from the first courtyard by a gate, where the prisoners were detained and only *Abteilung R* personnel could enter. During the entire stay in San Sabba, the Italian company members had practically no contact with the prisoners; the soldiers were strictly forbidden to enter the second courtyard and to communicate with the prisoners.

In addition to guarding the Risiera complex, the main task for the company was to contribute to guaranteeing security on the Trieste–Fiume road, under the orders of the *Sicherungskommandant der Karststrasse*, function held by Wirth and then by Allers.[82] This task included manning outposts and participating in anti-partisan actions. The main *Stützpunkt* manned by the company was Castelnuovo d'Istria (probably with a sub-post in Starada) and later Mattuglie; evidently the Italian soldiers were sent there to integrate and strengthen the elements of *Abteilung R* who were already based in these outposts.

On the *Stützpunkt* service there is very little information. Some data can be extrapolated from the personal registration cards that have been found for forty-two Italian soldiers of *6. Kp./SS-WMS-Btl.*, which list each soldier's movements from San Sabba to the Castelnuovo outpost and viceversa (no card mentions Mattuglie).[83] It appears that the first group of soldiers of this company was sent to the *Stützpunkt Castelnuovo* on May 18, 1944 (a date surprisingly close to the disarmament of *Battaglione Davide* and the integration of part of its men into the *SS-WMS-Btl.*). It was followed by a second group of soldiers on May 28. From this date, the command of the Castelnuovo detachment of *6. Kp./SS-WMS-Btl.* was taken up by *SS-Oberzugwachmann* (formerly *capitano*) Ernesto Sarzano;[84] from the same date also, *SS-Zugwachmann* (formerly *tenente*) Luigi Fulmine was in Castelnuovo. The men were billeted in the former Carabinieri barracks. Two sections for a total of twenty men were also sent to a *Casa cantoniera* (road inspector's house), probably near the village of Starada, also on the Karststrasse around three kilometers southeast of Castelnuovo; on July 23, most men serving in Starada deserted after contacting the local partisans, among them was *SS-Zugwachmann* (formerly *tenente*) Aldo Cerrato.[85] Still on the basis of the personnel cards, part of the Castelnuovo detachment was moved back to San Sabba on August 25, some other men on September 21, some more on October 23; they were replaced by other groups of men from *6. Kompanie*, who from the Risiera were sent to Castelnuovo on August 25, September 9 and 18, and October 23. A document dated November 8, 1944, confirms that on that day elements of the company, in the meantime renumbered *1. Kompanie* (see later), were still manning the Castelnuovo *Stützpunkt* under the command of Sarzano.[86] From the personnel cards it appears that the soldiers who arrived at the outpost on October 23, went back to San Sabba either on November 8 or 15; no other assignments to Castelnuovo were noted on the personnel cards after that date, so that it might be that the outpost was transferred to other units.

As for the outpost in Mattuglie, it seems that the first detachment from *6. Kompanie* was moved there on July 16; it consisted of two sections for a total of twenty men and was based in the building of the OMNI hospital, on the town main road, together with a German unit (probably men from section R II of *Abteilung R*). On July 28, following the desertion in Castelnuovo, most men of *6. Kompanie* in Mattuglie also went over to the partisans, including *SS-Zugwachmann* (formerly *tenente*) Mario Ferrero (brother of the former battalion commander "Davide"). The fleeing soldiers were chased by the Germans who had to retreat when attacked by partisans who, as agreed in advance, were awaiting the deserters.[87] It is likely, although not confirmed, that the Mattuglie outpost was left to other units from mid-November 1944. The company was then probably concentrated in San Sabba, where it surely was in April 1945.

Regarding the anti-partisan operations to which *6. Kompanie* (both the part that remained in San Sabba as well as the soldiers assigned to the *Stützpunkt*) participated, information is also scarce.

Elements of the company coming from San Sabba were engaged in an anti-partisan operation on June 21, 1944. It was a surprise action against the village of Calcizza, northwest of Castelnuovo d'Istria, an area where the partisans were constantly present and from where they threatened the Trieste–Fiume road. Probably only one platoon from the Risiera took part, led by Oberhauser together with Bolender. Participating in the operation was *2. Kompanie/3. Rgt. Brandenburg*, at that time based in Castelnuovo, which went into action on a larger area north of the Matteria–Castelnuovo road (between the villages of Merse–Slivia–Orecchia–Tatre–Cuie–Crussizza) where it tried to engage the partisans. The *Brandenburg* unit had some exchanges of fire with the partisans, while for the *SS-Wachmannschaften* the action ended with no contact with the enemy and no noteworthy incidents.[88] The *Kriegstagebuch* (war diary) of the *Brandenburg* company mentions the participation to the action of a platoon of "*landeseigene SS*" (local SS), which were most likely elements of *6. Kp./SS-WMS-Btl.* The description of the operation from the *Kriegstagebuch* is transcribed:

> 6/20–21/1944: operation in the area fifteen kilometers northwest of Castelnuovo. Around 2000, the combat elements [of *2. Kompanie/3. Rgt. Brandenburg*] set off.
>
> *I. Zug* starts out at 2200. At 2400, *I. Zug* is fired at by a partisan sentry at the crossroad 500 meters southeast of Merse.
>
> *II. Zug* marches through Crussizza. Civilians report that a reconnaissance squad with five bandits [= partisans] was in the village in the afternoon. The march continues via Cuie (completely burned down). North of Cuie six partisans in waiting position are spotted. After a short firefight they retreat towards Gabrega.
>
> *I. Zug* marches with compass from the crossroad towards Tatre. The platoon falls in an ambush and is stopped for a rather long time. Enemy strength around twenty men. Despite the significant difficulties caused by the terrain the platoon advances on the road towards Tatre via Orecchia. Some bandits are seen discussing with civilians in the centre of the village. One bandit is captured. Three civilians are also arrested. Another civilian, who declares to have been prisoner of the partisans, is taken with us. The bandits were in the village looking for food.
>
> During the march towards Tatre, *II. Zug* captures a civilian, who shows us the road. Gabrega is enemy free. At 0715 *II. Zug* arrives in Tatre.
>
> In the meantime at 0145 of 6/21/1944, *III. Zug* reaches the junction north of Slivia. A scout group explores the terrain around Slivia. No enemy forces are identified. At the Slivia church the platoon splits, the starting positions are reached. One group skirts the village, and 200 meters behind the church is taken under enemy fire. The village is searched and some weapons are found. Blood traces indicate that the enemy has suffered some losses. *Oblt.* Straub [commander of *2. Kp./3. Rgt. Brandenburg*] advances with two groups on Orecchia, outflanks the village and searches the houses. A bandits' supply cache is found. West of Orecchia a telephone cable is found and destroyed. Some observation posts on the Matteria–Castelnuovo road are also identified.
>
> *VI. Zug*, formed by local SS ("*landeseigene SS*"), marches during the night from Gradischie via Rittomece to Calcizza, surrounds the village and searches it at dawn. No contact with the enemy. The platoon marches on via Orecchia and makes contact with *Oblt.* Straub. At 1015, end of the operation, back to Castelnuovo.[89]

It is likely that *6. Kp./SS-WMS-Btl.* was often employed for actions of this type in areas close to the Karststrasse. The proposal for awarding Bolender the *Eisernes Kreuz II. Klasse* (Iron Cross Second Class), drawn up probably at the end of 1944 (the award was approved in January 1945) mentions his participation to numerous anti-partisan actions, probably conducted with men of *6. Kp./SS-WMS-Btl.* In particular, an action on Monte Lisina (in the Ciceria region, northwest of Mattuglie) that took place on August 19, 1944, is mentioned, during which, "a platoon of the *Kommando*, temporarily surrounded by the enemy, was relieved from its difficult predicament" thanks to Bolender's personal intervention.[90] The mentioned "*Kommando*" was probably an MDT platoon which participated in this operation; on this regard in fact the bulletin of the RSI *Guardia Nazionale Repubblicana* (= MDT) for the Fiume province reported on September 11, 1944:

> On August 18, thirty soldiers of *3. Reggimento MDT*, under the command of *Sottotenente* Aurelio Piesz, with two companies of German police and SS units conducted a sweep operation in an area between Starada and Vele Lasi. The [MDT] platoon, having received the order to occupy the Rossi hut on the Monte Lisina, reached the place and captured seven bandits, who were inside the

building and were taken by surprise. Shortly thereafter the outlaws, realizing that their headquarters had been occupied by the [MDT] soldiers, assaulted the hut with two companies, supported by the fire of machine guns and an 81 mm mortar. Our soldiers resisted bravely against this attack for around three hours, killing in the fighting five bandits. In the meantime German troops arrived and relieved our unit; the bandits however, having retreated to a more secure position, carried on the fight, but were overwhelmed by the fire of our artillery and by the élan of our soldiers. In this latter action it is presumed that the bandits had around sixty losses including dead and wounded.[91]

Elements of *6. Kp./SS-WMS-Btl.* belonging both to the Castelnuovo outpost and to the main group based at the Risiera, as well as elements of *Abteilung R*, participated in an action to relieve the German outpost of Elsane (village just north of the Rupa junction, on the Fiume–Postumia road), attacked by partisans on September 2, 1944. According to a detailed German report, in that period Elsane was occupied by *2. Kp./ Sicherungs-Bataillon (M) 1218*; however, on August 31, most of its forces were moved out to participate to the anti-partisan operations *Unternehmen Hochkönig* and *Traunsee*;[92] in Elsane remained only a group of around twenty men, divided in seven defensive positions. At dawn on September 2, the village was attacked by strong partisan forces, making it necessary for several other units to intervene to relieve the outpost. According to the report, the intervening forces were SS/*Polizei* from Castelnuovo (but actually reinforcements also came from the Risiera, consisting of one truck with 20–30 Italian and German soldiers) with two *Schützenpanzer* (armored troop transport vehicles, probably armoured trucks), a *Vierlingsflak* (anti-aircraft quadruple 2 cm machine gun), a *Nebelwerfer* (rocket-launcher), and one Italian 3.7 cm gun (probably recte: 4.7 cm) commanded by an unidentified *Oberstleutnant*. This officer was probably Allers and the unit was formed by elements of *Abteilung R* and Italians from *6. Kp./ SS-WMS-Btl.* According to the report, the commander of the Italian soldiers, a *capitano*, fell during the fighting in Elsane; this information is most probably not correct and originates because of a case of mistaken identity between *Capitano* Ernesto Sarzano (who was present during the action) and his brother Ettore Sarzano, who actually fell in Elsane on September 2, but was not an officer. Other forces that intervened to help the Elsane outpost were *6. Kp./Reserve-Gebirgs-Jäger-Rgt. 139* from Villa del Nevoso, the *mot. Pakgruppe* (motorized anti-tank unit) of *Gebirgs-Bataillon Heine* (belonging to *188. Reserve-Gebirgs-Division*) from Sappiane and a platoon from the Rupa outpost (Rupa junction) of *3. Reggimento MDT* led by *Tenente* Aurelio Piesz with two mortars. After heavy fighting these forces managed to repel the partisan attack by the end of the day.[93]

There is no further information on actions against the partisans which involved the men of the *Stützpunkt* of Castelnuovo or Mattuglie. However, the memoirs of an officer of *2. Compagnia* of *3. Reggimento MDT*, based in Mattuglie from mid-October, then (from the end of January 1945) in Giordani, and finally (from late March) at the Rupa junction, mention numerous anti-partisan actions carried out by his unit from October 1944 to March 1945, sometimes together with the SS from Castelnuovo or Trieste. These were made up, in addition to elements of *Abteilung R*, probably also by elements of *6. Kp./SS-WMS-Btl.* (at that time already re-numbered *1. Kompanie*). The places where these actions were conducted are not always named in the memoirs, but mentioned are Tatre, Tomigna, and the triangle Gabrega–Succorie–Prelose (all villages north of Castelnuovo) and upper Istria (i.e., probably the Ciceria south of Castelnuovo).[94]

In addition, elements of *6. Kp./SS-WMS-Btl.* were also sometimes used as escort during the arrests of Jews and confiscation of their properties operated by *Abteilung R*. The little information available on these activities comes from the memoirs of Dante Fangaresi, former member of *Battaglione Davide*, then integrated in *6. Kp./SS-WMS-Btl.* at the Risiera until July 16, 1944, when he deserted. Between late May and early July, parts of the company escorted German SS personnel during a night raid in the Trieste Jewish ghetto, during which numerous people were arrested, brought to the Risiera, and on the next day deported to Germany.[95] On June 5, around fifty company members were temporarily transferred to Abbazia, a famous holiday town on the coast of eastern Istria; on the next day they escorted German personnel in civilian clothes (belonging perhaps to *Abteilung R* or to the *Gestapo*) on a tour during which they inspected some luxurios villas in the area. The same happened the next day in the nearby town of Laurana. The purpose of these inspections is not known, but it seems—according to what was understood by Fangaresi (who—when possible—alerted the inhabitants to the danger)—that the objective was to plan future actions, perhaps the arrest of the inhabitants or the confiscation of their properties.[96]

Additionally, still according to Fangaresi, on June 15, company members were employed as security in the anti-aircraft bunker of the Servola hill, in Trieste, during an Allied air raid. On July 6, they participated in clearing damage at the Aquila oil refinery site, hit during an air raid on the city.

Kommando G.

At the beginning of 1944 some elements of the *SS-WMS-Btl.* were transferred to Gorizia under the command of *SS-Ustuf.* Kurt Franz, with the main task to train *Landschutz* recruits.[97] This group was indicated as *Kommando G.*, where *G* stood probably for Görz, the German name of Gorizia.[98]

Franz was trainer and platoon commander of a platoon of Italian recruits of the *SS-WMS-Btl.* in Trieste during winter 1943–44. In January 1944, with his trained platoon he was transferred to Gorizia. Here according to Franz (who was billeted on Via Leopardi) he was the only member of *Dienststelle* Wirth (Wirth's unit), that is of *Abteilung R*. His task was to set up a *Landschutzschule* to train local units' recruits; the school was based at the then-Opera Balilla (Fascist youth organization) building (today still hosting a school, on Largo G. Culiat).

Franz and his men also participated in propaganda and recruitment (voluntary or forced, as seen) actions for the *Landschutz*, targeting the inhabitants of the villages of the Gorizia province.[99] According to Franz, after 6–8 weeks of training the recruits were sent to their final units; probably they were mainly transferred to the SNVZ, but it is possible that part of them were also integrated in the *SS-WMS-Btl.* Still according to Franz, the recruits wore "*Waffen-SS* uniforms but other ranks," a definition that may hint (rather than at the rank insignia) at the specific rank names used by the *Landschutz* and the *SS-Wachmannschaften.*

A brief article, published in the German language newspaper *Deutsche Adria Zeitung* in Trieste on May 9, 1944, reported that two days earlier a company of Slovenian *Landschutz* had arrived in Gorizia, welcomed at the train station by the *SS-Wachmannschaft* based in the city (probably parts of *Kommando G.*, or perhaps of *1. Kp./SS-WMS-Btl.*) and by soldiers of the Slovenian *Landschutzschule.*[100]

Still according to Franz, his original platoon was progressively enlarged to the size of a company through the integration of trained recruits on a voluntary basis. It is not documented, however, that the unit led by Franz was ever formally elevated to company status in the *SS-WMS-Btl.*; it probably remained an independent unit inside the battalion, probably keeping the name of *Kommando G.* According to Franz's declarations, his company was employed to protect the building sites of the defensive lines around Gorizia, and later also to patrol a section of the Gorizia–Trieste railway line. It was also certainly used in anti-partisan operations.

In spring 1944, Franz also became *Sicherungskommandant* for the sector of San Daniele del Carso; despite its title he had his seat in Gorizia and was subordinated to the *SS-u.Pol. Kommandeur* in Gorizia, *SS-Sturmbannführer* Karl Tauss. In this function, Franz was responsible for the protection of the road and railway line Gorizia–Montespino–Rifembergo–San Daniele del Carso–Duttogliano–Opicina. Strangely, for this task he had at his orders—at least on June 20, 1944, the only date for which there are precise data—only Italian RSI units, but no forces from the *SS-WMS-Btl.*[101]

Franz was wounded during an action against the partisans probably in October 1944, and came back to Italy after a convalescence in February 1945. Assigned again to Gorizia, he was again used as *Sicherungskommandant* and as trainer for a *Brigate Nere* unit. According to Franz, during his absence his company had been decimated near Montespino; date and circumstances of this event are not known.[102]

Leichter Flakzug

No specific information is available on composition, dislocation, and employment of the leichter *Flakzug* of the *SS-WMS-Btl.* The only available piece of information is that in mid-September 1944 the *leichter Flakzug* and a *Vierling* quadruple anti-aircraft gun of *SS-WMS-Btl.* were subordinated to the *Höherer Sicherungsstab* (the headquarters tasked with the protection of the building sites of the defensive lines built under the responsibility of Rainer), which on September 17, ordered them to move to the area south of Mira (between Mestre and Padova, in the Veneto region).[103]

Elements of the battalion also manned the *Flak* weapons that defended the Gorizia airport; it is not known if they belonged to the *Flakzug, 1. Kompanie or Kommando G.*

4.5: Further Evolution of the *SS-Wachmannschafts-Btl./SS-Wachmannschaften* (Autumn 1944-45)

After summer 1944, information on the *SS-Wachmannschaften* of the OZAK is extremely scarce and their evolution is unknown. The last mention of the designation "*SS-WMS-Btl.*" which has been found is in a Verteiler dated August 27, 1944. After that date, in some documents dated from November 1944 to April 1945, only the designation "*SS-Wachmannschaften*" has been found, sometimes with the indication of the company number (for instance: *SS-Wachmannschaften, 1. Kp.*), but no reference to the battalion; also found is the designation *4. SS-Wachmannschafts-Kompanie*, used in March 1945. Despite the absence of information, it could be speculated that this change indicated a modification in the structure of the battalion: it is possible that its headquarters were disbanded, perhaps following its downsizing and the disbandment of some companies, and that the remaining companies became autonomous, operating under the control of the various *Sicherungskommandeur*.[104]

It is likely that during the summer the battalion strength was reduced because of personnel transfers to *24. Waffen-Gebirgs (Karstjäger)-Division der SS*, which was being formed starting from July 1944.[105] Combat losses and desertions must also have contributed to reducing the battalion size, but it is not possible to speculate on its strength after summer 1944.

It seems also that the *Trawniki* company, or *Wachmannschaft I (Ostvölker)*, at a certain point (probably during October 1944) was detached from the battalion; this was most probably the company indicated in various organization charts of forces subordinated to the HSSPF OZAK or in Verteiler, starting from the second half of October 1944, variably as *SS-Wachmannschafts-Kompanie, SS-Wachkompanie* or *Wachkompanie-HSSPF* (none of these organization charts or lists mentioned the *SS-WMS-Btl.*). The company existed until the end of the war, under the command of Eibisch; it remained based at the "Dante Alighieri" schools on Via Giustiniano, from where it continued to perform mainly guard and escort duties.

Additionally, surely already from late summer or early autumn 1944, at least some of the battalion's six companies formed by local elements (*Wachmannschaft II*) were re-numbered, probably also following the disbandment or merging of some of them. The *6. Kompanie* (formerly *Battaglione Davide*) became *1. Kompanie*, remaining under the command of Oberhauser. Probably the former *1. Kompanie* was disbanded or integrated in other companies.

An undated document, surely drafted later than January 1945, provided information for the "*SS-Wachmannschaften, 1. Kompanie*":

- *Kompanieführer* (company commander): *SS-Ostuf.* Oberhauser
- *Kompanieführer-Stellvertreter* (deputy company commander): *SS-Uscha.* Bolender
- *Stabs-Scharführer* (senior NCO, colloquially called *Spieß*): *SS-Uscha.* Baer
- *Furier* (quartermaster): *SS-Uscha.* Sporleder, *SS-Zugwachm.* Rosenke, A.

• 1. *Zug* (commander of first platoon): *SS-Uscha*. Bolender (with *1.*, *2.* and *6. Gruppe*, each with ten men).[106]

As it can be seen, all Germans and *Trawniki* serving in the company listed in this document belonged to *Abteilung R*. From the surnames of the thirty Italian soldiers belonging to *1. Zug* listed in the same document, it appears that all were Italians and that only a small part (four out of thirty) had belonged to the former *Battaglione Davide*; new recruits or soldiers coming from other companies of the battalion had therefore been inserted in the former *6. Kompanie* (formerly *Battaglione Davide*).[107] This must have been made necessary by losses and desertions; it is in fact ascertained that of the 122 names in the list of soldiers of *6. Kompanie* probably dating from May 1944 (but, many were excluded within a few weeks and deported to Germany, bringing down the number of soldiers in the company to around eighty-five), around forty were still serving in the *SS-Wachmannschaften* in early 1945, while at least forty-five had deserted, most of whom joined the partisans. All this indicates that in this phase the composition of the companies of the *SS-Wachmannschaften* (at least those formed mainly by Italians) had changed.

The *4. SS-Wachmannschafts-Kompanie* was apparently still based in Senosecchia on March 17, 1945 (company formed by Croats; evidently it was not re-numbered). Information on the other companies (possible re-numbering or disbandment) is completely lacking.

Hypothetically, the *SS-Wachmannschaften* may have consisted in 1945 of the following units:

• *SS-Wachkompanie* (*Trawniki* company)
• *1. Kompanie/SS-Wachmannschaften* (at the Risiera; formerly *6. Kp./SS-WMS-Btl.*)
• *2. Kompanie/SS-Wachmannschaften* (in the Udine province?)
• *3. Kompanie/SS-Wachmannschaften* (in Fiume?)
• *4. Kompanie/SS-Wachmannschaften* (in Senosecchia)
• *Kraftfahrstaffel*
• *leichter Flakzug*

Forced recruitment in the *SS-Wachmannschaften* continued practically almost until the end of the war. In December 1944, for instance, a group of workers employed for the construction of defensive positions near the village of Piedimonte del Taiano was taken to the Risiera and forcibly recruited.[108] A document has been found listing items delivered on January 25, 1945, by the *Bekleidungslager* (clothing depot) of Sagrado, near Gorizia, to a unit indicated as "*SS-Wachmannschaften Triest – Abt. R.*"[109] The items included various pieces of equipment (uniform elements, cartridge pouches, backpacks, haversacks, cutlery, etc.) for several hundred men (perhaps 200 or 300, the numbers vary according to the item) which may indicate the intention of inserting a new group of recruits in the *SS-Wachmannschaften*. It is not known if this happened.

Forced recruitment still took place even in April 1945: a group of people from Pirano and other nearby villages, arrested by the SS of Portorose because they had evaded labor service, was sent to the Risiera in early April. There, together with others arrested in other places, they were partly inserted in the *SS-Wachmannschaften* (the younger ones, while the older people were sent to work on the building sites of the defensive lines on the Carso plateau). According to the account of a member of this group recruited in the *SS-Wachmannschaften*, who remained at the Risiera only two weeks in the first half of April, at that time two SS companies were based there, composed 60% by Italians. In addition, there were German and Ukrainian SS, commanded by a German first lieutenant and a Ukrainian officer (most probably an NCO). Still according to this account, due to the increased partisan activity also in the city, every night groups of soldiers left the Risiera to patrol or search the surrounding area.[110]

Elements of the *SS-Wachmannschaften* participated the last large anti-partisan operation conducted by the Germans in the OZAK, *Unternehmen Winterende*, which from March 19 to April 5, 1945, involved the Bainsizza (Banjšice) plateau, the Chiapovano valley (Čepovanski dol), and the Tarnova plateau (Trnovski gozd), north and east of Gorizia.[111] A soldier belonging to *1. Kp./SS-Wachmannschaften* was reported fallen northwest of the Monte Signi (Sinji vrh, just north of Aidussina) on March 27, 1945.

According to an account, an *SS-Wachmannschaften* unit based in Trieste (led by Eibisch) took part in the parade that was held in the city on April 20, 1945, to celebrate Hitler's birthday, and on that occasion the soldiers were sworn in. A few days afterwards three Italians from the same unit (two from Istria and one from Trieste) tried to desert but were arrested and shot.[112]

The final destiny of the *SS-Wachmannschaften* remains largely unknown. With the penetration of the Yugoslav army in the area between Fiume and Trieste in the last ten days of April 1945, it is likely that the *SS-Wachmannschaften* units that might still have been located in that area were taken back to Trieste, although some elements may have taken part in the fighting against the Yugoslavs.

As the Yugoslavs came closer and closer to Trieste in the last days of April and when Globocnik abandoned the city with the SS/*Polizei* headquarters in the night between April 29–30, the parts of the *SS-Wachmannschaften* based in the city probably disbanded, but some elements followed the German retreat towards Austria. The same can probably be said also for the elements that might still have been based in the Udine province. In fact, an *SS-Wachmannschaften* identity tag has been found in the area of Portis, near Venzone, north of Udine; probably it was lost or discarded during the last days of the war.

Any precise information is absent, with one exception: according to one former member of *Battaglione Davide*, integrated in the *SS-Wachmannschaften* as a guard in the Risiera until the end of the war, when the Germans abandoned Trieste the Italian soldiers based at the Risiera were loaded on trucks which drove in the direction of Udine. In Faedis, northeast of Udine (the city was probably avoided due to the dangerous situation there), the column was attacked by Allied airplanes and in the following confusion some Italian soldiers managed to flee.[113] Numerous former members of *Battaglione Davide* (for the most part originating from the Piedmont region) who served in the *SS-Wachmannschaften* managed subsequently to return to their homes.

The same happened presumably to many *SS-Wachmannschaften* soldiers originating from the OZAK provinces, in particular those that had been forcibly recruited (like the recruits from Pirano that were transferred from the *Landschutz* to the *SS-Wachmannschaften*, who did not suffer any consequences after they returned to their town). Others, those more compromised with the Germans, probably thought best to hide or flee, at least temporarily, not to be tried or executed; it is not possible to refer to specific situations, because to date there are no known cases of former members of this unit recruited in the OZAK who have recounted their experience.

After the war several former *Trawniki* lived for shorter or longer periods in Trieste. Probably most had belonged to the *SS-Wachmannschaften*, although it cannot be ruled out that some had been attached to *Abteilung R* and had served in the Risiera. Some remained temporarily, obtaining residence permits from the Italian authorities until they resettled to other countries; some even obtained Italian citizenship and remained in Trieste or in Italy.[114]

Uniforms and Personal Equipment of *Abteilung R*, and the *SS-Wachmannschaften* of the OZAK

Part I: Uniforms, Equipment, Individual and Group Weapons

This section deals with uniforms, equipment, individual and group weapons that *Abteilung R* and the *SS-Wachmannschaften* used in the OZAK.[1] When needed, references to the previous time frame related to the activities in Poland have been inserted.

As far as possible the original spelling used at the time in German and Italian documents has been mantained. The description of the military uniforms and equipment is based on official documentation. Where this has not been possible for some terms, the international terminology of the militaria collectors' community has been used.

This photo was taken in Warsaw in 1942. Sitting are, from left, August Hengst in civilian clothes, his wife, Karl Pötzinger, and an unknown *Trawniki*; standing are, from left, the *Volksdeutsche Trawniki* Bienemann and Libodenko (both were later with *Abteilung R* in the OZAK). Being formally a civilian, Pötzinger wears an SS uniform modified by replacing the SS runic collar tab with a blank one. *LA NRW, Münster*

1: Uniforms and Insignia

Since no regulations or official orders regarding the uniforms supplied to these units have been found to date, a definitive analysis has not been possible. The data which are presented here are sometimes based on first-hand accounts, but mainly they are deduced from the analysis of the scarce available pictorial documentation; therefore they are sometimes hypothetical and may be subject to revision or update based on possible future discoveries.

In the analysis of the uniforms it is necessary to distinguish between those used by the members of *Abteilung R* (including the *Trawniki* attached to it)[2] on one hand, and those used by the Germans (*Reichsdeutsche*), the *Trawniki* and the *landeseigene Kräfte* of the *SS-Wachmannschaften* of the OZAK,[3] on the other hand.

1.1: *Abteilung R*

The men of *Abteilung R*, coming as they were from different military, paramilitary, or police branches, or even being civilians, used different types of uniforms despite serving in the same unit. Due to this heterogeneity, it is very difficult to describe all types of uniforms they used.

During the stay in Poland the members of *Aktion Reinhard*, if members of the *Orpo*, *Sipo*/SD or SS/*Waffen-SS*, used the uniforms of such branches.[4] Many were militarized civilians: in this case they received *feldgrau* (field gray) SS/*Waffen-SS* uniforms, but they had to remove the right collar tab with the runes and replace it with a "blank" one (it seems that the reason for this were the complaints by what trial depositions referred to as the "*aktive SS-Leute*," or "active SS-men," probably meaning the *Waffen-SS* members); consequently, their uniforms ended up looking very similar to the *Sipo*/SD uniform pattern. As headgear, they used *Schirmmütze* M37 or *Schiffchen* M40,[5] both in *feldgrau* color and always with the *Totenkopf* and the standard SS eagle affixed to the front. The militarized civilians received a rank corresponding to the one they had achieved in the *Allgemeine-SS*, the *Sturmabteilung*, or the NSDAP, in case they had been members of these organizations. In all other cases they were assigned a rank chosen at the discretion of the respective camp commander; it seems that most of them were given the rank of *SS-Unterscharführer*, in order for them to be higher ranked than the *Trawniki*. It also seems that the militarized civilians were authorized to wear the uniforms only inside the camp they were assigned to, while outside the camp they had to wear civilian clothes. At least some of them travelled to the OZAK in civilian clothes.[6]

Coming to the OZAK phase, the main types of uniform used by the members of *Abteilung R* in the region, are described in the following sections (in addition, the specific cases of the *Trawniki* attached to *Abteilung R* as well as the camouflage outfits and tropical uniforms are treated in specific sections).[7]

1.1.1: The *Sicherheitspolizei/ Sicherheitsdienst* Uniform

Some of the most well-known members of *Abteilung R*, such as Wirth, Stangl, Hering, and Reichleitner, came from the *Kriminalpolizei*, whose members wore the *Sipo*/SD uniform. The use of this uniform in the OZAK is photographically documented for Wirth, Stangl, and Hering, while it is very likely (but not sure, due to the absence of pictures) for Reichleitner. This uniform, of a color that can be ascribed to the wide *feldgrau* spectrum, belonged generically to the type use by the SS/*Waffen-SS*. It had the SS eagle on the left sleeve and black rhomboidal collar tabs (with piping in silver for the officers, without piping for NCOs and privates); the left collar tab showed the SS rank while the right one was blank. The absence of runes on the right collar tab distinguished *Sipo*/SD from SS/*Waffen-SS* members. During the war, in order to further differentiate between *Sipo*/SD and SS/*Waffen-SS* members, the former were also ordered to replace the *Waffen-SS*-style shoulder boards with those of the *Ordnungspolizei*, with *giftgrün* (toxic green) *Waffenfarbe*. Furthermore, *Sicherheitsdienst* personnel carried on the tunic left sleeve, at the level of the forearm, a small rhomboid made of black cloth with the SD letters sewn in gray thread, called SD-*Raute*. According to pictorial evidence and trial depositions, at least Wirth, Hering, and Stangl used this insignia.[8]

The headgear used with the *Sipo*/SD uniform was the same used with the SS/*Waffen-SS* uniform: *Schiffchen* M40 and *Schirmmütze* M37, both *feldgrau* and with the *Totenkopf* and the SS eagle affixed to the front.

Stangl pictured in the OZAK with the *Sipo*/SD uniform and the *SD-Raute* on the left sleeve.

1.1.2: The SS/*Waffen SS* Uniform

On the basis of pictorial evidence, the SS/*Waffen-SS* uniform saw limited use among *Abteilung R* members in the OZAK. This *feldgrau* uniform was characterized by the black rhomboidal right collar tab with runes and by the SS eagle worn on the tunic left sleeve. In the limited photographical documentation which shows the use of this uniform in the OZAK, it has been possible to identify Bolender, Dubois, Franz, Girtzig, Gomerski, Hackenholt, Oberhauser and possibly Schwarz. All of them had served at some point in the *SS-Totenkopfverbände* or the *Waffen-SS*.[9] Apparently the SS/*Waffen-SS* uniform was also used in the OZAK by some *Abteilung R* officers who, even if they were SS members, had not served in the *Waffen-SS*, as for instance Tauscher and Häusler.

The known pictures show the following headgear in use with this uniform: *Schiffchen* M40, *Einheitsfeldmütze* M43 and *Schirmmütze* M37, all of them in *feldgrau,* and always bearing the standard *Totenkopf* and SS eagle.

Franz in the OZAK wearing the standard *Waffen-SS* uniform, with *SS-Untersturmführer* rank.

Oberhauser in the *erdbraun* (earth-brown) M34 uniform of the *2. SS-Totenkopf-Standarte "Brandenburg."* The picture was taken very likely in 1937 after the *Sturm* were reorganized; apparently on the right collar tab, beneath the *Totenkopf*, is the number 16 which would identify the *16. Sturm* (company) of the *Standarte*. The *erdbraun* M34 uniforms were reserved to the *SS-Totenkopf-Standarten* units and were used for concentration camp guard duty.

1.1.3: The *Ordnungspolizei* Uniform

Upon arrival in the OZAK, those *Abteilung R* members who as militarized civilians had used in Poland the SS/*Waffen-SS* uniform carrying a right collar tab without runes (and that in some cases travelled to Italy in civilian clothes), received *Ordnungspolizei* uniforms. According to trial depositions, this happened a few days after the arrival in Trieste. These uniforms were possibly produced with *Polizei-Grün* (light-blue green) or some sort of field gray cloth.[10] The tunics were probably in the *Schutzpolizei* version, with *hellgrün* (light green) *Waffenfarbe* used for the arm eagle, the *Litzen* (collar tabs), and the shoulder boards' piping. From pictorial evidence it seems that most of them were non-standard tunics generally copying the cut of the German type. They had small rounded breast pockets, patch lower pockets with central reinforcement, six holes buttonings, straight cuffs imitating the style of the *Regio Esercito Italiano* (REI) mod. 40 tunics, elongated collar, and in some cases apparently Italian buttons. On the collar they carried obsolete *Litzen* with piping typical of the *Ordnungspolizei* M36 tunics, standard shoulder boards, and machine-embroidered arm eagle. Such tunics do not appear in photos of any other *Ordnungspolizei* unit employed in the OZAK; it can be therefore assumed that they were locally produced specifically for *Abteilung R*.

Bredow and Schneider photographed in the OZAK, wearing the *Ordnungspolizei* uniform specific to *Abteilung R*; note the peculiar elongated collar and the Italian-style cuffs.

Some members of the unit that originally belonged to the *Ordnungspolizei* kept on using the standard uniforms of this branch, including the M43 and the obsolete M36 model; these were evidently already in their possession when they arrived in Italy and were probably used until they were no longer serviceable.[11] On the basis of the available pictures, the *Ordnungspolizei* uniform seems to have been the most widely used by *Abteilung R* in the OZAK. For unknown reasons (maybe the replacement of worn or damaged items), it was sometimes used also by men who had previously served in the *Waffen-SS* (case documented photographically for Dubois).

Allers, according to his own deposition, wore the uniform of an *Oberregierungsrat der Verwaltungspolizei* (high rank official of the administrative police, corresponding to the rank of *Oberstleutnant der Polizei*); this was very likely a standard *Ordnungspolizei* uniform with insignia bearing the *lichtgrau* (light gray) *Waffenfarbe* specific for this branch.

The headgear generally worn by *Abteilung R* men with the *Ordnungspolizei* uniform was the *Einheitsfeldmütze* M43, which was the headgear most often used by the *Ordnungspolizei* units during the last war years. This fieldcap was made in *Polizei-Grün* wool cloth, and carried on the front an insignia composed of a tricolor cockade and the *Ordnungspolizei* eagle, probably always in the BeVo version.

1.1.4: The *Trawniki* of *Abteilung R*

No official regulations are known that could help clarify the of the uniforms used by the *Trawniki* in the *Distrikt Lublin* and later in the OZAK. For this reason it is very difficult to propose a definitive analysis. Nevertheless, based on the very scarce photographic documentation, it has been possible to produce a general analysis of the most widespread uniform patterns.

The *Trawniki* arrived in the OZAK in different groups at different times: with Globocnik's convoy, with the *SS-Wachmannschaften* company led by Schwarzenbacher (*Trawniki* company), together with members of *Abteilung R* and probably also with later arrivals during 1944. They were members of various units: some were practically part of *Abteilung R*, others were in the *Trawniki* company (or *Wachmannschaft I [Ostvölker]*), some in the *Wachmannschaft II (landeseigene Kräfte)*. Based on the little information presently available, it is difficult to establish what differences may have existed between the uniforms of the *Trawniki* serving in this or that unit in the OZAK.

This section addresses specifically the case of the small group of *Trawniki* that had served in *Aktion Reinhard* and in the OZAK were attached to *Abteilung R*. According to photographic evidence it seems that they arrived in the OZAK wearing the uniforms they had received in Poland. As far as known, the recruits training at the *Ausbildungslager Trawniki* wore the uniforms adopted by the *Wachmannschaften* of the *Distrikt* Lublin, namely tunics described as black or gray-green.[12] In general and based solely on photo material, a rather heterogeneous mix of garments was used, primarily made up of: black M32 *SS-Dienstrock* produced for the various SS branches *(Allgemeine-SS, SS-Verfügungstruppe,* and *SS-Totenkopfverbände*), already obsolete and maybe modified; standard SS-cut M37 tunics; tunics cut according to the style of the *Heer* M40/M41.[13] It also appears that old *erdgrau* M34 tunics originally used by the *SS-Verfügungstruppe* were

This and the next five photos illustrate the uniform patterns used by the *Trawniki* attached to *Abteilung R*. This picture, taken in Poland, shows the entirely black uniform with the short lower collar *Tresse*. The black *Schiffchen* (sidecap) seems to be the *Waffen-SS Panzertruppen* M40 type with standard insignia.

Another photo of the same man, identified as Bienemann, a *Volksdeutscher*, shows the collar *Tresse*. No known photos taken in the OZAK show the entirely black uniform being worn.

This picture, also taken in Poland, shows the gray-green uniform; the tunic is probably an SS-cut M37 tunic. This uniform pattern was later used also during the first months in the OZAK.

Taken in the OZAK, this photo documents the use by the *Trawniki* of the gray-green uniform that had been worn in Poland and was later worn unchanged during the first months in the OZAK. The *Trawniki* on the left, tentatively identified as *SS-Oberzugwachmann* Rosenholz, wears a tunic cut in the style of the *Heer* M40/M41, with short lower collar *Tresse* and three stripes of *Tresse* on the shoulder boards. The other *Trawniki* probably wears the same type of tunic, but since the lower pockets are not visible, it cannot be said with certainty. The photo was taken just outside the Risiera di San Sabba, in front of the camp entrance; the courtyard of the "Venezia Giulia" bar, still existing, is visible in the background, the door (see close-up) is still the same. *StA München*

This picture depicts *SS-Hauptzugwachmann* Kaiser, a Volksdeutscher *Trawniki*, in the OZAK, probably after spring 1944, wearing the old gray-green uniform already used in Poland. The tunic is probably cut on the style of the SS M37, with added black rhomboidal outlined collar tabs. This is the only known photo showing the SS rank *sterne* used by a *Trawniki* in the OZAK. Note that in this case the *Tresse* goes completely around the collar.

Trawniki-men wearing the black greatcoats produced for the *Schutzmannschaften* and black *Schiffchen* (sidecap), photographed in the OZAK in January 1944. This is the only known photo evidence showing the enduring use of *Schutzmannschaften* uniform items by the *Trawniki* in the OZAK.

re-used.[14] Additionally, according to some trial depositions, it seems that at least the *Trawniki* serving in Belzec were issued uniforms described as *erdbraun* or *lehmbraun* (clay-brown color);[15] it is likely that these were at least partly obsolete *erdbraun* M34 tunics used by the members of the *SS-Totenkopf-Standarten* employed for concentration camp guard duties. The various types of tunics were worn with black trousers or, in the case of gray-green tunics, also with trousers of the same color. Sometimes the *Trawniki* used military clothing of various and undetermined origin, such as German war-booty or personal equipment of the Soviet prisoners of war.[16] In some rare cases it would appear that they even used civilian clothes.

In almost all cases no collar tabs were worn on the tunics. NCOs wore a peculiar short lower collar *Tresse* (silver-colored) and rank stripes, also made of *Tresse*, on the black shoulder boards.[17] In some cases, the SS-style eagle was applied on the left sleeve of the tunics. From photo evidence related to the service in Poland it is also known that some men wore on the left sleeve of the black tunic a national shield bearing the colors of the Ukraine (yellow-blue).

Much less frequent but still confirmed by photos from the service in Poland was the use by the *Trawniki* of the bi-color combinations generally worn by the *Schutzmannschaften*.[18] These black uniforms, often obsolete *SS-Dienstrock* M32 originally produced for the various SS branches, had been modified by adding collars, cuffs, and lower pocket flaps of a lighter color (different sources state that the fabric was light-blue, bluish-gray, or green).[19]

Regarding the headgear, black *Schiffchen* were generally worn with a simple metallic tunic button affixed frontally.[20] In some rare cases, perhaps depending on availability, it seems that the button was replaced by a *Totenkopf* printed on a metallic button as originally produced for the obsolete *feldmütze* für SS M34, and sometimes even by the standard BeVo embroidered SS skull and eagle.

After the arrival in the OZAK, as far as it could be ascertained given the scarcity of documentation, the *Trawniki* attached to *Abteilung R* apparently kept for some time, probably until no longer serviceable and without any obvious modifications, elements of the uniforms used in Poland.[21] The use of the early gray-green uniforms in the OZAK is confirmed by photographic evidence, as well as the use, probably on a very limited scale, of the bi-color *Schutzmannschaften* uniforms. On the other hand, no pictures are known showing the use of full black uniforms in the OZAK.

These uniforms remained probably unchanged until some time during spring 1944. Photos taken during the parade for Hitler's birthday held in Trieste on April 20, 1944, and during Wirth's funeral in Opicina in late May 1944, show that by that time the uniforms used by the *Trawniki* attached to *Abteilung R* had been modified by adding SS-style collar tabs. These collar tabs were rhomboidal, black and outlined but carried no runes (as also used by the *Trawniki* serving in the *SS-Wachmannschaften* of the OZAK in the so-called "simil-*Sipo*/SD" uniform pattern, see section 1.2.2). It also seems that the NCO collar *Tresse* went now completely around the collar. It is not known how long this uniform pattern was used, possibly until the end of the war.

Regarding the headgear, it seems that a specific field gray sidecap was adopted, imitating the style of the *Schiffchen* M40, with standard SS insignia. In some rare cases the black *Schiffchen* was used after the arrival in the OZAK. A single photo shows that the *Einheitsfeldmütze* M43 was also used, probably very rarely; it is not possible to say which insignia were carried on it.

1.1.5: Camouflage, Tropical, and Winter Uniforms

At least from April 1944, *Abteilung R* personnel and the small number of *Trawniki* attached to it were issued a camouflage outfit produced in Italian mod. 29 camouflage fabric, consisting of tunic, trousers, helmet cover, and fieldcap (usually made on the style of the *SS-Tarnmütze* M42 or in some rare case of the *Einheitsfeldmütze* M43, with the flaps closed by buttons or a small metal buckle).

Many SS/*Polizei* units deployed in the Italian and Yugoslav war theaters were equipped with garments made of such polychrome fabric, which were usually worn on the standard field uniforms. The camouflage outfits issued to *Abteilung R*, while not all identical, were of a unique style compared to those used by other units. The tunics for instance were quite wide, with trapezoidal pectoral pocket flaps closed by flared buttons of

Karl Richter probably photographed in spring 1944, wearing the camouflage outfit produced for *Abteilung R* with Italian mod. 29 camouflage fabric. Richter was killed in Starada (now Starod) on August 18, 1944. *LA NRW, Münster*

Walter Novak wearing a camouflage tunic made with Italian mod. 29 camo fabric; it appears different from those generally used by *Abteilung R*. Note the Suomi KP/-31 sub-machine gun. *LA NRW, Münster*

Novak wearing the tropical shirt issued to *Abteilung R*, which was probably produced locally. *LA NRW, Münster*

the type used on shelter quarters (Italian or German *Zeltbahn*). They were probably locally produced, perhaps at the Risiera where some prisoners were used as forced labor in a tailor's workshop. Usually, no insignia were carried on the camo tunics or the headgear, except for a few documented cases of *Ordnungspolizei* shoulder boards worn on the camo tunics.

By warm weather, tropical sand-colored shirts were used; they had two chest pockets with trapezoidal flaps, closed by the same buttons as used on the camo tunics, and carried *Ordnungspolizei* shoulder boards. Also these shirts were probably produced locally, since they do not resemble any other standard garments used by the German or Italian armies. They were probably worn with shorts.

For winter duty, *Abteilung R* members were issued double-breasted gray greatcoats, possibly of German production, not carrying any insignia and only rarely seen with *Ordnungspolizei* shoulder boards. Also documented is the use by motorcyclists of the M34 *Kradschutzmantel* protective raincoat in rubberized cloth.

1.2: The *SS Wachmannschaften* of the OZAK

1.2.1: The *Reichsdeutsche*

Information on the *Reichsdeutsche* within the *SS-Wachmannschaften* of the OZAK is very scarce, but it is very likely that most of them used the SS/*Waffen-SS* or *Ordnungspolizei* uniforms. Pictures of *SS-Ostuf.* Schwarzenbacher taken in the OZAK show that he wore the standard *Waffen-SS* uniform, with M37 *Schirmmütze* bearing standard SS insignia.

Some men that had originally belonged to *Polizei-Begleit-Btl. "Steiermark"* served in the *SS-Wachmannschaften* of the OZAK, it is therefore very likely that in the latter unit they also wore the *Ordnungspolizei* uniform. The use of the *Ordnungspolizei* uniform in the *SS-Wachmannschaften* of the OZAK seems also confirmed by some pictures showing men (probably trainers) wearing this uniform, photographed with soldiers belonging to the *landeseigene Kräfte*.

1.2.2: The *Trawniki*

Although there is very little information about the *Trawniki* company, it is likely that the men initially wore the uniforms they had used in Poland (see description in section 1.1.4). According to some post-war accounts, the men wore black uniforms with (probably blank) SS-style black collar tabs, or black uniforms with gray cuffs and "old-style Russian collar tabs" (probably those produced for the *Schutzmannschaften* and described in section 1.1.4); some apparently even wore SS uniforms.

During spring 1944, probably around mid-April, the *Trawniki* of the *SS-Wachmannschaften* of the OZAK were issued new uniforms, very likely produced with Italian gray-green wool cloth. It seems that the tunic (although produced in slightly different variants) was cut on the style of the *Heer* M40/41 tunic, but had a distinctive and unusual collar made of black cloth (for a more detailed description see section 1.2.3).[22] With the new tunic, new black rhomboidal collar tabs with white outline were also introduced. They were SS-type tabs in the *Sipo*/SD pattern, with the right one without runes and the left one with rank indication (blank tab for the troops, with silver *Tresse* and/or *sterne* for the NCOs).[23] Because of these collar tabs, this uniform pattern will be called here for simplicity "simil-*Sipo*/SD." Based on photographic comparision, it appears that this tunic was the same as issued to the *landeseigene Kräfte* (see section 1.2.3), except for the color of the collar tabs (which was presumabily red for the latter).[24] The silver-colored collar *Tresse* remained in use, but now went completely around the collar and was probably only used from the rank of *SS-Zugwachmann* upwards. On this new tunic all ranks carried the black shoulder boards piped with (most probably) white *Waffenfarbe* also issued to the *landeseigene Kräfte* (see section 1.2.3), when necessary with the peculiar *Tresse* stripes. SS arm eagles were probably used, although there is only one known photo showing it with certainty on a "simil-*Sipo*/SD" uniform worn by a *Trawniki* (in this case the eagle appears smaller than the standard one, possibly it was the the BeVo version for the SS headgear).

Trawniki probably with the rank of *SS-Rottwachmann* wearing the "simil-*Sipo*/SD" uniform introduced for the *SS-Wachmannschaften* of the OZAK in spring 1944. The peculiarities of the tunic were the black collar and the rhomboidal outlined collar tabs, here in the black version used by *Trawniki*. Note the crossed *Tresse* stripes on the shoulder boards, whose meaning remains unknown, and the SS arm eagle of a smaller size than usual (probably the BeVo model for SS headgear). This is the only known picture showing a *Trawniki* wearing this type of uniform.

A photo taken on December 30, 1944, near Udine: next to a broken-down car are two SS men from the *Stabskompanie* HSSPF OZAK, on the right, and probably a *Trawniki* wearing a uniform mixing military and civilian clothes.

The field gray *Schiffchen* was adopted as headgear. At least in some cases it was the M40 (or perhaps locally produced copies), with SS BeVo eagle and *Totenkopf* affixed frontally.

Also some of the *Trawniki* attached to *Abteilung R* were transferred to the *SS-WMS-Btl.* (*Wachmannschaft II*). It is not clear whether they modified or replaced their uniforms (see section 1.1.4) after changing unit. In fact, there is no known image showing *Trawniki* from *Abteilung R* wearing the characteristic uniform used by the *SS-Wachmannschaften* of the OZAK.

1.2.3 The *landeseigene Kräfte*

All Italians (from Friuli, Venezia–Giulia, Istria, and those from other regions of Italy), Slovenes, Croats, and *Volksdeutsche* of the OZAK enlisted in the *SS-Wachmannschaften* were considered *landeseigene Kräfte*.

Unlike what happened to the *Trawniki*, who apparently arrived in the OZAK wearing the uniforms previously used in Poland, the recruits of the *landeseigene Kräfte* had to be equipped ex-novo. Their uniforms (as well as those, very similar, issued to the *Trawniki* of the *SS-Wachmannschaften* of the OZAK) were generally similar to the various models worn by the other *landeseigene Selbstschutzverbände* of the OZAK (*Landschutz*, *Selbstschutz* of the Valcanale and *Guardia Civica di Trieste*) and by equivalent units of the *Oberkrain* (*Oberkrainer Selbstschutz*) and *Untersteiermark* (*SA-Wehrmannschaft*).

In principle, it has been possible to identify three different uniform patterns specifically produced for the recruits of the *landeseigene Kräfte*. During winter 1943–44, thus prior to the conscription of March 1944, the recruits of the *SS-Wachmannschaften* were issued specific uniforms which were probably locally produced in some slightly different models, in some cases poorly tailored and lacking symmetry.[25] They were probably made of Italian Grigioverde wool cloth, whereby it is unclear whether they were assembled by using available war booty or newly produced. They are recognizable by some distinctive characteristics: in particular, the tunic was cut in the style of the German *Heer* M40/M41 with some references to the Italian mod. 40

tunic used by the REI and the *Milizia Volontaria per la Sicurezza Nazionale* (MVSN).[26] Peculiar to this tunic, which for simplicity will be called "*Heer* M40/M41 style," were the cuffs, inspired by the Italian mod. 40 tunic; sometimes the cuffs had buttons as on the German models. Other characteristic features of the tunic were the wide lapels resembling the German models, three or four buttonholes with Italian-made buttons, and four pockets with central reinforcement.

No insignia were worn on these tunics except for shoulder boards made of the same fabric as the tunic and piped with white *Waffenfarbe*. In some cases national tricolor shields were worn on the left sleeve, similarly to the foreign volunteers of the *Waffen-SS*. It would seem that during this early period national sleeve insignia were frequently worn by the recruits of the *landeseigene Kräfte*, although their use was by no means generalized; possibly the choice to be identified as member of a specific ethnic group was left to each soldier's discretion. Photographically documented are only two national shields: tri-color Slovenian (in two versions, with and without white outline) and Italian (with outline), both with national colors arranged transversally, sewn or printed on a support base.[27] The shields were probably all made in the same factory and had a peculiar shape, resembling those used by the Baltic volunteers of the German army.[28]

The use of this particular uniform pattern by the *landeseigene Kräfte* is documented with certainty until March 1944. It is almost certain that after this date this configuration was replaced or more correctly "upgraded," perhaps gradually, with a pattern that can be called for simplicity "transitional." With this term is meant a uniform composed of a tunic with black collar and black shoulder boards piped with (most probably) white *Waffenfarbe* but still missing the rhomboidal collar tabs which were adopted only later. It should be underlined that the "transitional" uniform does not seem to be a new model but rather an upgrading of the "*Heer* M40/M41 style" tunics already in use: apparently these were simply modified by adding the black collar and the black shoulder boards. The black shoulder boards with white *Waffenfarbe*, produced in at least two slightly different variants, were of SS-style, similar to those produced for the ranks between *SS-Schütze* and *SS-Rottenführer*. The black cloth used for the shoulder boards was probably the same as used for the collar; when necessary they carried the above-described peculiar *Tresse* stripes.

Based on the scarce photographic evidence, it would seem also that some "transitional" tunics were already issued during the early existence of the *SS-Wachmannschaften*, probably before the conscription of late March 1944, to a limited number of *landeseigene Kräfte* personnel. It is not known why some soldiers received these

Two soldiers belonging to the *SS-Wachmannschaften* wearing the "*Heer* M40/M41 style" tunic (used between late 1943 – March 1944). Note that the cuffs of the two uniforms are differently cut. *MNZS, NI11_656*

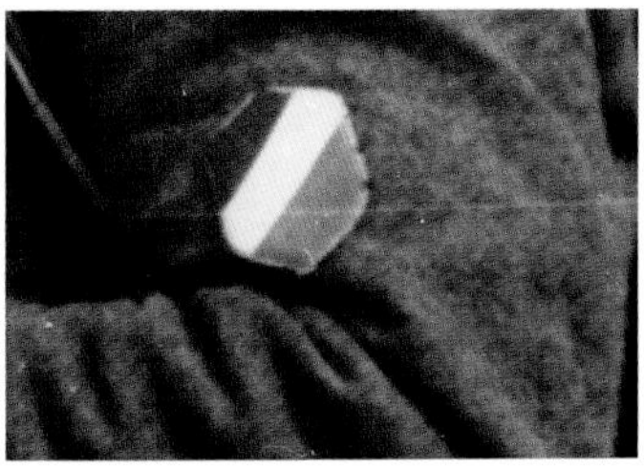

A soldier seen in March 1944, wearing the "*Heer* M40/M41 style" uniform, with shoulder boards made of the same fabric as the tunic with white *Waffenfarbe* piping and the outlined Italian national arm shield. He is carrying a 45 mm Brixia mod. 35 light mortar. *MNZS, 6113_13, NI5_677*

The "transitional" uniform pattern, with black collar and shoulder boards (used probably between January–February 1944 – mid-April 1944).

A soldier, probably Slovene, wearing the "transitional" uniform with an unusual SS arm eagle.

tunics rather than the "*Heer* M40/M41 style" tunics; it is possible that the "transitional" tunics were issued only to the personel who had already completed the training or, perhaps, to the trainers. It is also possible that the first photos showing these tunics were taken during the transition period when the "*Heer* M40/M41 style" pattern was being abandoned and the "transitional" one was being introduced, the latter possibly gradually replacing the former. The date of the (initially limited) introduction of the "transitional" tunic is not precisely known; from undated photos it appears that this probably happened during the first quarter of 1944 (maybe January or February), in any case during cold weather, when the "*Heer* M40/M41 style" uniform was still worn by the recruits of the *SS-Wachmannschaften* of the OZAK. Probably with the introduction of the conscription in March 1944, for reasons which are not precisely known (maybe in order to differentiate the *SS-Wachmannschaften* personnel from the other *landeseigene Selbstschutzverbände* units who had been using the very same uniforms), the "transitional" pattern replaced the "*Heer* M40/M41 style" for all members of the *SS-Wachmannschaften* of the OZAK.

Some pictures show the use of the Slovenian and Italian outlined national tricolor arm shields on the "transitional" tunic; their use seems to have been sporadic.

Probably during mid-April 1944 new tunics carrying "simil-*Sipo*/SD" black rhomboidal outlined collar tabs were introduced for the *Trawniki* of the *SS-Wachmannschaften* of the OZAK. Almost certainly during the same period, the same collar tabs were also introduced for the *landeseigene Kräfte* personnel; these were made in a clearer cloth, probably of red color.[29] It is possible that these were in some cases insignia originally produced for the *Luftwaffe Flak* units, simply modified with the addition of a piping—in some cases perhaps a simple underlayer—probably white.[30] Relying only on pictorial analysis, it seems that the new rhomboidal collar tabs were the only difference between the "transitional" tunic pattern and the new "simil-*Sipo*/SD"; at the same time, it seems that the different color of the collar tabs was the only substantial difference between the "simil-*Sipo*/SD" tunic issued to the *Trawniki* and the one issued to the *landeseigene Kräfte*.

The few available photos seem to show, in almost all cases, enlisted men with a blank left collar tab. Presently only one picture is known showing a *landeseigene Kräfte* soldier wearing a red (probably) rhomboidal left collar tab with rank indication, apparently a *stern* and a *Tresse* stripe (probably *SS-Zugwachmann* rank); the same man also wore shoulder boards with two stripes of *Tresse* (the maximum number ascertained for a *landeseigene Kräfte* soldier) and all-round collar *Tresse*. As for the shoulder boards, the "simil-*Sipo*/SD" tunic mantained those already used on the "transitional" one, with *Tresse* stripes when necessary.

Since no available photo shows clearly the use of national tricolor arm shields on the "simil-*Sipo*/SD" tunics, it is possible that these insignia, already probably used only sporadically, were gradually abandoned after the introduction of the collar tabs. They probably disappeared after the ordinance issued by the *Oberster Kommissar* in June 1944 which prohibited the use of national flags within the OZAK borders, except for the *Reich* flag.[31]

Only two photos show with certainty the use of the SS arm eagle by *landeseigene Kräfte* personnel, one on the "simil-*Sipo*/SD" tunic, one on the "transitional" pattern (in the former case the eagle appears to be smaller than the standard one, perhaps it was the BeVo version for the SS headgear; in the latter case it does not seem to be an SS eagle, but it was possibly a model from other *Wehrmacht* branches or even locally produced). The use of the eagle seems to have been limited and perhaps discontinued over time depending on the availability of supplies.

Regarding the headgear, since the introduction of the "*Heer* M40/M41 style" uniform until the end of the war, it seems that the *landeseigene Kräfte* widely adopted the *feldgrau Schiffchen* M40 (or maybe also locally made copies of it). Often, but not in all the cases, SS standard BeVo *Totenkopf* and eagle were affixed to the front of the sidecap. It would also seem that with the "*Heer* M40/M41 style" tunic gray-green sidecaps of unknown origin and carrying no insignia were also used; they were probably produced locally,

National arm shields worn by members of the *landeseigene Kräfte* on the "transitional" uniform, thus before mid-April 1944: on the first picture the outlined Italian model, on the second the outlined Slovenian model.

Two Slovenes and one Ukrainian *Trawniki* (in the middle, probably an *SS-Gruppenwachmann*) wearing the "simil-*Sipo*/SD" uniform (used at least from April 1944 onwards). Note the darker color of the collar tabs worn by the *Trawniki* compared to that of the two other soldiers. *Courtesy Branko Čermelj*

Close-ups showing three members of the *landeseigene Kräfte*, maybe Slovenes, portrayed in the "simil-*Sipo*/SD" uniform, probably after April 1944. Note the rhomboidal outlined collar tabs probably made of red cloth; the color is visibly lighter than the shoulder boards and the collar, which were both black. The soldier depicted in the two latter photos wears a rank collar tab with a *sterne* and a *Tresse* stripe, shoulder boards with two *Tresse* stripes and the collar *Tresse* (probably *SS-Zugwachmann* rank). He also carries a smaller-than-usual SS sleeve eagle (probably the BeVo model for SS headgear).

 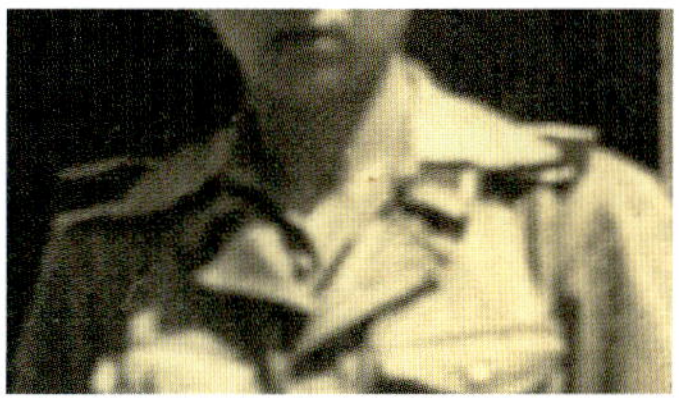

SS-Wachmann Ettore Sarzano from *6. Kp./SS-Wachmannschafts-Btl.* (former *Battaglione Davide* member) seen in summer 1944 wearing a tropical shirt. The rhomboidal outlined collar tabs, probably red, can be glimpsed beneath the collar of a lighter shirt he is wearing under the tropical one, which also carries black shoulder boards piped with white *Waffenfarbe*. The original photo has on the backside a handwritten dedication by Ettore's brother, *Capitano* Ernesto Sarzano, who served in the same unit, dated "San Sabba, 17.12.1944." *ARS Ljubljana*

This soldier guarding the *Landschutzschule* in Gorizia in early 1944 is wearing a gray-green greatcoat with black collar and cuffs. He may have belonged to the *SS-Wachmannschaften* but possibly also to the *Landschutz*, as in this phase both units appear to have worn the same uniforms.

imitating various models, in particular the *feldmütze für* SS M34, and were later widely used also by other units of the *landeseigene Selbstschutzverbände*.

The *landeseigene Kräfte* also used (mainly during training) Italian fatigue mod. 40 uniforms, dyed in khaki or sand color, without any insignia.[32]

Based on one piece of photo evidence, it appears that in summer the *SS-Wachmannschaften* of the OZAK were issued tropical shirts which were similar to, if not the same as, those already described for *Abteilung R*. Rhomboidal collar tabs and shoulder boards as used on the "simil-*Sipo*/SD" tunics were carried on these shirts. Light khaki shirts without any insignia and khaki shorts were also used, perhaps mainly as fatigues during training. Khaki *Schiffchen* were also used, at least in some cases with the double SS insignia affixed to the front.

As shown on some photos from early 1944, the soldiers guarding the *Landschutzschule* run by *Kommando G.* in Gorizia used German-style gray-green greatcoats with covered buttons. Almost certainly inspired by those of the *Schutzmannschaften*, they had collars and wide cuffs made in a very dark-colored cloth, almost certainly the black fabric also used for the collar of the "simil-*Sipo*/SD" tunic. They were devoid of any insignia except for the shoulder boards with white *Waffenfarbe* piping. Due to the absence of specific uniform features it is not known if these guards belonged to the *SS-Wachmannschaften* or to the *Landschutz*.

1.2.4: The *Battaglione Patrioti Davide*

Although the former members of *Battaglione Davide* integrated into the *SS-Wachmannschaften* were considered—for the German categorization—as *landeseigene Kräfte*, their uniforms are treated in a separate section because of the peculiar origin and characteristics of this unit.

According to one source, the members of *Battaglione Davide* used initially for identification, before the introduction of standard uniforms while still in the Piedmont region, a numbered armband, apparently with the colors of the Italian flag.[33] Such an armband, bearing the stamp of the SS headquarters in Asti (very likely the SD-*Aussenstelle Asti*), was worn on the partisan uniforms, which were not standardized but were composed of items of various origins. On February 28, 1944, probably in Canelli, *SS-Ustuf.* Grieser of the SD-*Aussenstelle Asti* delivered to Battaglione Davide new uniforms, cut on the style of the Italian paratroopers' gray-green mod. 41 uniforms. This new uniform is described by the same source as consisting of a, "collarless Sahariana tunic with incorporated belt, trousers with tight anklets, march boots, German fieldcap with visor, *Einheitsfeldmütze*,"[34] whereas, "the officers kept the REI uniforms and sidecap with rank insignia." This information is also broadly confirmed by an account from a former member of *Battaglione Davide*, who joined the unit in Venaria Reale, who additionally lists helmet, mess-kit, and rucksack, probably all Italian-made material.[35]

During the stay in Venaria Reale, but probably already in Canelli, the headgear, mostly REI sidecaps of various models, were decorated by the owners, in a totally spontaneous and unregulated way, with Italian tricolor ribbons and/or hand-witten slogans supporting the liberation of Italy from Fascism and in some cases the partisan movement. This headgear was worn until the unit disarmament and detention in the Risiera. The ribbons and slogans resulted in serious consequences for those who carried them: in the Risiera the Germans separated them from the other soldiers and they disappeared, most likely were deported to Germany.[36] At least during the stay in Venaria Reale the unit members wore collar tabs of various shapes (rectangular, trapezoidal, pentagonal) with the colors of the Italian flag, affixed vertically on the paratrooper-style tunic; in some cases they bear REI metallic stars. It seems that these collar tabs were still used in the OZAK.

During the first days or weeks of guard duty at the Risiera, the remaining former members of *Battaglione Davide* integrated in the *SS-Wachmannschaften* still used parts of the paratrooper-style uniform received in Canelli, such as the gray-green shirts and trousers. No distinctive insignia were carried on the uniform, and there was no headgear. After some time canvas khaki uniforms were introduced;[37] these were probably Italian fatigue mod. 40 tunics, devoid of insignia, and according to some accounts they were dyed in khaki or sand color. They were probably used primarily for guard duty at the Risiera.

It is considered very likely, although not certain, that the former members of *Battaglione Davide* later adopted the tunic with red (probably) rhomboidal collar tabs of the *landeseigene Kräfte*. A source, although not sufficiently clear, generally describes as "German uniforms" those worn for the guard duty at the Risiera in the weeks following the death of Wirth, i.e., after the end of May 1944.[38] Additionally, a picture from summer 1944 shows a former member of *Battaglione Davide* (Ettore Sarzano) wearing the tropical shirt described

Soldiers of *Battaglione Davide* photographed in Venaria Reale, in the Piedmont region, probably in March 1944. They wear uniforms cut on the style of the Italian paratroopers' gray-green mod. 41 uniforms, with trapezoidal tricolor collar tabs. *Courtesy Giuliano Giorcelli*

SS-Gruppenwachmann Dante Fangaresi from *6. Kp./SS-Wachmannschafts-Btl.* (former *Battaglione Davide* member), photographed on July 1, 1944, at the main gate of the Risiera during guard duty. He is wearing the khaki-dyed Italian fatigue mod. 40 tunic and Italian equipment for the Carcano mod. 91 rifle. He deserted two weeks later. *Courtesy Edizioni Polistampa*

A photo probably depicting a group of Italian soldiers, wearing partly the *SS-Wachmannschaften* "simil-*Sipo*/SD" tunic with collar tabs (second and fourth men from the right; therefore the photo was probably taken not before the end of April 1944), partly tunics made probably with Italian grigioverde wool cloth copying the cut of the *Heer* M40/41 tunics (the first three men on the left). The latter have collars that resemble those of the MVSN mod. 40 tunics. Interesting to note are the SS runic collar tabs and non-standard SS-style sleeve eagle. Which units these soldiers belonged to is not known; it is, however, possible that they were former members of the *Landschutz* of the Pola province transferred partly to the *SS-Wachmannschaften* (soldiers wearing the "simil-*Sipo*/SD" tunic) and partly to the *24. Waffen-Gebirgs (Karstjäger)-Division der SS* (unit to which perhaps the soldiers with the runic collar tabs belonged to).

for *Abteilung R*, with rhomboidal outlined collar tabs, probably red, and black shoulder boards piped with white *Waffenfarbe*; this would confirm that also former members of *Battaglione Davide* adopted the specific uniform pattern of the *SS-Wachmannschaften* of the OZAK. However, in a deposition Ernesto Sarzano said that he and his men received khaki uniforms with blank SS-style black collar tabs; consequently it remains unclear if the collar tabs issued to the former member of *Battaglione Davide* were actually black or (probably) red.

It is also likely that former members of *Battaglione Davide* wore the *feldgrau Schiffchen* with SS standard BeVo insignia, although confirmation is missing.

2: Personal Equipment

2.1: *Abteilung R*, and the *Trawniki* Attached to It

According to photo evidence, the personnel of *Abteilung R* and the *Trawniki* attached to it (and probably also the *Reichsdeutsche* in the *SS-Wachmannschaften* of the OZAK) were mainly issued German equipment and accoutrements, German M35/M40 steel helmets or even more frequently, the simplified M42 version without decals, SS M32 or *Ordnungspolizei* M36 metal belt buckles and pouches for the Mauser K98 ammunition.

Some photographs document the use of a particular type of Y-shaped suspenders: they look like German models but their origin could not be ascertained; it is possible that they were produced locally. Special pouches made for the Italian MAB mod. 38 sub-machinegun, again probably produced locally, and Carcano mod. 91 rifle ammunition pouches of unknown origin (maybe Czechoslovak) were also used. *Abteilung R* also used Italian aluminium canteens mod. 31 and mod. 33 and sporadically the Italian mod. 39 backpack. *Abteilung R* and the *Trawniki* used extensively knee-high boots from various sources. In some cases ankle marching boots with rolled up socks are also seen.

2.2: The *landeseigene Kräfte*

It seems that the soldiers of the *landeseigene Kräfte* (including the former members of *Battaglione Davide*) were almost exclusively equipped with Italian war booty supplies: belts with mod. 26 metal buckles, mod. 07/36 suspenders, Carcano mod. 91 rifle ammunition pouches and mod. 31 and mod. 33 aluminium canteens.

M35/M40 German helmets were used, some with single and double SS decals, double *Ordnungspolizei* decals and also single Heer decal; one single image also shows the use of an Italian mod. 33 helmet, without insignia. An inventory list dated February 15, 1945 lists "*300 italienische Stahlhelme*" and "*234 deutsche Stahlhelme*" as available to the *SS-Wachmannschaften* of the OZAK; it can possibly be assumed that there was approximately the same percentage of usage for the two types of helmet within the unit.[39]

German M35 helmet with double SS decal, painted in pre-war *apfelgrün*, or apple green (a rare sight so late in the war).

German *Heer* single decal M35/M40.

Series of pictures related to the use of the steel helmet by soldiers of the *landeseigene Kräfte*: Italian mod. 33 helmet without insignia.

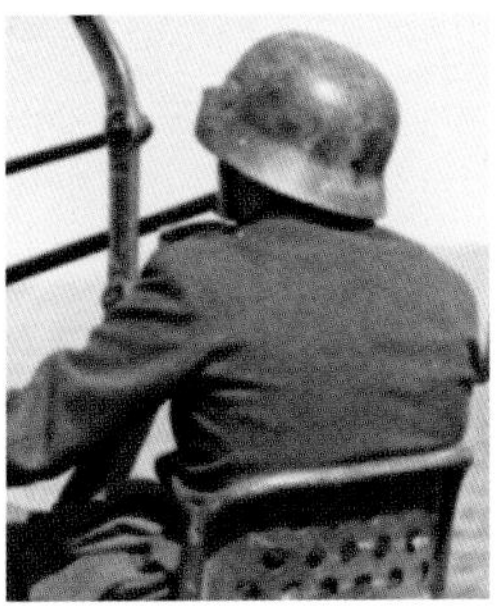

German camouflaged *Heer* single decal M35/M40 helmet.

German *Ordnungspolizei* double decal M35/M40.

German SS double decal M35/M40.

As to footwear, in almost all photographs the soldiers of the *landeseigene Kräfte* seem to have used Italian mod. 32 march boots and also in some cases Italian mod. 29 mountain boots, with puttees or socks rolled up at the ankles.

3: Individual and Group Weapons

Regarding weapons, there was a substantial difference between what was provided to *Abteilung R* and the *Trawniki* attached to it (and probably also to the *Reichsdeutsche* in the *SS-Wachmannschaften* of the OZAK), and what supplied to the *landeseigene Kräfte*.

The former were mostly armed with German Mauser K98 rifles, a good number of Italian Carcano mod. 91/38 rifles, and some Italian MAB mod. 38 sub-machine guns (and later versions). The men of *Abteilung R* also possessed a few dozen Finnish Suomi KP/-31 sub-machine guns[40] and a few Italian Breda mod. 30 machine guns.

The *landeseigene Kräfte* soldiers, on the other hand, were largely armed with Italian Carcano mod. 91/41 rifles, few MAB mod. 38 sub-machine guns (surely reserved for senior NCOs), and in some cases—as it would appear for example for guard duties at the Risiera—carbines, perhaps Italian Carcano mod. 91/38 TS.[41] As squad weapons, Breda mod. 30 and mod. 37 machine guns, Brixia 45 mm mod. 35, and Breda 81 mm. mod. 35 mortars were used.[42]

4: The Ranks of the *Trawniki*, and *landeseigene Kräfte*

The three columns on the right are are not confirmed by documents but are based on the analysis of the few available photographs, so they may not be entirely correct. The rank of *SS-Hauptzugwachmann* was probably a late addition, as originally the rank sequence seems to have ended with *SS-Oberzugwachmann*.

The officer ranks, not present in the sequence for the *SS-Wachmannschaften*, were reserved to the *Reichsdeutsche* only; senior NCOs ranks were preferably reserved for the *Volksdeutsche*.[43]

The officers of *Battaglione Davide* integrated into the *SS-Wachmannschaften* were given the highest ranks in the sequence, which in practice resulted into a demotion to NCO level; for instance, *Capitano* Ernesto Sarzano got the rank of *SS-Oberzugwachmann*.

SS-Wachmannschaften	**Left collar tab**	**Shoulder boards**	**Collar *Tresse***
SS-Wachmann	blank	blank	no
SS-Oberwachmann	blank	1 stripe of *Tresse*	no
SS-Rottwachmann	1 stripe of *Tresse*	1 stripe of *Tresse*	no
SS-Gruppenwachmann	2 stripes of *Tresse*	2 stripes of *Tresse*(or 2 crossed stripes?)	no
SS-Zugwachmann	1 *Sterne* + 1 stripe of *Tresse*	2 stripes of *Tresse*	yes
SS-Oberzugwachmann	2 *Sterne*	3 stripes of *Tresse*	yes
SS-Hauptzugwachmann	2 *Sterne* + 1 stripe of *Tresse*	3 stripes of *Tresse*	yes

Part II: Personal Documents, Letterhead, Stamps, and *Erkennungsmarke*

This section deals with the personal documents, letterhead, stamps, and *Erkennungsmarke* (identity tags) of *Abteilung R* and the *SS-Wachmannschaften* used in the OZAK. When necessary, references to the previous period of activity in Poland have also been included.

1: Personal Documents

1.1: *Abteilung R*

Based on trial depositions, it seems that at least in Poland the militarized civilians of *Aktion Reinhard* did not have any *soldbuch*. In Italy, according to a trial deposition, *Abteilung R* members received their *soldbuch* (military identity document) by an unknown entity, called "*Sicherungsgruppekommando Berlin-Mitte II*" or "*Sicherungsgruppenkommando Berlin II*";[44] there is no confirmation on the correctness of this statement.

At the present day there are no known examples of *SS-Soldbuch*, *Polizei-Soldbuch,* or *Polizei-Dienstpass* issued to *Abteilung R* members. However, a specimen of *Dienstausweis* (service document, valid for personal identification) belonging to a member of *Abteilung R*, Hödl, with serial number 01177, is known; it was issued by the HSSPF OZAK and signed by Allers.

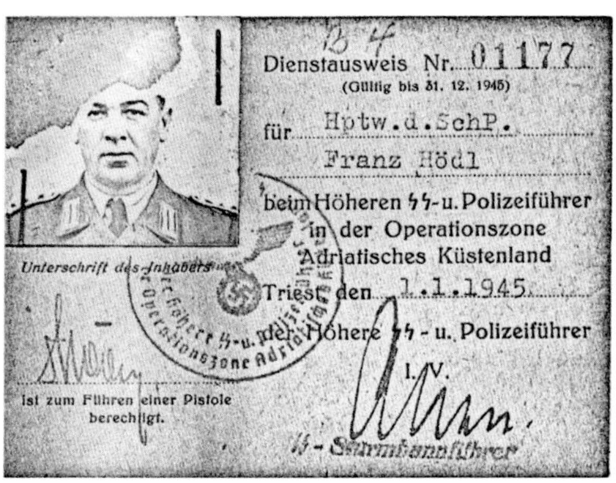

Dienstausweis Nr. 01177
(Gültig bis 31. 12. 1945)
für Hptw.d.SchP.
Franz Hödl
beim Höheren SS-u. Polizeiführer
in der Operationszone
Adriatisches Küstenland
Triest, den 1.1.1945
Der Höhere SS- u. Polizeiführer
I.V.
SS-Sturmbannführer
Unterschrift des Inhabers
Ist zum Führen einer Pistole berechtigt.

The *Dienstausweis* Nr. 01177 issued by the HSSPF OZAK to *Hptw.d.SchP.* Hödl on January 1, 1945, signed by Allers. Although the image quality is not optimal (a photocopy of the original), it is the only known personal document issued in the OZAK to a member of *Abteilung R.*

1.2: The *Trawniki*

As for the *Trawniki*, in Poland they were issued a beige-colored *Dienstausweis* with heading "*Der Beauftragte des Reichsführer-SS für die Errichtung der SS- und Polizeistützpunkte in neuen Ostraum – Dienstsitz Lublin Ausbildungslager Trawniki*" or in some rare cases "*Der SS- und Polizeiführer im Distrikt Lublin – Ausbildungslager Trawniki.*" Several examples of such *Dienstausweis* in Russian archives have been preserved, although their authenticity is currently a matter of discussion among historians and collectors. Noteworthy for this research is the *Dienstausweis* issued in Poland to *SS-Wachmann* Petro Nahorniak, a *Trawniki* who was later a member of the *SS-WMS-Btl.* (he was reported missing in action in Starada, near Castelnuovo d'Istria, during May 1944), which was used as evidence for the Demjanjuk trial. Since this *Dienstausweis* is apparently preserved in some Russian archive, it seems possible that these personal documents were handed back before departure from Poland and replaced with documents issued by the HSSPF OZAK at the arrival in Italy. A preserved list of *Trawniki* serving at the *Arbeitslager* Treblinka has a column indicating their "*SS-Soldbuch*" number; since in several cases the number on the list is the same as on the same man's *Dienstausweis*, it is not clear whether the *Trawniki* were also issued a *SS-Soldbuch* or if the numbers on the list were in fact those of the *Dienstausweis*.[45] At the present day there are no known specimens of *Dienstausweis* or *SS-Soldbuch* issued by *Abteilung R* or by the *SS-Wachmannschaften* to the *Trawniki* during their service in the OZAK.

1.3: The *landeseigene Kräfte*

No examples of *Dienstausweis* or *SS-Soldbuch* issued to members of the *landeseigene Kräfte* of the *SS-Wachmannschaften* of the OZAK are known. Known, however, is a type of bilingual "*Soldbuch für landeseigene Kräfte,*" of late SS typology but without runes on the cover, which was issued by the HSSPF OZAK, at least to the Slovenian *Landschutz,* and curiously to the Cossacks based in the Carnia region (Udine province); these documents were bilingual (respectively German–Slovenian and German–Russian, the latter written in Cyrillic) and had minor differences in printing and translation.[46] It is plausible that other units of the *landeseigene Selbstschutzverbände*, including the *SS-Wachmannschaften* of the OZAK, were issued a variant of this "*Soldbuch für landeseigene Kräfte*," most likely in the bilingual version corresponding to the soldier's ethnic group.[47]

According to a source, the officers of *Battaglione Davide* had been issued SS identification documents, possibly *SS-Soldbuch*, at the time when the unit was based in Canelli (Piedmont region);[48] assuming this is correct, it is possible that the officers integrated into the *SS-Wachmannschaften* kept this document. Another source claims that the soldiers of *Battaglione Davide* integrated in the *SS-Wachmannschaften* were issued identity badges with photo in German language, but there is no further confirmation.

2: Letterhead and Stamps

In the OZAK, *Abteilung R* used as its letterhead the formulation "*Der Höhere SS - u. Polizeiführer in der Operationszone Adriatisches Küstenland – Abteilung R*"; this was generally completed by typewriter indicating "*Der Inspekteur*," or I, II, or III (after the "R") depending on the section that produced the document. Also, a number of *haftschein* (detention forms) have been preserved, drawn up by the R I section of Trieste in the late 1943 and early 1944; they were produced using the standard *haftschein* of the *Sipo*/SD in Trieste but the heading "*Der Befehlshaber der Sicherheitspolizei und des SD in der Operationszone 'Adriatisches Küstenland' Triest*" was crossed out and replaced by "R 1" added by hand.

As to the service stamps, *Abteilung R* used the round stamp No. 5 of the HSSPF OZAK with the words: "* *Waffen-SS * Der Höhere SS-u. Polizeiführer in der Operationszone Adriatisches Küstenland* 5." Some sources claim that this was the stamp used at the Risiera di San Sabba, but it has been possible to ascertain its use only on

documents headed "*Der Sicherungskommandant der Karststrasse*" (signed by Allers) and "*Baustelle Wirth-West*" (signed by Schneider).

The *SS-Wachmannschafts-Btl.* used as its letterhead "D*er Höhere SS-u.Polizeiführer in der Operationszone Adriatisches Küstenland SS Wachmannschaftsbatl.*" It also used a round stamp with the words "*Der höhere SS-und Polizeiführer für das adriatisches küstenland*" [sic], as well as a round stamp with the words "*Dienstelle Feldpostnummer 01471*"; this was the *feldpostnummer* (military post number) of the HSSPF OZAK, also used by *Abteilung R*.

3: *Erkennungsmarke* (Identity Tags)

According to a trial deposition, in Italy *Abteilung R* members had identity tags bearing the inscription "*Sicherungsgruppekommando Berlin-Mitte II*" or "*Sicherungsgruppenkommando Berlin II*"; there is no confirmation on the correctness of this statement. In any case, if they had previously belonged to a military unit, *Abteilung R* members probably kept the *Erkennungsmarke* they had already received. Schwarz, who belonged to the *Waffen-SS*, had an *Erkennungsmarke* with inscription "*SS-Führungs-Hauptamt 3. Stabs-Kp.*" (the number 262).

Regarding the *SS-Wachmannschaften* of the OZAK, it is likely that *Reichsdeutsche* and *Trawniki* kept the *Erkennungsmarke* received by their respective former units, except in special circumstances. For the *Reichsdeutsche* the following *Erkennungsmarke* are documented:

- *1./8. SS-Totenkopf-Inf.Rgt. nr. 6* (assigned to Schwarzenbacher)
- two *Erkennungsmarke* from *Pol.Begl.Btl. Steiermark* (assigned respectively to an *Owm.d.SchP.* of *3. Kp.* and a *Zgw.d.SchP.* of *1. Kp./SS-WMS-Btl.*).

There is no information about the *Erkennungsmarke* that might have been used by the *Trawniki* in Italy (except in some cases where they received a new *Erkennungsmarke*, see below). For the *landeseigene Kräfte* a new *Erkennungsmarke* was introduced with the name of the unit followed by a progressive number, i.e., "*SS Wachmannschaften-Triest* + progressive number."[49]

This *Erkennungsmarke* was certainly used also by some *Trawniki* assigned to the *SS-Wachmannschaften*;[50] the reason for their replacing the original identity tag is not known.

No information is available on the identity tags used by the members of *Battaglione Davide* (if any), but it is very likely that those who were later drafted into the *SS-Wachmannschaften* also received the *Erkennungsmarke* for this unit.

The *Erkennungsmarke "SS Wachmannschaften-Triest 784"* found around Venzone (Udine province), along the State Road nr. 13 "Pontebbana," the road followed by *Abteilung R* and probably also by elements of the *SS-Wachmannschaften* to withdraw from Trieste to Austria during the last days of the war. *Private collection*

Uniforms and Insignia of the other *landeseigene Selbstschutzverbände* of the OZAK

In the category of *landeseigene Selbstschutzverbände* (local units) of the OZAK were included: the *SS-Wachmannschaften*, the units of the *Landschutz* (territorial defense, divided into *Aktiver Landschutz* and *Reserve-Landschutz* and formed on ethnic group basis) and other military units such as the Guardia Civica di Trieste and the *Selbstschutz* of the Valcanale.

After dealing with the *SS-Wachmannschaften* in the previous appendix, this one deals with the uniforms and insignia of the other landeseigene *Selbstschutzverbände* of the OZAK. Because of the special nature of these units, they were supplied with a heterogeneous mix of uniforms, insignia, equipment, and weapons coming from war booty stocks, mainly Italian (but also from other nations), as well as German materials and in some cases items produced specifically for these formations. For this reason only the most common uniform patterns shown on the very little available photographic evidence will be discussed. Considering the complexity of the topic, the contents of this appendix are not to be considered definitive and may be subject to changes on the basis of future discoveries.

1: The *Landschutz* in the Five Provinces Under the HSSPF OZAK[1]

1.1: The *Aktiver Landschutz* from December 1943 to March 1944

During this period, prior to the conscription of March 1944, *Landschutz* units wearing uniforms (*Aktiver Landschutz*) certainly existed but information about them is extremely scarce. They probably had few active soldiers. It seems that they used the same variants of gray-green uniforms as initially adopted by the recruits of the *SS-Wachmannschaften* of the OZAK. Initially the tunics did not bear any insignia except for shoulder boards piped with white *Waffenfarbe* and only in some rare cases national arm shields. During this time frame it is therefore difficult to determine on the basis of a photograph if a soldier belonged to the Landschutz or to the *SS-Wachmannschaften*, since neither unit used specific distinctive insignia. In the absence of reliable information it is impossible to say more in relation to the uniforms of the *Aktiver Landschutz* during this period.

1.2: The *Aktiver Landschutz* from March 1944 to May 1945

1.2.1: The *Landschutz* of the Udine province

Uniforms: From the available photos it would seem that this *Landschutz* made extensive use of the former REI Grigioverde mod. 40 tunics made of wool cloth;[2] in order to imitate the German models a white *Waffenfarbe* was applied on the fixed shoulder boards (as seen on the tunics produced for the SA-*Wehrmann-schaften* of the *Untersteiermark* – see appendix 3). It is not known whether these tunics were war booty or if they were newly produced. According to photo evidence, soldiers of this *Landschutz* were also equipped—in addition to mod. 40 tunics made of wool cloth—with mod. 40 tunics produced with the "tipo 343" fabric. There are also photos showing soldiers wearing a mix of uniform items, some made of wool cloth and some of "tipo 343" fabric. Photos also show members of this unit wearing Italian mod. 40 fatigue tunics (generally with the standard puttees of the REI), of the same model used by the *landeseigene Kräfte* of the *SS-Wachmannschaften* of the OZAK. During the summer, shirts or tropical tunics in khaki or olive drab color were used (also mixing items of different colors); these tunics had various origins, in some cases they seem to be similar to the Sahariana models of Italian or German production. The soldiers also used large leather belts with rectangular buckle without suspenders and the Italian made Armi a piedi mod. 32 walking boots.

Headgear: The members of this unit used sidecaps extensively, probably locally made with Italian Grigioverde or *feldgrau* cloth. These were apparently produced in some slightly different variants. The model most seen in photos was similar to both the *feldmütze* für SS M34[3] (similar cut of the foldable ear flaps) and the *Schiffchen* M40 (similar sidecap top). Also the Italian-made *bustina* mod. 34 and mod. 35 and the *berretto da campo* mod. 42 were certainly used, the latter perhaps preferably reserved to NCOs. Rarely used were *feldgrau* field caps with visor, similar to the *Einheitsfeldmütze* M43 (at least in one photo, a soldier seems to wear the *Ordnungspolizei* model with the police BeVo insignia type); some other field caps were similar to the cut of the *SS-Tarnmütze* M42 but made of Italian mod. 29 camo fabric (similar to what was supplied to the *Karstjäger-Division* at least since the summer of 1944). There is no known photographic evidence showing helmets used by the *Landschutz* of the Udine province.

Insignia: This unit was issued, probably as early as spring 1944, a provincial arm shield depicting the traditional eagle of the *Patriarcato di Aquileja* (the medieval ruler of the Friuli region, the Catholic patriarch based in Aquileja, south of Udine) on a blue field topped by a marquis crown; below the raptor's tail there was a scroll with the name "*Friuli*" written on it. The arm shield was embroidered in gold thread on a blue background and it was often sewn on an oval patch, probably in Grigioverde cloth. Presently at least two slightly different variants of this shield are known. Based on photographic evidence, it was carried on the left sleeve of the modified Grigioverde mod. 40 tunic, the Sahariana tunic, and sometimes also the Italian mod. 40 fatigue tunic. An identical but smaller shield was provided for the headgear but it was apparently more often used on field caps than on sidecaps, the latter having sometimes no insignia at all. At least one different model of the headgear badge is documented in photos: it would seem to depict a stylized eagle (bearing some similarity to the SS eagle) embroidered in a light-colored thread, perhaps yellow, which seem to form with its body the letter "F" (perhaps for "Friuli"). Sometimes a metallic *edelweiss* was carried on the side of the *Einheitsfeldmütze* M43, similar to the one used by the *Wehrmacht* but without the stem. As mentioned, this unit also wore shoulder boards made of the same cloth as the tunic, piped with white *Waffenfarbe*, and red unpiped rhomboidal SS-style collar tabs; the tabs were introduced at an unknown date but possibly after the introduction of the arm shield.[4] Apparently, the NCOs wore on the left collar tab the *sterne* indicating their rank; they were similar, if not identical, to those used by the SS.

Service documents: It is known that a type of nominative identity card titled *Dichiarazione*, devoid of picture, was used as personal identification by members of this *Landschutz* at least from the end of March 1944. It was printed on cream-colored cardboard in Italian only. The card was headed *Der Höhere SS-u.Polizeiführer in der Operationszone Adriatisches Küstenland – Der Beauftragte für die Provinz Udine*, and carried the printed signature of *SS-Oberführer* Feil, commander of the SS/*Polizei* for the Udine province from November 1943 to mid-1944. At least from late September 1944, the *Dichiarazione* identity card was replaced by the *soldbuch*, probably the *Soldbuch für landeseigene Kräfte*.[5]

1.2.2: The Slovenian *Landschutz* (SNVZ)

Note: For various reasons (in particular better career prospects), a considerable number of men transferred from the *Slowenische Landeswehr* (the Slovenian militia formed in the Ljubljana province by the HSSPF *Alpenland*) towards the SNVZ, most of them officers and NCOs who built the cadres of this unit. This fact gave rise to a uniformological mix as uniform items of the *Slowenische Landeswehr* were used together with those of the SNVZ. This has made it difficult to identify the specific uniforms adopted by the SNVZ.

Uniforms: In addition to the Italian-made mod. 40 modified tunics (in Grigioverde rough wool cloth, "tipo 343" or the fatigue model of the same type used by the *Landeseigene Kräfte* of the *SS-Wachmannschaften*), from the available photos it is clear that the SNVZ also used German-style tunics; the cut seems to be very similar to the *Heer* M40/M41 models, nevertheless presenting differences as to the number and type of buttons and the shape of the pocket flaps when compared to the standard German ones. It also seems to have been common to wear a mix of uniform items of different origin. In some cases camo tunics made of Italian mod. 29 fabric were used; they were generally similar to the standard four-pocket *Heer* M40/M41 tunics although the cut of the pockets was different from all other camo tunics used in the OZAK.

Also documented is the use by members of the SNVZ of German-style greatcoats with covered buttons but with collar and cuffs of the same black fabric already used for the collar of the "simil-*Sipo*/SD" tunic made for the *SS-Wachmannschaften* of the OZAK; it is very likely that the design of these greatcoats was inspired by the models used by the *Schutzmannschaften*.

Regarding the shoes, along with standard German and Italian models, footwear of civilian or unknown origin was also used. Belts from various sources were used: in addition to the widespread Sam Brown with shoulder strap adopted by many armies, also used were German or German-looking types with large rectangular metal buckles and M.10 types imitating the Austro–Hungarian simple buckle, produced and used also after the end of World War I by the states that had been part of the Habsburg Empire. In addition, standard German belts with plaque, in some cases in the *Heer* and SS versions, were used.

Headgear: This unit made massive use of side-caps from various sources: widespread was the Grigioverde or *feldgrau* model similar to the *feldmütze* für SS M34, but also the *Schiffchen* M40 and the *Einheitsfeldmütze* M43, in some cases even the traditional Yugoslav model Šajkača, were used. There is no known photographic evidence regarding the use of helmets by the SNVZ.

Insignia: At least since April 1944, the unit was issued a provincial arm shield (this insignia is visible on some photos taken during the April 20 parade in Trieste), apparently produced in two versions, printed or embroidered, depicting a red Illyrian ship (the coat-of-arms of the town of Ilirska Bistrica) on a white/blue background (representing the sky and the sea). This arm shield was carried on the left sleeve of all types of tunic, those made with Grigioverde cloth as well as those with Italian mod. 29 camo fabric. Additionally, some rare photographic evidence (including one dated July 21, 1944, depicting the 1st assault squad of the SNVZ Ceta based in Tolmin) shows members of this *Landschutz* wearing the Slovenian tricolor national arm shield, apparently produced exclusively for the *Landeseigene Kräfte* of the *SS-Wachmannschaften*; its use by members of the SNVZ was probably rare.

Some photos show the use of the typical "V" rank insignia of the German army (known by collectors as *Obergefreiter* chevron) affixed under the provincial arm shield, on all types of tunic, including camouflage. Some photographic evidence confirms the use, perhaps more sporadic compared to other units of the *landeseigene Selbstschutzverbände*, of rhomboidal unpiped SS-style collar tabs, very likely in red. The use of the collar tabs is also confirmed by a mimeographed publication produced by the SNVZ Ceta based in Aidussina, called *Umreti Nočemo*, which had on its cover a drawing of an SNVZ soldier with crimson-red rhomboidal-shaped collar tabs.[6] In some cases it would appear that such insignia were certainly of a darker color, probably black. In addition, some photo portraits used for the identity cards of the SNVZ show the use of rhomboidal unpiped collar tabs made with a very light colored cloth, possibly white or yellow, carried on the collars of Italian mod. 40 fatigue tunics; at present the meaning of these insignia is not known.

The Italian *griogioverde* uniforms of the SNVZ and the greatcoats with black collars and cuffs carried shoulder boards piped with white *Waffenfarbe*, made of the same fabric used for the garment. Officers used removable rectangular shoulder boards very similar to, if not the very same as, the model in use in the Yugoslav army in the period between the two world wars; unfortunately, the image quality does not allow us to analyze properly this type of shoulder board but it seems that they were identical to those used by the *Slowenische Landeswehr* (see below), i.e., made with wire trim and carrying rank stars; this could probably be explained by the fact that several cadres and trainers came to the SNVZ from the *Slowenische Landeswehr*. It seems that the NCOs too wore the same shoulder boards as the *Slowenische Landeswehr*, made with dark cloth with a variable number of horizontal white stripes in the center of the shoulder board. Again, these shoulder boards were used on all types of tunic, made with gray-green or camouflage fabric.

The hats sometimes carried on the front a circular, probably white/red, German-style cockade (resembling the model on the *Schirmmütze*) or a metal badge, triangular or oval, with the Slovenian flag colors arranged horizontally. For this unit also it has been noted that on the left side of the *Einheitsfeldmütze* M43 a solid *Wehrmacht*-style *edelweiss* was sometimes used, although lacking the stem (apparently the same type used by the *Landschutz* of the Udine province).

Service documents: A few bilingual (German–Slovenian) *Ausweis* with photo are known, made in a greenish-bluish colored cardboard; they were headed *Slovenski Varnostni Zbor na Jadranskem Primorju–Slowenischer Landschutz im Adriatisches Küstenland* and on their cover was depicted the provincial arm shield described above. These identity cards were issued by the HSSPF OZAK/ *SS-Inspekteur der Landschutzes*. Two examples of a bilingual (German-Slovenian) SNVZ *Soldbuch für landeseigene Kräfte* with photo are also known: they are of late SS typology but without runes on the front cover, made in light brown cardboard, and showing peculiar translation errors.[7]

1.2.3: The *Landschutz* of the Pola province (Istria)

Uniforms: This *Landschutz*—like some other *landeseigene Selbstschutzverbände* units—used Italian mod. 40 tunics modified to look similar to the *Heer* M40/M41. The most important changes concerned the collar which was modified to better fit the new type of rhomboidal tabs. Also in this case, the use of Italian war booty tunics made of wool cloth or "tipo 343" fabric is documented. It seems that Italian mod. 40 trousers were often used, worn with the standard puttees already in use in the REI. Also this *Landschutz* used in some cases greatcoats with covered buttons, whose collar and cuffs were made with black fabric as already described for the SNVZ. The shoes appear to have been of very heterogeneous models, mostly of German or Italian production.

Headgear: Sidecaps, probably produced locally with Grigioverde or *feldgrau* cloth, were widely used: in this case also they were hybrids imitating the style of the *feldmütze* für SS M34 and the *Schiffchen* M40. No photo is known showing the use of helmets by this *Landschutz*.

Insignia: This *Landschutz* was certainly issued at least since June 1944, but probably already by April–May, a provincial arm shield which was affixed on the left sleeve of the tunic; this was embroidered and outlined in white, and depicted the typical Istria white goat standing on a piece of land, probably in green or brown, with the sky as background, probably in blue. Again shoulder boards piped with white *Waffenfarbe* were used, produced in the same cloth as the tunic, and red rhomboidal unpiped SS-type collar tabs. The sidecaps showed, in most of the analyzed cases, what appears to be a simple metallic tunic button used as cockade (again, as already used by *Trawniki* in Poland).

1.2.4: The *Landschutz* of the Fiume Province

At the present day one photo is known showing a member of this *Landschutz*. The photo, taken in October 1944, shows a soldier dressed in the typical Grigioverde tunic of the *Landschutz*. The tunic is equipped with shoulder boards made of the same fabric as the tunic and piped with white *Waffenfarbe*, and red unpiped rhomboidal SS-style collar tabs. The tunic was modified by replacing the neck with a broader German-style one, of a slightly different color; probably this kind of collar fit better the German-inspired rhomboidal collar tabs used by the various *Landschutz* units. The tunic is held at the waist by a non-standard belt made of cloth with rectangular metal buckle. The trousers were similar to the mod. 41 introduced for the Italian paratroopers; more practical than the previous models, these trousers were widely used during the last period of the conflict by the army and militarized organizations of the RSI as well as by units operating in the OZAK. As often seen on MVSN soldiers, the man in the photo wears white socks rolled at the ankles. The shoes seem to be Italian Armi a Piedi mod. 32 standard infantry boots. The tunic has no arm shield and no headgear is visible.

1.2.5: The Croatian *Landschutz* (*Kroatischer Landschutz*)

Information regarding this unit is virtually non-existent. According to some sources, it was formed by regular soldiers of the NDH *Hrvatsko Domobranstvo* (the army of Independent State of Croatia). This seems also confirmed by some not very clear photographs taken in Istria and probably depicting soldiers of the Croatian *Landschutz* wearing the typical dark gray-blue uniform of the *Hrvatsko Domobranstvo*. From these photographs it can also be deduced that in the Croatian *Landschutz* there were also some members of the NDH police, wearing the peculiar uniform with peaked cap. A source, although very confused, argues that members of the Croatian *Landschutz* wore an arm shield with the red-white checkboard of the Croatian flag. It is very likely that this source actually refers to the *2. Kroatische Legion*, a unit organised by the Italian army from mid-1943, which after the Italian armistice sided with the Germans and was based in the OZAK from late September to early December 1943; indeed its men wore such insignia on their sleeve. Another source suggests on the contrary that the Croatian *Landschutz* used a tricolor arm shield with transversal national colors (red-white-blue), of the same shape as the shields used by the Italians and Slovenians in the *SS-Wachmannschaften* of the OZAK; at the present day this cannot be confirmed by photographic evidence.

1.3: The *Reserve Landschutz*

From an early phase during the German occupation and until the end of the war there also existed under the HSSPF OZAK a *Reserve-Landschutz* (auxiliary territorial defense, or civil guard), on which there is only very fragmentary information. Its members wore civilian clothes but carried red armbands with the inscription *Difesa Territoriale – Landschutz* (at least for the Italian-speaking units).[8] It seems that sporadically they also used military uniforms (tunics carrying shoulder boards with white *Waffenfarbe*).

Regarding the *Reserve-Landschutz* of the Udine province, a rectangular patch has been found with the words *DT Artegna* (*Difesa Territoriale Artegna*) and the municipal coat-of-arms of Artegna (a town north of Udine), enclosed within a bordered outline, printed in dark red on light blue cloth. The patch was probably meant to be stitched on the red armband. It is possible that such patches were provided to or at least planned for all municipalities where the *Reserve-Landschutz* was organized.

At least the *Reserve-Landschutz* of the Udine province used as identity document a *Mitgliedausweis* with HSSPF OZAK heading and photo; it was square and printed on cream-colored cardboard in German and Italian.

2: The *Landschutz* in the Ljubljana Province - the *Slowenische Landeswehr* (*Slovensko Domobranstvo*)

Uniforms: After the collapse of the former Italian army in September 1943, the members of the Bela Garda that remained under arms in the former Italian Provincia di Lubiana (Ljubljana province, now the German-occupied Provinz Laibach) were almost immediately re-organized by the German authorities. They formed the Slovensko Domobranstvo, which was further expanded in the following months. Initially, this militia used uniforms and headgear of various origins (Italian, German, Yugoslav, and according to some sources Dutch), but later it was equipped with its own distinctive uniforms and insignia. Although it is difficult to reconstruct with certainty when the various types of uniforms were distributed, two main supply batches can be identified: the first was made up of Italian mod. 40 uniforms, sometimes worn with the characteristic Šajkača sidecaps of the former Yugoslav army; the second apparently consisted of standard *Ordnungspolizei* M43 uniforms, with sidecaps of German model or similar. For the Italian uniforms it is possible that they were war booty distributed without apparent changes (unlike what happened for most of those distributed to other provincial *Landschutz* units). This would seem to have happened in quite an early phase because no provincial arm shield was worn on these tunics. Apart for a small badge on the headgear, no other distinctive insignia were worn on these uniforms. Probably because of the scarcity of available Italian material (maybe because it was mainly allocated to the various *Landschutz* of the other OZAK provinces) or with a view to standardizing the uniforms to German models, during 1944 the new model of *Ordnungspolizei* tunic was distributed to the *Slowenische Landeswehr*. This type of tunic, introduced in 1943, but available in large quantities only from 1944, was produced with the characteristic *Polizei-Grün* color cloth, was closed by six buttons and had four pockets of which only the upper ones had the central reinforcing fold. These uniforms were often devoid of shoulder straps and did not carry the specific *Litzen* collar tabs. Some photos from mid-1944 also show *Slovensko Domobranstvo* soldiers wearing rectangular epaulettes in dark cloth with the typical *Tresse* along the edge; they were used probably by NCOs and corporals. Among upper-rank officers it was relatively common to use a tunic made in the style of the Soviet Gymnasterka M35, buttoned up to the stomach, with rectangular shoulder pads of metallic wire braid and chest pockets with closing flaps. Upper-rank officers used rarely also former Yugoslav army uniforms. Lower-rank officers commonly used, like the other ranks, *Ordnungspolizei* M43 tunics with proper shoulder boards made of metal wire braid. Photographic documentation also show the use of camo uniforms made with Italian mod. 29 fabric; they were not standardized, sometimes reproducing the German anoraks with chest pockets used by the *Gebirgsjäger*, or the Italian tropical Sahariana tunics. Regarding the trousers, it is likely that both Italian mod. 40 and *Ordnungspolizei* M43 were used; in the field they were worn with standard German canvas gaiters or socks rolled at the ankles. During winter months, officers and other ranks used German greatcoats (perhaps also the *Ordnungspolizei* model) or German-style double-breasted greatcoats. Like the SNVZ, the *Slowenische Landeswehr* also used a wide variety of belts, probably based on availability: models similar to those used in the former Austro–Hungarian Army, made with reddish leather with simple rectangular metallic buckle, standard German models with plaque, and models with shoulder strap (perhaps even of the type used by officers in the former Yugoslav army).

Headgear: The headgear also was of heterogeneous origin: in the early phase the Yugoslav *Šajkača* sidecap, with its peculiar sloping central part, was certainly distributed. Later on, German-style sidecaps were used, perhaps in some cases *Ordnungspolizei* models made in *Polizei–Grün*, or the already described models imitating the *feldmütze* für SS M34 or the *Schiffchen* M40 (in some cases, probably for the NCOs or officers, they had a white or silver piping along the edge of the cap's upturned folded brim). It would seem certain that in some cases models similar to the *Einheitsfeldmütze* M43 were used. As to steel helmets, the Italian mod. 33 was largely used but also the German M35/40 and the mod. 32/4 of Czech production already used in large quantities by the former Yugoslav army. Helmets were sometimes camouflaged with sprayed reddish-brown and yellow stripes.

Insignia: All members of the *Slowenische Landeswehr* wore a provincial arm shield, printed or embroidered and outlined, depicting the stylized blue eagle of the *Herzogtum Krain* (the ancient Carniola region Marquisate) on a white background. The NCOs and corporals used special shoulder boards probably in dark green cloth; for the corporals, they were decorated along the perimeter with *Tresse*; higher grades were identified by adding at the center of the shoulder boards one, two, or three stripes, probably made with the same types of *Tresse*, and sometimes also rank stars. There were also other types of shoulder boards, made with dark cloth and bearing large Arabic numbers in light color, probably white, made from die-cut fabric or embroidered. The officers used special shoulder boards similar to the models used in the former Yugoslav army, probably made of metallic wire braid and bearing rank stars; for the ranks of junior officers, from lieutenant to captain, the braid was silvered and the stars were golden, while for senior officers, from major to colonel, the braid was golden and the stars silvered. Generals wore epaulets similar to German models with Prussian silvered knots on golden braid. On the headgear was initially carried, in most cases, a metal triangular badge with the Slovenian flag, with colors arranged horizontally; this model co-existed with another one, similar but oval in shape. Both were eventually replaced by an oval badge depicting the traditional Carniola eagle superimposed on the Slovenien flag colors, still arranged horizontally. On the left side of the Italian mod. 33 helmets a shield with the Slovenian tricolor was usually painted, again with horizontally arranged colors.

Service documents: Some specimens of *ausweis*, with photo, apparently made in light-gray paper, issued by the HSSPF *Alpenland* to the members of this unit, are known. These were almost identical to those issued to the SNVZ, but bear the traditional Carniola eagle on the cover and were headed *Slovensko Domobranstvo v Ljubljanski Pokrajini – Slowenische Landeswehr in der Provinz Laibach*.

3: Other landeseigene Selbstschutzverbände of the OZAK

3.1: The Selbstschutz of the Valcanale/Kanaltal in the Udine province

Uniforms: This unit adopted a particular type of uniform that was similar to the models in use in the various *Landschutz* but with some peculiarities. It is not known if the tunics were new models or if they were made using as a starting point the *Heer* M40/M41, to which they had a similar cut. In case they were new models, it is impossible to determine whether the fabric and the materials were of Italian origin; certain accessories such as the buttons would seem to point against this possibility. The tunic had four patch pockets with central reinforcement and was closed by six buttons. The sleeves had no cuff and had buttons as on German models. The peculiarity of these tunics was the long pointed collar reminiscent in some ways at that of the M.07 uniforms used by the five mountain regiments of the Austro–Hungarian Army during World War I. It should be noted that the long pointed collar was also seen on *Ordnungspolizei*-style tunics used by some members of *Abteilung R* in the OZAK which—as far as the cut is concerned—differed from those of the *Selbstschutz* only for the presence of Italian-style cuffs. The trousers used by members of the *Selbstschutz* were made of the same cloth as the tunic and were similar to the *Heer* M43 trousers. They were worn with knee-high boots or inserted in the standard canvas gaiters or with socks rolled at the ankles. The most popular shoes were mountain boots, probably of German production. Italian mod. 07/36 belts were often used, holding the leather bandolier consisting of two single pouches for the Mauser K98 ammunition.

Headgear: Unit members appear in some cases to have used the *feldgrau* standard *Einheitsfeldmütze* M43, but it seems that also widely adopted was a type of headgear very similar to the (*ersatz*) *feldkappe* M.07/15 model, made entirely of felt (including the visor), of Austro–Hungarian origin or also of the model used by the Austrian

Heimatwehr during the pre-*Anschluss* years. In all cases, headgear seems to have been worn without any kind of insignia. There is no known photographic evidence regarding the use of helmets by the *Selbstschutz*.

Insignia: The unit did not use an arm shield; in its place the typical SS embroidered eagle was often worn. On the collar, rhomboidal unpiped SS-style collar tabs were used, probably made with black or very dark-colored fabric. The field gray tunic of the *Selbstschutz* was fitted with shoulder boards made of the same fabric as the garment and piped with white *Waffenfarbe*, as it was common for almost all other units of the *landeseigene Selbstschutzverbände*. The *edelweiss* was sometimes used on the left side of the field cap, as customary for the *Gebirgsjäger*; it was apparently metallic, of unknown origin, very similar to those produced for the *Hitlerjugend* and the *Sturmabteilung*. However, it seems certain that, in some cases, also the metal version of the *edelweiss* produced for the *Wehrmacht* was used.

3.2: The Stadtschutz Triest (Guardia Civica di Trieste)

Uniforms: This unit used uniforms of very different origins. Photographic evidence confirms the widespread use of both Grigioverde mod. 40 (wool cloth and "tipo 343") and fatigue tunics similar to the model used by the *Landeseigene Kräfte* of the *SS-Wachmannschaften*. Tunics similar to the mod. 27 of the MVSN (the type where only the pocket flaps were visible and the front buttons were covered) were also seen. Additionally, some privately tailored tunics made of khaki canvas were used, probably mostly during the warm season, with shorts of the same color.

Headgear: In addition to the various standard Italian-made mod. 34 and mod. 35 sidecaps, mod. 42 field caps made with Grigioverde or gabardine cloth were also used. This headgear was probably locally made by private tailors (in fact, until the disintegration of the REI in September 1943, there was never any regulation for this type of headgear in Grigioverde cloth for the enlisted

This photo shows another example of how Italian uniforms were modified to be worn by German or local units in the OZAK. Taken in spring 1944, it depicts three South Tyrolean recruits of the *Waffen-Ausbildungs-und-Ersatz-Btl. der SS of 24. Waffen-Gebirgs (Karstjäger)-Division der SS* near the D'Incau Solideo barracks in Ugovizza (Udine province), wearing a mix of Italian and German material. The tunics seem to be REI and MVSN mod. 40 tunics modified to imitate the cut of the *Heer* M40/M41 tunics; the modification consisted mainly in shortening the tunic, tightening the sides and sometimes adding a button along the front opening. It is not excluded that these tunics were produced in the OZAK. The soldier in the middle uses, instead of the standard leather belt with metal buckle, a cloth strap from the Italian mod. 40 uniform. Also in this case the SS-style arm eagle seems to be non-standard. Also curious is the use of the *Feldgrau Schiffchen* M40 with standard insignia, a headgear rarely worn by *Waffen-SS Gebirgstruppen* during the late war years.

personnel, while those used by the officers in the metropolitan area were all private acquisitions). Additionally, field caps made of Italian mod. 29 camo fabric, with the same features as the *SS-Tarnmütze* M42, were also used. Photos show the use by the *Guardia Civica* of Italian mod. 33 helmets, with a black halberd painted on the front, and in some cases also of German M35/40 helmets.

Insignia: This unit was not issued any arm shield but on the headgear wore a badge depicting the city of Trieste coat-of-arms, a white or silver halberd on a red background, topped by a crown. This type of insignia was made in a large number of variants, sometimes entirely of fabric, sometimes metallic (of considerable size) and also in a mixed version with embroidered and metal parts. Dark-red rhomboidal unpiped SS-style collar tabs were adopted and worn on all types of tunic; the right collar tab often carried a small metal halberd, while the left one carried, as necessary, the rank insignia; these were of the SS type, using stripes of *Tresse* and/or six-pointed *sterne* (very similar to the specific variant intended for the *Einsatzstaffel der Deutschen Mannschaft in Kroatien*).

Service documents: Examples are known of a bilingual (German–Italian) *Dienstausweis–Legittimazione* identity cards with photo, with bluish-green cover on which the city coat-of-arms with the halberd was printed. They were issued by HSSPF OZAK and were probably produced by the Tipografia Riva of Trieste in 1944. Curiously, such identity cards were almost identical to the ones issued to members of the *Polizei-Freiwilligen-Bataillon "Triest,"* of which one surviving example is also known.

Men in civilian clothes, probably recruits for the *landeseigene Selbstschutzverbände*, seen in Gorizia during 1944. This photo comes from the personal album of Franz, seized by the German authorities during the investigations of the Treblinka extermination camp.

Uniforms and Insignia of the *Oberkrain* and *Untersteiermark* Militias

In order to free combat units from onerous internal security duties in the occupied areas, a number of anti-partisan and anti-communist rural territorial militias were formed by the Germans along the southeastern border of the *Reich*. This project replicated the organization of the ethnic *Grenzer* (*Grenzjäger*) regiments that were used successfully for about 300 years by the Austro–Hungarian Empire in the same areas for anti-Turkish and anti-guerrilla warfare, along the so-called *Militärgrenze* (Vojna Krajina, military border). The references to these units and their traditional operational context are evident in the German propaganda produced in the OZAK. The propaganda efforts, aided by a massive circulation of publications written in the various local languages, were aimed primarily at promoting or awakening the self-awareness of the various local ethnic groups which for centuries had lived in the southern regions of the former Habsburg Empire.[1] For the sake of completeness it has been decided to briefly describe here also the German-sponsored units created near the OZAK, in the *Oberkrain* (Higher Carniola) and *Untersteiermark* (Lower Styria) regions, both annexed to the Reich in 1941 after the Yugoslav capitulation, but limited to the period from the Italian armistice until the end of the war. These units are certainly comparable to the *landeseigene Selbstschutzverbände* of the OZAK, with which they had some interesting similarities as far as their uniforms are concerned. They were in part also sporadically employed in the OZAK.

1: The Oberkrainer Selbstschutz (Gorenjsko Domobranstvo)

Uniforms: From the scarce and often unclear photographic documentation, it seems that the *Selbstschutz* organized by the *Kommandeur der Sicherheitspolizei* (KdS) Veldes (now Bled) in the *Oberkrain* wore a fairly heterogeneous mixture of uniforms. It seems, however, that their cut was always similar to German models. There were, for instance, tunics made on the style of the M37 used by the SS, apparently in a rather light color, devoid of any distinctive insignia and worn with open collar, as was common for the *Sipo*/SD. Also in this unit, towards the end of the conflict, *Ordnungspolizei* M43 tunics were widely used; also in this case, any insignia was absent. Also used were tunics, probably of local production, varying in cut and made with Italian camo mod. 29 fabric or with *Waffen-SS* camouflage fabric in its many variations of colors and patterns. Also documented is the use of reversible *Wehrmacht* parkas made with *Splitterntarn* camouflage fabric. Further on winter equipment, standard double-breasted greatcoats, perhaps of the *Ordnungspolizei* type, were distributed.

Headgear: The *Einheitsfeldmütze* M43 of German production was heavily used, however, there are also clear photographic evidences related to the use of field caps imitating the M43 but produced with various types of *Waffen-SS* camouflage fabric.

Insignia: On the tunic left sleeve an outlined provincial shield was carried, depicting the traditional blue *Herzogtum Krain* eagle on a red/white background with colors arranged vertically. It would appear that it was produced in both a printed and an embroidered version. In some cases, it seems that the arm shield was replaced by the SS sleeve eagle, although no photographic evidence has been found. Some sources also mention the use, by members of the assault troops of this unit, of the black rhomboidal SS-style right collar tab with *Totenkopf*, but also in this case photographic evidence confirming this is missing. On the left side of the *Einheitsfeldmütze* M43 the SS headgear eagle in BeVo was sometimes affixed, while on the front different badges were used, such as the metal tricolor oval insignia also supplied to the *Slowenischer Landeswehr* or rarely also the typical SS metal *Totenkopf*.

Service documents: Some examples of *ausweis* for the members of this *Selbstschutz* are known, printed or typewritten and with photo, issued by the various *Stapo-Aussendienststelle* of the Oberkrain. They all bear the stamp *Der Kommandeur der Sipo/SD in den wiedereroberten Gebieten von Kärnten*.
Note: From some very rare photographic evidence it seems clear that some *Oberkrainer* certainly wore the SS-type uniform with *Sipo*/SD insignia (black rhomboidal collar tabs of which the right one without runes) both with and without the SD-*Raute* on the sleeve. It is not clearly known why this type of uniform was used, but according to some sources those who wore it were members of the *Oberkrainer Selbstschutz* under the command of the *Grenzpolizei* of the *KdS Veldes*. In this regard it is interesting to mention that the so-called "*Gegenbande*" (*Protibande*, or counter-bands), special *Jagdkommando* units formed by the *KdS Veldes* with members of the German police together with local *Oberkrainer* guides, also used the *Sipo*/SD uniform pattern, as well as civilian clothes or partisan uniforms during counter-guerrilla actions.

2: The SA Wehrmannschaften of the Untersteiermark

Uniforms: This unit used special tunics made of cloth of a characteristic brown color, very similar to the pattern used by the *SA-Wehrmannschaften* in other districts of the *Reich* but lacking any bottom pockets and carrying five large metal front buttons. Trousers were similar, if not identical, to the model used by *SA-Wehrmannschaften* and made with the same cloth as the tunic; they had tight anklets for use with canvas gaiters or with rolled socks. Standard brown leather belts with rectangular metal buckle and mountain boots were widely used. In winter German-style double-breasted greatcoats, made with the same cloth as the uniform, were distributed.

Headgear: This unit used extensively the *SA-Tuchmütze* in brown cloth also adopted by the *SA-Wehrmannschaften* of the Alpine districts of the *Reich* (which was almost identical to the *Einheitsfeldmütze* M43 apart from the color); it lacked the characteristic colored band, and the foldable ear flaps were held above the visor with two buttons, also painted brown.

Insignia: Fixed shoulder boards piped with a silvered *Waffenfarbe* were worn on the tunic; rhomboidal brown collar tabs in a very similar hue as the uniforms, piped with a white braid, were carried on the collar. The *SA-Tuchmütze* carried the NSDAP M37 metal eagle on the front, while the SA metal *edelweiss* sewn on a backing of red cloth was affixed to the left side of the cap. Small patriotic insignia of the *Steierischer Heimatbund* were sometimes used. Probably, only during official events or celebrations, the unit wore special arm bands; one model was a green-white (the colors of Styria) band on which was applied a white circular badge on which were printed in black the Styrian coat-of-arms with a rampant panther, a swastika and the writing *Steierischer Heimatbund*. Later, towards the end of the conflict, this arm band was replaced by a green one with two white outlines at the edges and a golden band in the middle, superimposed with a white diamond outlined in gold, inside of which was printed a large black swastika with a white panther on it. In addition to these two arm bands there was also a third model, similar to the latter one, but with green-white-green colors and a black swastika in the center of a white diamond, similar to the model used by the *Hitlerjugend*.

Service documents: The members of this unit used the specific *Wehrmannschaftspass* of the *Steierischer Heimatbund*, in green cobalt color.

APPENDIX 4

Vehicles of *Abteilung R*; the *SS-Wachmannschaften*; and Unit Insignia

1: Vehicles

Abteilung R had a number of vehicles, which were parked in the SS garage on Via San Francesco in Trieste (at the then-number 21, where later—at least in the 1970s—there was a Lancia car dealership). This vehicle park was, however, not used exclusively by the unit; the vehicles belonged to the HSSPF and *Abteilung R* made use of them when needed.[1]

The unit also had (probably for its exclusive use) some combat vehicles, such as armored trucks, and at least one truck armed with a quadruple 20 mm gun. The armored trucks were probably acquired during winter 1943–44. The first photographs that show them in action date from the end of April 1944, during the anti-partisan operation *Unternehmen Braunschweig*. From available photographs it seems that there were at least three of them, perhaps four, with slight differences distinguishing one from the other. They were jury-rigged, using armored plates from various sources, including Austrian trench shields from World War I.[2] In their general lines they imitated the Fiat 665 NM armored truck produced for the Italian Army before the Italian armistice, and later widely used by the Germans. At least two armored trucks of *Abteilung R* were however produced on the chassis of the Fiat 626 truck, which was smaller and lighter than the Fiat 666 on which the Fiat 665 NM was based. They were mainly used to patrol the Trieste–Fiume road and to escort convoys travelling back and forth between these two cities. It seems that one was assigned to the group based in Castelnuovo;[3] another one was used by section R II in Fiume for liaison with Trieste.[4] One more armored truck, perhaps two, was probably based at the Risiera (where there was a garage) and was used by section R I.[5] They were all painted in a camouflage scheme consisting of a network of (probably) green stripes sprayed on a sand yellow base color. The characteristics of each identified truck are described further down with reference to the available photographs.

It is also possible, although not certain, that the Sd.Kfz. 253 half-track photographed during the parade of April 20, 1944, in Trieste, showing a large SS-style skull painted on the front (see photo on page 12), belonged to *Abteilung R* (or was at least used by it). *Abteilung R* also mounted at least one 2 cm *Flakvierling* 38 quadruple anti-aircraft gun on the flatbed of a non-armoured Fiat 626; it was already in use in the second half of April 1944.[6]

As far as the *SS-Wachmannschaften* of the OZAK are concerned, there is no specific information on their motor pool. Apparently, they were allocated a certain number of their own vehicles; a document by the HSSPF OZAK mentioned that the vehicles of the *Wachmannschaften*, like those of the *Landschutz*, had to carry registration plates starting with the LEV abbreviation (for "*landeseigene Verbände*") and numbers from 001 to 200. Additionally, it seems that the *SS-Wachmannschaften* also used when necessary (in particular for anti-partisan actions) vehicles put at their disposal by the HSSPF, by other SS/*Polizei* units, or even by the *Wehrmacht*.

According to a trial deposition by Oberhauser, the *Trawniki* company initially led by Schwarzenbacher in Trieste had a Soviet T-34 tank, but any other confirmation is missing.

2: Unit Insignia

Some photos show vehicles used by *Abteilung R* or the *SS-Wachmannschaften* of the OZAK carrying an insignia representing a globe, this being a clear hint to Globocnik's nickname, "Globus." It is not clear if this was the insignia of *Abteilung R* and/or the *SS-Wachmannschaften*, or if it belonged to the HSSPF OZAK.

On one occasion, Allers declared that a "Münchhausen" (probably a drawing of the Baron Münchhausen), was the tactical symbol used by the *SS-Wachmannschafts-Btl.*[7]

A rendering of the "Globus" insignia.

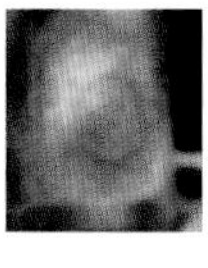

Close-up from another photo taken in Abbazia (see page 71): just visible on the car's right fender is apparently the "Globus" insignia. Note that the car has no registration plate.

The "Globus" insignia as seen on a vehicle (close-up from a photo of the Fiat 621 truck with registration number SS-965047, taken in Abbazia) (see the section on the *Unternehmen Braunschweig*, page 73).

Two images of a Fiat 626 truck with SS registration plate and the "Globus" insignia painted on the tailgate, photographed on the Trieste Ljubljana road near Vrhnika on January 28, 1944, while carrying cigarettes from Ljubljana to Trieste. Travelling on the truck were some *Trawniki* (wearing the black *Schutzmannschaften* coats), and members of the *Stabskompanie* of the HSSPF OZAK.

An Italian M15/42 tank that had been used by a German unit photographed in a captured equipment collection camp near Villa Vicentina, south of Udine, towards the end of 1945. The insignia painted on the turret rear depicts "Baron Münchhausen" flying on a cannonball. It is not known if this was the insignia that, according to Allers, was used by the *SS-Wachmannschafts-Btl. DeH, 14198*

The German cross (*Balkenkreuz*) painted on the tank is unusual in that the colors are inverted (white center and black borders) compared to normal practice. In the background is a *Panzer-Attrappe*, or tank mock-up, probably made of wood, used for training. *DeH, 8208 and 8209*

Vehicles belonging to the *SS-Wachmannschaften*, photographed inside the barracks of Via Besenghi in Trieste. Recognizable are three Benelli solo motorbikes, a motorbike with sidecar, a light truck, an OM 36 truck, a camouflaged Fiat 626 truck, and probably a car. The motorbikes have no registration number. The men wear uniforms with black collars, and two of them carry the national arm shield, respectively (from the right) Slovenian and Italian; on this basis the photo was probably taken before April 1944. *MNZS, NI11-508*

3: Armored Trucks of Abteilung R

Note: The numbers 1 to 4 are only used to distinguish the vehicles on the basis of the characteristics identified on the photos; these numbers were not used by *Abteilung R*.

Armored truck number 1: built on the chassis of a FIAT 626, with registration number SS 965034, it is recognizable from the front vision ports of different size and from the vertical, slanted and then again vertical flatbed side armour plates. It was armed with a French 8 mm Saint Etienne mod. 07T16 machine gun dating from World War I.

The armored truck with registration number SS 965034 belonging to *Abteilung R* on the Trieste–Fiume road (or Karststrasse) during the *Unternehmen Braunschweig*.

The same truck stopped in Castelnuovo d'Istria (now Podgrad, Slovenia), on the Karststrasse, almost certainly in the days of the *Unternehmen Braunschweig* operation (see the *Unternehmen Braunschweig* map, Then and Now point "A"). None of the men on or around the vehicle is identified. In the background an ambulance is parked in front of a dressing station, on the street leading to the village church.

The same armored truck number 1 in Trieste on April 20, 1944.

Armored truck number 2: built on the chassis of a FIAT 626, it is recognizable for the peculiar armored cover in front of the radiator. Also this vehicle was armed with a Saint Etienne mod. 07T16 machine gun.

The *Abteilung R* armored truck number 2 on the Karststrasse during the *Unternehmen Braunschweig*. Two more photos of the same vehicle are in the section dedicated to this operation.

This photo taken at the entrance to the Risiera complex shows Philip Post wearing an *Ordnungspolizei* uniform and behind him the armored truck number 2; as it can be seen, it had an SS registration plate but the number is not known. *LA NRW, Münster*

Men from *Abteilung R* taking cover on the ground next to a road, probably during contact with the partisans (the man in the foreground is identified as Erich Schulz, but more likely he is Gustav Münzberger). In the background on the left is armored truck number 2. *LA NRW, Münster*

Armored truck number 3: apparently carrying the registration number SS 965042, it is recognizable for having a particularly high vertical section of the flatbed side armor plates, and for a small rectangular welded plate connecting the cabin armor with the flatbed armor.

In the foreground is Paul Bredow, armed with a Finnish-produced Suomi KP/-31 sub-machine gun, behind him are men from *Abteilung R* wearing the characteristic camo outfit used by the unit and the armored truck number 3. *LA NRW, Münster*

A different cropping of the previous photo, showing a bit more of the same armored truck; the side of a second armored truck can just be seen in the background. The first man from the left is identified as Sporleder (but could also be Bolender), the second as Barbl; the second man from the right could be Rum. *LA NRW, Münster*

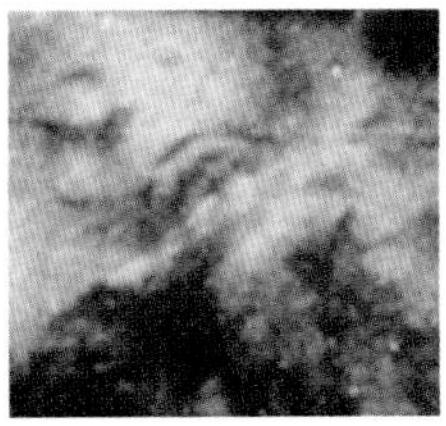

The men in this photo, taken in the first courtyard of the Risiera complex probably in spring 1944, are identified as (from the left) Hackenholt, Hering, Wirth, Stangl; the officer on the right is sometimes indicated as Oberhauser, but this appears incorrect. Behind them the armored truck number 3 is on the right, while number 4 is on the left. Note above Hackenholt's left shoulder the "Globus" insignia painted on the truck rear. *LA NRW, Münster*

The same armored truck number 3 in Trieste on April 20, 1944.

Armored truck number 4: only two photos of this truck are known (one of which shows it with armored truck number 3), both taken from behind, so its peculiarities cannot be determined. Although not certain, it seems that this was a different vehicle than the armored trucks 1 and 2.

A group of men from *Abteilung R* photographed with armored truck number 4: starting from the left on the ground are Kaiser (a Volksdeutscher *Trawniki*), Hödl, and Gomerski (the latter with *Waffen-SS* uniform); on the truck from the left are Dachsel, Pötzinger, and an unidentified man. On the right edge of the picture a small part of the "Globus" insignia can just be seen. *LA NRW, Münster*

A Fiat 626 truck armed with a quadruple *Flakvierling* 38 gun mounted on the flatbed, used by *Abteilung R*. The photo was made on the Trieste quay during the parade of April 20, 1944. The soldier standing on the truck on the left is a *Trawniki*, identifiable by the collar *Tresse*, rank strips on the shoulder boards, and black collar tabs with white piping. The driver wears on his right arm the *Ehrenwinkel der Alten Kämpfer*, the award for SS members that had joined this organisation or the NSDAP before January 30, 1933.

Personnel of *Abteilung R* lined up in the first courtyard in the Risiera, probably in March or April 1944. Recognizable in the first line are, from the left: Stadie, Bolender, ?, Lambert, Jührs. In the second line, behind Jührs is Gringers, behind Lambert is Schluch. Most men wear the *Ordnungspolizei* uniform; only two of them wear a uniform with SS collar tabs (Bolender with the runes and another man behind him, in the third line, apparently wearing a *Totenkopf* on his collar tab). Noticeable are also some *Trawniki* with the short lower collar *Tresse*. Behind the men is the same Fiat 626 truck with *Flakvierling* (covered by a camouflage cloth) as in the previous photo. In the foreground on the left is probably the access door to an armored truck. *LA NRW, Münster*

In the same place three men of *Abteilung R* (on the right is Fritz Küttner, wearing an old *Ordnungspolizei* M36 uniform) observing an Italian 20 mm anti-aircraft Breda 20/65 gun. Behind them is a *Flakvierling* 38 on a Fiat 626 truck, probably the same as in the two previous photos. *LA NRW, Münster*

Another photo probably taken on the same occasion, showing from the left Gentz, Bredow, Bolender, Gomerski, and Pötzinger. Gentz and Pötzinger wear *Ordnungspolizei* uniforms, Bolender a *Waffen-SS* one, Bredow and Gomerski motorcycle overcoats. Pötzinger is armed with a Suomi KP/-31 sub-machine gun, the others with Carcano mod. 91/38 rifles. On the left is probably the same truck as in the previous photos, with the *Flakvierling* hidden by a camouflage cloth. In the background in the middle, wearing no headgear, is probably Küttner. *LA NRW, Münster*

The same Sd.Kfz. 253 as seen earlier is being recovered from a vehicle dump in Casarsa, near Udine, in early 1946. *DeH, 14348*

Note that the half-track is missing its armored front plate decorated with the *Totenkopf*. The vehicle (still minus its front plate) is now part of the De Henriquez collection in Trieste, and is awaiting restoration. *DeH, 7792*

APPENDIX 5

List of Men Belonging to *Abteilung R* in the OZAK

Note: These lists are probably not complete, and not necessarily fully correct. Officer names are in **bold**.

Germans					
	Surname	Name	Rank in the OZAK	Was in	Notes
1	**Allers**	Dietrich	*SA-Stubaf.* + *Oberstltn.d.Pol.*	Trieste	commander of *Abteilung R*
2	Arndt (Arendt?)	Kurt		Trieste (?)	
3	Baer	Rudolf	*SS-Uscha.* (*Waffen-SS*)	Trieste	
4	Barbl	Heinrich		Trieste	
5	Bauer	Erich		Fiume, Trieste	
6	Becher	Werner			in Italy?
7	Beelitz	Willi		Udine	left Italy at unknown date
8	Bischkopf	Erich			
9	**Börner**	Gerhard	*SS-Ustuf./Ltn.d.Pol.*	Fiume	commander of R II; missing or killed in 1945?
10	Bolender	Kurt	*SS-Uscha.* (*Waffen-SS*)	Fiume, Trieste	
11	Bollert			Udine	in the Val Fella end 1944–45
12	Bredow	Paul		Trieste	
13	Dachsel	Arthur	*Owm.d.SchP.d.R.*	Fiume, Trieste	at the Risiera (warder)
14	Dietze	Erich	*Owm.d.SchP.d.R.*	Trieste	
15	Dubois	Werner	*SS-Scha.*, from January 1944 *SS-Oscha.* (*Waffen-SS*)	Trieste	
16	Eisold	Johannes		Trieste	left Italy in autumn 1944
17	Fels			Udine	in the Val Fella end 1944–45
18	Fettke	Erich		Trieste	courier Trieste/Berlin
19	**Fischer**	Helmut	*Polizeimeister*, from late June 1944 *SS-Ustuf.* (*Allgem.-SS*)	Fiume, Udine	possibly at the Sappiane and Castelnuovo outposts; commander of R III; in the Val Fella end 1944–45
20	Forker	Alfred		Trieste	

21	**Franz**	Kurt	*SS-Ustuf.* (*Waffen-SS*)	Trieste, Gorizia	
22	Frenzel	Karl		Fiume	
23	Geis	Albert		Trieste	arrived in Italy in autumn 1944; at the Risiera (warder); in Val Fella end 1944–45
24	Geng	Konrad	*Hptwm.d.SchP.*	Trieste	
25	Gentz	Ernst		Udine	
26	Girtzig	Hans	*SS-Rttf.*, from November 1944 *SS-Uscha.* (*Waffen-SS*)	Trieste	
27	Gley	Heinrich		Trieste	left Italy in July or August 1944
28	Godenschweig	Gerhard			in Italy?
29	Gomerski	Hubert	*SS-Oscha.* (*Waffen-SS*)	Fiume, Veneto	at the Mattuglie outpost; also in Lombardy/Piedmont
30	Gringers	Max	*Hwm.d.SchP.*	Trieste	died on 4/30/1944
31	Grossmann	Willy	*Owm.d.SchP.d.R.*	Trieste	in Tolmezzo end 1944
32	Hackenholt	Lorenz	*SS-Hscha.* (*Waffen-SS*)	Trieste	in Tolmezzo end 1944
33	**Häusler**	Willy	*Polizeimeister*, later *SS-Ustuf.* (*Allgem.-SS*)	Trieste	also in Lombardy/Piedmont; left Italy in March 1945
34	Hengst	August		Trieste, Udine	
35	**Hering**	Gottlieb	*SS-Hstuf.* (*Allgem.-SS*) + *Kriminalinspekteur* (*Kripo*)	Trieste, Udine	commander of R I and of the Risiera; left Italy in August 1944
36	Hiller	Richard		Fiume	
37	Hirtreiter	Josef		Udine (?)	
38	Hödl	Franz		Fiume, Veneto	
39	Horn	Otto		Trieste	at the Risiera (warder); left Italy in autumn 1944
40	Jührs	Robert	*Hwm.*	Trieste	
41	Kamm	Rudolf		Fiume	
42	Kielminsky	Otto		Udine	at the Castelnuovo outpost
43	Klier	Johann		Trieste	
44	Köhler	August	*Owm.*, later *Hwm.*	Trieste	arrived in Italia in September 1944
45	Koschewski	Fritz		Trieste	at the Risiera (warder)
46	Küttner	Fritz	*Polizeimeister*	Udine	temporary commander of R III; also in Lombardy/Piedmont; left Italy in March 1945
47	Lambert	Erwin	*Owm.*	Trieste, Fiume (?)	at the Mattuglie outpost; in Tolmezzo end 1944, in the Val Fella end 1944–45

48	Löffler	Alfred	*Rev.Owm.d.SchP.*	Trieste	died on 4/30/1944
49	Ludwig	Karl		Fiume	
50	Mätzig	Willy	*SS-Scha.* (*Waffen-SS*)	Trieste, Udine	at the Castelnuovo outpost
51	Matthes	Arthur		Trieste	
52	Mentz	Willy	*Hwm.*	Udine	at the Castelnuovo outpost
53	Miete	August	*Owm.*	Trieste, Udine	in the Val Fella end 1944–45
54	Möller	Robert			
55	Müller	Adolf (Karl?)			
56	Münzberger	Gustav	*Hwm.*	Udine	at the Castelnuovo outpost; in the Val Fella end 1944–45
57	Nowak	Walter		Trieste	
58	**Oberhauser**	Josef	*SS-Ustuf.*, from January 1945 *SS-Ostuf.* (*Waffen-SS*)	Trieste	commander of R I and of the Risiera
59	Orlyewski	Eduard		Trieste (?)	
60	Plikat	Karl-Heinz		Trieste	also in Lombardy/Piedmont; left Italy summer/autumn 1944
61	Pötzinger	Karl	*Hwm.*	Udine	died on 12/22/1944
62	Post	Philip	*Owm.*	Trieste, Veneto	also in Lombardy/Piedmont; left Italy in March 1945
63	Rehwald	Fritz (Wenzel)		Trieste	
64	**Reichleitner**	Franz	*SS-Ustuf.* (*Allgem.-SS*) + *Kriminalsekretaer* (*Kripo*) + *Hptm.d.Pol.*	Fiume	commander of R II; died on 1/3/1944
65	Richter	Karl	*Hwm.d.SchP.*	Fiume	died on 8/13/1944
66	Riedel	Kurt		Trieste	
67	Rose	Walter		Trieste	courier Trieste/Berlin
68	**Rost**	Paul	*Polizeimeister*, from November 1944 *Revierltn.d.SchP.* + *SS-Ustuf.* (*Allgem.-SS*)	Trieste	
69	Rum	Franz	*Hwm.*	Trieste	left Italy in February 1945
70	Schiffner	Karl		Trieste	
71	Schluch	Karl		Trieste	
72	Schmidt	Fritz		Trieste	
73	Schneider	Gerhard	*Hwm.d.SchP.*	Trieste	at the Risiera (warder)
74	Schrottmayer	Anton			

75	Schulz	Erich		Trieste	accounts mention two people named Schulz at the Risiera, a warder and one responsible for warehouses (mentioned first names are Adolf and Franz); one may have been a *Trawniki* (*Volksdeutscher*), or Schulze
76	Schulze			Trieste	see above
77	**Schwarz**	Gottfried	*SS-Ustuf.* (*Waffen-SS*)	Trieste	died on 6/19/1944
78	Seidel	Kurt	*Owm.d.SchP.d.R.*	Trieste	
79	Seidler	Ernst			left Italy at unknown date
80	Seifert	Rudolf	*Owm.d.SchP.*	Trieste	
81	Siebert	Gerhard		Trieste	left Italy in early 1944
82	Sporleder	Erich	*SS-Uscha.* (*Waffen-SS*?)		
83	Stadie	Otto	*Hwm.*	Fiume, Trieste	at the Risiera (warder)
84	**Stangl**	Franz	*SD-Hstuf.* (*Allgem.-SS*) + *Kriminalsekretaer* (*Kripo*) + *Obltn.d.Pol.*	Udine, Fiume, Veneto	commander of R II, R III, and R IV; also in Lombardy/Piedmont; left Italy in March 1945
85	Steubl	Karl	*Hptwm.d.SchP.*	Fiume	
86	Suchomel	Franz		Trieste, Udine, Veneto	also in Lombardy/Piedmont
87	Sydow	Hermann			
88	**Tauscher**	Fritz	*Oberltn.d.Pol.* + *SS-Ustuf.*	Trieste	
89	Thiel	Erich			missing in March 1945
90	Unverhau	Heinrich		Trieste	left Italy in March 1944
91	Vey (Fey)	Kurt	*Owm.d.SchP.d.R.*	Trieste	died in April (?) 1945
92	Wagner	Gustav		Fiume, Veneto	left Italy in March 1945
93	**Walther**	Arthur	*Revier-Ltn.d.SchP.*	Udine	arrived in Italy in March 1944; commander of R III; at the Castelnuovo outpost, later in Sesana
94	Wendlandt	Willi		Fiume, Trieste	died on 12/28/1944
95	**Wirth**	Christian	*SS-Hstuf.* (*Allgem.-SS*) + *Kriminalrat* (*Kripo*)	Trieste	commander of *Abteilung R*; wore *SS-Stubaf.* uniform; died on 5/26/1944
96	Witt	Wilhelm			
97	Wolf	Franz		Fiume, Trieste	
98	Zänker	Hans	*Owm.d.SchP.d.R.*	Trieste	
99	Zierke	Ernst		Fiume	at the Mattuglie outpost

Trawniki attached to *Abteilung R* in the OZAK				
	Surname	**Name**	**Rank in the OZAK**	**Notes**
1	Andrejewski			
2	Antonow	Wasyl (?)		
3	Bienemann			probably *Volksdeutscher*
4	Buziak			*Volksdeutscher*
5	Dahlke	Helmut		*Volksdeutscher*
6	Hellmuth			probably *Volksdeutscher*
7	Kaiser	Alexander	*SS-Hauptzugwachmann*	*Volksdeutscher*
8	Kostenko	Emil/ Emiljan	*SS-Zugwachmann*	died on 5/15/1944
9	Kostenko			brother of Emil/Emiljan
10	Libodenko	Dimitri		also spelled Lebodenko or Lebedenko; deserted
11	Makoda	Nikolay (?)		
12	Maurer		*SS-Zugwachmann*	probably *Volksdeutscher*
13	Prochorenko	Wasyl (?)		
14	Razenko			= Rosenke?
15	Rosenke	Arnold	*SS-Zugwachmann*	probably *Volksdeutscher*; missing in action in March 1945
16	Rosenke	E.		probably *Volksdeutscher*
17	Schalajew	Nikolay (?)		
18	Schmidt	C.	*SS-Zugwachmann d.SchP*. (sic)	*Volksdeutscher*; died on 4/9/1944
19	Schneider	Friedrich (?)	*SS-Hauptzugwachmann*	*Volksdeutscher*
20	Schütz			*Volksdeutscher*
21	Schulz		*SS-Zugwachmann*	probably *Volksdeutscher*; deserted?
22	Siewert			*Volksdeutscher*
23	Szpliny	Heinrich		*Volksdeutscher*

APPENDIX 6

Comparative Rank Table: *Heer, Waffen-SS, Ordnungspolizei*, Italian Army, US Army

Heer	*Waffen-SS*	*Ordnungspolizei*	Italian Army	US Army
Mannschaft	***Mannschaft***	***Mannschaft***	***Truppa***	**Enlisted men**
Schütze (Grenadier, Pionier, etc.)	*SS-Schütze* (*SS-Grenadier, SS-Pionier*, etc.)	*Anwärter*	*Soldato*	Private
Oberschütze (*Obergrenadier, Oberpionier*, etc.)	*SS-Oberschütze* (*SS-Obergrenadier, SS-Oberpionier*, etc.)		*Appuntato*	Private 1st class
Gefreiter	*SS-Sturmmann*	*Unterwachtmeister*	*Caporale*	Lance Corporal
Obergefreiter	*SS-Rottenführer*	*Rottwachtmeister*	*Caporalmaggiore*	Corporal
Unteroffiziere	***Unteroffiziere***	***Unteroffiziere***	***Sottufficiali***	**NCOs**
Unteroffizier	*SS-Unterscharführer*	*Wachtmeister*	*Sergente*	Sergeant
Unterfeldwebel (*Unterwachtmeister*#)	*SS-Scharführer*	*Oberwachtmeister*	*Sergente maggiore*	Sergeant Major
Feldwebel (*Wachtmeister*#)	*SS-Oberscharführer*	*Revier-Oberwachtmeister/ Zugwachtmeister*	*Maresciallo ordinario*	Technical Sergeant
Oberfeldwebel (*Oberwachtmeister*#)	*SS-Hauptscharführer*	*Hauptwachtmeister*	*Maresciallo capo*	Master Sergeant
Stabsfeldwebel (*Stabswachtmeister*#)	*SS-Sturmscharführer*	*Meister*	*Maresciallo maggiore*	Staff Sergeant Major
Offiziere	***Offiziere***	***Offiziere***	***Ufficiali***	**Officers**
Fähnrich			*Aspirante*	Officer candidate
Leutnant	*SS-Untersturmführer*	*Leutnant der Polizei*	*Sottotenente*	Second Lieutenant
Oberleutnant	*SS-Obersturmführer*	*Oberleutnant der Polizei*	*Tenente*	First Lieutenant
Hauptmann (*Rittmeister*#)	*SS-Hauptsturmführer*	*Hauptmann der Polizei*	*Capitano*	Captain
Major	*SS-Sturmbannführer*	*Major der Polizei*	*Maggiore*	Major
Oberstleutnant	*SS-Obersturmbannführer*	*Oberstleutnant der Polizei*	*Tenente Colonnello*	Lieutenant Colonel
Oberst	*SS-Standartenführer*	*Oberst der Polizei*	*Colonnello*	Colonel

SS-Oberführer			Senior Colonel	
Generalmajor	*SS-Brigadeführer und Generalmajor der Waffen-SS*	*Generalmajor der Polizei*	*Generale di brigata*	Major General
Generalleutnant	*SS-Gruppenführer und Generalleutnant der Waffen-SS*	*Generalleutnant der Polizei*	*Generale di divisione*	Lieutenant General
General der ... (Infanterie, Artillerie, Gebirgstruppen, etc.)	*SS-Obergruppenführer und General der Waffen-SS*	*General der Polizei*	*Generale di corpo d'armata*	General
Generaloberst	*SS-Oberstgruppenführer und Generaloberst der Waffen-SS*	*Generaloberst der Polizei*	*Generale d'armata*	General of the Army
Generalfeldmarschall			*Maresciallo d'Italia*	
# = Cavalry ranks				

APPENDIX 7

Place Name Equivalents in Italian, Slovenian, and Croatian

The following list includes towns and villages whose Italian names are used in the text (as they were inside Italy's borders at the time of the events, the Italian names were used in official documents and maps), but which are now in Slovenia or Croatia, with their present name.

Italian name	Slovenian/Croatian name
Abbazia	Opatjia (Croatia)
Aidussina	Ajdovščina (Slovenia)
Albona	Labin (Croatia)
Antignana	Tinjan (Croatia)
Antignana	Tinjan (Slovenia)
Apriano	Veprinac (Croatia)
Arsia	Raša (Croatia)
Aurania	Vranja (Croatia)
Baccia di Matteria	Bač pri Materiji (Slovenia)
Barbana	Barban (Croatia)
Becca	Beka (Slovenia)
Brdo	Brdo (Croatia)
Bergut Grande	Veli Brgud (Croatia)
Bergut Piccolo	Mali Brgud (Croatia)
Bogliuno	Boljun (Croatia)
Braicovici	Brajkovići (Croatia)
Bresa	Breza (Croatia)
Buie	Buje (Croatia)
Cacitti	Kačiče (Slovenia)
Calcizza	Kovčice (Slovenia)
Canale d'Isonzo	Kanal ob Soči (Slovenia)
Capodistria	Koper (Slovenia)
Caporetto	Kobarid (Slovenia)
Capriva del Carso	Kopriva (Slovenia)
Càrie	Harije (Slovenia)
Castel Lupogliano	Lupoglav (Croatia)
Castelnuovo d'Istria	Podgrad (Slovenia)
Castua	Kastav (Croatia)
Cattuni	Katun (Croatia)
Cere	Cere (Croatia)
Cerreto	Cerovlje (Croatia)
Chersano	Kršan (Croatia)
Chiapovano	Čepovan (Slovenia)
Circhina	Cerkno (Slovenia)
Clana	Klana (Croatia)
Clenosciacco	Klenovšćak (Croatia)
Cosina	Kozina (Slovenia)
Cottesevo	Kuteževo (Slovenia)
Crepegliano	Kreplje (Slovenia)
Criva	Kriva (Croatia)
Crussizza	Hrušica (Slovenia)
Cuie	Huje (Slovenia)
Danne	Dane (Croatia)
Divaccia	Divača (Slovenia)
Draguccio	Draguć (Croatia)
Duttogliano	Dutovlje (Slovenia)
Erpelle	Hrpelje (Slovenia)
Elsane	Jelšane (Slovenia)

Fabice	Fabci (Slovenia)
Felicia	Zatka Čepić (Croatia)
Fianona	Plomin (Croatia)
Fiume	Rijeka (Croatia)
Gabrega	Gabrk (Slovenia)
Gabrovizza	Gabrovica pri Črnem Kalu (Croatia)
Gelovizza	Jelovica (Croatia)
Giavorie	Javorje (Slovenia)
Gimino	Žminj (Croatia)
Giordani	Jurdani (Croatia)
Gradischie	Gradisce pri Materiji (Slovenia)
Grisignana	Grožnjan (Croatia)
Iscra	Lisac (Croatia)
Lanischie	Lanišće (Croatia)
Laurana	Lovran (Croatia)
Lipa (or Lippa)	Lipa (Croatia)
Loce Grande	Velike Loče (Slovenia)
Magnadorsi	Manjadvorci (Croatia)
Marcossina	Markovščina (Slovenia)
Matteria	Materija (Slovenia)
Mattuglie	Matulji (Croatia)
Merse	Mrše (Slovenia)
Montemaggiore d'Istria (or Villamonte) Grande	Vela Učka (Croatia)
Montemaggiore d'Istria (or Villamonte) Piccolo	Mala Učka (Croatia)
Montespino	Dornberk (Slovenia)
Moschiena	Mošćenice (Croatia)
Mucici	Mučići (Croatia)
Mune Grande	Vele Mune (Croatia)
Mune Piccolo	Male Mune (Croatia)
Nazire di San Dorligo della Valle	Nasirec (Slovenia)
Novocracina (or Graccina Nova)	Novokračine (Croatia)
Obrovo	Obrov (Slovenia)
Occisla	Ocizla (Slovenia)
Opacchiasella	Opatje Selo (Slovenia)

Orecchia	Orehek pri Materiji (Slovenia)
Passiaco	Pasjak (Croatia)
Passo	Paz (Croatia)
Piedimonte del Taiano	Podgorje (Slovenia)
Pinguente	Buzet (Croatia)
Pirano	Piran (Croatia)
Pisino	Pazin (Croatia)
Plezzo	Bovec (Slovenia)
Pobese	Podbeže (Slovenia)
Podicrai	Podkraj (Slovenia)
Pola	Pula (Croatia)
Portorose	Portorož (Slovenia)
Postumia	Postojna (Slovenia)
Prapozze	Praproče pri Podpeč (Slovenia)
Pregara	Pregarje (Slovenia)
Prelose	Prelože (Slovenia
Prestrane	Prestranek (Slovenia)
Prevacina	Prvačina (Slovenia)
Prevallo (or Preval)	Preval (Slovenia)
Prodol	Prodol (Croatia)
Racia	Račja Vas (Croatia)
Raspo	Rašpor (Croatia)
Recizza	Rečica (Slovenia)
Rifembergo	Branik (Slovenia)
Rittomece	Ritomece (Slovenia)
Rovigno	Rovinj (Croatia)
Ruccavazzo	Rukavac (Croatia)
Rupa (or Ruppa)	Rupa (Croatia)
Sambasso	Šempas (Slovenia)
San Daniele del Carso	Štanjel (Slovenia)
San Pietro del Carso	Pivka (Slovenia)
San Pietro di Gorizia	Šempeter (Slovenia)
San Pietro di Madrasso	Klanec pri Kozini (Slovenia)
San Sergio	Črni Kal (Slovenia)
Santa Croce di Aidussina	Vipavski Križ (Slovenia)
Santa Domenica di Albona	Nedešćina (Croatia)

Santa Lucia di Tolmino	Most na Soči (Slovenia)
Sappiane	Šapjane (Croatia)
Sasseto	Saksid (Slovenia
Sasseto	Zazid (Slovenia)
Seiane	Žejane (Croatia)
Senosecchia	Senožeče (Slovenia)
Sesana	Sežana (Slovenia)
Sicciole	Sečovlje (Slovenia)
Sinadole	Senadole (Slovenia)
Slivia	Slivje (Slovenia)
Sottomerischie	Podmerišće (Croatia)
Starada	Starod (Slovenia)
Storie	Štorje (Slovenia)
Studena	Studena (Croatia)
Succorie	Suhorje (Slovenia)
Sucodru	Jasenovik (Croatia)
Sumbresi	Šumber (Croatia)
Suonecchia	Zvoneće (Croatia)
Sussa	Susak (Slovenia)
Susak (o Sussa)	Sušak (Croatia)
Tatre	Tatre (Slovenia)
Tolmino	Tolmin (Slovenia)

Tomigna	Tominje (Slovenia)
Trestenico di Raspo	Trstenik (Croatia)
Valdarsa (or Susgnevizza)	Šušnjevica (Croatia)
Valsantamarina (or Draga di Moschiena)	Mošćenička Draga (Croatia)
Vele Lasi	Vele Lasi (Croatia)
Veliacchi	Veljaki (Croatia)
Vertoiba	Vrtojba (Slovenia)
Villabassa di Senosecchia	Dolenja Vas (Slovenia)
Villa Decani	Dekani (Slovenia)
Villa del Nevoso	Ilirska Bistrica (Slovenia)
Villa di Rovigno	Rovinjsko Selo (Croatia)
Villanova	Nova Vas (Croatia)
Villa Podigraie	Podgraje (Slovenia)
Vodizze di Castelnuovo	Vodice (Croatia)
Volosca	Volosko (Croatia)
Vosilla	Vozilići (Croatia)
Zaielse	Zajelšje (Slovenia)
Zolla	Col (Slovenia)

Endnotes

Chapter 1

1. The camps' commanders were: in Belzec, Christian Wirth, from spring 1942, Gottlieb Hering; in Sobibor, Franz Stangl, from September 1942, Franz Reichleitner; in Treblinka, Irmfried Eberl, from September 1942, Franz Stangl, from August 1943, Kurt Franz. All took part in *Aktion T4*.

Chapter 2

1. On the OZAK, and in particular on the military aspects of the German occupation, see Stefano Di Giusto, *Operationszone Adriatisches Küstenland. Udine Gorizia Trieste Pola Fiume e Lubiana durante l'occupazione tedesca 1943–1945,* IFSML, Udine, 2005 (see www.panzer-ozak.it).

2. The *Sicherheitspolizei* included the *Kriminalpolizei* (*Kripo*, criminal police) and the *Geheime Staatspolizei* (*Gestapo*, state secret police).

3. The *Ordnungspolizei* included several components, among which the main ones were the *Schutzpolizei* (*SchP*. or *Schupo*, state protection police), the *Gendarmerie* (*Gend*., police for rural areas), the *Verwaltungspolizei* (administrative police), the *Verkehrspolizei* (traffic police), the *Wasserschutzpolizei* (water police), as well as several branches of auxiliary police.

Chapter 3

1. Initially it was just sixteen men in total; among them some of his closest collaborators, such as Ernst Lerch, Georg Michalsen, Gustav Hanelt, Adolf Bareuther. In the convoy travelled also around thirty *Trawniki* (deposition by Alexiej Mihalic, who was one of them, of 16.1.1976, during the investigations for a second Risiera di San Sabba trial).

2. During his stay in the OZAK, Wirth signed as *SS-Sturmbannführer* and wore an *SS-Sturmbannführer* uniform. In April 1943, Globocnik wrote to the SS personnel office (*SS-Personalhauptamt*) that Himmler had promoted Wirth to *SS-Sturmbannführer* during his visit to Lublin in February 1943, and he requested this promotion to be formally acknowledged. However, the *SS-Personalhauptamt* pointed out that according to official documentation Wirth was only *SS-Obersturmführer* and therefore he could not be directly promoted to *SS-Sturmbannführer*. Accordingly, Wirth's last rank was officially *SS-Hauptsturmführer* and he was indicated as such in the documents referring to his death and in the official death announcement published in the *Befehlsblatt des Chefs der Sipo*/SD (Wirth's personal file, BA Berlin).

3. The relationship between Wirth and Oberhauser is not completely clear: in several depositions by former members of *Abteilung R*, Oberhauser is defined as Wirth's aid or orderly officer; in others, his role is described as more limited, such as Wirth's assistant, orderly, or escort. The option that he was an assistant and escort seems more likely; in any case Oberhauser accompanied Wirth in all his movements and was evidently his closest collaborator. According to Oberhauser, in Poland he was also liaison officer between Wirth and the *Stab* of the SSPF Lublin, Globocnik.

4. Geng was Wirth's driver. On the presence of Baer in the group (mentioned in a deposition by Geng) there is some uncertainty, because at least two other former members of *Abteilung R* (August Hengst and Willy Häusler, both contradicting themselves in different depositions, though) stated that they travelled to Trieste with Wirth.

5. Deposition by Oberhauser of 24.9.1973 (HHStA, Wiesbaden, Abt. 631a, Nr. 1330).

6. It was planned that Wirth would later take up command of this and other similar battalions that Globocnik intended to set up in the other provinces of the OZAK region. However, no other SS battalion was formed, and Wirth was destined to lead *Abteilung R* and to other tasks. On the *SS-WMS-Btl*. and in general on the *SS-Wachmannschaften* of the OZAK—units that had significant links with *Abteilung R*—see the specific chapter.

7. Deposition by Stadie of 9.7.1962 (LA NRW, Münster, Q234, Nr. 4275).

8. Letter from Globocnik to von Herff dated October 27, 1943 (Globocnik's personal file, BA Berlin).

9. The often-cited figure of ninety-two members of *Abteilung R* present in the OZAK is not correct. It comes in fact from the mentioned letter by Globocnik, in which however this figure—as seen—is referred to the men seconded from Hitler's Chancellery for *Aktion Reinhard* in Poland.

10. According to Geng, the unit name in Italy was *Einsatzstab Reinhard*, but no confirmation to this statement has been found. The documents from HSSPF OZAK generally use, as far it could be ascertained, the name *Abteilung R*. According to Suchomel, later (under Allers, Wirth's successor) the term "Reinhard" was replaced by "Münchhausen," but this was denied by Allers, who stated in a deposition that a "Münchhausen," i.e., probably a drawing of the Baron Münchhausen, was just used as unit insignia of *SS-WMS-Btl*.

11. Among the men who lived in the villa were Wirth's orderly, Rum, and his driver, Geng. Rum was later also Allers' orderly. Also Geng was initially Allers' driver, but was later replaced by a Ukrainian *Trawniki*, Libodenko, who subsequently deserted.

12. Formally they remained however civilians: in a letter sent by the T4 office to Pötzinger's wife (following his death in Italy on 22.12.1944) in February 1945 one can read: "It is generally known that your husband, although he was employed in a special assignment (*Sondereinsatz*), is fallen as a civilian employee (*Zivilangestellter*)." (LA NRW, Münster, Q234, Nr. 4271).

13. See on this also the appendix 1 on uniforms.

14. On the *Trawniki* see primarily Peter Black, "Foot Soldiers of the Final Solution: The Trawniki Training Camp and Operation *Reinhard*," in *Holocaust & Genocide Studies*, vol. 25, nr. 1 (spring 2011).

15. They will be indicated here as "*Trawniki* attached to *Abteilung R*."

16. The complex is generally indicated as Risiera di San Sabba. As in the common use, here it will also be indicated just with the terms of Risiera or San Sabba.

17. Of these, at least the following came from *Aktion T4* without having taken part in *Aktion Reinhard* in Poland: Fettke, Fischer, Geis, Köhler, Riedel, Rose, Schneider, and Siebert.

18. According to a deposition (Bauer, 12.2.1963, StA München, Nr. 33033/8) there was a base in Fiume and one in Sušak, but further confirmation is missing; another deposition (Gomerski, 27.8.1965, HHStA, Wiesbaden, Abt. 631a, Nr. 887) indicated both Sušak and Mattuglie as Stützpunkt, or outpost (on Mattuglie see later). On section R II see in particular the depositions by Stangl of 12.3.1971 and by Wolf of 3.5.1971 (both in IRSML-FVG, Risiera collection, box 88).

19. Of these, only Fischer came from *Aktion T4* without having taken part in *Aktion Reinhard* in Poland.

20. Of these, Bollert, Fels and Fischer came from *Aktion T4* without having taken part in *Aktion Reinhard* in Poland.

21. On section R III see in particular the depositions by Mätzig of 8.10.1968 and 14.9.1970, by Münzberger of 7.8.1967, by Suchomel of 10.8.1967 and by Walther of 22.6.1967 (all in IRSML-FVG, Risiera collection, box 88), and by Fischer of 27.6.1969 (HHStA, Wiesbaden, Abt. 631a, Nr. 1320).

22. Account by Suchomel in Pier Arrigo Carnier, *Lo sterminio mancato. La dominazione nazista nel Veneto orientale 1943–1945*, Mursia, Milano, 1988, pg. 67 and 95.

23. Of these, at least the following came from *Aktion T4* without having taken part in *Aktion Reinhard* in Poland: Bischkopf, Godenschweig, Schrottmayer, Thiel, Witt.

24. According to a deposition by Häusler (of 20.3.1962, LA NRW, Münster, Q234, Nr. 4271) he, Stangl, Küttner, and Wagner were sent back to Germany in March 1945 for disciplinary reasons. This is also confirmed by Suchomel (deposition of 24.1.1962, LA NRW, Münster, Q234, Nr. 4269), who also added the name of Post, sent back for the same reason. However, in other depositions Häusler declared to have gone to Berlin on leave; here at the T4 he was then told not to go back to Italy. In a deposition Stangl claimed to have been repatriated in February 1945 because of illness.

25. The dead of *Abteilung R* were buried at the German military cemetery of Opicina, near Trieste. After the war the bodies were transferred to the military cemetery of Costermano, near

Verona. The presence in this cemetery in particular of the bodies of Wirth, Reichleitner, and Schwarz caused heated discussions at the end of the 1980s. In the early 1990s, these three names were therefore removed from the book of honor and their ranks deleted from the tombstones.

26. On the episode see Tone Ferenc, *Satan, njegovo delo in smrt*, Ljubljana, 1979 (Wirth's biography, consulted in an unpublished Italian version). A description of the episode is also in the history of the partisan unit that carried out the ambush: Maks Zadnik, "Istrski odred," *Nova Gorica*, 1975, pp. 317–323 (it is not possible to comment here on the reliability of this reconstruction, in particular the claim that a Ukrainian named Nikolai died with Wirth; in any case one element of the reconstruction, i.e., the claim that Geng was heavily wounded to the stomach, is not correct, as—according to his own account of the episode—he was wounded but only lightly). Geng recalled the episode in his deposition of 1.9.1970 (IRSML-FVG, Risiera collection, box 88, also published in Adolfo Scalpelli, *San Sabba. Istruttoria e processo per il Lager della Risiera*, Aned-Lint, Trieste, 1995, vol. 2, pg. 97).

27. Fischer declared in a trial deposition (of 27.6.1969, HHStA Wiesbaden, Abt. 631a, Nr. 1329) to have arrived in the OZAK during August 1944, but this is perhaps not correct. He was possibly the "Captain Fischer" that according to Yugoslav documents (prosecution file for war crimes) commanded the Sappiane outpost, and apparently also the one of Castelnuovo d'Istria, already at least from the second half of March 1944 (see the section on the Lipa massacre).

28. According to a trial deposition by Münzberger of 26.1.1962 (LA NRW, Münster, Q234, Nr. 4272), at the arrival in Trieste of his group Wirth explained to them that their task was to, "make the provinces of Trieste, Udine, Fiume and Pola free of Jews ("*judenfrei*")" and additionally to, "acquire and administer the properties and goods of the Jews."

29. Deposition by Dubois of 2.8.1967 (IRSML-FVG, Risiera collection, box 88, also published in Italian translation in Adolfo Scalpelli, *San Sabba*, vol. 2, pp. 21–25) and deposition by Wolf of 3.8.1967 (IRSML-FVG, Risiera collection, box 88); it is not clear if this is the same episode, but it seems likely.

30. Dante Fangaresi, *Dieci settimane a San Sabba*, Edizioni Polistampa, Firenze, 2003, pp. 82–84 and pp. 85–88.

31. Deposition by Oberhauser of 24.9.1973 (HHStA, Wiesbaden, Abt. 631a, Nr. 1330) and of 3.5.1971 (IRSML-FVG, Risiera collection, box 88, also published in Italian translation in Adolfo Scalpelli, *San Sabba*, vol. 2, pp. 31–35). See also the deposition by Stangl of 12.3.1971 (IRSML-FVG, Fondo Risiera, busta 88).

32. Deposition by Suchomel of 10.8.1967 (LA NRW, Münster, Q234, Nr. 4269) and his letter to Carnier published in Pier Arrigo Carnier, *Lo sterminio mancato*, pg. 360. A hint of this is also to be found in the deposition by Dubois of 2.8.1967 (IRSML-FVG, Risiera collection, box 88, also published in Italian translation in Adolfo Scalpelli, *San Sabba*, vol. 2, pp. 21–25).

33. Also the properties of emigrated Jews, stored in the warehouses of the Trieste port, were seized.

34. Deposition by Häusler of 11.6.1971 (HHStA, Wiesbaden, Abt. 631a, Nr. 1316). According to Pier Arrigo Carnier, *Lo sterminio mancato*, pg. 108, Stangl, Häusler, Suchomel and others were in Turin; Küttner, Plikat, Gomerski, Post, and others in Milan. Carnier says that these groups had the task of acquiring materials for the construction of the defensive lines coordinated by *Sonderauftrag Pöll* (see section 3.4.5); it is likely that they also had this task, but Häusler's deposition indicates that they also seized Jewish property.

35. Deposition by Oberhauser of 3.5.1971 (IRSML-FVG, Risiera collection, box 88, also published in Italian translation in Adolfo Scalpelli, *San Sabba*, vol. 2, pp. 31–35).

36. There were in *Abteilung R* at least two Schulz (one of them was named Erich, the other one was a *Volksdeutscher Trawniki*) and one Schulze; it is not clear who was the warder, perhaps the *Trawniki*.

37. Hackenholt was apparently responsible for the vehicle park as well as a kind of "factotum" (he received the *Eisernes Kreuz II. Klasse* in Italy in April 1944, motivated as it seems by his talent as an "organizer"); Bolender was seconded to *6. Kp./SS-WMS-Btl.* (see next chapter).

38. Around April 20, 1945, around 285 Italian RSI soldiers belonging to *16. Battaglione Costiero da Fortezza* (coast fortress battalion) were

imprisoned in the Risiera (around 200 recruits from 2. Company arrived at the Risiera in the night between April 20–21, around eighty-five soldiers from 1. Company arrived the next night); they came from Fiume, where in the previous months they had manned part of the city external defense belt. They were disarmed by the Germans on April 16–17, after discovering a plan for the unit to go over to the resistance movement and, if necessary, fight against the Germans. An officer, *Sottotenente* Raoul Sperber, considered the author of the plan, was shot in Fiume on April 18; other officers were arrested. The soldiers brought to the Risiera were probably spared because it was considered that they were not aware of the plan or not actively involved in its implementation. The soldiers were imprisoned in the large rooms on the second and third floor of the building on the left of the second courtyard; through slits in the wooden floor they managed to speak to civilian prisoners (Jewish men and women and Slovenian women) who occupied the first floor. Some days after their arrival, the soldiers were asked if they were ready to fight with the Germans or go for work service; all chose the latter option, but remained imprisoned until April 28, when they were sent by tram to a barracks in the center of the city. Because of the weak surveillance and the news of the imminent end of the war gathered from civilians, most of the soldiers fled during the transfer. On this unit see Carlo Cucut, *Alpini nella città di Fiume 1944–1945*, Marvia, 2012.

39. Much of the information on the Risiera di San Sabba is taken from the depositions of former inmates made during the trial celebrated in Trieste in 1976, published in Adolfo Scalpelli, *San Sabba*, vol. 2.

40. On *Kommando G.* and Franz's activities see the chapter on the *SS-Wachmannschaften*.

41. Depositions by Stangl of September 1947 (HHStA, Wiesbaden, Abt. 631a, Nr. 1331a), of 27.6.1967 (summarized in HHStA, Wiesbaden, Abt. 631a, Nr. 1315) and of 12.3.1971 (IRSML-FVG, Risiera collection, box 88). A report by the *Sonderkommando "Adria" – Einsatztrupp Fiume* (operational section based in Fiume) dated June 2, 1944 mentioned the participation of the "*Stützpunkt Mattuglie, SS-Hstf. Stangel*" (very likely it was meant Stangl) to an action where leaflets were distributed and propaganda posters affixed in the Fiume province in the previous days.

42. The Karst Plateau or the Karst region, also simply known as the Karst (Italian: Carso; Slovene: Kras), is a limestone plateau region extending north, east, and southeast of Trieste.

43. BA-MA Freiburg, RH 20-14/83 (AOK 14, Ic Meldungen, where the name of Reichleitner is erroneously indicated as Reitleithner). The next day, probably in response to the ambush, unidentified German forces, among which probably also members of *Abteilung R*, carried out a sweep operation in an area thirteen kilometers north of Castelnuovo, killing five partisans.

44. Deposition by Suchomel of 24.1.1962 (LA NRW, Münster, Q234, Nr. 4269).

45. Deposition by Schneider of 11.7.1967 (IRSML-FVG, Risiera collection, box 88).

46. A prosecution file for war crimes put together by the Yugoslav authorities against a "Captain Fischer," first name unknown (Hrvatski Državni Arhiv, fund nr. 306, Zemaljska komisija za utvrđivanje zločina okupatora i njihovih pomagača Hrvatske (State commission for the investigations on the crimes of the occupiers and their supporters in Croatia), file Zh 25543), indicated that he was present in Sappiane already in late March; it reports that on March 26, German troops under his orders raided the villages of Mune Grande, Mune Piccolo, and Seiane. Despite the rank discrepancy, the "Captain Fischer" can possibly be identified with Helmut Fischer of *Abteilung R* (who was Polizeimeister, later *SS-Ustuf.* from the end of June 1944, according to his personal file).

47. If *Abteilung R* ever had a presence in Sappiane, it is not known if it kept it beyond spring 1944.

48. Befehl 16/44, transcribed (without date) in *Mitteilungsblatt des Befehlshabers der Sipo und des SD* in Triest, Nr. 21, 27 May 1944, ARS, AS 1931, box 756, sheet 94 and 147. The nomination used the title "*Sicherheitskommandant für die Strasse Trieste–Fiume*," while the security commander's own letterhead was "*Sicherungskommandant der Karststrasse*." *Sicherheitskommandant* and *Sicherungskommandant* are practically equivalent terms, but in the military vocabulary the latter term was more common.

49. The order made in fact reference to a previous order, Befehl 15/44, probably issued on

the same day or little before, which regarded the creation and tasks of the security commanders.

50. Deposition by Allers—who from early June took up all tasks previously assigned to Wirth, among which also that of *Sicherungskommandant der Karststrasse*—of 24.11.1970 (IRSML-FVG, Risiera collection, box 88, also published in Italian translation in Adolfo Scalpelli, *San Sabba*, vol. 2, pp. 25–31).

51. Deposition by Walther of 22.6.1967 (IRSML-FVG, Risiera collection, box 88).

52. In addition to Walther, the following men of *Abteilung R* were for at least some time in Castelnuovo: Kilminsky, Mätzig, Mentz, and Münzberger.

53. The *Milizia per la Difesa Territoriale* (MDT; Militia for Territorial Defense, or *Landschutz-Miliz* in German) originated from the Fascist *Milizia Volontaria per la Sicurezza Nazionale* (MVSN). The MDT was the OZAK equivalent to the *Guardia Nazionale Repubblicana* (GNR) that existed in the rest of the RSI, and initially also its units were denominated GNR; but the Germans ordered that the name was changed into MDT, in order to underline the factual separation of the region from the RSI territory. There were five MDT regiments, one per province (*1. Rgt.* in Trieste, *2. Rgt.* in Pola, *3. Rgt.* in Fiume, *4. Rgt.* in Gorizia, *5. Rgt.* in Udine); additionally, some units of the *Milizia Confinaria* (Border's Militia, which was originally a border police but was later used against the partisans) plus some other *Milizia* specialities (railway militia, road militia, port militia, forestry militia, etc.) were also active in the OZAK.

54. In the deposition of 24.11.1970, Allers confirmed that under his orders as *Sicherungs-kommandant* were the listed units, i.e., a company of *3. Rgt. MDT,* a company of the *Guardia di Finanza* and the company of the *SS-Wachmannschafts-Btl. Triest* based in San Sabba (i.e., *6. Kp./SS-WMS-Btl.*); Allers did not mention, however, the elements of *Abteilung R*, even stating not to know that name. Allers' deposition is very reticent on the activity of *Abteilung R* in the OZAK, and seems incorrect on several aspects: his statements that he had no command authority in the Risiera, and that the company of the *SS-WMS-Btl.* based in San Sabba was only tactically subordinated to him, but not as far as disciplinary questions were concerned, does not seem credible; equally not credible is his statement that his tactical tasks did not include arresting civilians of the local population, and that he did not know about Jews being detained at the Risiera.

55. According to a deposition by Oberhauser (of 24.9.1973, in HHStA, Wiesbaden, Abt. 631a, Nr. 1330) the employment of *6. Kp./SS-WMS-Btl.* on the Karststrasse was caused by the high losses sustained by the *Guardia di Finanza*, but there is no confirmation to this statement.

56. Pierpaolo Meccariello, *La Guardia di Finanza sul confine orientale*, Museo Storico della Guardia di Finanza, Paravia, Torino, 1997, pp. 224–225.

57. Vincenzo Cerceo, *La Guardia di Finanza nel "Litorale Adriatico" 1943–1945*, Dossier nr. 14 of "La Nuova Alabarda," 2014, pp. 16–17. During the night of January 12–13, 1944, the *Guardia di Finanza* men manning the Matteria outpost were disarmed by the partisans and some of them were killed.

58. In Yugoslav documentation Rolleri is accused of participating to the evacuation of the civilian population from the villages of Danne, Vodizze di Castelnuovo, Trestenico di Raspo, Raspo, Mune Grande, Mune Piccolo, and Obrovo and their subsequent burning in August 1944 (together with Allers and Walther); he is also accused of having committed, together with his men, violences and abuses against the civilian population of the villages along and near the Trieste–Fiume road (Komisija za ugotavljanje zločinov okupatorjev in njihovih pomagačev za Slovenjo, Commission for the investigations on the crimes of the occupiers and their supporters in Slovenia, file Z-1000-P).

59. MDT – Headquarters of *3. Rgt. "Quarnaro" (61. Legione)*, *Ordine del giorno* (order of the day) nr. 2 of 1 August 1944, signed by the regiment commander, *Ten.Col.* Giuseppe Porcu.

60. Additionally, the company had outposts in Ruccavazzo and some villages of the Ciceria region where there were building sites for defensive positions (see the specific section), such as Seiane, Suonecchia, and Mune Grande. On *2. Compagnia "Arditi"* of *3. Rgt. MDT* in the period late 1944–45 see the memoirs of Torquato Dalcich (anagram of Aldo Quattrocchi), *Un diario (1944-1945)*,

Firenze, 1997, available on the webpage: www.isses.it/diario4occhi.htm.

61. According to a deposition (by Geng of 1.6.1971, in HHStA, Wiesbaden, Abt. 631a, Nr. 1316), "it practically happened that unit members participated to operations together with other units when the *Wehrmacht* carried out anti-partisan operations."

62. BA Berlin, R 70 Italien/23, sheet 155–156. The mentioned memoirs of Dalcich recall the participation of the MDT unit to sweep operations in unspecified locations of "upper Istria" in the days around December 21, 1944, together with *Ltn.* Walther.

63. BA Berlin, R 70 Italien/32, sheet 106.

64. BA Berlin, R 70 Italien/30, sheet 1 and 37. In particular on the Starada ambush: BA Berlin, R 70 Italien/20, sheet 85, 92, 95–96 and 175. The dead was an NCO from the *Ski-Kommando* of the *Befehlshaber der Sipo*/SD in Italien; the missing in action were another NCO from the *Ski-Kommando*, a Ukrainian, and three members of the *Landschutz*.

65. *Kriegstagebuch* (war diary) of *2. Kompanie/3. Rgt. Brandenburg*, which mentions a meeting between the company commander and a *Ltn.* Walther from the "*Polizeistützpunkt Castelnuovo*" to prepare the action. Elements of *6. Kp./SS-WMS-Btl.* were employed with *2. Kp./3. Rgt. Brandenburg* in the following days (June 20–21), and it is not excluded that also elements of *Abteilung R* participated to this action (described in the chapter on the *SS-Wachmannschaften*).

66. Adolfo Scalpelli, *San Sabba*, vol. 2, pp. 41–42, and 93–95.

67. Torquato Dalcich (anagram of Aldo Quattrocchi), *Un diario (1944–1945)*, Firenze, 1997, available on the webpage: www.isses.it/diario4occhi.htm.

68. Depositions by Allers of 19.9.1962 (HHStA, Wiesbaden, Abt. 461, Nr. 36346/9) and of 16.5.1963 (BA Ludwigsburg, B162/18096) (in the two depositions Allers gave different information relating to the changes to his responsibilities, so it is not clear what happened).

69. Deposition by Walther of 2.9.1965 (HHStA, Wiesbaden, Abt. 631a, Nr. 886).

70. Pierpaolo Meccariello, *La Guardia di Finanza sul confine orientale*, Museo Storico della Guardia di Finanza, Paravia, Torino, 1997, pg. 242.

71. Lerch was an old friend of Globocnik's from the time of the clandestine political activity in Carinthia in the mid-1930s, and was later with him in Lublin and became his right hand. In Trieste, Lerch was Leiter (head) of Globocnik's *Persönliches Büro* (private office), which had coordination and control powers over the activities of all entities subordinated to the HSSPF OZAK.

72. The *Cetnik-Dinara-Division* was a Serbian Chetnik unit that had arrived in the OZAK between late December 1944 and early January 1945, under the orders of Vojvoda Momcilo Djujic.

73. Serbian Military Archives, box K-32 A/II, folder 17.

74. Among those that were awarded the *Bandenkampfabzeichen* was Schiffner, who attended a six-week course on fighting the partisans at the *Bandenkampfschule* in Duino (according to his own declarations). Also, Münzberger attended a similar course for around ten days, probably at the same school.

75. Documents and sources used for this section: BA-MA Freiburg, RH 24-87/40 and /61; BA Berlin, R 70 Italien/19 sheet 93–94, R 70 Italien/20 sheet 84–85, R 70 Italien/23 sheet 73 and 167, R 70 Italien/30 sheet 1 and 37, R 70 Italien/31 sheet 199, R 70 Italien/32 sheet 102, 104, 106 and R 70 Italien/35 sheet 33–38; Soldbuch of a soldier from the Stabskp./SS-Karstwehr-Btl., reproduced in Rolf Michaelis, *Die Gebirgs-Divisionen der Waffen-SS*, Michaelis Verlag, Berlin, 1998, pg. 286; Ludwig Heymann, *Geschichte des Gren.Rgt. 992 (Berlin–Brandenburg)*, Pohl Verlag, Celle, 1959, pg. 19.

76. According to some sources it would seem that the operation may have continued until May 13, but further details in this respect are missing.

77. Liaison officer with the FSBB for the *Wehrmacht* was the Ia (operations' officer) of the *278. Infanterie-Division, Major i.G.* Wolfgang Klennert.

78. In the operation's initial phases, in the early afternoon of 25 April, a German motorized medical column (with five trucks) coming from Trieste was attacked by partisan forces around two kilometers from Vele Lasi–Casa Cantoniera (on the Trieste–Fiume road, between Sappiane and Mucici). Also the Milizia Confinaria outpost at the Casa Cantoniera (near the present Bergut train station) was attacked at the same time, but the

partisans were repulsed. In the same afternoon a German–Italian unit (the Italians were MDT troops from Mucici, led by a company commander *tenente* of the *Milizia*, most probably Oscar Battestin, commander of *2. Compagnia* of *3. Rgt. MDT*) came to the rescue of the medical column; however, the column had been destroyed and had suffered heavy losses, among which were eight dead. Also attacked by the partisans in those days were the outposts of the Guardia di Finanza in Valsantamarina (April 27) and Matteria (April 30).

79. Although *I. Btl./SS-Pol.Rgt. "Bozen"* was based in Abbazia, the first photos of the sequence show the unit motorized column, with the battalion commander *Major* Kretschmer, stopped near the *Milizia* outpost between Giordani and Mucici on the Karststrasse, heading south. It is not known where the column was coming from. It is documented that *3.* and *4. Kp./SS-Pol.Rgt. "Bozen"* had losses in the area of Castelnuovo–Passiaco–Recizza on April 25, so the column may have been coming back from operations in this area; it is not clear however if they were carried out in the context of the *Unternehmen Braunschweig*.

80. Additionally, on April 28, elements of the *Einsatzgruppe* of the *Sipo*/SD were in action on the Monte Alpe Grande, while on April 29, unidentified forces mopped-up the area of Monte Lisina (around five kilometers west of Giordani).

81. The *2. Kp./SS-Pol.Rgt. "Bozen,"* employed in the protection of the *Sicherungsbereich Arsia* (Arsia security sector), took part in the operation as *Sicherungsgruppe* (security group) from the area of Valdarsa, probably as blocking force trying to stop the partisans from retreating and escaping from the encirclement.

82. Members of *1. Kompanie* were photographed near the Učka Pass very likely on April 28; members of *4. Kompanie* on Monte Maggiore on April 28, and in Valsantamarina on May 1; members of *2.* and *4. Kompanie* in Abbazia on May 2.

83. It is also documented that a soldier belonging to *4. Kp./SS-WMS-Btl.* was wounded in Mattuglie on May 3, 1944.

84. Also on May 4, units from the *Befehlshaber der Sipo/SD* in the OZAK were in action in Sottomerischie, near Draguccio, but further information is missing.

85. Apparently, together with the Germans, also elements of the *Guardia di Finanza* company based in Castelnuovo participated in the pillage and evacuation of the civilian population from the villages of Baccia di Matteria, Marcossina, Orecchia and Giavorie.

86. In general, civilians who were able to work were often deported to Germany, sometimes after being detained for some time in the Risiera di San Sabba.

87. According to the prosecution files compiled by Yugoslav commissions for the investigation of war crimes for two Germans identified as "Captain Fischer" and "Lieutenant Walter" (sic) (in both cases first names are unknown; see endnote 104), and indicated as commanders of the outposts of Sappiane and Castelnuovo, they were in charge during the evacuation of the villages and their subsequent burning. The latter can be very likely identified as Arthur Walther, the former possibly with Helmut Fischer, both from *Abteilung R*. Also according to the account of an Italian MDT officer, Torquato Dalcich (quoted by Decleva in his writings, mentioned in the section on the Lipa massacre), the villages of Seiane, Mune Piccolo, and Mune Grande were burned on orders from "First Lieutenant Arthur Walther." On the mentioned Yugoslav prosecution files, and the account of the Italian officer, see the section on the Lipa massacre.

88. ARS, AS 1760, box 200/V and BA Berlin, R 70 Italien/10.

89. According to Croatian sources there were two survivors: a woman who managed to hide and a man who was wounded and pretended to be dead. Rodolfo Decleva mentions in his writings (see later), in addition to the wounded man, a woman who survived because she came across a Blackshirt (*Milizia* soldier) who urged her to run away (this was reported by people from the village). The survivors may then be three. Numerous other civilians escaped the massacre because when it happened they were not in the village; at least one of them, Josif Smajla, saw what happened while hiding at the edge of a wood, a few hundred meters away from the village.

90. Torquato Dalcich (anagram of Aldo Quattrocchi), *Un diario (1944–1945)*, Firenze, 1997, available on the webpage: www.isses.it/diario4occhi.htm

91. Ivan Kovačić, Vinko Šepić Čiškin, Danica Maljavac, *Lipa pamti*, Naklada Kvarner, Rijeka, 2014.

92. For the Italian side the research of Rodolfo Decleva, who published the article *L'eccidio di Lipa* (The Lipa massacre) in the periodical *Fiume–Rivista di studi adriatici*, nr. 1–6, year XXIII, Società di Studi Fiumani, Roma, 2003, deserve mention; this writing was later re-published in various Internet websites in slightly different versions, the most recent of which to date on www.rigocamerano.it/testodecleva13.htlm.html (April 2014); see also his interview in *La Voce del popolo*, April 30, 2015 (http://editfiume.com/lavoce/cultura/12865-non-posso-dimenticare-quell-orrore). For the Croatian side, Antun Giron has briefly dealt with the episode in various writings (among them Antun Giron, *Zločin u Lipi 1944. godine*, Liburnijske teme: Zbornici čakavskog Sabora knjiga 3, Opatijsko područje u NOB-u i oslobođenju, Opatija, 1978, pp. 75–83, and Antun Giron, *Narodnooslobodilačka borba na opatijskom krasu 1941–1945 godine*, Liburnijske teme: Zbornici čakavskog Sabora knjiga 5, Opatijski kras, Opatija, 1983, pp. 83–98). The most recent and probably the most detailed research from Croatia is the already mentioned *Lipa pamti*.

93. It seems that the association of the *SS-Karstwehr-Btl.* with the Lipa massacre was originally made in an article by the late Slovenian historian Tone Ferenc, later quoted by other authors.

94. Apparently the same units (or at least elements of *Abteilung R* and Italians from the Rupa junction outpost) burned the village of Iscra (a few kilometers east of Lipa) the next day; during this action three civilians were killed, and eighteen were deported.

95. From early December 1943 to mid-March 1944, a German tank company, the *3. Panzer-Sicherungs-Kompanie*, was based in Castelnuovo; a part of one of its platoons, with two tanks and their crews, was detached to the Rupa junction. On March 15, however, the entire company (including the elements at the Rupa junction) were transferred to Mossa, near Gorizia; it is not known if another German unit replaced it in Castelnuovo right away, but at the end of April elements of *Abteilung R* were probably based in the village (see later).

96. The headquarters of *2. Compagnia* were most probably in the outpost located half way between Giordani and Mucici (see photos in the section on the *Braunschweig* operation). Apparently, the outpost was sometimes indicated as based in Mucici, other times in Giordani (it looks unlikely that there were MDT outposts in both villages). It seems therefore more correct to indicate it as the Giordani–Mucici outpost.

97. Although very scarce information is available on the Chetniks in the OZAK, it is confirmed that at least one unit of Croatian Chetniks arrived in the region in early 1944; it had detachments in Postumia, Giordani (in the Flondar barracks), Mattuglie, Abbazia, Laurana, on Monte Maggiore (the last three were later disbanded). They were Croatian Chetniks from the Lika region (western Croatia) who as a consequence of the Italian armistice had crossed the Adriatic sea to Italy to escape from the partisans, arriving in Pesaro; from here the Germans had transferred them to Bologna and then to Trieste. It is documented that a Chetnik unit called by the Germans "*Einheit Welzin*" (Welzin unit, from the name of its commander, a German officer), participated in summer 1944 in anti-partisan operations in Istria; it was probably a group of Croatian Chetniks.

98. Ivan Brozina, *Put prve Istarske brigade "Vladimir Gortan,"* vol. 1, Kotarski odbor Saveza boraca, Pula, 1963, pg. 117. Actually the junction was not attacked by Partisan infantry, but only bombarded by mortar fire (personal account of Vinko Surina to the authors).

99. Letter to Rodolfo Decleva of August 1966 (kindly provided to the authors). Some excerpts from the letter are published—with small variations compared to the original which is reproduced here—in the writings from Decleva, where the officer's name is not mentioned; that he was Torquato Dalcich was confirmed by Decleva in an interview published in *La Voce del popolo*, April 30, 2015. Although Dalcich wrote "we, meaning the outpost soldiers," according to his memoirs (cited above) at the time of the massacre he was not in Rupa and not even in the OZAK, but rather at the school of the *Guardia Nazionale Repubblicana* in Modena as an officer cadet; he was later assigned to *3. Rgt. MDT* and from the second half of March 1945, he was the commander of the outpost at the Rupa junction. Evidently, his intention is to absolve the Italians from participation

in the massacre, throwing the full responsibility to the Germans; on this point see later in the text.

100. Account of Vinko Surina to the authors (August 2014). Surina saw two trucks stopped in front of his house (the restaurant) but no armored car. His vision was limited by the small street-level cellar window through which he was looking; therefore he cannot exclude that there was also an armored car among the halted vehicles. Surina is second cousin to Decleva, who also quotes him in his writings (naming him only in the most recent version).

101. The wounding of Schneider (grenade splinter to the neck) is mentioned by him in several occasions (deposition of 3.11.1965, HHStA Wiesbaden, Abt. 631a, Nr. 890 and of 11.7.1967, IRSML-FVG, Risiera collection, box 88, also published in Italian translation in Adolfo Scalpelli, *San Sabba*, vol. 2, pg. 13); although stated from memory, the date should be correct because—as mentioned by Schneider himself—it was the day after his birthday, and as such he could remember it precisely.

102. The place of death is indicated as Opicina in the *Grabmeldung* (death and burial declaration) for both Gringers and Löffler (it is to be noted that near Opicina was located the war cemetery where German soldiers who died in the area of Trieste were buried, including Gringers and Löffler). In the register of the Opicina cemetery it is indicated as Cosina. In the burial cards of the Costermano war cemetery (where bodies were transferred from most German war cemeteries in northern Italy, including Opicina, after the war), the place of death is indicated for Gringers as *"in der Gegend von Triest"* (in the vicinity of Trieste) and for Löffler as *"Raum Triest"* (area of Trieste). There seems to have been an intention not to be precise as to the place of death.

103. According to Decleva the village inhabitants had been warned by a *Carabiniere* that they were at risk of reprisal actions because of their support for the partisans.

104. Hrvatski Državni Arhiv, fund nr. 306, Zemaljska komisija za utvrđivanje zločina okupatora i njihovih pomagača Hrvatske (State commission for the investigations on the crimes of the occupiers and their supporters in Croatia), file Zh 25543 (Fischer); file Zh 25546 (Walter). Walther is indicated in these prosecution files as Fischer's adjutant, but this seems unlikely. Neither Fischer nor Walther are explicitly accused in these files to have taken part personally in the massacre; it is just indicated that the units they commanded took part in it. Regarding the presence of Fischer in the area, in a deposition (of 27.6.1969, HHStA Wiesbaden, Abt. 631a, Nr. 1329) he declared to have arrived in Italy in August 1944; this seems, however, not to be supported by an element of his own deposition: Fischer said to have taken up command in Udine after Walther was transferred to Castelnuovo, but if he had actually arrived in Italy in August it appears unlikely that he could have known that Walther had left Udine the previous April to go to the Karststrasse. It seems rather more likely that Fischer was already in Sappiane (or Castelnuovo) when Walther arrived there and that later (possibly in August 1944) he replaced him in Udine. On the other hand, according to his personal file Fischer was serving with *SS-Pioniersturmbann 9* (an *Allgemeine-SS* engineer unit, based in Dresden) when he was promoted to *SS-Ustuf.* on June 21, 1944, so this point remains unclear.

105. The prosecution file on Piesz of the Istria commission for war crime investigations (see endnote 110) mentions the participation in the massacre of SS elements coming from Fiume led by Stangl, but it is not clear whether the element of Stangl's presence is reliable.

106. Lists of units allegedly involved in the massacre have been published in Yugoslav and Croatian publications, but they seem only partially reliable. Antun Giron (*Zapadna Hrvatska u Drugom svjetskom ratu*, Adamić, Rijeka, 2004, pg. 304) put forward the following list (apparently on the basis of data gathered by the Croatian commission for war crime investigations): elements of *2. Compagnia* [of *3. Rgt.*] *MDT* led by Piesz, *Carabinieri* from Rupa, elements of *3. Compagnia* [of *3. Rgt.*] MDT from Giordani, elements of *Res. Geb.Jg.Rgt. 137* of *188. Res.Geb.Div.*, elements of the *SS-Karstwehr-Btl.* and police element led by Stangl coming from Fiume. This list appears surely incorrect as far as *Res.Geb.Jg.Rgt. 137* is concerned (see next endnote) and most probably also for the *SS-Karstwehr-Btl.*; in addition it seems that at least in this period there was no outpost of *3. Compagnia del 3. Rgt. MDT* in Giordani, where

actually *2. Compagnia* had its headquarters. The recent and already mentioned *Lipa pamti* has a similar list (pg. 96): elements of *2. Compagnia* [of *3. Rgt.*] *MDT* led by Piesz, *Carabinieri* from Rupa, elements of *3. Compagnia* [of *3. Rgt.*] *MDT* from Giordani, elements of *Res.Geb.Jg.Rgt. 137*, elements of the *SS-Karstwehr-Btl.*, elements of *SS-Pol.Rgt. "Bozen"* and around thirty Chetniks or Domobranci.

107. According to the prosecution files of the Croatian commission for war crime investigations, the German troops that carried out the reprisal came from Villa del Nevoso and Sappiane; in the latter village, in addition to the *Gebirgsjäger*, there were apparently also personnel of *Abteilung R* (based on the fact that the commander of the Sappiane outpost is indicated as a "Captain Fischer," possibly to be identified as Helmut Fischer from *Abteilung R*). It should be also noted regarding the *Gebirgsjäger* that the prosecution file on Piesz from the Istria commission for war crime investigations (see endnote 110) contains an almost certainly incorrect piece of information, that is the presence in Lipa of *3. Kp./Res.Geb.Jg.Rgt. 137* of *187. Res.Geb.Div.* (sic, but should be *188. Res.Geb.Div.*): at that time *Res.Geb.Jg.Rgt. 137* was almost certainly still based in the area of Caporetto–Tolmino–Cividale, and only towards mid-May moved to Opicina; evidently *Res.Geb.Jg.Rgt. 137* is confused with *Res.Geb.Jg.Rgt. 138*, whose *I. Btl.*, was based in Villa del Nevoso.

108. In addition to the Blackshirt, who according to Decleva saved a woman by urging her to flee, one source mentions an account from a civilian from Rupa who right after the reprisal saw some Blackshirts upset by the slaughter they had assisted and perhaps taken part in (account by Danica Maljavac in http://www.uni-regensburg.de/Fakultaeten/phil_Fak_III/Geschichte/istrien/route-lipa.html).

109. In his writings Decleva insists on the concept of "German massacre" as opposed to "Italo-German massacre," maintaining that the Italian soldiers that participated were probably forced to do it and in any case only had a secondary role. On the basis of what is known of the massacre, it is not sufficiently clear what the specific role of the Italians was; sufficient facts to support Decleva's position seem therefore to be missing.

110. Hrvatski Državni Arhiv, fund nr. 306, Zemaljska komisija za utvrđivanje zločina okupatora i njihovih pomagača Hrvatske (State commission for the investigations on the crimes of the occupiers and their supporters in Croatia), file Zh 25512 (Piesz); it contains reports from the Croatian commission as well as from the Istria commission. With "Giordani outpost" it is probably meant the outpost which was located between Giordani and Mucici (see endnote 96).

111. This statement, apparently made by a soldier identified as Umberto Scalle, is reported in secondary sources. He could have been Piesz's adjutant, whose surname according to Surina was Scala; he is reported to have been arrested by Yugoslav partisans near Rupa in the last days of the war while trying to reach Trieste, brought to the partisan headquarters in Castua, questioned and then probably killed. In the prosecution file on Piesz his adjutant is named as Sergente Maggiore Giuseppe Scalli; Dalcich/Quattrocchi mentions a Sergente Maggiore Scali belonging to the Rupa junction outpost, who was apparently killed by the partisans at the end of the war.

112. The files of the Croatian commission for war crime investigations on "Captain Fischer" and "Lieutenant Walter" (sic) mention the Lipa massacre and the participation of German troops from the Sappiane outpost, of which they were indicated as commanders; however neither Fischer nor Walter/Walther are explicitly accused in these files of having directly taken part in the reprisal. Any other Yugoslav prosecution files on other soldiers that may have participated in the massacre have not been found.

113. The prosecution file on Piesz contains the names of thirty-four Italian soldiers accused of having participated in the massacre. An additional sixteen names (plus seventeen more already mentioned in Piesz's file) are listed in reports contained in Državni Arhiv u Rijeci, JU 41, kut. 1, fasc. 269. Another list of "fascists from Fiume" (eight names, six of whom also listed in Piesz's file) accused of having participated in the reprisal is published in Amleto Ballarini and Michael Sobolevski (ed.), *Le vittime di nazionalità italiana a Fiume e dintorni 1939–1947*, Ministero Beni e Attività Culturali, Roma, 2002, pp. 63–64; the source of this list is indicated as a report drafted by a Commission for war crimes investigations from Albona dated October 10, 1945, from Državni

Arhiv u Rijeci, Komisija za mine zlocine (Commission on war crimes), JU 41, b. 6 (now in JU 41, kut. 1, fasc. 269). The names are often written in slightly different ways in different lists.

114. Sometimes the equivalent term of *Sicherheitskommandant* was also used.

115. For instance some *Gebirgs-Jäger* units from *188. Reserve-Gebirgs-Jäger-Division*, probably some *Sicherungs-Btl.* or—in the area of Pordenone—*Luftwaffe* units.

116. ARS, AS 1931, box 765, sheet 94 and 147.

117. According to a deposition by Allers, when he took up this task he had under his command one company of *3. Rgt. MDT*, one *Guardia di Finanza* company and one company of the *SS-Wachtmannschafts-Btl.* (for more details see the chapter on *Abteilung R*).

118. In spring 1944, it was *SS-Untersturmführer* Gottfried Schwarz, belonging to *Abteilung R* and probably commander of *2. Kp./SS-WMS-Btl.*, killed on June 19, 1944. His successor was perhaps *SS-Obersturmführer* Adolf Garlich.

119. On June 20, 1944, it was *SS-Untersturmführer* Kurt Franz, based in Gorizia, belonging to *Abteilung R* and commander of *Kommando G.*, a unit belonging to the *SS-Wachmannschafts-Btl.* In March 1945, it was *Leutnant d.SchP.* Bade (as *stellv. Sicherungskdt.*, i.e., as deputy commander).

120. The *Sich.Kdt. Adelsberg* (Postumia) was based at times, in addition to Postumia, also in Storie and Senosecchia (at least until the subdivision of the sector in four parts). In May 1944, it was *Hauptmann d.Gend.* Rieck; at least between June and August, *Hauptmann d.Gend.* Lehnick; in December, *SS-Hauptsturmführer* Bareuther; in April 1945, *Hauptmann d.SchP.* Müller. On June 20, 1944, the forces in the sector included, among others: an *SS-Wachmannschaften* unit (with one officer, one NCO and forty-seven troops) [these were elements of *4. Kp./SS-WMS-Btl.*] and *5. Kompanie* of the SNVZ (with one officer and seventy-six troops) in the *Stützpunkt Storie*; an unidentified company in San Pietro del Carso [probably *7. Kompanie* of the SNVZ]; an unidentified company in Postumia [probably 4. Company of the SNVZ] (Roland Kaltenegger, *Zona d'operazione Litorale Adriatico*, Libreria Editrice Goriziana, 1996, pg. 120, where the name Lehnik is erroneously spelled Lehnich).

121. Of these, twenty were in the Udine province, eight in the Gorizia province, six in the Trieste province, three in the Fiume province, and none in the Istria province (from where in 1945 the SS/*Polizei* were withdrawn and replaced by *Wehrmacht* forces).

122. The various mobilization orders for work service issued by Rainer from July 1944, progressively came to concern civilians from 16 to 60 years; on this aspect see Roberto Spazzali, *Sotto la Todt. Affari, servizio obbligatorio del lavoro, deportazioni nella Zona d'Operazioni "Litorale Adriatico" (1943–1945)*, Libreria Editrice Goriziana, 1998, pp. 169–192.

123. The Führerweisungen 60, 60a and 60b are in Walther Hubatsch, *Hitlers Weisungen für die Kriegsführung 1939–1945*, Bernard & Graefe Verlag, Frankfurt a.M., 1962, pp. 267–272; a contemporary summary of the directives is in Percy Ernst Schramm, *Kriegstagebuch des Oberkommandos der Wehrmacht*, vol. 4/1 (1944), Bernard & Graefe Verlag, Frankfurt a.M., 1963, pp. 591–593.

124. The formulation "*blaue Vorfeldlinie I (Adriatic coast–Tschitschen–Boden and Fiume)*," used in the contemporary summary by Percy Ernst Schramm, *Kriegstagebuch des OKW*, vol. 4/1, pg. 594, does not seem correct as far as the path of the *blaue Vorfeldlinie I* is concerned (it looks very unlikely that the *Karststellung* and Fiume were part of the *blaue Vorfeldlinie I*), and has been corrected here.

125. Percy Ernst Schramm, *Kriegstagebuch des OKW*, vol. 4/1, pp. 593–594.

126. Percy Ernst Schramm, *Kriegstagebuch des OKW*, vol. 4/1, pp. 563–564.

127. The letterhead used on official documents was "*Der Gauleiter und Oberster Kommissar – Sonderauftrag*" (*Gauleiter* and Highest Commissar – Special task).

128. Deposition by Geng of 1.6.1971 (HHStA, Wiesbaden, Abt. 631a, Nr. 1330; "*Einsatzstab beim Gruppenstab Böll*" in the text of the deposition).

129. Deposition by Allers of 19.9.1962 (HHStA, Wiesbaden Abt. 461, Nr. 36346/9); this deposition stated that the "*Stellungsbau*" works (i.e., the construction of the defensive lines) started in June on the *Karststellung*, but probably they actually started later.

130. Deposition by Allers of 24.11.1970 (IRSML-FVG, Risiera collection, box 88, also published in Italian translation in Adolfo Scalpelli, *San Sabba*, vol. 2, pp. 25–31).

131. Roberto Spazzali, *Sotto la Todt*, Libreria Editrice Goriziana, 1998, pg. 217. Examples of both types of documents, on headed paper of the Sicherungskommandant der Karststrasse and concerning workers of the *Oberabschnitt Wirth-West* (indicated in both cases as *Bauunternehmen Wirth-West*, or building company) are reproduced here.

132. Roberto Spazzali, *Sotto la Todt*, Libreria Editrice Goriziana, 1998, pg. 219.

133. ARS, AS 1769, box 203 (HSSPF OZAK, Tgb.Nr. 572/44 g, December 7, 1944, signed by Michalsen); the order is also reproduced entirely in Ricciotti Lazzero, *Le Brigate Nere*, Rizzoli, Milano, 1983, pp. 138–140.

134. In this period (from summer 1944 to February 1945) some men also guarded a fuel depot in Möllbrück, Carinthia, near the border with Italy (deposition by Schluch of 11.4.1962, LA NRW, Münster, Q234, Nr. 4272).

135. Deposition by Geng of 1.6.1971 and Köhler of 28.11.1961 (both in HHStA, Wiesbaden, Abt. 631a, Nr. 1330).

136. Serbian Military Archives, box K-32 A/II, folder 17.

137. IFSML, collection *III. Btl./SS-Pol.Rgt. 12*, folder 5137.

138. In another document of the same period the unit was in fact indicated as *II. halb.Pol.Btl. "Italien,"* that is half-battalion. The headquarters and the other two companies of *II. Pol.Freiw.Btl. "Italien"* (*1.* and *4. Kp.*) were based at that time in San Daniele del Carso and Capriva del Carso, near Trieste, in the OZAK region.

139. IFSML, collection *III. Btl./SS-Pol.Rgt. 12*, folder 5137.

140. On September 17, 1944, Herrmann ordered the *leichter Flakzug* and *Vierling* to be transferred to the *Oberabschnitt "Seestern I,"* in the area south of Mira (IFSML, collection *III. Btl./SS-Pol.Rgt. 12*, folder 5137).

141. *Oberabschnitt "Feuerstein"* was divided in several sectors, of which the first one (*Abschnitt "Feuerstein" I*) included the village of Valvasone.

142. IFSML, collection *III. Btl./SS-Pol.Rgt. 12*, folder 5138. In that period *III. Btl./SS-Pol.Rgt. 12* was in Friuli on the Tagliamento, *I. Pol.Freiw.Btl. "Italien"* probably in Pravisdomini (its headquarters were based there on February 2), the two companies of *II. Pol.Freiw.Btl. "Italien"* in an unknown area probably in eastern Veneto; a few days later, on February 11, 1945, *Gend.Hauptmannschaft "Umbrien"* was in Ormelle (near Oderzo), *Gend. Hauptmannschaft "Toscana"* in Mira.

143. IFSML, collection *III. Btl./SS-Pol.Rgt. 12*, folder 3200. In that period (mid-March 1945) *III. Btl./SS-Pol.Rgt. 12* was in Friuli on the Tagliamento, *I. Pol.Freiw.Btl. "Italien"* probably still in Pravisdomini, the two *Gend.Hauptmannschaft* probably in eastern Veneto; on *II. Pol.Freiw.Btl. "Italien"* (i.e., the two companies that had remained in the Veneto region with the *Höherer Sicherungsstab*, not the other two companies that in the same time were based in San Daniele del Carso and Capriva del Carso, near Trieste, in the OZAK region) no precise data is available.

144. The troops of *97. Armee-Korps* (the new name of *General-Kommando Kübler*) deployed to defend Fiume were surrounded by the end of April in the area of Villa del Nevoso (Fiume had been abandoned during the night of May 2–3), and forced to surrender on May 7. On the military operations of the last weeks of war in the OZAK see Stefano Di Giusto, *Operationszone Adriatisches Küstenland*, pp. 641–715.

145. As mentioned in the chapter on the *SS-Wachmannschaften*, according to an account also the Italian soldiers who were billeted at the Risiera were put on trucks and followed the German retreat towards Udine; in Faedis their column was attacked by Allied aircraft, and in the confusion some Italian soldiers managed to flee.

146. Deposition by Geng of 1.9.1970, published in Adolfo Scalpelli, *San Sabba*, vol. 2, pg. 98.

147. Grossmann also was wounded in an aircraft attack at the end of April 1945, perhaps during the retreat.

148. Some were detained in the camp of Bad Aibing in Bavaria, others—mainly from section R III—in Habach near Weilheim, also in Bavaria, others in Aalen in Baden–Württemberg. Allers was in the British camp of Federaum near Villach, later in the Wolfsberg camp, then in the work camp of Weissenstein an der Donau from where he was released in February 1947.

149. For some time after the war Geng lived in Trieste, before moving to Milan.

150. Reproduced in Pieri Stefanutti, *Novocerkassk e dintorni. L'occupazione cosacca della Valle del Lago (ottobre 1944 – aprile 1945)*, IFSML, Udine, 1995, pp. 190–196.

151. The report is in AORF, P3-67-3/1 and is also reproduced in Pieri Stefanutti, *Novocerkassk e dintorni*, pp. 171–174.

152. See mainly Pier Arrigo Carnier, *Lo sterminio mancato*, pp. 211–220, and Pieri Stefanutti, *Novocerkassk e dintorni*, pp. 112–128. An additional hypothesis, that of a reprisal for the attack on a German and Cossack column coming from Spilimbergo that passed through Peonis heading north on 1 May, does not seem plausible: it is documented by various accounts that this column, shot at by isolated snipers who killed a German soldier near Alesso, executed some partisans and civilians on the road in retaliation and took some hostages to avoid other attacks; it then proceeded to Tolmezzo without stopping in the Valle del Lago Valley.

153. In *Lo sterminio mancato* and in various articles, among which more recently (and mentioning the names of the German witnesses whose testimonies on the episode were collected by Carnier; see below) in the periodical *Asou Geats*, August 2003, and in the daily newspaper *Il Gazzettino*, November 14 and 21, 2005.

154. Excerpt from the diary of Don Francesco Zossi, AORF, P 3-67-5, also quoted in Pieri Stefanutti, *Novocerkassk e dintorni*, pg. 121 and in Pier Arrigo Carnier, *Lo sterminio mancato*, pg. 214. On April 29, there was also an isolated attack by a Partisan who fired on a passing German motorcycle; this caused an immediate reprisal (seven people were executed in Taboga, near Gemona), the episode therefore does not seem to be connected to the attack on Avasinis (see Gianfrancesco Gubiano, *"Gemona liberata,"* Link edizioni, 2004, pp. 129–134).

155. See Stefano Di Giusto, *Operationszone Adriatisches Küstenland*, pp. 495–498.

156. This was already asserted by Pier Arrigo Carnier in *Lo sterminio mancato*. Later, in the articles published in *Asou Geats*, August 2003, and in *Il Gazzettino*, November 14 and 21, 2005, apparently on the basis of accounts by a former trainer in the *Bandenkampfschule* of Duino and by the former officer of the *Karstjäger-Division,* Erich Kühbandner, Carnier again attributed the responsibility for the massacre to units of the *Karstjäger-Division* (among them some Spaniards that had been integrated in the division), together with units from the *Feldgendarmerie*, the *7. SS-Gebirgs Division "Prinz Eugen"* (probably meaning the *SS-Geb.Ers.u.Ausb.Btl. 7*, a training unit, which was the only unit linked with the "*Prinz Eugen*" division that that was based in the OZAK, in Gradisca) and *Gebirgsjäger* (perhaps with this term are meant again the same units from the *Karstjäger-Division* and the *SS-Geb.Ers.u.Ausb. Btl. 7*, which were both mountain units). However, Carnier has never presented any proof or facts to support these claims. Investigations by the German police in the early 2000s on the Avasinis massacre, concentrated on the *Karstjäger-Division*, could not ascertain any responsibility and were closed in 2007.

157. Despite being designed at this stage as a division (official name: *24. Waffen-Gebirgs (Karstjäger)-Division der SS*), the unit was little more than a reinforced regiment, formed by the *Waffen-Gebirgs (Karstjäger)-Regiment der SS 59* (on two battalions) and a few support units. On this unit see Sergio Corbatti and Marco Nava, *Karstjäger*, Heimdal, 2010.

158. One of the few survivors of the slaughter (Cesarino Venturini, his testimony is inserted in the film *Avasinis luogo della memoria*) said that the two soldiers he saw (one spoke German, the other one Friulian) were "SS," wore a, "camouflage uniform made of shelter quarters cloth" ("*una divisa mimetica di telo tenda*"), a cap with a skull insignia and SS collar tabs. The term "*divisa*" (uniform) seems to indicate both tunic and trousers in camouflage cloth, as they were used by *Abteilung R*, rather than the camouflage smock of the *Karstjäger-Division*. The term "telo tenda" (shelter quarters) could mean that the camouflage cloth was the Italian mod. 29, colloquially called "*telo tenda*" also in civilian use, that is again the cloth used for *Abteilung R* outfits, but not for the *tarnjacke* of the *Karstjäger-Division*. On the other hand, the cap with a skull insignia and SS collar tabs were not generally worn by members of *Abteilung R*, except for those who belonged to the *Waffen-SS*. The members of the

SS-Wachmannschaften often carried the skull on the sidecaps; it is not known however if they used camo uniforms. Some other survivors stated that the perpetrators wore camouflage uniforms with large spots, again referring probably to the mod. 29 camouflage cloth.

159. An account by Suchomel, member of *Abteilung R* (quoted in Carnier, *Lo sterminio mancato*, pg. 215), confirms that its men went into action against the partisans during the retreat; the account is, however, too vague ("The partisans wanted to block the retreat (May 1, 1945). They were successfully overcome by my unit, during the night") to identify the area where the episode took place, which should be between Udine and the border with Austria; it is not excluded that he was making a reference to the Avasinis massacre.

160. On the trials for the crimes committed during *Aktion Reinhard,* see Sara Berger, *NS-Prozesse gegen Personal der Vernichtungslager der "Aktion Reinhardt,"* in *Einsicht 02*, autumn 2009.

161. On the investigations and trial for the Risiera in Italy, see Tristano Matta, *Il Lager di San Sabba. Dall'occupazione nazista al processo di Trieste*, Beit – IRSML-FVG, Trieste, 2012.

162. Copies of the depositions are in IRSML-FVG, Risiera collection, box 88. Some are published in Adolfo Scalpelli, *San Sabba*, vol. 2.

Chapter 4

1. Probably the name of *Wachmannschaften* derived from that of the *SS-Wachsturmbann* units employed to guard the concentration camps in Germany, later renamed in *SS-Totenkopfverbände* (SS-TV, death's head units).

2. For more information on the *Trawniki* see the chapter on *Abteilung R*.

3. The SS- suffix was introduced also for the *Wachmannschaften* in Poland in autumn 1943.

4. Literally *Ostvölker* means "eastern peoples"; the term indicated the peoples belonging to the various nationalities within the Soviet Union.

5. Well-known organization charts dated from July and October 1944 (BA Berlin, R19/451, provided in Stefano Di Giusto, *Operationszone Adriatisches Küstenland*, pp. 481–482 and 485–486) are limited to *Ordnungspolizei* units only.

6. In the charts and *Verteiler* starting from October 1944, an *SS-Wachmannschafts-Kompanie* (also indicated as *SS-Wachkompanie or Wachkompanie des HSSPF*) based in Trieste is always present. On this basis some have concluded in the past that in this phase the battalion had been reduced to a company. However, it seems rather that—as it will be mentioned later in the text—the *SS-Wachmannschafts-Kompanie* was the Trawniki company that had arrived in Trieste from Poland in 1943 under Schwarzenbacher, which was initially inserted in the structure of the *SS-WMS-Btl.* and later probably detached from the battalion.

7. The presence of other nationalities of the then Soviet Union is likely but not confirmed.

8. Letter from Globocnik to von Herff dated October 27, 1943 (Schwarzenbacher's personal file, BA Berlin): "As I moved to Trieste I took with me seventy men from the *Wachmannschaften* of the *Ausbildungslager Trawniki* otherwise I would have had no forces. I nominated *SS-Ustuf.* Schwarzenbacher as commander of this troop." Born in Munich in 1909, Schwarzenbacher was member of both the Nazi party and SS; he was not involved in *Aktion Reinhard.* Having served in the *SS-Totenkopfverbände* in 1941, he was assigned to the SSPF Lublin, and was company commander in *Trawniki*. In January 1942, he was promoted *SS-Untersturmführer* (*Allgemeine-SS*) and became commander of a *Trawniki Wachbataillon* based in Lublin, which he led into action during the repression of the Warsaw ghetto uprising from April to June 1943. At the time just before leaving Poland for Italy, he was commanding three companies of foreign volunteers (*fremdvölkische Wachmänner*, probably *Trawniki*) tasked with guarding the *Arbeitslager Poniatowa* (work camp). Formally he was assigned to the *Stabskompanie beim HSSPF Ost* until 20.11.1943, then to the *Stabskompanie der Waffen SS beim RSHA*, finally from 1.5.1944 to the *Stabskompanie der Waffen-SS beim HSSPF OZAK*.

9. Depositions by Oberhauser of 3.5.1971 (IRSML-FVG, Risiera collection, box 88, also published in Italian translation in Adolfo Scalpelli, *San Sabba*, vol. 2, pp. 31–35) and 24.9.1973 (HHStA, Wiesbaden, Abt. 631a, Nr. 1330). In the first deposition Oberhauser said he belonged to this company when he arrived in Trieste but this does not seem correct and is in fact contradicted by Oberhauser himself in the second one. Oberhauser had been platoon

commander of a *Wachmannschaften* unit in the first phase of his stay in Poland (where he arrived in summer 1941), in Lublin and Belzec; later (probably after Wirth relinquished the command of Belzec to become inspector of the three extermination camps in summer 1942) he was Wirth's assistant as well as escort, a role that he kept also in Italy.

10. Perhaps Globocnik only quoted the number of *Trawniki* that remained in the *Wachmannschaft I (Ostvölker)*, after some of them had been transferred as cadres to the companies of the *Wachmannschaft II*, mainly formed with local elements, and to another unit subordinated to the HSSPF and based in Pola (see below).

11. It is very likely that the around thirty *Trawniki* who had travelled to Trieste with Globocnik's convoy in September 1943 were all or mostly integrated in this company upon its arrival (at least this was the case for one of them, Alexiej Mihalic).

12. The initial intention was to form a battalion of *SS-Wachmannschaften* for each of the five Globocnik's provinces (Trieste, Pola, Fiume, Gorizia and Udine) and to put them under Wirth's command (deposition by Oberhauser of 24.9.1973, HHStA, Wiesbaden, Abt. 631a, Nr. 1330). One battalion in each province is also shown in an organization chart of the HSSPF [OZAK] – IVa, not dated but probably from February–March 1944, which reported plans rather than the actual situation. This plan was probably soon abandoned and reduced to a single battalion, with companies distributed in the various provinces.

13. The designation of *SS-Wachmannschaften-Triest* was used on the unit *Erkennungsmarke* (identity tags; see the specific section in appendix 1).

14. This formulation meant acting commander (it indicated an officer who was in command despite not having a sufficient rank or the formal qualifications, or who was temporarily in command before being confirmed or replaced), in opposition to the formulation *Btl.Kommandeur* which indicated a battalion commander.

15. Letter from Globocnik to von Herff dated October 27, 1943 (Schwarzenbacher's personal file, BA Berlin): "Schwarzenbacher is setting up a battalion of local forces (*ein Bataillon fremdvölkischer Kräfte*)."

16. Depositions by Dorotea Schäfer (who had been clerk and interpreter at the *SS-WMS-Btl.* headquarters) of 17.8.1970 and 30.4.1971 (IRSML-FVG, Risiera collection, box 90) and by Oberhauser of 3.5.1971 (IRSML-FVG, Risiera collection, box 88, also published in Italian translation in Adolfo Scalpelli, *San Sabba*, vol. 2, pp. 31–35; he mentioned a school in the San Sabba city quarter, probably meaning the one on Via Combi).

17. Depositions by Oberhauser of 3.5.1971 (IRSML-FVG, Risiera collection, box 88, also published in Italian translation in Adolfo Scalpelli, *San Sabba*, vol. 2, pp. 31–35) and 24.9.1973 (HHStA, Wiesbaden, Abt. 631a, Nr. 1330).

18. Letter from Globocnik to the SS-FHA dated 13 March 1944 (Schwarzenbacher's personal file, BA Berlin): "Here in the *Adriatisches Küstenland*, Schwarzenbacher has set up a new *SS-Wachmannschaftsbataillon*, demonstrating remarkable skills in the area of commanding local units (*fremdvölkische Einheiten*), as he has managed to create the battalion with especially weak cadres (*ungewöhnlich schwache Führungskräfte*)."

19. Cartellieri report, BA-MA Freiburg, RW 4/689, Anlage 10. In the document the battalion was indicated as "*SS-Wacht-Mannschafts-Btl.*," in a slightly different way than the designation normally used (*Wacht-* instead of *Wach-* , the meaning of the two terms is practically the same), perhaps because the author of the report was a *Wehrmacht* officer (who came to the OZAK on a fact-finding mission on behalf of the *Oberkommando des Heeres*) and was not used to the SS terminology.

20. According to Oberhauser (deposition of 24.9.1973, HHStA, Wiesbaden, Abt. 631a, Nr. 1330) around thirty men belonging to the *Trawniki* company were transferred to the "*Aussenstelle HSSPF* in Pola." Probably this was the *Aussendienststelle Pola* (or *Aussenstelle Pola*, i.e., Pola office) of the *Befehlshaber der Sipo*/SD, which had a company used for anti-partisan activity in Istria, formed by Germans, Italians and Byelorussians (referred to as *Weissruthenen*) and commanded by *SS-Ostuf.* Helmut Prasch. In post-war interrogations, Prasch claimed (deposition of 23.11.1963, HHStA, Wiesbaden, Abt. 631a, Nr. 1330) that his company in Pola had nothing to do with the *Gestapo* or the SD, but action reports signed by him in May 1944 referred to his unit as *BdS-Aussenkommando Pola* or as *SD-Einsatzkommando Pola*; also, documents are known dated from March 1944 and January 1945, signed

by Prasch, written on headed paper of the *Befehlshaber der Sipo u.SD i.d. OZAK Triest – Aussendienststelle Pola* (all mentioned documents are in ARS, AS 1760, box 200/V and box 202). On this regard it is also interesting to mention that another company formed by Byelorussians serving under the SD, called *3. Kp./(weissruth.) Schutzmannschafts-Bataillon der SD 13* (in short: 3./Schuma-Btl. 13), was employed in the OZAK, probably since summer 1944. Almost nothing is known about its activities, but it is documented that in September 1944 it was in San Daniele del Friuli (where there was a *Sipo*/SD detached headquarters), and between the end of that month and early October it was transferred to Pola, where it was also put under Prasch's orders. The transfer order specified that the company had to be used to collect information and fight the partisans, not for guards or protection of buildings or infrastructure. On this battalion see Jerzy Grzybowski, "An Outline History of the 13th (Belarusian) Battalion of the SD Auxiliary Police (*Schutzmannschafts Bataillon der SD 13*)," in *The Journal of Slavic Military Studies*, vol. 23, Issue 3, 2010, pp. 461–476; the transfer order of *3. Kp./Schuma-Btl. 13* from San Daniele to Pola is in ARS, AS 1931, box 756, sheet 212.

21. Depositions by Alexiej Mihalic of 16.1.1976, during the investigations for a second Risiera di San Sabba trial.

22. It is also known that on July 16, 1944, a Croatian soldier from *4. Kompanie* who had deserted and defected to the partisans was executed by a *Sipo* unit from Gorizia in Preval.

23. Deposition by Carlo Grini, in Adolfo Scalpelli, *San Sabba*, vol. 2, pg. 51.

24. "... as cadres for the formation of local units in the *Adriatisches Küstenland*" *("... als Stamm für die Aufstellung landeseigener Verbände im Adriatischen Küstenland")*, BA Berlin, NS 19/2245.

25. Report by the partisan unit Južnoprimorski odred dated June 3, 1944, published in *Zbornik dokumentov in podatkov o narodnoosvobodilni vojni jugoslovanskih narodov*, vol. VI, part 14, document number 18.

26. Unusually, news of the ambush was reported by the *Deutsche Adria Zeitung* newspaper, published by the Germans in Trieste, in the article *Gefallen für die Heimat. Feierliche Beisetzung von Obersturmführer Schwarzenbacher und zehn Landschutzmännern,* published on June 7, 1944.

27. *Befehlsblatt des Befehlshabers der Sipo und des SD* in Trieste, Nr. 23, 5 July 1944, in ARS, AS 1931, box 756, sheet 163. According to Tone Ferenc, *La polizia tedesca nella Zona d'Operazioni "Litorale Adriatico" 1943-1945*, in *Storia Contemporanea in Friuli*, nr. 10, IFSML, Udine, 1979, pp. 24–25, before Hornof the battalion temporary command had been assigned to *SS-Hauptsturmführer* Gustav Hanelt (who was a member of the HSSPF headquarters, charged with personnel matters), but no confirmation of this statement could be found.

28. Deposition by Allers of 21.3.1962 (LA NRW, Münster, Q234, Nr. 4271).

29. Depositions by Dorotea Schäfer (clerk and interpreter at the SS-WMS-Btl. headquarters) of 17.8.1970 and 30.4.1971 (IRSML-FVG, Risiera collection, box 90).

30. Document dated April 7, 1944 (ARS, AS 1878, box 4). Another document dated May 23, 1944, was signed "*Der Führer des SS-Wachmannschafts-Btl., i.A. Eibisch, Ltn.d.SchP.*" where "i.A." ("*im Auftrag*," i.e., "by order") indicated that Eibisch signed on behalf of Schwarzenbacher.

31. Depositions by Franz of 9.8.1967 (IRSML-FVG, Risiera collection, box 88) and of 3.12.1959 and 30.12.1959 (LA NRW, Duisburg, Rep. 388, Nr. 743); also, deposition by Allers of 19.4.1960 (LA NRW, Duisburg, Rep. 388, Nr. 747) and Franz's personal file in BA Berlin. See also the essay of Tone Ferenc, *Kurt Franz*, in Siegfried Pucher, *Il nazista di Trieste. Vita e crimini di Odilo Globocnik, l'uomo che inventò Treblinka*, Beit, Trieste, 2011, pp. 229–242.

32. His burial report (Grabmeldung) contained the following data: *Erk.M.* (identity tag) *262 SS-Führungs-Hauptamt 3. Stabskp.*; *Truppenteil* (unit): *Einsatz R – SS-Wachm.Batl. FP 01471*. The place of death is indicated on the *Grabmeldung* as "San Pietro," a place name which is quite common in the region; the identification of San Pietro di Ragogna is certain on the basis of a report by the Prefettura of Udine on the "rebels' [= partisans] activity" according to which, "the German SS Lieutenant commander of the SS in Gemona" was killed in a firefight in San Pietro di Ragogna on June 19, 1944 (Archivio di Stato in Udine,

Prefettura–Archivio di Gabinetto, box 044 folder 156). According to a report by the Carabinieri, the firefight started when the car in which a German officer, the driver, and a woman were travelling, stopped near a van parked at the side of the road to identify the people in it; the officer was killed and the woman was wounded while among the truck passengers there were one dead and two wounded (the latter, members of the MDT from Udine, claimed they had been kidnapped by the partisans). On the episode there is also a partisan account: according to Ermes Brezzaro, *Ragogna nella Resistenza*, 1997, pp. 259–260, in the evening of June 19, a pick up truck carrying some partisans driving toward the Pinzano bridge crossed paths with a German car near the San Pietro hairpin turn (Giron); in the resulting firefight a German officer was killed, the woman travelling with him was wounded by bullets and then killed when run over by the partisans' truck, while the German driver escaped; three partisans were wounded, one of whom died shortly afterwards. According to documents on the burials at the Udine cemetery, a Luftwaffe auxiliary woman is reported as killed in the same way described by Brezzaro (wounded by bullets and run over by a car) in Gemona on July 4, 1944; it is not known if this was the same woman who died two weeks after being wounded, or if these were different episodes and Brezzaro mistakenly inserted in his reconstruction an element of an episode on July 4 (the death of the woman caused by a car) in his reconstruction of the episode on June 19 in San Pietro.

33. The names are: *Hwm.d.SchP.* Josef Horvath, seconded from the *Feldkommandostelle RFSS*; *Hwm.[d.SchP.]* Steffen; *Zgw.d.SchP.* Franz S., *1. Kp.*, reported missing in action during an anti-partisan action in Vertoiba, near Gorizia, on 23.5.1944; *Owm.d.SchP.* Heinz R., *3. Kp.*, wounded on the Senosecchia–Storie road on 2.6.1944. The latter two had *Erkennungsmarke* issued by the *Pol. Begl.Btl. Steiermark*.

34. The names are: *SS-Zwchm.d.SchP.* (sic) C. Schmidt, Russian *Volksdeutscher*, who committed suicide in Trieste on 9.4.1944; *SS-Zwchm.* Emiljan Kostenko, Ukrainian, *6. Kp.*, fallen in Trieste on 15.5.1944; *SS-Owchm.* Mychailow Sawka, Ukrainian, *5. Kp.*, fallen on the Senosecchia–Storie road on 2.6.1944 (he was probably one of the *Trawniki* that had arrived in Trieste with Globocnik in September 1943); *SS-Wchm.* Petro Nahorniak, Ukrainian, *5. Kp.*, captured by partisans near Castelnuovo on 24.5.1944 (all the previous four had *Erkennungsmarke* issued by the *SS-WMS-Btl.* and marked "*SS-Wachmannschaften*-Triest"); *SS-Zwchm.* Arnold Rosenke, Russian (probably *Volksdeutscher*), *6. Kp.* (later *1. Kp.*; he was *Furier*, or quartermaster, in this company in 1945); Helmut Dahlke (Ukrainian *Volksdeutscher*) and Siewert (probably Ukrainian or Russian *Volksdeutscher*); the latter two were both in San Sabba as members of *1. Kp.* (former *6. Kp.*) at the end of April 1945.

35. The names of the probable *Trawniki*, apparently both Ukrainians, on the *Auszahlungsliste* are: Arendartschuk (*Wchm.*), Sawka (*Wchm.*; probably the same person listed in the previous endnote, later transferred to *5. Kp.*). More names of "Ukrainians" who served in German units in Trieste were collected during the investigations for a second Risiera di San Sabba trial and most appeared in the article *Ex SS accolti come "probi e onesti,"* published in the newspaper *Il Piccolo di Trieste*, June 5, 1994: Adamov (apparently an officer), Michael Bolukalo, Bruch (Russian Volksdeutscher), Elmach (Ukrainian), Juri Gjubanov (Ukrainian), Nikolaus Gorobej (Russian), Grizka (or Grigori) Jahns (Russian), Stjepan Korovin, Josip Kultschek, Juri Kuvanov, Madomov (Ukrainian), Alexiej Mihalic (Ukrainian), Vasilj Mrekalo (Ukrainian), Michahil Sauka (Ukrainian; most probably the Sawka mentioned in the previous endnotes), Juri Soltis (Ukrainian), Josip Susanskj (Galitian). Most of them probably served in the *SS-Wachmannschaften*, it is not known if some were employed in the Risiera.

36. The ordinance was published on the *Verordnungsblatt* (official journal) nr. 54 of December 25, 1943 (some corrections were published on the *Verordnungsblatt* nr. 20 of 6 May 1944). The German text is also included as an annex to the cited Cartellieri report (BA-MA Freiburg, RW 4/689, Anlage 12).

37. The ordinance was published on the *Verordnungsblatt* (official journal) nr. 54 of December 25, 1943 (where the date is given, it seems erroneously, as December 16). The German text is also included as an annex to the cited Cartellieri report (BA-MA Freiburg, RW 4/689,

Anlage 12; the date here is December 6). After March 1944, the option to volunteer applied of course only to the classes which were not drafted; the draftees could opt to serve in this unit rather than in other ones.

38. At least in the five OZAK provinces under Globocnik's authority, i.e., Trieste, Gorizia, Pola (or Istria province), Fiume (or Quarnero province), Udine (or Friuli province). In the Ljubljana province (Provinz Laibach, in German; formally part of the OZAK, but placed under the responsibility of HSSPF Alpenland as far as SS/*Polizei* matters were concerned) the *Slovensko Domobranstvo* (Slovenian National Guard, or Slowenische Landeswehr in German), was formed starting immediately after the Italian armistice on the basis of existing militias, and had already 5,000 men in December 1943. It counted around 12,000 men in the phase of its maximum expansion during summer 1944.

39. The other units included for instance the *Guardia Civica di Trieste* (Civic Guard of Trieste, created in the city on a voluntary basis starting from January 1944) and the militia called *Selbstschutz* ("auto-defense") formed from the German-speaking local population of the Valcanale, a valley near the border with Austria north of Udine.

40. The existence of *Landschutz* units during winter 1943–44 is certain only for the Italian *Landschutz* in the provinces of Friuli and Istria, and for the Slovenian SNVZ; there is no confirmation as regards Italian *Landschutz* units in other provinces, or as regards Croatian *Landschutz* units, that may have been formed before the introduction of the conscription.

41. Excluding thus the Ljubljana province, where as mentioned Slovenian recruits went to the Slovensko Domobranstvo.

42. Not to be confused with the *Milizia per la Difesa Territoriale* (MDT, or *Landschutz-Miliz* in German), which—as mentioned—originated from the *Fascist Milizia Volontaria per la Sicurezza Nazionale* (MVSN). As far as the *Landschutz* consisting of Italians is concerned (the *Difesa Territoriale*), after the training phase its men were assigned to outposts, of which a network was built which included all towns and villages of some importance. They were armed only with rifles and did not have heavy weapons; their tasks were generally limited to guard and surveillance, only rarely some units took part in sweep operations or anti-partisan operations, generally with a secondary role. In general its men had low motivation and were often unreliable. It seems that the many draftees chose this unit because they were persuaded that they could serve in their place of residence. A widespread opinion at the time was that the Difesa Territoriale had been created with the main purpose of keeping young people under control and to avoid them joining the partisans. In fact its members sometimes sympathized with the partisans and joined up with them at the moment of the partisan uprising at the end of April 1945.

43. The fact that documents produced by the *Leitstab* were also sent to the *SS-WMS-Btl.* is additional proof that also this unit was considered as falling into the category of *landeseigene Selbstschutzverbände*. Also the men of *SS-WMS-Btl.* were sometimes indicated as *Landschutzmänner* (*Landschutz* men), see for instance the article *Gefallen für die Heimat. Feierliche Beisetzung von Obersturmführer Schwarzenbacher und zehn Landschutzmännern* published on the newspaper *Deutsche Adria Zeitung* on June 7, 1944.

44. The Duino school was inaugurated by Globocnik on May 14, 1944, see the article *Schulungsburg des Landschutzes*, in *Deutsche Adria Zeitung*, 16 May 1944.

45. The ordinance was published on the *Verordnungsblatt* (official journal) nr. 10 of March 2, 1944, and again on nr. 22 of May 6, 1944. In July 1944, all classes from 1914 to 1926 were drafted for military service.

46. As an example a report drafted by a member of the *Sonderkommando "Adria" – Einsatztrupp Görz* (task force based in Gorizia of the "*Adria*" unit of the *SS-Standarte "Kurt Eggers,"* a propaganda unit) can be mentioned, related to an action called "*Propaganda- und Zwangsrekrutierungsaktion*" (propaganda and forced recruitment) that took place in the villages of Tolmino, Santa Lucia and Canale (in the Isonzo River valley) on February 9, 1944, where one can read: "After arriving in Santa Lucia (...) I was ordered to carry out the recruitment action in Tolmino. (...) In the village cinema hall were gathered the around 500 male inhabitants of all ages from Tolmino and nearby villages. As agreed, after forty people were recruited for intelligence-gathering purposes

("*Abwehrzwecke*") by *Oberleutnant* Koeppke, I held a brief speech to the people, using an interpreter, in which I spoke about the sense and aims of the *Slowenischer Landschutz*. My invitation to enter voluntarily the *Slowenischer Landschutz* did not bear any results, so I went over to forced recruitment. Leaving out the classes above forty years, cripples and disabled and the youngsters below fifteen years, out of the remaining 80–90 men I could recruit for the Landschutz thirty-three usable men aged between 16 and 33 years" (ARS, AS 1760, box 202). To this action participated also a group of soldiers of the "*slowenische SS-Wachmannschaft*" (probably belonging to *1. Kp./SS-WMS-Btl.* or to *Kommando G.*) with security tasks. Also elements of the *SS-WMS-Btl.* and *Abteilung R* were used in the recruitment and training of the *Landschutz*. A report of the *Sonderkommando "Adria" – Einsatztrupp Görz* on a propaganda action carried out in Aidussina on March 10, 1944, mentioned the participation of Franz (who at that time led *Kommando G.* of the *SS-WMS-Btl. in Gorizia*) (ARS, AS 1760, box 202). Additionally, an award proposal for *Hwm. d.SchP*. Josef Horvath belonging to the *SS-WMS-Btl.* mentioned his participation to a fight against the Partisans on the island of Krk during a recruitment propaganda action, carried out together with "*fremdvölkische SS-Wachmänner*" (evidently *SS-WMS-Btl.* soldiers) (BA Berlin, R 70 Italien/23). On the participation of Stangl in the same kind of activities see the chapter on *Abteilung R*.

47. Mario Bonifacio, *La leva del marzo 1944 a Pirano*, in *Tempi e Cultura – Rivista dell'Istituto Regionale per la cultura Istriana*, year III, winter 1998 – spring 1999.

48. The accounts are: 1) Marino Palcich: transported with other workers from the Organisation Todt building site of Piedimonte del Taiano to the Risiera in early December 1944, he was inserted in the *SS-Wachmannschaften* in the Risiera (see the article *Risiera, parla il regista delle evasioni*, in the newspaper *Il Piccolo di Trieste*, June 28, 1994); 2) Italo Contento: arrested in Pirano in early April 1945, because he had failed to present himself for work service, he was inserted in the *SS-Wachmannschaften* in the Risiera (*"a unit of Italian SS which was based at the Risiera,"* as he wrote in his account); he remained with this unit only two weeks, then he could go back home with a permission for study reasons (IRSML-FVG, Venezia Giulia collection, box XX, folder 702).

49. ARS, AS 1618, box 216. Several lists are available, but only one is complete.

50. On the unit history see: Roberto Gremmo, *I partigiani alleati dei nazisti. Il "Battaglione Davide" dalla Resistenza astigiana alla Risiera di Trieste*, Storia Ribelle, Biella, 2015; Giuliano Giorcelli, *Il Battaglione "Davide." Piemonte, Trieste San Sabba, Jugoslavia 1944–45. Cronaca e storia*, Edizioni dell'Orso, Alessandria, 2014; Cosimo Vuerich, *Il battaglione Patrioti Davide*, in *Storia e battaglie*, nr. 61, September 2006; Lutz Klinkhammer, *L'occupazione tedesca in Italia 1943–1945*, Bollati Boringhieri, Torino, 1996, pp. 325–327; Ricciotti Lazzero, *Le SS italiane*, Rizzoli, Milano, 1982, pp. 77–80 and 377–380. For the period April–July 1944 is also available the autobiographical account of Dante Fangaresi, *Dieci settimane a San Sabba*.

51. Enrico Ferrero had been corporal in the Italian *Regio Esercito*. Born in Savona in 1910, he had been convicted for theft and draft dodging, in the 1930s he had been sent to internal exile for attempted fraud and later again arrested for the same crime in early 1943. He came out of prison soon after Mussolini's fall on July 25, 1943.

52. Indicative about these sentiments is that many soldiers felt that the unit disarmament by the Germans (see later) was a "betrayal" and "Davide" was accused by some of his men to have "sold them to the Germans."

53. Reproduced in Giorgio Pisanò, *Storia della guerra civile in Italia 1943–1945*, Edizioni FPE, 1966, pg. 863.

54. Only later (May 1944) were these units fully integrated in the *Waffen-SS*: the *Italienische Freiwilligen Legionen* became *Italienische Waffenverbände der SS*, or *Legione SS italiana*. In particular, the *1. Sturmbrigade* was transformed into *1. Waffen-Grenadier-Brigade der SS (italienische Nr. 1)* and later in *29. Waffen-Grenadier-Division der SS (italienische Nr. 1)*. On the history of these units see Sergio Corbatti and Marco Nava, *Sentire pensare volere. Storia della Legione SS italiana*, Ritter, Milano, 2001.

55. Bulletin of the GNR (called MDT in the OZAK) for the Gorizia province, 9.5.1944 (acces-

sible on the website of Fondazione Luigi Micheletti: www.notiziarignr.it). According to the bulletin the unit, whose name was given as "*Legione Volontari Italiani – 1. Brigata d'Assalto – Battaglione Patrioti Davide*," counted 250–260 men; on the basis of other sources this figure appears excessive.

56. War diary of *32. Comando Militare Provinciale italiano* in Gorizia, 10.4.1944 (AUSSME, RSI collection, box 9); at this date the battalion was indicated as based in Gradisca with 400 men, but this figure is surely exaggerated.

57. ARS, AS 1618, box 216. Also the GNR bulletin dated 9.5.1944 stated that the unit was directly subordinated to Globocnik.

58. War diary of *32. Comando Militare Provinciale italiano* in Gorizia, 3.5.1944 (AUSSME, RSI collection, box 9) and report by the *Ispettorato Speciale di Pubblica Sicurezza per la Venezia Giulia* to the Head of the Police, 10.5.1944. According to other unconfirmed rumors, "Davide" acted under instructions by the *SS- und Polizeikommandeur* for the Gorizia province, *SS-Sturmbannführer* Karl Taus, who aimed at obtaining the liberation of German prisoners held by the partisans.

59. This figure is mentioned in various accounts, and seems consistent with the strength reached by the unit in June, after various selections (see later). According to the account by Dante Fangaresi, *Dieci settimane a San Sabba*, the number of imprisoned soldiers was 168 (pg. 45), but he may have inverted figures by mistake, also considering that he writes later (pg. 81) that initially "around 180 men" from *Battaglione Davide* were prisoners in the Risiera.

60. Those that disappeared after these initial selections were in total around 75–80 men according to Fangaresi, but rather they were probably around sixty, which (taking also into account the execution of Pairolero and Battistini; see below) brought down the number of soldiers to the 122 contained in the list mentioned later on. A group of seventeen soldiers (among them the officers Mario Ferrero and Cerrato), taken from the group and meant to be shot, were pardoned after a couple of days in detention (see Giuliano Giorcelli, *Il Battaglione "Davide,"* pp. 40–42 and 133).

61. The war diary of the RSI military command for the Gorizia province, stated that seven officers of the battalion, including the commander "Davide," were executed, but in reality Ferrero was deported to Dachau, where incredibly he was treated as an important prisoner; after the end of the war he came back to Italy and later disappeared, probably eliminated by old enemies in the area of Alessandria (see Roberto Gremmo, *I partigiani alleati dei nazisti*, pp. 113–162).

62. According to Fangaresi, these were *Capitano* Ernesto Sarzano and three *tenente/sottotenente*, but it seems certain that the unit, after the disarmament and selections, had five Italian officers (see below).

63. The list (ARS, AS 1760, box 203, folder 9) had on its cover the writing "*SS-Wachbataillon – 6 Komp. – Ruolino per appello*" (roll call roster). It included 126 names, but four of these were cancelled (one officer, two NCOs, one enlisted man), and at the end it was indicated "*Forza: 122 uomini*" ("strength: 122 men"). Another note at the end of the list mentioned that three men were in hospital and forty-two in "*blocco*" (block), the latter formulation is not clear but perhaps it indicated those eliminated through the medical examination (see later) and earmarked to be deported to Germany; evidently not all forty-two were deported since the total number of soldiers who finally remained in the unit was around eighty-five (see below). The entire list was published (with numerous transcription errors) in the Trieste newspaper *Il Piccolo* of June 1, 1994 (it seems very unlikely that the list came from Lerch, as stated in the article). On June 5, 1994, the same newspaper published a note from the ANPI (former Italian Partisans' association) of Gorizia according to which twenty-seven persons mentioned in the list later deserted to the partisans. In addition to Enrico Ferrero ("Davide"), the names of three other identified officers who had belonged to *Battaglione Davide* before its disarmament do not appear in the list: *Capitano* Piras, Audano, and Ruggero; for the first two the reason is not known, it may be that they did not follow the battalion to the Gorizia area or they had been deported to Germany with "Davide," while Ruggero had probably already left the unit and had been assigned by the Germans to other tasks. In a report dated May 13, 1944, signed by Franco Frattarelli, leader of the Fascist party in Gorizia, it is written: "Yesterday, *Capitano* Ruggero with other soldiers from the *Battaglione "Patrioti,"* accompanied by

a German NCOs and two soldiers, came to Gorizia. *Capitano* Ruggero stated to Commissar Carelli that he had been nominated battalion commander and that from now on he would work in true comradeship" (Archivio Centrale dello Stato, SPD, Carteggio riservato, box 12, folder 11, sheet 79185). Apparently, Ruggero remained very briefly in the former *Battaglione Davide*, since as said his name does not appear in the list of 122 names; his further employment is not known. Despite the similar surname, it seems that he is not the same person as *Capitano* Ernesto Ruggiero belonging to *5. Rgt. MDT*, who from November 1944, as commander of the regiment's 2. Company, based in Palmanova (south of Udine), was active in the suppression of the partisan movement, becoming notorious for killing and torturing (for these actions he was tried and convicted after the war); it is in fact known that Ernesto Ruggiero was *tenente* in *5. Rgt. MDT* in June and August 1944.

64. It is known from accounts that only these five officers, among those mentioned in the list of 122 names, actually served in the company. Probably, the other four officers in the list (*Capitano* Piano and Gonella, *Tenente* Spaccaferro, *Sottotenente* Sanfelice), considered insufficiently motivated or trustworthy, were eliminated, probably deported to Germany. The figure of sixty-five men left in the unit after the last selection quoted by Fangaresi (pg. 81) seems too low (probably it was obtained subtracting those eliminated via the selections from his initial figure of 168 which, as mentioned, was probably incorrect); at least eighty-five men from the list of 122 are in fact confirmed as members of the *SS-WMS-Btl.*, although of these at least forty-five later deserted (including three officers, Mario Ferrero, Cerrato and Sarzano; the latter, according to his own words, left Trieste for leave in late January 1945, but then went into hiding and never came back to the unit), for the majority going over to the partisans (of the remaining two officers, Fulmine remained in the unit until the end of the war, for Ranalli information is missing).

65. It is to be noted that elements of all the first five companies were still in Trieste in early June, as visible from the fact that fallen, wounded, and missing in the ambush of June 2, where Schwarzenbacher was killed, belonged to all these companies (in particular to the *2.* and *4. Kp.*, with respectively eleven and eight losses), as well as to the *Stabskompanie*.

66. List of losses for the *SS-WMS-Btl.* are in *Deutsche Dienststelle/Wast, Verlustmeldungen*, Band 534. It is not clear if under the *fremdvölkische Angehörige* also the *Trawniki* were included, or only the locals.

67. In Gorizia there was also *Kommando G.* of the *SS-WMS-Btl.* commanded by Franz; no information has been found pointing to the fact that *Kommando G.* could be a part of *1. Kp./SS-WMS-Btl.*, so it is dealt with in a separate section.

68. He was the already mentioned *Zgw.d.SchP.* Franz S., indicated as belonging to *1. Kp./SS-WMS-Btl.*

69. The *Compagnia Autonoma di Sicurezza* of the *Guardia di Finanza* was commanded by *Tenente* Giuseppe Osana. With a strength of 235 men, it had just been formed in mid-May 1944, presumably on German request especially to serve under the orders of the *Sicherungskommandant*. Company outposts are documented in Gemona (where the company headquarters were based), Flagogna (disarmed by the partisans within a few days), Cimano, Provesano, San Martino al Tagliamento, as well as in the Osoppo ammunition depot. Right after the arrival in Gemona on May 18, Osana started to cooperate with the partisans of the area, to whom he went over at the beginning of August. See the report by Osana published in Pierpaolo Meccariello, *La Guardia di Finanza sul confine orientale 1918–1954*, Museo Storico della Guardia di Finanza, Paravia, Torino, 1997, pp. 228–232; the report mentions the presence of Schwarz in Gemona in May 1944, and his command authority over the *Guardia di Finanza* unit (it also mentions an *SS-Obersturmführer* Adolf Garlich, who might have been Schwarz's successor).

70. According to the description of the episode provided by Giorgio Brusin, *Nella bufera. Memorie di "Sandro,"* 1973, the capture of the two partisans took place near Travesio in the morning of June 20; according to the diaries of the partisan units quoted in Bruno Steffè, *La guerra di liberazione nel territorio della Provincia di Pordenone 1943–1945*, ANPI Pordenone, Edizioni ETS, Pisa, 1996, pg. 69, it happened in the area of San Daniele on June 18 (but the episode described seems to be the one of the death of Schwarz, so

it is possible that some confusion was made between different episodes).

71. Leonardo Picco, *Partigiani sovietici nella Val d'Arzino*, ANPI Spilimbergo, 2002, pg. xviii.

72. See the reconstruction by Lino Pinter "Bores" in *La Resistenza Osovana nell'Arzino e nella Val Tramontina*, Arti Grafiche Friulane, Udine, 1975, pp. 45–49; see also Ermes Brezzaro, *Ragogna nella Resistenza*, 1997, pp. 101–102 and 107 and Bruno Steffè, *La guerra di liberazione nel territorio della Provincia di Pordenone 1943–1945*, pp. 75–76.

73. IFSML, collection *III. Btl./SS-Pol.Rgt. 12*, folder 5137.

74. A report from the *Kommando "Adria" – Einsatztrupp Fiume*, belonging to the *SS-Standarte "Kurt Eggers,"* mentioned the participation of a "*Werbetrupp der SS-Wachmannschaften*" (propaganda section of the *SS-Wachmannschaften*) to a propaganda mission (which included leaflet distribution, hanging of posters, speeches to the population) on February 1, 1944, in the villages around Fiume; it is not known if these were elements of *3. Kp./SS-WMS-Btl.* or if the company was already in Fiume in early February (ARS, AS 1760, box 202).

75. BA-MA Freiburg, RH 28-188/12.

76. Other German units in the area included parts of *Reserve-Gebirgs-Jäger-Rgt. 139* (*Rgt. Stab, Pionier-Kp./139, Nachrichten-Kp./139, Sanitäts-Kp./139* and the regiment's entire *II. Btl.* with its five companies), led by *Oberst* Christl and based in Postumia (Christl was also *Stadtkommandant* Adelsberg) and *Sicherungs-Btl. 705* based in San Pietro del Carso (with elements at the Postumia train station). Since mid-July, *I. Btl./SS-Polizei-Regiment 10* was also based in Prestrane and Postumia.

77. Report by *Leutnant* A. Cerne dated 28.7.1944, ARS, AS 1878, box 4, folder 33.

78. The admission card to the military hospital of Postumia for a soldier wounded in Prevallo in the night between June 5–6, indicated that he belonged to the "*Kroatische SS-Mannschaft Triest*" (ARS, AS 1878, box 4, folder 38); the soldier's name also appears in the list of losses of the *SS-WMS-Btl.* where he is indicated as a member of its *4. Kompanie*.

79. Roland Kaltenegger, *Zona d'operazione Litorale Adriatico*, Libreria Editrice Goriziana, 1996, pp. 119–120.

80. ARS, AS 1931, box 839 (Slovenian transcription of a German document).

81. Bolender had commanded the *Wachmannschaften* in Sobibor, after the uprising of August 2, 1943.

82. In a deposition Allers confirmed that he had under his orders as *Sicherungskommandant* a company of the *SS-WMS-Btl.* (deposition of 24.11.1970, IRSML-FVG, Risiera collection, box 88, also published in Italian translation in Adolfo Scalpelli, *San Sabba*, vol. 2, pg. 27). It is plausible that the company was formed specifically with the intention to use it for the security of the Trieste–Fiume road; right in the days of the disarmament of *Battaglione Davide*, in fact, Wirth was nominated *Sicherungskommandant der Karststrasse*, and probably found himself in need of forces for this task.

83. The list of forty-two soldiers (two officers—Sarzano and Fulmine—five NCOs and thirty-five enlisted personnel) is published in Ricciotti Lazzero, *Le SS italiane*, Rizzoli, Milano, 1982, pp. 377–380. All but one (Agrippino Nascente, who joined the unit in August 1944) had belonged to *Battaglione Davide*.

84. On Sarzano's personal card is noted: *"Sarzano führt seit dem 28.5.1944 den Stützpunkt Castelnuovo"* ("Sarzano leads the Castelnuovo outpost since 28 May 1944"); it seems unlikely that he commanded the entire outpost, more probably he only led the group of Italians. His card is also printed in *Gente*, March 15, 1976.

85. Among the fugitives from the *Casa cantoniera* was also Ettore Sarzano (brother of Ernesto), who went back to the SS unit and was later killed in combat against the partisans (see later) (depositions by Ernesto Sarzano of 23.2.1976 and 23.2.1978, during the investigations for a second Risiera di San Sabba trial). A personal account of a soldier that deserted from the Casa cantoniera is in Giuliano Giorcelli, *Il Battaglione "Davide,"* pp. 63–64; however, the location of the Casa cantoniera as being near the village of Passo, on the old stretch of the Mattuglie–Pisino road between Aurania and Cerreto, west of the Monte Maggiore, mentioned in this account, is not considered correct. According to another personal account in the same book (pg. 55), another group of soldiers from *6. Kompanie*

deserted on 11 June, but where this happened is not known.

86. ARS, AS 1618, box 216. In the document the company is indicated as "*SS-Wachmannschaften – I. Kompanie*."

87. See the notes written by Adelmo Deregibus, a soldier of *6. Kompanie* who deserted from Mattuglie on July 28, published in Dante Fangaresi, *Dieci settimane a San Sabba*, pg. 135: 16 July: "transfer to Mattuglie; 18 July: night bombardment, a fire bomb detonates four meters from our billets"; 23 July: "those of Castelnuovo [probably recte: Starada, as a sub-post of Castelnuovo] have gone over to the partisans"; 25 July: "the *panzer* [probably an armored truck] has been attacked in Castelnuovo, nothing serious; 28 July: escape towards the Monte Maggiore in Istria. " See also Giuliano Giorcelli, *Il Battaglione "Davide,"* pp. 55–57.

88. Dante Fangaresi, *Dieci settimane a San Sabba*, pp. 91–96. The "Mongols" mentioned by Fangaresi were probably Ukrainians and Caucasians who were serving in *3. Rgt. Brandenburg*, see on this Hinrich-Boy Christiansen, *Mit Hurra gegen die Wand*, 2010, pp. 16 and 61.

89. *Kriegstagebuch* of *2. Kp./3. Rgt. Brandenburg*, kindly provided by a former unit member, Hinrich-Boy Christiansen; place names have been corrected when necessary. This excerpt is also partially published in Helmuth Spaeter, *Die Brandenburger. Eine deutsche Kommandotruppe zbV 800*, W. Angerer, München, 1978, pp. 410–411, but here the term "*landeseigene SS*" was modified in "*Landesbewohner*" (local inhabitants). It is not clear what is meant by "*VI. Zug*" (6th platoon), but it may mean a platoon from *6. Kp./SS-WMS-Btl.*

90. BA Berlin, R 70 Italien/23, sheet 155–156.

91. The bulletins of the GNR (called MDT in the OZAK) are accessible on the website of Fondazione Luigi Micheletti: www.notiziarignr.it Despite the one day discrepancy in the date, this is evidently the same action mentioned in Bolender's award proposal.

92. *Sicherungs-Btl. (M) 1218* had arrived in the area during August 1944. Operations *Hochkönig* and *Traunsee* (parts of a larger operation called *Unternehmen Tschitschenboden*, or *Ciceria* operation, on which there are no further details) took place in early September respectively in the areas of Monte Lisina, and in the area northeast of Fiume, with the participation of the following units: *3. Rgt. Brandenburg*, *Res.Jg.Btl. 499*, *Geb. Btl. Heine*, *Sich.Btl. (M) 1218* and *I. Btl./Res.Geb. Jg.Rgt. 139* (the latter called *Kampfgruppe Huber*).

93. Report by the commander of *2. Kp./Sich. Btl. (M) 1218* (BA-MA Freiburg, RH 28-188/4). See also the personal account by a former soldier of *Battaglione Davide* serving in *6. Kp./SS-WMS-Btl.* at the Risiera who participated in this action, in Giuliano Giorcelli, *Il Battaglione "Davide,"* pp. 61–62.

94. Torquato Dalcich (anagram of Aldo Quattrocchi), *Un diario (1944–1945)*, Firenze, 1997, available on the Internet page: www.isses.it/diario4occhi.htm.

95. Dante Fangaresi, *Dieci settimane a San Sabba*, pp. 82–84.

96. Dante Fangaresi, *Dieci settimane a San Sabba*, pp. 85–89.

97. As mentioned, in Gorizia there were also parts of *1. Kp./SS-WMS-Btl.*, at least in the first half of 1944; no information has been found to support the possibility that *Kommando G.* was part of this company, therefore it is treated separately.

98. This name is used in a note sent by Franz to the *SS-Personalhauptamt* in Berlin on May 13, 1944, where the unit he belonged to is indicated as "*SS-Wachmannschaftsbatallion – Kommando G.*" (Franz's personal file, BA Berlin).

99. See endnote 46.

100. *Slowenischer Landschutz*, in *Deutsche Adria Zeitung*, May 9, 1944.

101. On June 20, 1944, were in fact under Franz's control as Sicherungskommandant the following *Stutzpünkt* (outposts), with strength and—if known—unit and commander (from a document transcribed in Roland Kaltenegger, *Zona d'operazione Litorale Adriatico*, Libreria Editrice Goriziana, 1996, pp. 120–121): San Pietro di Gorizia (commanded by Maggiore De Ferri; one officer and twenty-six enlisted personnel from the Milizia = MDT); [Mount] San Marco (one officer, five NCOs, and seventy-seven *Alpini* enlisted personnel from *Rgt. "Tagliamento"*); Prevacina (four NCOs and thirty-three *Alpini* enlisted personnel from *Rgt. "Tagliamento"*); Montespino (one officer, ten NCOs, and eighty-five *Alpini* enlisted personnel from *Rgt. "Tagliamento"*); Tabor (two officers, three NCOs, and forty-eight *Alpini* enlisted personnel

from *Rgt. "Tagliamento"*); Rifembergo (commanded by *Capitano* Arturo Vettorini, commander of *2. Compagnia/5. Rgt. MDT*; three officers and forty enlisted personnel from *5. Rgt. MDT*); Sasseto (one officer and thirty-two enlisted personnel from the *Milizia* = MDT); Viadotto (one officer and fifty enlisted personnel from the *Milizia* = MDT); Duttogliano (one officer and fifty enlisted personnel from the *Milizia*); Crepegliano (twenty-six enlisted personnel from the *Milizia* = MDT); Monrupino (two officers and forty-six enlisted personnel from the *Milizia* = MDT).

102. For the sources on Franz and *Kommando G.* see endnote 31.

103. IFSML, collection *III. Btl./SS-Pol.Rgt. 12*, folder 5137. It is not known if also other parts of the *SS-WMS-Btl.* were subordinated to the *Höherer Sicherungsstab*, in the Veneto region or in the OZAK. On the *Höherer Sicherungsstab* see the specific section.

104. From this point on therefore the term *SS-Wachmannschaften* is used instead of *SS-Wachmannschafts-Bataillon*. It must be noted that the term *SS-Wachmannschaften* was used also before, during 1943–44, in parallel with the term *SS-WMS-Btl.*

105. In addition to the case of the members of the *Landschutz* from Pirano, who were transferred to the *SS-WMS-Btl.* and from this in part to the *Karstjäger-Division*, confirmed is also the case of a *Trawniki* transferred from the *SS-WMS-Btl.* to the division. He was a Ukrainian born in a village near Sobibor and had an *Erkennungsmarke* issued by the *SS-WMS-Btl.*, which he kept also after moving to the *Waffen-SS*; he was transferred to the division apparently in December 1944, and integrated in *3. Kompanie/Waffen-Gebirgs (Karstjäger)-Regiment der SS 59*. The man is reported as killed in the area of Gemona, north of Udine, in the last days of the war.

106. ARS, AS 1618, box 216. The *3.*, *4.* and *5. Gruppe* were probably in *2. Zug*, not listed in the document.

107. It can be mentioned on this regard that Fangaresi wrote in appendix to the second edition of his book *Dieci settimane a San Sabba* (pg. 138) to have been contacted after the appearance of the first edition by at least two persons (one from Tarvisio with a German surname, one from Trieste with a Slavic surname) claiming that they had served in the former *Battaglione Davide* at the Risiera from late 1944. One of them told Fangaresi that he had been part, "of that group of 100 young people that came to the Risiera di San Sabba in December 1944 to integrate the *Battaglione David*" (i.e., actually *1. Kp./SS-Wachmannschaften*, formerly *6. Kp.*).

108. Personal account by Marino Palcich in the article *Risiera, parla il regista delle evasioni*, in the newspaper *Il Piccolo di Trieste*, June 28, 1994. According to a contemporary document Palcich was integrated in *1. Kp./ SS-Wachmannschaften*.

109. ARS, AS 1618, box 219.

110. Account by Italo Contento, IRSML-FVG, Venezia Giulia collection, box XX, folder 702.

111. On this operation see also the chapter on *Abteilung R*.

112. Mario Bonifacio, *La leva del marzo 1944 a Pirano*, in *Tempi e Cultura – Rivista dell'Istituto Regionale per la cultura Istriana*, year III, winter 1998 – spring 1999.

113. Account by Tommaso Scaglione in the article *"Non siamo criminali di guerra,"* in *Gente*, March 29, 1976.

114. See the article *Ex SS accolti come "probi e onesti"* published on the newspaper *Il Piccolo di Trieste*, June 5, 1994.

Appendix 1

1. The name of *SS-Wachmannschaften* (literally "guard units") of the OZAK is meant to include:

a) the company of *Wachmannschaften* that arrived in the OZAK from Poland, commanded by Schwarzenbacher, formed in the majority by *Trawniki* and by some *Reichsdeutsche* (*Trawniki* company); initially integrated into the *SS-Wachmannschafts-Btl.* and indicated as *Wachmannschaft I (Ostvölker)*, it was probably later detached and renamed *SS-Wachmannschafts-Kompanie*;

b) the *SS-Wachmannschafts-Btl.*, formed (at least initially) by two parts: the *Wachmannschaft I (Ostvölker)* and the *Wachmannschaft II (landeseigene Kräfte*); the latter consisted of several companies and was formed—in addition to some *Reichsdeutsche* and *Trawniki*—mainly by locally recruited elements, called by the Germans *landeseigene Kräfte* (literally local forces). This term, that for clarity is also used in this analysis, included both soldiers recruited in the OZAK region and belonging to its various ethnic groups (Italians, Slovenes, Croats and some *Volksdeutsche*, i.e., ethnic Germans living outside the Reich's borders), as well as Italians from others regions (for instance the former members of *Battaglione Davide*).

2. The uniforms worn by the *Trawniki* attached to *Abteilung R*, although in some cases they were seconded to the *SS-WMS-Btl.*, are dealt with in the section related to *Abteilung R*.

3. The term *landeseigene Kräfte* is used from now onwards in this appendix to indicate the *landeseigene Kräfte* of the *SS-Wachmannschaften* of the OZAK.

4. From September 1939, the *Sicherheitsdienst* (security service of the SS, shortened in SD) and the *Sicherheitspolizei* (security police, or *Sipo*), the latter formed by the *Geheime Staatspolizei* (secret police, or *Gestapo*) and by the *Kriminalpolizei* (criminal police, or *Kripo*), were brought into the *Reichssicherheitshauptamt* (central office for the Reich's security, or RSHA), with the aim of uniting all criminal and political police forces, secret services and public security forces under the control of Reinhard Heydrich. The name *Sipo* und SD (*Sipo*/SD) was used to refer to the forces of the RSHA until the end of the war. The *Waffen-SS* ("Armed-SS") were basically the SS army, which during the war fought on the front line like the regular army, the *Wehrmacht*.

5. Since the "*SS-Feldmütze neuer Art M40*" is described also as "*Schiffchen-form*," the term *Schiffchen M40* will be used here for simplicity.

6. Depositions by Hödl of 30.3.1963 (LA NRW, Münster, Q 234, Nr. 4424), Münzberger of 26.1.1962 (LA NRW, Münster, Q 234, Nr. 4269), Bolender of 27.9.1963 (LA NRW, Münster, Q 234, Nr. 4293), Frenzel of 12.11.1963 (LA NRW, Münster, Q 234, Nr. 4294) and Oberhauser of 6.12.1961 (StA München, Nr. 33033/18).

7. According to a deposition by an Italian interpreter employed by *Abteilung R* in Trieste, Augusta Reiss (of 10.2.1976, during the investigations for a second Risiera di San Sabba trial), the members of *Abteilung R* as well as the *Trawniki* attached to it wore some insignia on their arm with a German word written on it, probably an arm band or a cuff title; however, this statement could not be confirmed by pictorial evidence.

8. This is particularly odd in the case of Hering, who apparently was not even an SS member (at least until May 1943). According to depositions at the Nuremberg trials of 1945–46 (in particular those of *SS-Stubaf.* Walther Schellenberg and *SS-Ostuf.* Rolf-Heinz Höppner on the RSHA and the *Einsatzgruppen*), it seems that, at least in the eastern territories conquered by Germany, the SD-*Raute* was also used by *Sicherheitspolizei* members, in particular those attached to the *Einsatzkommandos*. This may also explain why some *Aktion Reinhard*/*Abteilung R* members wore this insignia.

9. Dubois, Gomerski, Hackenholt, Oberhauser, and Schwarz had belonged to the *2. SS-Totenkopf-Standarte "Brandenburg"* (during the first phases of World War II Oberhauser was also in the *Leibstandarte Adolf Hitler*). Franz had belonged to the *3. SS-Totenkopf-Standarte "Thüringen,"* Bolender to the *I./7. SS-Totenkopf-Standarte*. Mätzig and Baer had also served in the *Waffen-SS*, but it is not known what kind of uniform they used in the OZAK since no pictures of them in this region are known.

10. According to a deposition by Schiffner (of 18.2.1972, HHStA, Wiesbaden, Abt. 631a, Nr. 1316), these tunics were made of an unfamiliar cloth; this could mean they were not made in the standard *Polizei-Grün* cloth, so it is possible they were actually produced locally with Italian *Grigioverde* (gray-green) wool cloth.

11. As far as known, the following men were Ordnungspolizei members: Dachsel, Dietze, Fischer, Küttner, Rost, Seidel, Vey/Fey, Walther, Zänker.

12. According to a source, "the *Trawniki* were issued initially gray-green (*grau-grüne*) uniforms, after the end of the training period they received black uniforms" (*Urteil der 1. Strafkammer des Landgerichts München II als Schwurgericht in der Strafsache gegen Demjanjuk Iwan Nikolai*, Lfd. Nr. 924 LG München II 12.05.2011, JuNSV Bd. XLIX pg. 237); with the term "*grau-grüne*" it was very likely meant the *erdgrau* (earth-gray) or *feldgrau* color. However, photo evidence seems to show that gray-green uniforms supplied by the *Ausbildungslager* were used by *Trawniki* also during their early days in the OZAK, so obviously long after the training in Poland.

13. The term "*Heer* M40/41" refers to the standard *Wehrmacht* tunic distributed after the initial phases of the war. It was a simplified model compared to the previous M36 *feldgrau* model: while the M36 had collar and shoulder boards made of dark green cloth, on the M40/41 they were made of the same wool cloth used for the rest of the garment. The only difference between the M40 and the M41 was the number of buttons: five for the M40 and six for the M41. Apparently, in the OZAK a local production of uniforms was initiated in order to supply the units formed in the region (see appendix 2). As the locally produced tunics imitated the main features of the standard *Heer* M40/41 models, in this analysis they are referred to as *Heer* M40/41 style.

14. An order issued by Globocnik on May 10, 1943, stated: "The *Wachmannschaften* are issued until further notice black or earth-gray (*erdgrau*) uniforms" (*Urteil der 1. Strafkammer des Landgerichts München II als Schwurgericht in der Strafsache gegen Demjanjuk Iwan Nikolai*, Lfd.Nr. 924 LG München II 12.05.2011, JuNSV Bd. XLIX pg. 281); it is very likely that the term black uniforms referred at least in part to the already mentioned *SS-Dienstrock* M32, while the term *erdgrau* referred to the obsolete *SS-Verfügungstruppe* M34 tunics.

15. Deposition by Oberhauser of 12.6.1973 (HHStA, Wiesbaden, Abt. 461, Nr. 36346/12).

16. According to a thorough research on the topic (Peter Black, "Foot Soldiers of the Final Solution: The Trawniki Training Camp and Operation *Reinhard*," in *Holocaust & Genocide Studies*, vol. 25, nr. 1 (spring 2011), pg. 12 and footnote 95), the *Trawniki* initially received Polish uniforms dyed in black, that apparently had belonged to the dissolved *Lublin Selbstschutz*; starting from 1942 the *Ausbildungslager Trawniki* was issued earth-brown uniforms from the Belgian army. The same study also emphasizes that *Trawniki* used the most varied combinations of items from different types of uniforms.

17. Photos show a maximum of three *Tresse* stripes worn by *Trawniki* (also in the OZAK) on the shoulder boards to indicate ranks. These *Tresse* stripes were probably of the same type as used by the *SS-Unterführer-Anwärter* of the *Waffen-SS* and were used to indicate ranks by several foreign units such as the *Osttruppen*, the *Sonderdienst* of the *Generalgouvernement*, the *SS-Wachmannschaften* of the OZAK and the *Guardia Civica di Trieste*, sometimes together with collar piping or with collar *Tresse*. The collar *Tresse* seems to be the standard one for the NCOs of the German army; a peculiarity of the *Trawniki* was that the *Tresse* started at the tip of the collar and ended at shoulder level ("short lower collar *Tresse*").

18. The *Schutzmannschaften* were auxiliary police forces formed by the Germans in Lithuania, Latvia, Estonia, Belarus, and Ukraine; these units, organized in batallions along rigid ethnic lines, were employed for internal security and sweep operations.

19. These *Schutzmannschaften* uniforms used by *Trawniki* can be seen in photographs taken during the suppression of the Warsaw ghetto uprising in April–May 1943, as well as in a photo taken at the funeral of *Aktion Reinhard* men killed during the uprise of October 1943, in the Sobibor extermination camp.

20. Such sidecaps were probably obsolete *Feldmütze für SS* M34 produced for the *Allgemeine-SS*, the *SS-Verfügungstruppe,* and the *SS-Totenkopfverbände* and fallen into disuse during the late 1930s, as well as locally produced models. In some rare cases it seems that the black *Schiffchen* were also of the *Waffen-SS Panzertruppen* M40 model, with standard SS BeVo insignia. It seems that only the *Volksdeutsche* used in some cases the *Feldgrau Schiffchen* M40 with *Totenkopf* and eagle affixed frontally.

21. In a deposition (of 18.2.1972, HHStA, Wiesbaden, Abt. 631a, Nr. 1316), Schiffner said that the *Trawniki* attached to *Abteilung R* were still wearing the *erdbraun* uniforms in Italy.

22. It is likely that the new tunics were inspired by those produced for the *Sonderdienst*, an auxiliary police force set up in the *Generalgouvernement* and active also in the *Distrikt Lublin* during Globocnik's presence. On this, see Jan Rutkiewicz, *Il Sonderdienst*, in *Uniformi & Armi*, nr. 133, May 2007; the article mentions a regulation issued on 11.6.1940 by the *Hauptabteilung Innere Verwaltung – Abteilung Inspektion des Sonderdienstes* which set out that soldiers of this auxiliary police were to wear *feldgrau* tunics and greatcoats, with black collars. Andrew Mollo (*Uniforms of the SS*, Windrow & Greene, 1992, vol. 5, pg. 55) quotes a *Verordnung über die Errichtung eines Sonderdienstes* issued

on 6.5.1940 and came into effect on 11.5.1940, that in paragraph four described the Sonderdienst tunics with black collar. This tunic with a black collar was almost a unicum in the wide spectrum of uniforms used by German regular or auxiliary army/police forces.

23. These black collar tabs were reminiscent of those produced in the 1930s for the various SS branches.

24. It is not known if both the black and red (probably) collar tabs were issued at the same time, but this is certainly possible. Such insignia were certainly already in use on April 20, 1944, as they are seen in pictures taken during the parade for Hitler's birthday held in Trieste on that day; it is even possible that they were introduced for the first time on the occasion of this parade. From the black and white image it is not clear if it shows the black or red version or both.

25. Based on photo evidence it appears that at least until the conscription of March 1944, this same type of uniform was used by all or most units of the *landeseigene Selbstschutzverbände*. This should have made it hard or impossible to identify members of different units and may explain why changes were subsequently adopted in order to differentiate the uniforms of the *SS-Wachmannschaften* from those of the other units of the *landeseigene Selbstschutzverbände* (for instance the *Landschutz*).

26. It would seem that in some cases the Italian standard mod. 40 tunic was also used, but without white *Waffenfarbe* on the shoulder boards. The evidence on this regard is very scarce and it is thought that this may have happened rarely.

27. It is not known what kind of arm shield (if any) was used by the *Volksdeutsche* and Croatian soldiers of the *SS-Wachmannschaften*. With regard to the latter, a drawing has been published of an arm shield identical to those described but with the Croatian national colors (red-white-blue), with the indication that it was used by the *landeseigene Selbstschutzverbände*. However, no photo evidence of this Croatian shield is known to the authors.

28. It can be assumed that the national tricolor arm shields were produced for exclusive use by the *landeseigene Kräfte* of the *SS-Wachmannschaften*; in fact, except for some limited photo evidence referring to the *Slovenian Landschutz*, no evidence has been found showing the use of national shields by other units of the *landeseigene Selbstschutzverbände*. Among the latter, the *Landschutz* had already adopted provincial arm shields by early May—as mentioned in a report by 1. Rgt. MDT dated May 3, 1944—therefore, it had no reason to use national shields. The same report also mentions the use of national tricolor shields, probably by the *landeseigene Kräfte* of the *SS-Wachmannschaften*.

29. It is conceivable that the red (probably) collar tabs were meant to distinguish at first glance the *landeseigene Kräfte* members from the *Trawniki*. According to personal accounts (in Mario Bonifacio, *La leva del marzo 1944 a Pirano*, in *Tempi e Cultura – Rivista dell'Istituto Regionale per la cultura Istriana*, year III, winter 1998 – spring 1999, pg. 25), some recruits from Pirano (Istria), forcibly transferred from the *Landschutz* of the Pola province to the *SS-Wachmannschaften* between April and May 1944, received, "black collar tabs without the double S"; it is unclear whether this is an error (possibly caused by the fact that some of these recruits were later transferred to the *Karstjäger-Division*, where in some cases locally recruited soldiers used black rhomboidal collar tabs without runes) or if indeed even some of the *landeseigene Kräfte* personel of the *SS-Wachmannschaften* were issued the black collar tabs usually reserved for *Trawniki*, perhaps due to logistical problems or while awaiting to receive the red ones.

30. Some sources claim that the rhomboidal tabs used by the *Flak* units was the same used by the *Italienische Waffenverbände der SS* (Italian SS Legion) and apparently—according to photo comparison—also by the *Guardia Civica di Trieste*, the SNVZ and the *Landschutz* of the provinces of Pola, Fiume and Udine. From the generally poor and unclear photo evidence it is impossible to confirm or refute these claims. In any case, it is possible to notice a significant difference between the various shades of red of the cloth used for the collar tabs adopted by the various *Landschutz* units; it is not known if this was simply due to different production lots or if it had any specific meaning. The red rhomboidal non-outlined collar tabs used by the various *Landschutz* units, which were part of the *landeseigene Selbstschutzverbände*,

are very likely the same tabs used, after the addition of the outline, also by the *landeseigene Kräfte* of the *SS-Wachmannschaften*.

31. About the collar tabs and national arm shields it is interesting to quote a first-hand account by a former member of *Battaglione Davide*, later transferred to the *SS-Wachmannschaften*, referring to an episode at the Risiera di San Sabba in mid-May 1944: "I remember (because this seemed very strange to me) that there were SS soldiers wearing the Italian tricolor [arm shield] but also [SS soldiers] with the French one and others that I was told wore Slovenian collar tabs" (deposition by Gottardo Milani, in Adolfo Scalpelli, *San Sabba*, vol. 2, pg. 129). It is very likely that the term "Slovenian collar tabs" described the red (probably) rhomboidal outlined tabs used by the *landeseigene Kräfte*. Regarding the arm shields, it seems certain that the witness mistook the Slovenian (or, if actually used, Croatian) tricolor for the French, which all had the same colors (there is no information about French SS units operating in the OZAK).

32. These comfortable uniforms were made of robust gray cotton fabric; before the armistice they were widely used during the summer months by the Italian army in order to preserve the dwindling stocks of gray-green uniforms. There are photos showing these tunics in use in the OZAK also by the *Waffen-Ausbildungs-und-Ersatz-Btl. der SS* stationed in the Valcanale (Udine province), the *Landschutz* of the Udine province, the SNVZ, *Polizei-Freiwilligen-Btl. "Fiume"* and the *Guardia Civica di Trieste*.

33. Cosimo Vuerich, *Il battaglione Patrioti Davide*, in *Storia & Battaglie*, nr. 61, September 2006, pg. 18.

34. Being the "German fieldcap with visor" the correct translation of the term "*einheitsfeldmütze*," it is likely that the author has mentioned twice the same headgear, surely the *Einheitsfeldmütze* M43.

35. Dante Fangaresi, *Dieci Settimane a San Sabba*, pg. 31. The two mentioned sources are in disagreement only regarding the use of the *Einheitsfeldmütze*: it is not clear in fact if, until *Battaglione Davide* arrived in the OZAK, the unit members used the German fieldcap as claimed by Vuerich, or instead mainly the REI sidecap, as Fangaresi would seem to indicate.

36. Dante Fangaresi, *Dieci Settimane a San Sabba*, pg. 47.

37. Dante Fangaresi, *Dieci Settimane a San Sabba*, pg. 70.

38. Dante Fangaresi, *Dieci Settimane a San Sabba*, pg. 85.

39. The list was drafted by *1. Kp./SS-Wachmannschaften* and signed by Oberhauser. The number of helmets so improbably high for a single company seems to suggest that probably the document actually listed the entire stock of helmets available to the *SS-Wachmannschaften*, stored at the Risiera, where in this period its *1. Kompanie* was based.

40. Accordingly to the little information available, including some rare pictures, it seems that these weapons were at least in some cases of the model chambered for the Parabellum 9 x 19 mm cartridge without muzzle, produced for export after February 1943. Apparently, at least three stocks of Suomi KP/-31 were ordered by Germany during the war: 1,742 pieces in March 1942, 1,100 pieces in June 1942, and finally 200 pieces in August 1943; the latter, ordered directly by the *Privatkanzlei des Führers*, seem to have been delivered at the beginning of 1944 and apparently issued to the *Waffen-SS* (Markku Palokangas, *Sotilaskäsiaseet Suomessa 1918–1988*, The Arms Historic Society of Finland, 1991, vol. 2, pg. 267). According to a trial deposition by Gomerski, the Suomi KP/-31 were probably already in possession of *Aktion Reinhard* in Poland; apparently some of them were kept at the Sobibor camp armory. According to another source (Pier Arrigo Carnier, *Lo sterminio mancato*, pg. 34), it was *SS-Oberführer* Viktor Brack of the *Kanzlei des Führers*, one of the highest people responsible for the Euthanasia program and *Aktion Reinhard*, that obtained these weapons for the unit. It can be noted that some Suomi KP/-31 were also used by men of the SSPF *Warschau* (*SS-Gruppenführer* Jürgen Stroop) who were photographed together with *Trawniki* during the destruction of the Warsaw ghetto in April–May 1943; such pictures were used by Stroop in his report on the operation ("*Es gibt keinen jüdischen Wohnbezirk in Warschau mehr!*," better known as the *Stroop Report*).

41. Dante Fangaresi, *Dieci Settimane a San Sabba*, pg. 64.

42. On an inventory list of weapons drafted by *1. Kp./SS-Wachmannschaften* and signed by

Oberhauser, dated February 15, 1945, were listed: "2 heavy mortars (81 mm) (complete), 1 heavy mortar (81 mm) with 60 shells, 4 Breda 8 mm heavy machine guns, 1 German MG34 machine gun, 1 German MG42 machine gun, 8 Italian 6,5 mm machine guns, 131 Italian short rifles, 260 Italian long rifles, 12 Italian Carabinieri rifles, 3 Italian old model rifles, 11 pistols, 44 Italian bayonetts (....), 6 Beretta sub-machine guns (...), 61 Italian long rifles, zurück Br. Nero" (the note "*zurück Br. Nero*" probably meant that the rifles had been handed over by the Brigata Nera of Trieste). As already seen for helmets (see above), the high number of weapons in this inventory list seems to suggest that it included the entire stock of weapons available to the *SS-Wachmannschaften*, stored at the Risiera, where in this period its *1. Kompanie* was based.

43. "The entry rank of a *Trawniki* man was "*Wachmann*." According to ability and performance he could be promoted to *Oberwachmann*, *Gruppenwachmann*, *Zugwachmann*, *Rottenwachmann* and *Oberzugwachmann*. As a rule, the higher ranks were attributed to the *Volksdeutsche*" (*Urteil der 1. Strafkammer des Landgerichts München II als Schwurgericht in der Strafsache gegen Demjanjuk Iwan Nikolai*, Lfd. Nr. 924 LG München II 12.05.2011, JuNSV Bd. XLIX, pg. 237).

44. Deposition by Jührs of 8.4.1964 (HHStA, Wiesbaden, Abt. 631a, Nr. 1329) and of 5.11.1963 (StA München, Nr. 33033/16).

45. With regard to this subject it can be added that Rudi Bittner, who led the *SS-Standortverwaltung Lublin–Zweigstelle Trawniki*, said at the Demjanjuk trial that in his view the men trained at the *Ausbildungslager* were issued an *SS-Soldbuch*. He added also that he did not remember the type of *Dienstausweis* as Nahorniak's.

46. A similar *soldbuch*, also bilingual but with the words "*Soldbuch zugleich Personalausweis – Libretto Personale*" on the cover, was issued in two slightly different versions to the members of the *Legione SS Italiana* and to the Italian soldiers recruited in the OZAK and assigned to the *24. Waffen-Gebirgs (Karstjäger)-Division der SS*.

47. There are substantial similarities among the personal documents issued to the locally recruited members of the units subordinated to the HSSPF OZAK. In particular the "*Dienstausweis*" for *Polizei-Freiwilligen-Btl. "Triest,"* the "*Soldbuch für landeseigene Kräfte*," the "*Soldbuch zugleich Personalausweis – Libretto Personale*" in the version for the soldiers recruited in the OZAK serving in the *Karstjäger-Division*, and the identity card for MDT soldiers, all show similar features. Since the latter was surely printed by Tipografia Riva of Trieste, it is likely that this company produced the other three documents as well. They all look similar for the type of paper and fonts used, sometimes some small translation and spelling mistakes and a standardized code referring to the production lots, often printed on the cover. According to the analysis of the survived specimen, it seems that the Tipografia Riva produced at least part of the printed material used by the offices of the *Oberster Kommissar* and the HSSPF OZAK in Trieste.

48. Cosimo Vuerich, *Il battaglione Patrioti Davide*, in *Storia & Battaglie*, nr. 61, September 2006, pg. 18.

49. The *Erkennungsmarke* with the lowest number, *SS-Wachmannschaften-Triest 1*, was assigned to a *Volksdeutscher* from Trieste assigned to *4. Kp./SS-WMS-Btl.*; the highest known number is 1399, which was given to an Italian soldier from *1. Kp./SS-Wachmannschaften* killed in action on March 27, 1945. On the around 700 names of *Trawniki* and *landeseigene Kräfte* soldiers of the *SS-Wachmannschaften* of the OZAK that are known, only fifty-two *Erkennungsmarke* are identified, assigned to members of the *Stabskompanie*, *Kraftfahrstaffel* and *1., 2., 4., 5.* and *6. Kompanie*. There are also some cases in which the *Erkennungsmarke* seems not to have been assigned (this is documented for three Croats of *4. Kp.* and four Italians of *2. Kp./SS-WMS-Btl.*).

50. Known are the cases of two Ukrainians of *5. Kp.* and of a Ukrainian and a Russian *Volksdeutscher* of *6. Kp./SS-WMS-Btl.*

Appendix 2

1. These were the provinces of Trieste, Gorizia, Pola (or Istria province), Fiume (or Quarnero province), and Udine (or Friuli province; it included the present provinces of Udine and Pordenone). The Ljubljana province (Provinz Laibach, in German) was formally part of the OZAK, but was placed under the responsibility of HSSPF *Alpenland*

as far as SS/*Polizei* matters were concerned, and is treated in a separate section.

2. The Italian Army used several types of cloths for its uniforms. The "Grigioverde" wool cloth was the standard gray-green rough wool cloth widely adopted by the Italian troops. The "tipo 343," also known as "double-sided autarchic cloth," mentioned later in this section, was also of gray-green color but was different in terms of texture from the standard wool cloth; it was introduced in 1942 because of the scarcity of virgin wool.

3. The similarity to this model was probably not accidental since it had already been widely adopted by the *Trawniki* in Poland.

4. The only known German source mentioning the color of the collar tabs used by the various units of the landeseigene *Selbstschutzverbände* of the OZAK, though lacking precise references to a specific unit, describes such insignia as "*hellrote Kragenspiegel*"; the term hellrot, or light red, referred to the hue known as scarlet red (*Freiwillige im Landschutz* in *Adria – Mitteilungsblatt für die deutschen Einsatzkräfte im Adriatischen Küstenland*, pg. 7, issue nr. 3, September 1944). In a report by *1. Rgt. MDT* of Trieste dated May 3, 1944, units defined as "*Guardie Territoriali*" were reported to be wearing red collar tabs on German-style uniforms. These SS-type red rhomboidal-shaped collar tabs had been adopted by the SNVZ, the *Landschutz* of the Udine, Fiume and Pola provinces, the *Guardia Civica* and the *Landeseigene Kräfte* of the *SS-Wachmannschaften* (in the latter case with white outline). From photographic evidence it would seem that there were several shades of red used by members of the same *Landschutz* unit, which could range from a very light red, sometimes maybe rosy, to a much darker color, almost crimson: it is not clear whether these differences had any particular meaning or if they were simply due to variations in different lots of fabric used for the production of the tabs. Also, a color drawing on the cover of *Umreti Nočemo*, a publication produced by the SNVZ Ceta (company) of Aidussina, depicts an SNVZ soldier wearing red rhomboidal collar tabs tending to a crimson hue.

5. See endnote 7.

6. The soldier depicted wears an M35/M40 German helmet with the Slovenian tricolor shield with colors arranged horizontally affixed on the right side, in the same way as shown on some *Slowenische Landeswehr/Slovensko Domobranstvo* propaganda posters.

7. The document, probably produced by the Tipografia Riva print shop of Trieste in 1944, show some lines in Italian that were probably forgotten by mistake during the composition of the print prototypes; from this it can be inferred that an identical document in German–Italian intended for the *landeseigene Selbstschutzverbände* units formed with Italian speaking soldiers also existed. According to the bulletin *Besondere Anordnungen* Nr. 3 issued by the *HSSPF OZAK – Der Führer der deutschen Rahmenkräfte für den Landschutz im Leitstab Ia*, dated September 9, 1944 (ARS, AS 1931, box 824, sheet 34), all members of the *Aktiver Landschutz* of the OZAK would have to replace their own *Mitgliedsausweis* (probably meaning the various models of *Dienstausweis* described in this appendix) with a *soldbuch* provided by the Abt. IIa/b of the HSSPF OZAK; this was probably the *Soldbuch für landeseigene Kräfte* described here.

8. According to a report by *1. Rgt. MDT* of Trieste dated May 4, 1944, the *Reserve-Landschutz* units wore over the red arm band the municipal coat of arms and in some cases even the provincial arm shields. The bulletin *Besondere Anordnungen* Nr. 3 issued by the HSSPF OZAK confirmed what stated on the MDT report, adding that the arm band must also have the word "*Landschutz*" on it.

Appendix 3

1. With regards to the marked similarities between the organization of the landeseigene *Selbstschutzverbände* and the multi-ethnic territorial units (*Grenzer*, *Streifkorps,* and *Gegenbande*) employed to fight the Ottomans during the Austro–Hungarian Empire, some interesting writings can be mentioned that were published in the collection of propaganda writings and essays *Drehscheibe Triest*, published by the Deutscher Verlag Adria–Triest in April 1945; in particular the articles by *Generalmajor* Hugo Kerchnawe, *Die k.k. Gegenbande* (in the chapter *Bandenkrieg*, pp. 167–168) and by Dr. Robert Ofner, *Südostwall aus Grenzern* (in the chapter *Sicherung*, pp. 201–204).

Appendix 4

1. Deposition by Geng of 3.9.1970 (IRSML-FVG, Fondo Risiera, box 88, also published in Adolfo Scalpelli, *San Sabba*, vol. 2, pg. 109). Vehicles used by *Abteilung R* often had registration numbers that started with SS-965 ...; it seems that at least the number blocks SS-950, 960, 965 and 966 were assigned to the HSSPF OZAK and its units.

2. According to Carnier, *Lo sterminio mancato*, pg. 109, two "armored vehicles" were produced in the Trieste shipyards, following a design by Hackenholt who also oversaw their realization.

3. Deposition by Mätzig of 14.9.1970 (HHStA, Wiesbaden, Abt. 631a, Nr. 1330), according to whom the armoured truck's driver was Kilminsky (who was also Walther's personal driver). In the memories of Delia Biasi (*I fiori azzurri*, Lint, Trieste, 1999, pg. 10), who at that time was a young girl in Castelnuovo, "the driver for the SS that patrolled the area with an armored car was named Prohorenko and was eighteen years old"; this was probably Prochorenko, a *Trawniki* attached to *Abteilung R*.

4. According to the deposition by Wolf of 3.8.1967 (IRSML-FVG, Fondo Risiera, box 88), the armored truck used by section R II was produced under the guidance of Bauer.

5. According to the deposition by Allers of 24.11.1970 (IRSML-FVG, Fondo Risiera, box 88, also published in Italian translation in Adolfo Scalpelli, *San Sabba*, vol. 2, pp. 25–31), there were three armored trucks based in Trieste, Castelnuovo, and Fiume.

6. Two *Flakvierling* guns were given to *Abteilung R* by a *Kriegsmarine* (navy) unit stationed in Trieste, that also trained some of its men (one of whom was Jührs) to use them.

7. Deposition by Allers of 21.3.1962 (LA NRW, Münster, Q234, Nr. 4271).

Selected Bibliography

This list only mentions the few available books and articles dealing directly with *Abteilung R* in the OZAK. References to other published sources are mentioned in the endnotes.

Berger, Sara. *Experten der Vernichtung. Das T4-Reinhardt-Netzwerk in den Lagern Belzec, Sobibor und Treblinka.* Hamburg: Hamburger Edition, 2013.

Carnier, Pier Arrigo. *Lo sterminio mancato. La dominazione nazista nel Veneto orientale 1943–1945.* Milano: Mursia, 1988.

Di Giusto, Stefano. *Operationszone Adriatisches Küstenland. Udine Gorizia Trieste Pola Fiume e Lubiana durante l'occupazione tedesca 1943–1945.* Udine: IFSML, 2005.

Fangaresi, Dante. *Dieci settimane a San Sabba.* Firenze: Edizioni Polistampa, 2003.

Ferenc, Tone. "La polizia tedesca nella Zona d'Operazioni 'Litorale Adriatico' 1943–1945," in *Storia Contemporanea in Friuli*, nr. 10. Udine: IFSML, 1979.

Fölkel, Ferruccio. *La Risiera di San Sabba. L'Olocausto dimenticato: Trieste e il Litorale Adriatico durante l'occupazione nazista.* Milano: Rizzoli, 2000.

Matta, Tristano. *Il Lager di San Sabba. Dall'occupazione nazista al processo di Trieste.* Trieste: Beit – IRSML-FVG, 2012.

Scalpelli, Adolfo (a cura di). *San Sabba. Istruttoria e processo per il Lager della Risiera.* Trieste: Aned-Lint, 1995.

Wedekind, Michael. *Nationalsozialistische Besatzungs- und Annexionspolitik in Norditalien 1943 bis 1945. Die Operationszonen Alpenvorland und Adriatisches Küstenland.* München: Oldenbourg Verlag, 2003.

Archives

Croatia:
Hrvatski Državni Arhiv, Zagreb
Državni Arhiv u Rijeci, Rijeka

Germany:
BA Berlin (Bundesarchiv, Berlin)
BA Ludwigsburg (Bundesarchiv, Ludwigsburg)
BA-MA Freiburg (Bundesarchiv Militärarchiv, Freiburg i.B.)
Deutsche Dienststelle (Wast), Berlin
HHStA, Wiesbaden (Hessisches Hauptstaatsarchiv, Wiesbaden)
LA NRW, Duisburg (Landesarchiv Nordrhein-Westfalen, Abteilung Rheinland, Duisburg)
LA NRW, Münster (Landesarchiv Nordrhein-Westfalen, Abteilung Westfalen, Münster)
StA München, Staatsanwaltschaften (Staatsarchiv München)

Italy:
Archivio Centrale dello Stato, Roma
AUSSME (Archivio Ufficio Storico dello Stato Maggiore dell'Esercito, Roma)
Archivio di Stato, Udine
AORF (Archivio Osoppo Resistenza Friuli, Udine)
DeH (Civico museo di guerra per la pace "Diego De Henriquez," Trieste)
IFSML (Istituto Friulano per la Storia del Movimento di Liberazione, Udine)
IRSML-FVG (Istituto Regionale per la Storia del Movimento di Liberazione del Friuli-Venezia Giulia, Trieste)

Serbia:
Serbian Military Archives, Belgrade

Slovenia:
ARS (Arhiv Republike Slovenije, Ljubljana)
MNZS (Muzej Novejše Zgodovine Slovenije, Ljubljana)

USA:
NARA (National Archives and Records Administration, Washington)